GROUP DYNAMICS AND SOCIETY

eit

EIT—the European Institute for Transnational Studies in Group and Organizational Development—is a professional association of social scientists with members from Austria, Belgium, Denmark, England, Germany, Holland, Italy, Norway, Spain, Sweden, Switzerland, and the United States. The Institute has undertaken responsibility for running programs to develop international trainers. It has also given information to official authorities when group dynamics has arisen as a conflicting issue. A further presentation is best offered by referring to article I in the constitution of EIT:

ARTICLE I, Aims and Mission

To bring into being a transnational body of professionals in the social sciences under conditions which will foster the development of a distinctive competence to undertake research, training, and consultation activities concerning inter-group and cross-cultural phenomena and problems arising in transnational organizations and environments.

This objective entails the institute maintaining its own forum to interchange field experiences, collect information, and hold scientific discussions. It commits the members of the institute to a regular examination of their own direct group experience in developing the institute—itself a transnational organization—as an essential means of acquiring relevant knowledge and skills. It further requires the institute to undertake its own program of research, training, and consultation activities. Last, it requires the institute to cooperate with, and encourage the work of, other organizations whose aims and activities accord with its own central objective.

Group Dynamics and Society
A Multinational Approach

Edited by
Trygve Johnstad

Published for

THE EUROPEAN INSTITUTE **eit** FOR TRANS-NATIONAL
STUDIES IN GROUP AND ORGANIZATIONAL DEVELOPMENT

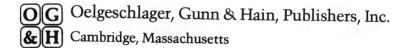

Oelgeschlager, Gunn & Hain, Publishers, Inc.
Cambridge, Massachusetts

International Standard Book Number: 0–89946–070–4

Library of Congress Catalog Card Number: 80–24932

Printed in the United States of America

Library of Congress Cataloging in Publication Data
Main entry under title:

Group dynamics and society.

    Bibliography: p.
    1. Organization—Addresses, essays, lectures. 2. Social structure—Addresses, essays, lectures. 3. Organizational change—Addresses, essays, lectures. 4. Social groups—Addresses, essays, lectures.
I. Johnstad, Trygve. II. European Institute for Trans-National Studies in Group and Organizational Development.
HM131.G7178   302.3   80–24932
ISBN 0–89946–070–4

Contents

v

Editor's Preface

     This is a European book. This statement may sound a little pretentious, knowing the extent to which we are indebted to American colleagues for the development of modern social sciences. But according to our own theories it is not surprising that a distinct European accent is emerging.

     One of the differences lies in the magnitude of work. Whereas in the United States thousands of greater and smaller social scientists have spent considerable amounts of money in countless research projects, the European contribution must in comparison be said to have been rather modest. This has led to an eager transfer of theoretical and methodological approaches, combined with a series of visits to Europe by American social scientists and a stream of students of all ages going the other way.

     We have learned that the methodological refinement and the level of theoretical sophistication could be—and certainly still is—highly impressive. But we have also learned—slowly—that Europe is different. The pragmatic American orientation, the laboratory character of the United States, the never-ending enthusiasm for implementing changes while at the same time regretting the lack of a basic theory of change—all these seemed more and more like ingredients relevant to a searching culture, one marked by a conspicuous need for having things better than they were before.

Obviously this situation must have something to do with the way the United States has been built up by people who wanted it their own way, left Europe because of persecution and poverty, and headed for a new and better life. They would be likely to combine next this American dream with European nightmare, thus throwing a tinge of suspicion on traditions as such.

This may be part of the reason that undercurrents of European traditions are not much looked into by social scientists, even when these traditions clearly manifest themselves in the very core of the American culture, in its educational system, its ability to stimulate identity formation, its power distribution, its economical arrangements, and its missionary attitude toward the rest of the world. With few exceptions the trend seems to be toward a basic acceptance of given conditions, with critical voices only concerned with ways and means, and offering applied social science in an effort to improve these conditions.

In Europe we have never been able to forget about traditions, and we are becoming increasingly aware of their impact. In recent years we have been witnessing quite a few well-planned and solidly grounded projects honestly supported by the right persons. They go through a sequence of initial, at times enthusiastic, acceptance followed by a period of committed experimentation and learning, only to end up as interesting bits of history, slowly suffocated by powerful social forces unforeseen in the projects.

Consequently, we have to take a closer look at our traditions. How much power is hidden there? How much regulatory impact do they have? How much choice do *we* really have? A large part of this book will deal with these questions, and in doing so build on experiences from the application of group dynamics in consultation and research over a period of twenty years. We hope some points made can be used by colleagues elsewhere in their efforts to come to grips with *their* traditions and cultural undercurrents.

Traugott Lindner's opening chapter deals with the authoritarian system as it is expressed in the hierarchic model of organization. The model is here presented in its ultimate form. The author shows how it is constructed and how it functions, as well as the ideas of the empire; the role of the king; and the values, norms, and social structures belonging to this system. The actuality and common acceptance of the hierarchic model is emphasized, whereby the realistic picture of a crisis emerges, a crisis determined by the simultaneous existence of political ideals of democracy confronting the penetrating effects of our hierarchically structured organizations.

Gurth Higgin describes in the following chapter the span of time required for more profound cultural changes. By introducing the concepts of "social projects" and "leading part" he shows how Western European societies developed a new social project that replaced religious economic values, and how manufacturing industry replaced the church as the leading part. Again a crisis is pointed up, this time caused by a growing dissatisfaction with the economic values inviting us to dedicate our lives to being merely instruments of work.

Eric Trist, one of the European pioneers, covers another aspect of tradition by representing in review the development of group dynamics as a joint European-American enterprise. He shows the historical development in ways of thinking and practical approaches in the field of organizational change. He points to the mixture of heritages from both sides of the Atlantic and puts some of the more central experiments and projects into an historical frame, where the history itself is the development of the relation between the social scientist and the client system.

Peter Heintel is occupied by the same problem but sees it in another context, namely the need for a scientific model relevant to social processes. He sees group dynamics as an alternative to the traditional model inherited from the natural sciences and finds that it is also able to offer a method of communication whenever there is a wish for more emancipation and freedom. This educational aspect of group dynamics represents to the author a revival of the forgotten connection between perception, reality, and theory. He also presents a theory of communication in which he starts with some basic contradictions in our societies today and goes further by demonstrating how these contradictions influence the communication process on all levels and at all stages—from the globally oriented power clusters to the man-to-man communication.

Gerhard Schwarz is also occupied with the formulation of an alternative scientific model. He justifies his claim by going all the way back to our hunting and scaring tribes, and then describes the slow emergence of villages, markets, and towns and how this geographical map bears in itself the germ of the hierarchic model of organization. He defines our common methods of abstraction and our classical models of logic as functions of an hierarchic system. This implies that the traditional models of science are intrinsically hierarchic and consequently of little use when the objective is to develop nonhierarchic organizations. He finds group dynamics to be a relevant alternative.

Kurt Buchinger is interested in using group-dynamic theory to describe and explain social processes in and around group psychotherapy. He deals with therapeutic process and different concepts of the group, and analyzes problems actualized by transferring psychoanalytic concepts and techniques to group therapy. He sees the therapeutic setting as an organization that reflects—like any other organization—the structures of its social surroundings, and that shows how neurotic structures in the wider society can be unwittingly introduced into the group—even by therapists. He analyzes the consequences of working with a therapeutic culture in a setting that is hierarchically organized. He points out consequences and risks for the training of therapists as well as for the treatment of patients, for example, the risk of developing a subject-object relationship or a new double standard.

Bernard Pesendorfer deals with Marxism as a theory of social change and tries to show how group dynamics can supplement Marxist theory. He discusses power distribution, different and alternative social structures, and models of freedom, seen both from a Marxist and a group-dynamic viewpoint. In the same context he deals with the formation of social structures, the regulatory forces behind longductive conditions—in a Marxist sense. But first and foremost he examines how crucial social processes like authority, dominance, privilege seeking, protection of private property, and the development of solidarity and freedom, are illuminated in the light of small-group work.

Max Pàges has seen the importance of exploring unconscious resources, and his work has helped us to use these resources better. In addition to the collective deferences as described in psychoanalysis and Bion's "basic assumptions," the author describes the more constructive elements in group energy such as collective desires and collective goals, perceptible as drives for autonomy and solidarity. He sees in these elements the germ of a global reorganization of human relations, and his work can be said to constitute the subconscious counterpart to Peter Heintel's more rationally based theory of communication. He also explains the appearance of counterforces in this unconscious collective system, like generalized paranoia and terrorism, which he sees as hiding the unconscious group goals.

Ramon Meseguer is certainly not trying to hide anything in his candid description of the Spanish people, a group of which he is proud to be a member. He gives a colorful and vivid picture of these peopel—or rather peoples—on their way to becoming a nation, and shows to what they have been exposed through the years of fanaticism, anarchy, glorification, humor, hand-to-hand combat, envy, lack of group formation, inquisition, and unconscious fantasies in the fight for power, as a Dantesque vision of heaven and hell. He gives at the same time—indirectly—a picture of what group dynamics can look like in a country where T-groups suffered under severe restrictions.

Ronald Markillie introduces the part of this book that is concerned with application. He does so by considering the ethical issues always inherent in a helping or consulting contract. In this article the author presents a pragmatic view of ethics as something that should be operationally valid in an environment and not necessarily part of a system of belief. To him a working contract has the mediating function of balancing the needs on both sides. Both the consultant's and the client's needs are seen within the prescribed ethical frame. Whereas ethics generally is associated with control and tranquility, it is interesting to see how the author emphasizes the courage to work with anxiety—and on both sides. This is an ethic relevant to the kind of group-dynamic work so emphatically presented by the Austrian contributors to this book.

Arne Derefeldt, like Ramon Meseguer, describes a whole nation in his contribution, but this time the T-group is certainly not forbidden. On the contrary, he shows how group dynamics fitted into the national scheme for wide-ranging development of democratic methods in various domains of Swedish society. A new legislation in the industrial relations field provides a formal background for substantially intensified training activity. A main part of the article describes development in Sweden leading up to the situation as it is today, and adds to this a prediction of what is most likely to happen through the 1980s.

Harold Bridger, another European pioneer, commits himself to a different kind of task when he reports from a multinational group of wives of executives in the international organizations. They were given a chance to prepare themselves for the move to another country by taking part in a course arranged for the couples, where the wives had a separate program. As a consultant to the wives, the author describes the way they worked in order to come to grips with the group's international cultural borders. He outlines the clarification of differences and similarities, various aspects of the process they encountered, and how this experience could be used to understand and adapt to an unfamiliar cultural background.

Hanne Sjelle Ernst and **Peter Holbøll** are also occupied with cultures, not as national characteristics reflected in an individual's behavior, but with more locally bounded organizational cultures. They invite us to a learning experience where the idea is to utilize the resources available when three different cultures confront each other in order to compare and analyze and learn about themselves. Their model is an answer to the uneasiness they felt when working either with people from one organization only, or with single individuals from a multitude of organizations. Their "third road" offers additional learning possibilities.

Svein M. Kile reports from a long-term organizational development program. It is presented as a live-trust model where group dynamics are introduced in careful and kind ways. This certainly comes through in the report, where it is made clear how the emotional realities in the organization are approached almost with caution, which tells us how deeply the author is aware of the risks connected with a too brusque introduction of unfamiliar emotional themes in a fact- and task-oriented group.

Trygve Johnstad also presents a report, but this time it concerns a specific problem formulated by a company that definitely wanted help. A group of fishermen working for the company created serious problems daily, and the question was what to do. An investigation led to a transfer of the problem from the ships alone to the relationship between the ships and those on shore, whereby the lack of identity in the group of fishermen was exposed as the cause of the problem. Consequently, the action steps taken in the project were chosen to support the development of a relevant identity in the group of fishermen. Once this was secured, it produced a series of surprising results.

The articles described here are not intended to give a full picture of the role of group dynamics in Europe. Rather, the intention is to give samples of group-dynamic explorations in a part of the world where traditions are still living realities, where language borders are at times insurmountable, where participation in anything that could be called a common culture differs immensely from country to country, and consequently where group dynamics, bound to be influenced by local culture, cannot possibly be portrayed as a coherent picture, but has to be a vividly composed picture of various styles with colors from different painters' palettes.

There are countries missing from this book, like Holland, Belgium, and Switzerland. This is caused by the fact that this book is sponsored by EIT—the European Institute for Transnational Studies in Group and Organizational Development—and there are only a few EIT-contacts in those countries.

There is a good reason to be grateful to many people for the realization of this book—not least to the contributors. But one person deserves to be personally mentioned: Mrs. Inge Hagen in Copenhagen. She has not only taken the bulk of all that has had to be done, but has been partly responsible for the translation and has been truly a partner with whom I could share excitements and uncertainties as they came.

Trygve Johnstad

Chapter 1

The Monarchic-Aristocratic Model of Organization

Traugott A. Lindner

For thousands of years we have been living in groups, and we construct organizations of all kinds. All the same we have—up to the nineteenth century—hardly been able to penetrate the presuppositions of our organizational efforts. Even Sigmund Freud, the great unveiler of human behavior, repeatedly assumes in his social psychological works that the monarchy (or the Almighty Father) is the only possible model for social order.

An Austrian politician was much mistaken when he recently declared on TV: "Monarchic ideas are once and for all dead in Austria." On the contrary, monarchs are still enthroned everywhere; they have survived all revolutions and are in the midst of us. They govern in private and public offices, in schools and hospitals, in political parties and unions, in congregations and associations, in the West as well as in the East. Indeed, especially where a political monarchy has never been an autonomous form of government—namely in the United States—we find a monarchic-aristocratic commitment in business and public administration to be more heavily pronounced than in Europe, with all its traditions.

This chapter, originally titled "Das monarchisch-aristokratische Organisationsmodell," was translated from the German by Trygve Johnstad.

But then what is it all about when we inquire into the presuppositions of the monarchic-aristocratic model of organization?

THE IDEA OF THE EMPIRE

Model: Every monarchy has as its last justification a leading concept at its disposal—"The idea of the empire." This is absolute, that is, requiring allegiance from everyone and fundamentally not to be questioned. The idea of the empire is the best possible so far, and through this idea is the existence of the social reality of the people justified.

The important thing in this fiction is that justification for the existence of the people is derived from the monarchy, and not conversely that the monarchic system is solely a cultural contribution of organization by the citizens. This conversion is determined by the fact that the origin of the system whereby every monarchy is given metaphysical foundations must necessarily be found outside of the social reality.

Practice: In the industrial society of today it is unlikely that things happen in such a grand and venerable way, but nevertheless political ideologies in the West and East claim absolute submission to their ideas, which in their own opinion are the best so far. Those who do not accept these ideas no longer belong to the system and must therefore be expelled. Leaders in offices and factories speak in similar ways about the idea of the institution or the goals of the company. It is not for the lower ranks to question these, and the justification for staying in the system is undoubtedly derived from the company goals.

It is also possible in a more modest way to compare the monarchic-aristocratic idea of empire with the image of the company. Such an image is formed both inside and outside the company, namely in all people who in one way or another need the company and take advantage of its services. The better the company fulfills its functions to meet the needs of its employees, its investors, its customers, and the public interest, the better the image will be. The management can derive its claim to power only from this service-giving function, and yet this group as well is only fulfilling more complex social needs.

Just as in many of the monarchic-aristocratic systems known from history, we find the managers today paradoxically trying to defeat the only legitimate grounds for their claim to power. They try indefatigably to gain control over the various groups upon which they are dependent. They are struggling with their dependence on employees, investors, and customers, and are invariably looking for manipulative techniques in order to reduce —or even better to reverse—the existing degree of dependence. Many top managers are striving for a situation where people are unable to find their way without their "company," at first locally, then regionally, and finally internationally. The service function of meeting needs is perverted to a power function of controlling these needs—whereby indeed any credibility is gone.

THE CONTINUATION OF THE KING'S ROLE

Model: In the monarchy the sovereign is the first and only representative of the idea of the empire. He is possessor of the whole truth, he knows the goal better than anyone else, he alone is the mediator to the origin of all power and the source for all formations of the national will. Theoretically there are no limits to the wisdom of the king, and when he interprets the idea of empire, he does so by means of a charismatic talent giving him infallibility.

Listen to the instructions of Pharao Ammenemes I to his son (12th dynasty, approximately 2000 b.c.): "You who have stood forth as God, listen to what I say to you in order that you may reign as a king and govern the countries and preserve an abundance of delight. Keep far away from those under you, who are nothing and whose needs should not be considered. Never approach them in your solitude. Do not fill your heart with a brother. Avoid knowing anyone as a friend, and do not provide for yourself any confidant, since nothing will come of it." (Wolf: *Das alte Ägypten*, Deutscher Taschenbuch Verlag, 1971).

The king is bound to govern and to defend his power whenever it is questioned. It is worth mentioning that the most frequent reason for the fall of chiefs in primitive cultures was continuous misinterpretation of the reality of the tribe and the failure to exercise power, while misuse of power was more easily tolerated.

Practice: The private owner of a company and the administrative leader of an old-style office will see themselves as kings, even today. They regard themselves as completely in possession of the whole truth and look upon themselves as better equipped than anyone else to formulate the goals of the company and, if necessary, to interpret them. They are centers for the ultimate formation of what the people wish to accomplish, not only de jure but also de facto.

Also many employees see their top man as the master. He is certainly not as well equipped with charismatic talents as the monarchs of the past, yet he should belong to the eminent company of personalities who, because of their intuition, always find the right solutions, even against any advice from highly qualified professionals.

This need of ours to subject ourselves to one single person as the center of all authority is deeply rooted in us. Even in joint stock companies, where the legislation lets the highest responsible executive face a collective as the last resort for a decision, many general managers hopefully expect that the general assembly, manipulatively linked together, will not reach an independent conclusion.

Kings are elected for a lifetime, whereas general managers are not. The exceptions are private owners in family companies where the senior of the family is the administrator, and joint stock companies where a leading executive has control over a considerable amount of the stocks or over an actively blocking minority group of stockholders. In such cases the company often grows old with its head, and quite a few people consequently have had to retire from business. The royal role of many a management is often seen as meaningless, but even so it is so deeply rooted in our thinking that we do not attack it openly. The way to withdraw from a leader who has become incompetent is rather by escape than by attack, be this leader a shareholder, employee, customer, or counselor.

Absolute command by one single person is today more and more rarely seen. The old-style manager who could really rule within his own company has become a social fossil—a circumstance many certainly regret. But nevertheless, sometimes this final arbiter is found with all the characteristics of the absolute monarchy. While the power link in the political area goes from dictator to parliament, it goes from private owner to joint stock company in the business world. The final arbiter can always be found— fixed by legislation. Since the majority are of the opinion that it cannot be organized differently, the least they can do is to act as if these legislative agencies possess the whole truth and as if their wisdom knows no limits. This fiction is not fully believed by anyone anymore, and therefore parliamentary deputies or leaders make it evident every now and then by their statements that they are neither charismatically gifted nor infallible. This reduced credibility in our highest agencies is certainly a symptom of the decline of the monarchic-aristocratic system.

Consequently the authorities are challenged—openly or secretly—in their right to represent the final arbiter and to lay claim to obedience. However, this decline does not imply that the authorities, now under more pressure, cease to govern, or that they voluntarily give up their positions of power. This way of acting is thoroughly consistent with the system, even if it is regretted by those who consider themselves or a couple of others as better substitute kings.

THE OBLIGATION TO BE AT THE KING'S DISPOSAL

Model: As a consequence of the monarchic structure the whole population has to be totally dependent on the king. Whatever is delegated to anyone as task or authority is from the king and is something to which no one can lay claim. This is not a free choice, it is system-consistent. As the center of all formations of will, only the king can delegate. In principle he is the one to confirm every goal expressed by others in his name. But in order for the king to delegate it is necessary that all others are at the disposal of the royal service. Once a goal is declared it cannot be rejected, since then the foundations of the system would be shaken.

In every monarchy it has happened that a few of the people are promoted and placed in a proper hierarchy, whereby their closeness to the king decides their rank; that is, an aristocracy is created. What this is really about is a division of functions in society—one of the greatest cultural contributions of man.

According to this principle the king delegates a small area of his all-embracing task to one or some functional executives. These functional executives are given the power to rule over a number of others. For the benefit of those so empowered he gives up his immediate power of disposal of the people. Those members of society who are distinguished in this way receive with their task a royal authority and are thereby made into an elite. Now they have the right to decide on the disposal of others by delegating further tasks. At the same time they are obliged to let the king dispose of their resources and to keep those in good shape.

In this connection it is important that the royal task is not given once and for all (that belongs to later forms of privilege). If, for example, he who has a task does not live up to expectations, he can be deprived of all offices and is again to be regarded as an ordinary man.

Faced with this, the nobility very wisely chooses to monopolize certain areas of function, which has the consequence that the king's disposal of nobility now becomes more restricted, that is only outside certain areas of privilege. The nobility claims the right of succession, full jurisdiction over their subjects, and so on. In this way it is the nobility itself that after all starts the dissolution of the monarchy within its structure. This is the group that has forced itself between the king and the people. And the more indispensable this noble hierarchy becomes, the more the king loses of his right to have his subjects at his immediate disposal. He loses in power and esteem until he himself becomes dependent on his princes.

Practice: The dependence of everybody on the king—which is settled in the monarchic structure—can be demonstrated either directly or with minor changes in every business enterprise. The same holds true for the privileges running through the system. Just as on a farm, where the farmhand can be installed at any time in a certain job by the farmer, in a big enterprise the management decides who shall carry on a task. The person in question neither has the right to choose a certain task, nor can he prevent the function from being taken away from him should he not live up to the expectations of the management. Anyone in an institution today who rejects a transfer knows what that means for his career. A rejection hurts the principle of disposal, whence dependence on the management is thoroughly called into question. This particular aspect of monarchic government, still altogether intact, implies that offenses of this kind will be suitably punished. Even when there is a possibility of protest against a transfer, or of restoration of earlier functions with the help of agencies outside of the system, the management's persistence in the decision will either prevail or the whole system will break down. The reaction of the highest levels is particularly sensitive when the reason for refusal is loyalty to others (family, friends, and so on). Such reasons are simply classified as "insufficient." The duty of the employees to be at the disposal of the employer is one of the most vulnerable points in monarchic-aristocratically organized systems.

For a person to reject work is in most countries a reason for inevitable dismissal. On the other hand, the hard-won right to strike (making possible a collective laying down of work) has led to the most forceful shaking of hierarchical structures. Above all, these systems are especially vulnerable when their very defenders withdraw their duty to be at disposal, that is when officials, police, or the armed forces lay down their work. In most countries this is forbidden.

THE UNWANTED INITIATIVES

Model: The individual in the monarchic structure is of no significance in relation to the common task—indeed, he receives his total significance from his connection with his royal task. Personal initiative, although immanent in the system, is therefore not only uninteresting but also unwanted, even if according to objective standards it may be genial. Initiative from below hurts the principle of dependence and jeopardizes the system.

In the monarchic-aristocratic system initiatives not coming from above must be announced in due time and accepted in advance. If they are simply courageously carried through, it is up to the sovereign whether he will later separately confirm them or will interpret them as resistance toward his person and thus in opposition to the idea of empire.

Practice: In the monarchy everything is regulated from above, even the existence of the monarch himself. Many superiors in industry and public administration are thinking along the same lines. In a chemical concern the chief chemist once said to me: "A chemical worker who on his own initiative will take a risk in these complex chemical processes has to be dismissed immediately, even if his action were to produce extraordinary results."

One of the higher officers in public service puts it in a similar way: "Because of the political consequences private initiative can be utterly damaging—indeed, it can be inconceivably disgraceful for the whole ministry. It simply does not fit into the bureaucratic apparatus."

THE DIFFICULT RELATIONSHIP BETWEEN PEOPLE AND RULER

Model: One of the most important principles for every monarchic system is that everyone has an immediate and personal relationship with the king. This binding to the king is fundamentally more important than any other human relationship. The all-inclusive social unity of a monarchic system can only be guaranteed through the king. This principle has a double effect.

In the first place it opens up a possibility for appeal against decisions taken by agencies in between. This possibility follows the entire ladder of hierarchy all the way up to the king, where it ends. The highest representative of the common task—the king—has to be at everyone's disposal as the last and final instance of judgment when a conflict cannot be resolved at a lower level.

In the second place, a logical consequence of the principle is that it jealously forbids the binding of one to another. This is because powerful subgroups reduce the willingness to be at the king's disposal and cool the love for the monarchy or transform it into distant respect, whereas exactly the contrary should happen. Only as long as you can happily leave parents, friends, wives, and small children, when the king calls, is the king sovereign and able to wage wars.

Interpretation: The personal relationship with the top leader is a very efficient construction (in mass-psychological terms), which after all has a certain manipulation of information as its presupposition. Everybody has something like a self-ideal, which can be personalized through eminent personalities. An actual contact with the gods is for the self-ideal rather disappointing and is therefore taboo. Only in fantasy is it possible to pass through all the stages in between and thereby reach them and talk with them directly. This dialogue, however, is a dialogue with oneself. If you really stand there as the little man facing the top leader, it is almost impossible to say anything of importance.

Thereby a problem has come up for the rulers. They have to be popular, but are not allowed to meet the people. (K. Michalowsky relates from the Pharaos: "God-like honor was bestowed upon him. Personal contact with him was only allowed to his family and the highest ministers of religion and officials. The ordinary man seldom saw his ruler, and then only at a great distance. . . . His family life was also restricted to the palace. His "Great, Royal Spouse" lived concealed, just like the king's numerous second wives." ("Ägypten, Kunst und Kultur," *Herder Verlag* 2, Auflage 1971).

So when the rulers appear in public they will continuously perform benevolent deeds: by inaugurating many things which are practical for others, by giving pardon where others in their names have sentenced, or by inviting to celebrations.

When actions in grand style like these are also being preserved in words and pictures and widely published through the mass media we call it today "public relations," while it was earlier called "historical writing." The fact that a historical document is contemporary is not the important thing about it, rather it is that it represents the development of an image with which it is possible for others to identify. This image must burst with kindness, wisdom, and strength, and tends therefore every now and then towards the ridiculous. It is interesting from this viewpoint to read company newspapers, prints from associations, and printed matter from political parties.

CONSEQUENCES OF OWNERSHIP

Model: In the absolute monarchy there is theoretically no property. And if all property and means of production do not already belong to the king personally, they will ultimately be managed by him. This implies that every member of the society is bound to poverty, that is fundamentally without means. Certainly the king can lend land to individuals, but for this they have to pay rent or keep soldiers and munitions ready when needed. The ruler can at any time recall the granted feudal estate, and does when he calls in the property of an unfaithful prince. Duty-free estate and right of succession of ownership to a greater landed area later characterizes the position of a free citizen, that is, one who has grown independent of the king. In this way the principle of absolute monarchy is clearly broken.

Practice: This is not the place to discuss problems around property. Let it only be referred to our modern industrial states where everyone's dependence on certain forms of property increases so rapidly that we really have to pay attention to a balance between the operative forces before it is too late. Through the concentration in the business world some few companies swallow more and more of the small and middle size firms. Thereby certain professions are monopolized to a degree that makes it impossible for many experts to choose where they want to work. This will be reinforced in the future as we specialize more and more.

In addition there is the enormous rise in the costs involved in the development and maintenance of the single man's place in the workshop. For a long time now we have seen how the wages for a whole lifetime are insufficient for certain groups to be able to buy the tools necessary for their own work. The working people's dependence on the owners of the means of production, however, is only a particular aspect, one which has been specially emphasized by Marxism. For example, the citizen is theortically, and now and then also practically, abandoned to a total lack of means whenever the highest executive power wishes it. Therefore the property one has is at the most a gift to every single individual from the state, but given in such a way that it can be recalled at any time through relevant manipulations of value or tax reforms. And every so often it really is.

THE UNEASINESS ABOUT OBEDIENCE AND SANCTIONS

Model: In order that a society—constructed according to monarchic principles—may be able to function fully there has to be strict discipline, since absolute obedience is demanded from the hierarchy as well as from the people. Should the principle of obedience be breached, evaded, or somehow or other not sufficiently fulfilled, than it is necessary for the system to devise adequate sanctions simply in order to enforce obedience.

Practice: All the great institutions of the past drafted according to the monarchic-aristocratic model—the state, the church, the army, and even the guilds—have in reality developed their own jurisdiction in the economic area. Only from industries was the right to their own jurisdiction withheld. They had to find their means within the general civil rights, even when statutes and acts relating to trade constitute today the greater part of the work of legislators.

Societies drafted according to the monarchic-aristocratic model—as are almost all great institutions today—have therefore a need to maintain the principle of obedience. If disobedience against superiors cannot be punished, the leaders have no power.

Repressive measures generally culminate in the expulsion of the insubordinate. This was earlier tantamount to the withdrawal of social and economic means of survival for people in business and public administration. Today measures of this kind only hit the weak ones—the unskilled and the old, even the unemployed and the socially sick can survive. Younger and more competent manpower may now and then improve considerably when they change their working place. But what can institutions do when they can no longer afford to expel the insubordinates, when this leads to a shrinking of the work force, shortage of personnel, or scarcity of highly qualified people? What use finally is control when the master (superior) is dependent on the servant (the expert)? Who is controlling whom in the long run?

If we then break the monarchic-aristocratic principle to pieces—or if it dissolves itself—every hope of superintending human behavior must be abandoned at the same time, and the goal must be self-control. That we are still considerably far away from this is not least proved in our education system with its giving of the marks, in our business with its standards of achievement, in public administration with its job descriptions, and in the state with its legislation. Maybe such dignified oldfashioned arrangements are still necessary for a while to secure order—the future is meant for somebody else.

In a man-to-man relationship there is no need for standards of achievement, marks, job descriptions, or laws. Anyone who is not of this opinion should try, indeed, to subject the behavior of his family, his friends, or the really creative power of his country, to a norm.

Here we are faced with the peculiar dilemma of finding ourselves in circumstances where it is exactly the norm-giving and institutionalized control arrangements, installed for the purpose of temporarily keeping order, which prevent people from maturing to powerful self-control.

THE SLAVES OF TODAY

Model: Once and for all let it be said that it definitely does not belong to the model conception of monarchic-aristocratic principles to have a bottom layer of subjects obliged to total drudgery—comparable with slave work. However, those in power have always known how to institute such groups. They make up the broad base of the hierarchical pyramid. Legally they are clearly separated from the aristocracy, now and then even totally outlawed. This pariahlike group in society has no proper membership in the system. They are not to be taken into consideration, in spite of the fact that they support the entire fabric of the monarchic structure.

Practice: It is possible to avoid the fate of slavery only when the lowest layer can organize themselves and carry out their ideas. Even in the highly industrialized countries there is no guarantee of this, since the slaves of modern times are no longer to be found among the workers but rather among the consumers. A business system oriented toward maximum profits will simply not offer what the consumer needs (for example, durable goods), but rather look for what raises the investment return. It is evident that the consumer is in this sense placed outside the system, but he still has to support it.

ABSTRACT

There exists a power and wisdom continuity that in every respect is condensed to omnipotence in the monarchs, and then down the hierarchic ladder is so diluted that total powerlessness is left to the ordinary man, that is, political indolence and economic impotence. The people therefore need direction, which the monarch offers with the help of his nobility. The dependence of his subjects and their obligation to be at his disposal, as well as the upper layers' willingness to direct, is the basis for every order. Nothing can be changed in these dependence relationships, since the authority of the monarch and of those he has appointed is not to be touched.

The essence of the monarchic-aristocratic structure is the coordination of individuals and of groups through a superior agency. For individuals to have consideration for one another, or for one group to relate to another group, is a threat to the system and has to be prevented.

Before we raise the question whether or not the monarchic-aristocratic model of society is able to function today, and whether the signs of crisis are connected with a general and historically necessary decline of this system, we must have a clear understanding of the following:

Throughout history it has been shown that people have used this model concept to organize themselves, and that immense cultural achievements have been brought forward by this system.

The monarchic order of society is deeply connected with individual genetic viewpoints, so that in our thinking in many respects we are inclined to rely on this model.

Considerable remnants of this system are still visible and active, and it has not been possible to replace them with anything better.

The monarchic-aristocratic order of society has to be evaluated differently when seen in highly industrialized cultures than when seen in developing countries and in primitive cultures.

So far it can hardly be said that alternative systems have been presented that have been sufficiently proved and confirmed in their practical achievements and that are conclusively different from the monarchic-aristocratic system. And even when successful experiments do occur, it cannot be ascertained how it would have been without the multitude of remnants from the old system; for example, the legal framework and the police established to keep law and order within it.

SYSTEMS CRITICISM

The monarchic-aristocratic model of society exists in its pure form nowhere today, and has probably never existed. Not only would it have implied that the monarch should be omnipotent, but also that he would have to live in a social vacuum from his individual subjects. Because the absolute power claim is decisively broken as soon as anyone else but the king influences somebody—and this must happen inevitably through every other subject—the monarchy is a social fiction, never to be totally realized.

In spite of this it is today more realized than any other system, and with all its serious defects it is still beyond doubt the decisive theoretical foundation of the major part of management thinking in church, business, and public administration.

We know now that great associations and entire peoples undergo a maturing process similar to the individual process of development. In primitive cultures the strong leader of a tribe acts as a model, whereas the model in the developed countries will be the wise statesman, just as in the family the father is the naturally given model. To be dependent on him means social security. However, in the course of further development it emerges that this habitual omnipotence is insufficient and a hindrance to self-development.

Through juvenile forms of resistance and opposition a maturation process begins, leading to acceptance of responsibility. This stage does not imply independence, because in the social area this does not exist. Rather it is a renewed dependence experienced as a free decision arising out of a willingness-to-be-there-for-one-another in the sense of "love." This level of consciousness can no longer stand any dependence rooted in reason but is essentially an autonomous decision taken by a mature individual.

The comparison with the individual genesis has been chosen to show that the monarchy as an organizational model has a level of consciousness corresponding to the impotence of the subjects.

As consciousness continues to develop through history this stage will be overcome and lead to the survival of potency. Nevertheless, the social psychology of today is unable to say when the monarchic-aristocratic system will be completely displaced, even if there is no doubt about its increasing decline.

Through the development of science and its application to daily life, the dependence of people becomes multilateral and complex; there is no longer only one king. The same holds true for the increasing number of new power centers like unions, political parties, professional associations, and citizen federations. They all break with the required loyalty to one exclusive figure at the top.

Increased communication in quantity and quality across boundaries leads to a breakdown of these boundaries, which were installed to separate empires in the past. This applies to physical boundaries in time and space as well as to social boundaries in thought and feeling. Fractionizing the globe into separated empires becomes increasingly impossible.

Old value systems that have directed people throughout centuries have become obsolete in almost all large institutions: the church, government, the army, the universities, industry, and so on. The right to rule is itself in question from top to bottom in society, leaving not even the family untouched.

All tendencies to internationalize systems like news distribution, traffic, law, capital distribution, energy, raw materials, food, and so on must lead either to the establishment of a world government with new forms of centralization, or to chaos; or a completely new form of decision-making process has to be learned by mankind.

Chapter 2

Scarcity, Abundance, and Depletion: The Need for Continuing Management Education for Managers

Gurth Higgin

Most away-from-the-job education for managers is undertaken on an extramural basis by institutions specializing in this activity. Work in this field by university schools and departments of management is very typical. In this traditional model, however, there is a discontinuity in education, in learning between the parties. For the university tutors and others involved, the role is more that of a catalyst in bringing knowledge to students in whom it is hoped some learning processes will be stimulated. The university people concerned are not themselves directly involved in any learning.

This model, when applied to management education, presupposes a situation of stability both within organizations and in their economic and social environments. In a stable situation knowledge and skills can be slowly established and passed on and found useful in application. The product of the experience of one generation can be codified and found useful by the next generation. We are, however, no longer in conditions of stability. We are discovering that the conditions that we have always taken for granted as fixed, and the implicit and explicit principles and standards about them that we have always accepted, are decreasingly valid. This condition of instability has been well documented by others, particularly by Donald Schon in his recent Reith Lectures.[1] The common experience today is of turbulence, both within the organization and within the environment.

A model that allows some conceptual understanding of this condition and of the most usual forms of reaction to it has been elaborated by Emery and Trist.[2] They show that in conditions of turbulence it is impossible for a single system, whether it be a single psychological system or a single social system, to be able to control its own goals or even its own boundaries as an independent autonomous unit. It is impossible in such conditions for the independent system to decide unilaterally what to relate to and what to ignore in its environment when this is changing, turbulent and unknown. In these conditions long-term strategy is impossible. For short- and medium-term activity, the best strategy is to optimize at the tactical level. This implies a constant monitoring of the environment and a readiness at all times to change the pattern and the objects of its interactions.

In this situation an educational institution such as a university will decreasingly be able simply to offer its knowledge to the outside world. Now knowledge is hardly codified before it is out of date. All that it can offer is its skills and knowledge of the means to analyze and to understand the problems encountered by those trying to manage them. Obviously it must do this in a relationship of interdependence, not for but with the other system that is struggling with the problem. This means that for both parties there must be constant inquiry, constant learning—in short, continuing management education.

So much then for a brief general statement of what I believe to be a useful form of reaction for the future.

I would like now to put some flesh on this rather meager skeleton. By flesh, I mean ideas, values—a view of reality. In doing this, I do not feel that I need provide any justification in terms of my university role. It is a prime function of people in universities to deal with ideas. If we are to justify the support that society gives us, it is incumbent upon us to have ideas, to discuss them, to argue about them, to test them, and to disseminate them.

If further justification is needed, I would make the case on two bases. First, that ideas, particularly general ideas about the nature of reality, are important, often more important than we realize; second, that these general ideas are manmade artifacts, do not have the universal and abiding truth we often credit them with, and so should be under constant scrutiny. They do, however, have a very important influence on us, which is a matter of little importance when we all accept them, when they are working as shared beliefs about reality. But when they begin to falter, when belief is not secure and universal among us, when in terms of gestalt psychology they are no longer a generally accepted ground but become figures competing with other figures, in these circumstances we often become painfully aware of them—they certainly preempt attention.

Let me give a simple illustration of these points. When men believed the world was flat, it was logical, it stood to reason, that if you kept going long enough in one direction you would fall off the edge. When they believe it is round, it is logical, it stands to reason, that by going long enough in one direction you come back to where you started. To bring it closer to my theme, if you believe in original sin different things will be axiomatic and stand to reason for you than if you believe in primal innocence. From a belief in original sin there logically flows a need for coercion, control, and discipline in society, for what would be released without these would be evil and destructive. If on the other hand you believe in primal innocence, you may regret any present necessity for social controls and will see them as due to evil and destructive reasons produced in human beings by manmade imperfections in society.

These general ideas or maps of reality that we have in our hands are only of philosophical or academic interest when we all share the same ones. But when we do not, they can be of very immediate relevance. I have on several occasions been involved in practical management decisions that boiled down to a confrontation between these two views of reality. On the one side were those who believe it is impossible in any situation not to have some element of imposed discipline and authoritative leadership. For them an open situation of trust is not logical, it is against human nature. On the other side have been those for whom openness and trust and the minimizing of imposed control are the only way to release involvement, cooperation, and creativity that is inherent in man but which our organizational struc- tures suppress. There is no logical way of resolving such a situation, simply because there are two different logics involved depending on what basic belief about the nature of reality is held. Moreover, both parties to the dispute would be likely to declare that analysis to this level was irrelevant. They would disdain it as too theoretical for practical men and return to their inherently unreasonable conflict trying to find a common logic to resolve it. Their belief would be, as is so often the case, that logic is logic and has nothing to do with beliefs about sin and innocence.

Let me now briefly return to an earlier illustration. If we were to meet, a group of intelligent, educated, and inquiring people, we would have the security of the knowledge of a shared and comfortable belief in the fact that the world is round. Had we been a similar meeting of our forefathers of five or six hundred years ago, which in terms of human history is a very short time, we would have had the same secure and comfortable feeling in a shared belief that the world was flat.

Now the map of the world as flat and the map of the world as round are both manmade. Our grandchildren may well come up with quite a different map, a map which to us today is impossible outside of science fiction, a map which may make us look as naive and as blind as we believe our forefathers were.

I have labored this point because I want to present the thesis that the central problem in management of our affairs in the future will be to do with changes at this level, at the level of the general ideas, the maps of reality that lie behind the explicit and particularly the implicit assumptions we bring to our management activities.

When changes of this nature begin, the problem for the individual is less one of accommodating to the new than one of disengaging with the past. As we know from experiments initiated by Hebb[3] and the philosophy of Sartre,[4] one of the greatest terrors a human being can contemplate is an eternity of unstructured time. Similarly terrifying and difficult to accept is the possibility of no longer being able to structure one's everyday experience, to face the possibility that what one has always taken as the bedrock of reality may be wrong, that what one always took as axiomatic no longer stands to reason. I believe that we will not be able to manage our affairs in the future unless we have the courage to face a challenge of this kind. In the words of the psychologist Erich Neumann, "In our age, as never before, truth implies the courage to face chaos."[5]

I would like to start my excursion into ideas by introducing two concepts, that of social project and that of the leading part. The former I take from existentialism, the latter from Fred Emery, a former colleague at the Tavistock Institute, now of the National University in Canberra.

A "social project" is a quality that can be observed in any settled society, although it often requires cultural or temporal distance to discern it clearly. It is a pattern of beliefs and values, the pursuit of which gives a society its distinctive character. It provides for a society's members a basic model or reality, and an explanation of and a meaning in living. It is very similar to Max Weber's concept of the sanction for a social order, but more dynamic than Weber's static concept.

I can illustrate this by taking the cultural and temporal distance between our age and Europe of the Middle Ages. Medieval society had religion as its social project. Understanding God's will and its application to the world and living and manifesting these in everyday life was what gave meaning to life for people at that time. The beliefs about reality, the sanctions for social order, and the reasons behind all activities were seen quite simply as bring derived from religion; and adherence to them was seen as serving religion.

Emery describes his concept of the "leading part" as the part of a system "whose goals tend to be subserved by the goals of other parts."[6] In settled societies the leading part is fairly easy to discern. In societies in a state of instability and change, a failing leading part may be easily discernible, but the emerging leading part or parts may not. In the Middle Ages the church was very much the leading part. It defined morality and law, supervised all activities and relationships, and was the most powerful institution in society, even more powerful than any temporal institution. We all know the story of what happened to Henry II when he challenged the power of the Church. Thomas a Becket was murdered, but it was Henry who finally had to submit and to do penance. Even more dramatic was the confrontation of the Holy Roman Emperor Henry IV and Pope Gregory VII. Henry had defied the power of the Church, in which he was unsuccessful, and was made to do penance barefoot and in a penitent's shirt in the snows of Canossa. Gregory used the occasion to produce what must be a prime example of the arrogant confidence of the voice of a settled leading part serving a settled social project when he declared to the world, "The Church of Rome has never erred, nor will it err to all eternity."

During the Middle Ages people did not, of course spend all their time contemplating the works of the Almighty. They did provide for themselves within an economic system. But being subservient to the religious leading part, they paid little attention to this aspect of their lives. In our terms it was a very unworldly world. During these centuries there was practically no change or development in the economic system. In spite of its inherent incapacity to provide for the population at all adequately, little attention was applied to raising its productivity or developing its technology. The Church, however, did not stand still. It grew in power and in the extent of its dominance of society. In its physical setting it moved from the small Saxon church and the Norman chapel to develop the great Gothic cathedrals we know today.

Between five and six centuries ago things began to change. The settled religious social project of the Middle Ages began to lose its power, and in spite of a bitter and vigorous rear-guard action, its leading part, the Church, also finally suffered decline. Western European societies were developing a new social project, a social project that replaced religious by economic values. In its most developed form, the form that we have known for the last two or three centuries, this new social project can be seen to be dedicated to overcoming material scarcity in our societies. Its leading part has become manufacturing industry. As this leading part became established, the goals of all the other parts of society, our noneconomic institutions, became subservient to its needs. As we know from R. H. Tawney's "Religion and the Rise of Capitalism," even religion and the Church suffered a change to a form that supported the emerging new order.

Before moving on to consider this new order, I would like briefly to mention something of its origins in the old. Social developments are never sudden and dramatic, in spite of the radical change that revolutions and *coups d'etat* often claim. In all cases the seeds of the emerging future can be seen in the present or the past. So it is in this case. During the Middle Ages the origins of the new social project and its institutions existed. These were the money lenders and the merchants of the time. Both these roles, however, were never granted much esteem or significant privileges in medieval society. The peddlers and usurers were always marginal men, often foreigners. They were tolerated but despised. That a medieval contemporary should envisage the possibility that the successors of these men from below the salt would become the great capitalist entrepreneurs, the princes of a new era, would have been simply not credible. As A. N. Whitehead has remarked, "Great ideas enter into reality with evil associates and with disgusting alliances."[7]

To return to the bourgeois capitalist world, or more accurately the modern industrialized world—my remarks apply equally as much to its Eastern Marxist forms as to its bourgeois capitalist forms that we know. Its social project was a dedication to overcoming material scarcity. Its leading part was manufacturing industry, which dominates the lives of all through the relationship we call "work." In its developed form as we know it all the other parts of our society can be seen to be subservient to the goal of its leading part. Religion I have already mentioned. The form of religious belief that was developed in line with the rise of the new project provided that set of qualities that we know as the Protestant ethic. These were the personal traits needed by a society dedicated to work, and moreover, to work that in turn was dedicated in the name of progress to producing ever-increasing quantities of material goods. The wealth these goods represented was not for present consumption. The task of man was to labor through life in the vineyard of the Lord, postponing his reward to the hereafter. Morality and justice changed to fit the new dispensation. Whereas in the Middle Ages the most heinous crimes were blasphemy, heresy, witchcraft, and other crimes against religion, in the new order the most serious crimes are those against property, and in particular its symbol, money. In the same way marriage, childrearing, education—all our social institutions—were modified to suit the new project.

Although it is not very prevalent today, when I was in school the end of education was seen as character training. A good charater was taken to mean a belief in work as a value in its own right; a belief that wealth should be saved and not used for indulgence; a strong belief in the need to suppress spontaneity, expressiveness or emotion, which were defined as the expressions of original sin; a strong belief in the supremacy of the intellect. The intelligence test and its product, the I.Q., were the most usual and often the only index used in the educational system. Finally, good character required an unquestioning acceptance of authority and habits of automatic obedience. There was, of course, some instruction in the 3 R's and other basic skills thought to be necessary to equip the young for work, the main activity of their adult lives. However, the medium of character training was at all times more important than any message of instruction. Instructional activities would be suspended if the situation called for an exercise in character training, usually in the form of an outburst of moral disapprobation followed by public chastisement for infringements against the basic canons of good character. Nonconformity, even to the details of school uniform, was a very usual cause for such outbursts.

The upshot of such training was to produce individuals who were willing to use themselves as instruments for outside purposes, centrally those of work. A parallel to this was of course that within the life space of the individual the leading part became his work activities. All his other activities became subservient to this, a situation Marcuse very accurately described as being that of a "one dimensional man."[8] However, such training did have the advantage of releasing an enormous amount of social and psychological energy channeled through work to society's leading part. And it was a very successful undertaking. When one considers the whole span of history, the achievements of industrial societies over the last few centuries in terms of producing a supply of technically ever more complicated goods for man's consumption, it is truly a breathtaking achievement.

My central thesis today is that our society's traditional social project, that of overcoming scarcity, is, in its turn, withering, and along with it its leading social part, manufacturing industry, and its leading psychological part, an alienating willingness to dedicate one's life to being merely an instrument of work.

This is not a new idea. As early as 1930, in the depths of the worst depression our economy has ever known, the economist John Maynard Keynes speculated about the economic possibilities for his grandchildren and found them very promising. The adult generation today is that of Keynes' grandchildren. Speaking at that time, Keynes looked forward, basing his prophecy on what he called "the true interpretation of the trend of things," to the conclusion that his grandchildren would discover that "the economic problem is not the permanent problem of the human race." In other words, he foresaw even then that the social project of industrial society had within it the seeds of its own destruction. These seeds were not in a Marxist type of reaction against an unequal distribution of scarcity, but in the situation that would arise when our purpose of overcoming scarcity was felt by enough people to have been achieved. Keynes was by no means certain that the arrival of such a situation would be the panacea of universal contentment that it always had been thought to be. He said, "If the economic problem is solved, mankind will be deprived of its traditional purposes. Will this be a benefit? If one believes at all in the real values of life the prospect at least opens up the possibility of benefit, yet I think with dread of the readjustments of the habits and instincts of the ordinary man, bred into him for countless generations, which he may be asked to discard within a few decades." He foresaw too the problems that would arise for those most committed to and active in guiding our leading part. He said, "The strenuous purposeful money-makers may carry all of us along with them into the lap of economic abundance . . . but the rest of us will no longer be under any obligation to applaud and encourage them for we shall enquire more curiously than is safe today into the true character of this 'purposiveness' . . . for purposiveness means that we are more concerned with the remote future results of our actions than with their own quality or their immediate effects on our environments. . . ."[9]

I believe that the uncanny foresight of Keynes was accurate both as to its content and as to its timing. I believe that the main cause of our current instability is a breakdown in the unquestioned allegiance to the social project of industrial society.

I see the main precipitating cause of this development in the change of rate in the production per capita of goods that our industrial societies have experienced over recent decades.

These diagrams illustrate this point. They show the rise in the capacity of Western industrial societies to produce goods. This has been going on for several centuries, indeed ever since the Industrial Revolution. During this time whatever we thought of as being enough of the goods of the world for people to enjoy the good life was always rather ahead of production.

Beginning with the 1950 level it can be seen that, over the next two decades to 1970, our capacity to produce rose with dramatic steepness. Taking 1950 as 150 percent, by 1970 the United States and Canada, which of course had started off at a higher level than the rest of us, had achieved an increase of 200 percent. The countries of Europe were between 250 percent and 260 percent. Russia, starting even further behind, was at 430 percent. The acceleration in the speed of this increase is the point here. To be a living reality, a social project requires more than just an intellectual acceptance of the logical case that can be made for it. It also needs continuous confirmation in everyday experience. Thus a social project dedicated to overcoming material scarcity could only remain credible, in an experimental sense, when scarcity was a ubiquitous reality. The experience during the two decades from 1950 to 1970 for those living in industrialized societies provided the opposite experience. Every year brought more goods and brought more new and exciting goods, cars and refrigerators for all, automatic washers, stereo reproducers, color television, and the electric toothbrush. Alvin Toffler estimated at the time "that the child reaching teenage in any of these (industrialized) societies is literally surrounded by twice as much of everything newly man-made as his parents were at the time he was an infant . . . by the time the individual reaches old age the society around him will be producing thirty-two times as much as when he was born."[10]

The result was to accelerate and to clarify in the minds of many the change that started very much earlier, certainly for some in the time of John Maynard Keynes. Those born since the last war, those who have lived all of their conscious lives in societies experiencing these sharply rising curves of production, such people do not really believe in scarcity. They know it as a concept but not as a meaningful threat, in the way those of us who started life before the war know it. It is no good pointing out to these young people that illness, bad housing, and even poverty still exist in our societies. They see this merely as a reflection of how badly "they" or the establishment organize our affairs. They do not believe scarcity exists. They believe it is bad management and wicked inequalities of distribution that produce such a situation. It is certainly difficult to believe that an economy hard pressed to produce new novelties for "the man who has everything" does not have the means to feed and house its needy. This reaction is illustrated in Figure 2-1 by what I have called the scarcity barrier—the point at which the rapidly rising curves of production cross the line representing what is felt to be enough.

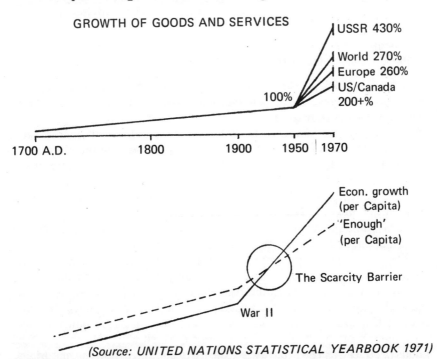

Figure 2–1. Growth of goods and services. Source: *United Nations Statistical Yearbook* 1971.

There have always been rebellious groups in society, usually spearheaded by the young. But with the present generation of young people, there is, I believe, a distinct change in the quality of their rebelliousness. In the past rebelliousness has usually been within the system. If only we the socialists, or we the fascists, or some other "we," could grasp the levers of power from the hands of the present selfish elite, we would produce the millennium in very short order. The existing pattern of institutions and their power levers were not themselves attacked. Today's rebelliousness, however, which labels itself as a counterculture, has a different quality. It is not interested in who controls our institutions; it wants to do away with them and their values, particularly our economic institutions and the highly sophisticated, if often impersonal, techniques we have developed to serve productivity. I have no systematic data from England but from the United States there is information about what the student population rejects as the bad words about current society. These are:

> Professional . . . system . . . planning for the future . . . conceptual framework . . . experiment . . . organization . . . detachment . . . management . . . verification . . . facts . . . technology . . . cost-effectiveness . . . theory . . . rationalization . . . efficiency . . . measurement . . . statistical controls . . . manipulate . . . mechanization . . . institutions . . . power . . . determinism . . . intelligence testing . . . abstract thought . . . programming . . . calculate . . . objectify . . . behaviorism . . . modification of the human environment . . . liberal . . . molded to specification . . . genetic planning . . . achievement.[11]

In addition, 76 percent of the sample thought there should be less emphasis on money, and 80 percent that there should be more emphasis on self-expression in our lives.

From this it can be seen that in America, and I believe the situation is very similar in any industrial country, the rising generation of students, from whose ranks the leaders of our institutions will be drawn in the future, show a positive rejection of society's current central values. This, I believe, is the result of their sense of being out of a condition of basic scarcity and into a condition of postscarcity.

The same phenomenon can be seen in the Paris uprisings of 1968. In this affair there were many aspects, but dominant among them was the cry for liberation. This cry was not the traditional political call for social and economic emancipation, it was a call for psychological emancipation, liberation from the Protestant ethic bonds of industrial one-dimensional man. The urge for freedom that was the essence of that revolt was freedom from all the forces, social as well as psychological, that lock industrial man into being a prisoner of the requirement to work with only the material goods produced as reward. It was a desire to get away from the materialist world and to recontact all the human emotional elements in man that industrial society had for so long suppressed. Their posters defined freedom as "the consciousness of our desires," and to quote from the literature of the time, "the authentic wealth of human beings reduces material wealth instantly to a drab back-cloth of objects."[12] The experience of postscarcity had mobilized enough people to take action on Wordsworth's 170-year-old lament, in "getting and spending, we lay waste our powers."

This erosion of the acceptance of economic man, the being at the heart of classical economics and of the materialist acquisitive society he represents, is, I believe, now endemic in our societies. Although one hears some economists, the high priests of industrial society, still roundly declare that the laws of the market have never erred, nor will they err to all eternity, the contrary evidence is nevertheless overwhelming. According to classical economic theory high unemployment means lower wage demands; high prices mean less consumption; inflation and unemployment cannot both happen at once; more pay means more output. In no industrial society today are these things any longer true. It is not surprising, therefore, that there are other economists who are a lot less confident of the validity of their dismal science. Lord Balough has said that "recent years have shattered a large number of economic fetishes. The whole accumulated conventional wisdom of orthodox economists seems menaced."[13]

The position of the more orthodox at this time who insist that economic man is not dying but merely suffering a passing ailment, is an example of the difficulties of disengagement I have already mentioned. Such people cannot envisage that the behavior of economic man, the key to which is that he can be relied upon singlemindedly to pursue the objective of maximizing his material gain in any economic transaction, is not fixed in the reality of human nature, but could be bred into us by our society. Economics as we know it is essentially the science of the distribution of scarcity, a condition that we have known throughout the 200 odd years of the life of the discipline. Scarcity is the datum point of the map of reality it is derived from. If this datum point becomes unsure, then all that is derived from the map becomes unreliable. The main parameters of this map, the laws of the market, obviously will only hold so long as scarcity is a reality that will dominate our economic behavior. When enough of the economic behavior of enough people is qualified by other considerations than those of holding off or building up a material defense against scarcity, then these laws will no longer explain our behavior adequately. They are, after all, not laws of nature, but merely generalizations about the behavior of economic man. When economic man has a change of heart, they obviously will no longer hold true. Some of our economists may not have seen the change, but those who are in touch with what we really do have not missed it. Even as hardheaded an operator as the late American trade union leader Walter Reuther said: "The relationship between people which was historically based on dividing up scarcity must be changed to manage abundance."[14]

I would suggest that the analysis I have presented allows us to explain several other phenomena that otherwise remain puzzling. It is only during the last ten or fifteen years that the question of the alienation of people from work and the problem this gives rise to, has been a subject attracting serious attention and research. During recent years it has preoccupied not only social scientists, but also many managers in all types of organizations in many countries. A considerable amount of research and experimentation has been done, increasingly under the auspices of the International Council for the Quality of Working Life, a founder and prime mover in which is Albert Cherns of Loughborough University. What appears puzzling at first sight is the fact that for centuries, indeed since the time of the Industrial Revolution, the conditions giving rise to the phenomenon of work alienation, particularly the instrumental use of human beings in work, have been very much with us. Indeed, this was described by Marx as early as 1842. Yet it is only since the early to mid-1960s that we have taken this problem seriously. The reason, I would suggest, is that, given a sense of postscarcity, we can now afford to take it seriously. Previously the need to work at the production of wealth to overcome scarcity had such priority that we could not afford the luxury of attempting to humanize work at the possible expense of productivity.

By a strange paradox I also believe that this analysis helps us to understand why so many efforts toward improving the quality of working life which this belated recognition of alienation has stimulated have not been more successful. There must be others here who, like myself, have been involved in these sorts of activities connected with job enlargement, job enrichment, increased participation, and the like, and have also read accounts of many such projects. With so many of these projects, when they are viewed at a later point, one is puzzled at how little real change they have produced. I believe there are several reasons for this.

The process of the movement from scarcity to postscarcity, and what one might expect to be the developments following this, have been confused by a change in the total situation in which this development was occurring. The change I am referring to is not so much a change in external conditions as in our perception of them. The problem during the period of scarcity was to find the means to produce from nature sufficient to provide enough for everyone. The change to conditions of postscarcity started when we began to feel that, largely through the application of science and technology, we had achieved these means. The assumption behind both of these situations was that the resources which these means were to draw on were infinite. Scarcely had we begun to feel that we were getting on top of scarcity than we became aware of the fact that the resources of the world were not infinite, but frighteningly finite. These facts had been pointed out to us for many years but we chose to ignore them. Recently they have intruded on us so powerfully that we no longer ignore them. Just as we seemed to move into an idyllic age of abundance, we became aware that the means we achieved are not enough. Now we face a much more intractable problem of scarcity, which indeed would be made considerably worse if we were to proceed to use our new-found productivity to its full. In short, conditions of postscarcity had barely emerged before we realized that we are in a period that could be called "neoscarcity." This is a new situation compared with the traditional conditions of scarcity because now we have the means but we do not have the resources. I believe that this new sense of scarcity has dampened the ardor of our rush into the postscarcity paradise of abundance for all, satisfied workers, and fulfilled people.

You will recall my quotation from Walter Reuther about the need to think about managing abundance rather than scarcity, in which he seemed to be unaware of the problem of neoscarcity. Walter Reuther said that several years ago, before we became as fully aware of neoscarcity as we are today. A common reaction to this renewed awareness of scarcity is a call to return to the old scarcity virtue, to revitalize the belief in work, and to resuscitate ailing economic man. In many ways this would be the most comfortable solution. It would allow us to to avoid a lot of tension and strife that I believe otherwise lie ahead of us. But I do not believe such a return is any longer possible. There are too many people in industrial societies today, particularly among the young, who no longer believe sufficiently in work as the central moral imperative of life. Moreover, if we were to return fully to work using the massively productive technology we now have in industrial societies, we would use up world resources at such a rate as to leave the cupboard bare for our grandchildren, thus defeating the original objective.

Currently the only productive resource of which the world supply is increasing is manpower. This fact would seem to indicate that the only way ahead must be some program that includes such things as a selective return to more manpower-intensive intermediate technology; a search for alternative types of resources, most immediately alternative sources of energy; and a willingness by those of us in the rich countries to accept a significantly lower standard of living. Such a program is obviously impossible except on a basis of agreement, cooperation, and sharing. Thus competitive, acquisitive economic man must give way to some different paradigm that puts caring for people ahead of personal getting and spending.

I also do not believe that a return to the old ways, or even our continuance in them in some ameliorated form, is a practical possibility in the modern world. All I have said so far applies to those of us who live in the industrialized countries—some 20 percent of the world population. It has affected the other 80 percent of mankind only marginally, but they are well aware of what is going on and increasingly cannot be denied some say. I do not believe that this hungry 80 percent of mankind will tolerate, as indeed many in our societies would not, an attempt by the affluent and powerful minority to impose a program on the world based on our attachment to economic man and his holy laws of the market, a program that is likely to end up with a struggle to the death between the Russians and the Americans for the last barrel of Chinese oil.

But to return to my theme about the difficulties experienced in attempts to improve the quality of life. A further reason, I think, is quite simply the fear of change, the difficulties of disengagement. It has been established for many years that one-dimensional industrial man has a very real fear of freedom. When he is offered programs designed to improve the quality of his working life, that is, an invitation to move away from a position of using himself as an instrument and to grow more autonomous, expressive, and self-activating in his work, he furrows his brow. This invitation implies a tremendous change in his view of his relation to work, to authority—indeed, to his very identity—the picture of himself and the patterns of behavior he has built up to maintain its integrity in his dealings with the world. He has after all been molded to believe that work and obedience to the demands made in its name are good and moral and that to be self-willed and expressive is sinful. For many this challenge, this demand for dread readjustments, is too great, and as always in conditions of doubt and confusion there is an inevitable tendency to retreat to the simpler familiar ways.

There is, I believe, a deeper difficulty involved in this phenomenon of the relative lack of success in the application of programs for the improvement of working life. This arises from the unrecognized use of a paradigm from the old order as a basis for attempting to build the new. We have seen that work in the service of the production of wealth is the leading part in our traditional system, and also that within the life space of the individual his work activity is likewise the leading part. Any approach toward improving the quality of life that is based on the assumptions of the old paradigm with economic man as its datum, whether such thinking takes the bourgeois or Marxist form, will take work as its leading part. If we are in the process of developing a new social project as a more relevant paradigm for postscarcity and neoscarcity, a process of which many people are aware, if not very consciously, then it will be for some part of their experience other than work that they will be searching as a new leading part in their lives. No aspect of life other than work has yet become sufficiently clarified to attract the social and psychological energy of a new leading part—indeed, no social project has emerged clearly to replace the battle with scarcity. Nevertheless, in spite of this lack of a new focus the pull of interest and energy away from the centrality of work in our lives is a fact. For many people, the idea of improving the quality of their work lives, although not unattractive, does not seem to be of central relevance to their current experience. They are more concerned with finding a new and more satisfying focus for their lives than in reenforcing the declining old. In short, the quality of life is not divisible. If it considers only work, if it does not cover the total life space, for many it loses its relevance.

I believe that an increasing number of people are experiencing something of this kind. The incidence of apparently senseless and irrational strikes over recent years, I suggest, indicates that there is an element of disturbance in the inner world of the working man that would not be possible if the traditional inoculation of moral and psychological work discipline was acting as it should. The quality of their family relationships, some recreational or artistic pursuit, or more commonly, at the moment, an interest in communal activity—for many, such things are becoming the center and main interest of their lives.

The existence of this phenomenon is supported by research being carried out at London University to investigate what is significantly called "work shyness."[15] This phenomenon, not yet a major form of reaction but an increasingly common one, is found in many large organizations. People are refusing promotion or advancement if this means an interruption of some other aspect of their living, particularly their family lives, which they value more than money or career advancement. We are all aware of the increasing number of people, particularly middle-class people, who are dropping out of the work force to go off and run a small business, join a commune, or otherwise find a life activity that is more personal and expressive than alienated work. Only last month, on 24 November, the *Business Guardian* had a leader on this question. In the course of it the city editor remarked: "Some sort of half-understood change has been taking place in our social attitudes during the last few years. Wealth, pure and simple, is no longer the goal of the professional and managerial classes." Recently the same phenomenon has been reported from the United States by Richard Walton of the Harvard Graduate School of Business Administration. He says: "Even stockbrokers, advertising agency executives and business managers whose work lives would have scored high amongst the criteria for a high quality of working life, have made the news by dropping out of the 'rat race' in order to redress the imbalance between work and the other aspects of their lives."[16] For such people something else has already replaced work as the leading part of their lives.

If, as I have suggested, we are in the throes of a change in our basic social project from an economic flat-earth paradigm to a more rounded one concerned more with other aspects of human potential than interest in bread alone, what are the implications?

For those who manage our affairs it would obviously call for more awareness of the basic assumptions they are making and their implications whenever they set up an organization or define its objectives. They will need to be similarly sensitive about the work systems they use, with their assumptions about motivation of people at work, and the relationship of people's work experience to other areas of their lives. I think that inevitably managers, whose job is to ensure work, will need to learn to tolerate what will appear to be irrational behavior. People find it much easier to be clear about what they do not want than what they do. To ask in exasperation what they do want is unlikely to be satisfactory. It will probably be some time before anyone is at all clear. I think things will get worse before they get better. The clarifying process will generate a lot of tension and, I expect, conflict.

Any experienced manager knows about and expects conflict. Every organization is riddled with politics. Scheming, pleading, intriguing are going on all the time. We all know it but pretend not to. When society has a settled project, from which we can all derive a common view of reality and so share beliefs about values and objectives, organizational politics can be fairly easily handled. We can at least agree about where the organization should be going and what logically follows from this. Apart from the more immediate politicking about which person or which group should get more power or money, organizational politics tend to be about the means for achieving agreed ends. And it is surprising how heated we can become about getting things done our way, even when we do agree about what is to be done. But in this case we at least have a common view of reality. We do share a fall-back position. But things are different when a society is experiencing a failing social project and no clear alternative has developed, surely the most trying situation a society can experience.

I am suggesting that this is the situation we are heading for, a situation in which managers will have to deal, not only with the politics of promotion and money, nor even of means, but with confrontations about ends, about values and objectives and, most intractable of all, with the clash of the different views of reality from which these derive. The name of the game in the Middle Ages was religion. The name of the game in the industrial era is economics. What it might be in the distant future nobody knows. But we can be pretty certain that in the near future, while we are struggling to find it, probably for the lifetime of all of us, the name of the game will be "the politics of reality." And there is no nastier game.

Some of our managers have experienced it already—a liberal vice-chancellor, for example, when confronted with the militant vanguard of the postscarcity counterculture view of reality. Part of him shares their view about the exploitive, alienating, and humanity-suppressing nature of current society. But part of him knows that other things he and many others genuinely value can only be protected, at least until the day of general liberation arrives, by his continuing to run his university as he does. He is deeply wounded when he is called a fascist pig. He knows he is not. Similarly with the rebellious students; they have been genuinely and altruistically converted to the counterculture. But they are children of the present order that brought them up. There are still parts of it within themselves that they value. But they must harry themselves with the painful and integrity-destroying experience of distorting and denying these parts. In the politics-of-reality game everybody suffers. There will be winners and losers, but no villains. Everyone is fighting for what he knows is the only right, moral, and possible cause. But those of us who currently manage will have the worst of it. If my analysis is correct, today's managers will lose, but they will suffer as much hurt as anyone else in the process. Moreover, through it all they will have to be responsible for keeping the housekeeping going for all the protagonists. The psychosocial processes involved in these developments are discussed in greater detail in my book, *Symptoms of Tomorrow.*[17]

With respect to management education, I see these changes having two effects, on our teaching and on our research. In both cases the key is that we need to introduce an appropriate degree of uncertainty. On the teaching side, we too often give the impression that there is a body of known and decided knowledge and skills that we can make available to students. All the students need to do is to master this and then to go forth having completed their education to exploit it for achievement—a result which I think we too often produce. If ever we did have a body of fixed and useful knowledge to pass on, we certainly cannot claim to have one today. I do not suggest that we should reject all that we have, but I think we should be increasingly alerting our students to the fact that it does not have the certainty that we once, rightly or wrongly, claimed for it. We should make clear to them the assumptions arising from the view of reality embedded in much of our material, and the effect these assumptions have on the conclusions we draw from it. We should alert them to other interpretations that can be drawn if the assumptions of different paradigms are taken as a starting point. The sort of process I have in mind is that in which the research workers on the classic Hawthorne Experiment had the courage to become involved.

It will be remembered that halfway through their experiment the researchers had the courage to change their starting assumptions from those of a stimulus-and-response model of experimental psychology to those of a more process-oriented model from social psychology, with the result that they arrived at a quite different and much more insightful perception of the data they were collecting. If our students as managers of the future will need, willy nilly, to deal with the developing effects of changes in our approach to life and work, they will indeed be lost if they are unfamiliar with what these might be. We hope to produce more young people who, although uncertain, are aware when they leave the university of the need for constant inquiry and relearning, and are aware that their education must continue.

I believe, too, that we need more uncertainty in our approach to research. We cannot, as we so often do now, pretend ahead of time that we know where our research is taking us and how we are going to get there. Too much current research only confirms the suppositions that went into it. We need to become rather more disreputable. This will undoubtedly create difficulties for the advisory committees of our research councils, whose decisions often give the impression that they are more concerned with respectability than with new ideas. Their insistence on having precise but conventional hypotheses, their demand for a detailed statement on research methodology and techniques, and their deep suspicion of anything not in line with the maxims of the current literature, leave the impression that many exciting research possibilities go unsupported. Furthermore, this approach does inevitably lend weight to the common view that, in this field at any rate, much research is merely the laborious rediscovery of the obvious. To be of value a research project must follow where the inquiry leads, if necessary against traditional canons. Whether those of us in this field can live with the dread readjustments this may lead to, I do not know. Certainly it will not be easy. There is bound to be a backlash from the traditional mandarins who, one can imagine, will castigate any such activity as a rationalization for sloppy scholars and for lazy and irresponsible researchers. This will undoubtedly be true in some cases. But the researchers themselves will know. If they find what they are doing exciting and challenging, the chances are they are onto something. I would always take the researchers' reaction as one criterion in judging a research project. Cool and unmoved researchers tend to produce cool and unmoving conclusions, and uncertainty is anything but cool.

With respect to one's view of the future, I believe that a stance that says that we cannot know the future but can only wait to see what time unveils is not the only possibility. We have considerable freedom to invent our own futures. This means that if we are inevitably in for basic changes, then to understand something of them ahead of time is very necessary if we are to take a hand in inventing the future to which such developments are taking us. We must be willing, to return to the words of Keynes's essay, "to enquire more curiously than is safe today into the true character of this purposiveness." He was, you will remember, speaking of the purposiveness of the social project of forty-five years ago.

When people come under the influence of a dominating social project, as we have seen, they change their institutions and values to bring them in line with its requirements. These changes will include morality and what is taken as decorum and good taste. It is therefore to be expected that a change as basic as the one I have been describing is necessarily going to grow from starting points that, in the old order, are probably considered, if not immoral, certainly in bad taste. We have already seen the case of the medieval peddlers and usurers. Thus, in the areas we research, as well as in our techniques, we may need to be a bit disreputable. If we are to take a hand in inventing our future, we must be ready to become involved in knowing about and exploring what, by currently established standards, would be considered marginal and even deviant, for the simple reason that it is here that the chances are highest of discerning the seeds of the future. Indeed, in my opinion, and I believe anybody currently in contact with psychotherapy would agree, we already have some painful indications of this. In our psychiatric clinics and even in our mental hospitals, there are people today who can be considered as victims of the future. They are people who find it quite impossible to arrive at any *modus vivendi* with the present state of things which they find intolerably immoral or inhuman in many ways, but who cannot find any solution except what we would call irrational or deviant behavior. Too often therapists attempt to condition such people back to an acceptance of current reality, instead of giving them the more valid advice, "Do not adjust your mind; there is a fault in reality."

I would like to give some examples of what I mean. Although we cannot foresee with any clarity what the future may bring, we do already have some indications of what are likely to be the characteristics of any future patterns of the relationship of people to work, that is, to those activities necessary to all of us if we are to manage our affairs and to produce the wealth we need. These characteristics will be different, probably in many ways the reverse of those of the current situation.

I would like to return again to Keynes's 1930 essay. After speaking of the inevitability for his generation of living with the purposiveness of material progress, he continues:

> Meanwhile there will be no harm in making mild preparations for our destiny, in encouraging and experimenting in the arts of life as well as the activities of purpose . . . it will be those people who can keep alive and cultivate into a fuller perfection the art of life itself and do not sell themselves for the means of life, who will be able to enjoy the abundance when it comes . . . those walk most truly in the paths of virtue and sane wisdom who take least thought for the morrow. We shall once more value ends above means and prefer the good to the useful. We shall honor those who can teach us how to pluck the hour and the day virtuously and well, the delightful people who are capable of taking direct enjoyment in things, the lilies of the field who toil not, neither do they spin."

Whatever the characteristics of work in the future, they will almost certainly not allow work activities to be the leading part and to dominate the life space of the individual. This place will be taken by some other interest or activity. In this area of his life the individual will be willing to be the instrument of its demands, because the pursuit of its activities and its values will be for him the most highly prized possibility in living. He will dedicate himself to it as the medieval man dedicated himself to religion and industrial man to the pursuit of material goods. Work will be seen as an adjunct to this, which at a minimum provides its economic basis. Work activity will take on something of the "take it or leave it" quality that we now usually associate with nonwork activities. If this seems a little far-fetched, let me give you an example from contemporary society in which work is the leading activity. If nobody took education beyond the compulsory school-leaving age, the work of our technically complex society could not be done. Although higher education is not compulsory, and is on a take-it-or-leave-it basis, enough people undertake it to ensure that our work gets done. Finally, in the future, one would expect that in the work area the individual would be quite unwilling to use himself as a pure instrument to achieve his limited end. In such a situation one would guess that we will not need projects designed to raise the quality of working life. If it is too unattractive, it will not get done.

I cannot claim to be a prophet, so the cases I am about to mention are presented only to illustrate my theme. I am currently working with an educational development in Sheffield which is an attempt to do something with the dropouts from the top end of the secondary school system. These boys and girls on the whole are dropping out physically as truants; but there are many who are, in fact, internal dropouts. They may attend school but are in no way part of it. The development I am speaking of is an attempt to combine teams of youth workers and school teachers in providing, during school time but away from the school and in youth club premises, some sort of partial education more in line with the needs of such young people who, not just in Sheffield but throughout our school system, are being turned away from school and from contemporary society, which they find offers them little that speaks to their condition. The strategy is to provide them with a supportive atmosphere and the bases of self-respect that the traditional school system has tended to destroy. Once some degree of relaxation and openness has been developed, they are offered a range of activities that it is hoped will stimulate their interest in learning. This range is very wide and even includes help with arithmetic and literacy problems, very common in this group. The essence of the scheme is that there is no compulsion to work. It has a free-school atmosphere. Any work the students do is entirely on their own volition; the pace at which they learn is entirely determined by themselves; even attendance is not compulsory.

This development has released a surprising amount of commitment, both in the young people and in the adults involved. The social workers and teachers give to the scheme much more time and energy than would be called for in the normal line of duty. They are in part sustained by the long-term aspiration that if they can make it work, it may have effects on the school system so that even the stunted academics in the scholarship streams may get a fuller education. It is, however, not without its critics. There are many members of the educational establishment who criticize it sharply as being an indulgence for lazy students.

I would also like to draw your attention to the so-called lump, the men known officially as individual labor contractors in the construction industry; and to the existence of the system of temporary secretaries, particularly in London. Both these activities suffer from exploitation. The subcontractors who run the "lump," and the agencies who organize the temporary secretaries, often tend to make a very good profit. Also, there are those working in this way who would prefer not to. They do it because they cannot find a more respectable or established means of earning a living. Nevertheless, there are many involved in these activities who are there from choice. The reasons for their choice are that it allows them so much more control over their working lives. They can work when they wish and, within limits, can earn what they wish. In short, they have moved toward acting out a resolve not to allow work and their economic needs to dominate their lives, which have become centered on the pursuit of some interest other than work. Typical is the secretary who will work all the hours she can for a time and then take time off to pursue some personal interest, or the building worker who will work hard through the summer and then spend the winter enjoying the Mediterranean sun. Both these modes of working are not without their critics. There have been demonstrations in Whitehall by civil servants against the use of temporary secretaries, and there are moves, particularly from the unions, to have the government legislate against the "lump."

It can be seen, however, that in all three examples something of the emerging qualities of a new relationship to work along the lines I mentioned earlier are present, and all three are the subject of vilification from those in established positions. Are they, for us, what the peddlers and usurers were for the Middle Ages? Using the Whitehead criteria mentioned earlier, if these activities do indeed contain the seeds of a great idea for our future reality, they do pass his test. For many they certainly have evil associations and are making disgusting alliances. But I cannot offer these cases as more than illustrations. I do not know, and do not know anybody who even pretends to know, what the shape of the future may be. The only thing that is certain is that for some time there will be uncertainty and that we will need to monitor constantly and to be prepared to learn and to change. Thus for those who manage our affairs, and for those of us who attempt to help them do it—for all of us—education will need to be continuing.

REFERENCES

1. Schon, D. *Beyond the Stable State.* New York: Random House, 1971.
2. Emery, F. E., and Trist, E. L. "The Causal Texture of Organizational Environments." *Human Relations* 18 (1965).
3. Beston, W. H.; Heron, W.; and Scott, T. H. "The Effects of Decreased Variation in the Sensory Environment." *Canadian Journal of Psychology* 8 (1954).
4. Raina, R. D., and Cooper, D. G. *Reason and Violence: a Decade of Sartre's Philosophy.* London: Tavistock, 1964.
5. Neumann, Erich. *Art and the Creative Unconscious.* London: Routledge & Kegan Paul, 1959, p. 112.
6. Emery, F. E. "The Next Thirty Years: Concepts, Methods, and Anticipations." *Human Relations* 20 (1967).
7. Whitehead, A. N. *Adventures of Ideas.* New York: The Free Press, 1967, p. 18.
8. Marcuse, H. *One Dimensional Man.* Boston: Beacon Press, 1964.
9. Keynes, J. M. "Economic Possibilities for Our Grandchildren." In *Essays in Persuasion.* New York: Norton Library, 1963.
10. Toffler, A. *Future Shock.* London: Bodley Head, 1970, p. 25.
11. Yankelovic, D. *The Changing Values on Campus.* New York: Washington Square Press, 1972, p. 171.
12. Quattrochi, A., and Nairn, Ian. *The Beginning of the End.* London: Panther Books, 1968.
13. *The Guardian,* 22 May 1972. Since this was written Wilfred Beckerman has repeated and extended Balogh's criticism in *New Statesman,* 23 January 1976.
14. *The Guardian,* 11 May 1970.
15. Williams & Guest, *New Society,* 1 July 1971.
16. Walton, R. E. "Criteria for Quality of Working Life." In *The Quality of Working Life,* edited by L. E. Davis and A. B. Cherns, vol. 1, p. 98.
17. Higgin, Gurth. *Symptoms of Tomorrow.* London: Plume Press/Ward Lock, 1973.

Chapter 3

The Professional Facilitation of Planned Change in Organization

Eric Trist

1. The facilitation of planned organizational change as a process involving collaborative relationships between client systems and social science professionals may now be said to have emerged as a recognized though still precarious activity in human affairs. The action-research studies that provide its first models were undertaken during World War II independently and against the background of distinct traditions in the United States and Britain when conditions of crisis compelled rapid change. Subsequently, work of this kind has made its appearance in most Western and in one or two Eastern European coutries, and in developing countries as different as India and Mexico.

After the immediate postwar years came a lull, during which the different norms of the academic and practical worlds were separately reasserted; but in manifold ways pressures toward change continued to mount and from the late 1950s onward collaborative activities have grown in frequency, while increasing their variety, their depth, their scope, and their duration.

Their persistence and elaboration over the past quarter of this century suggests that they represent a response, however groping, to a widespread "felt need" in the contemporary world. This need arises from the continuous presence in the social environment of a more rapid change rate (stemming from an acceleration of technological innovation and scientific advance), which has created higher orders of complexity and interdependence and a higher level of uncertainty than have previously characterized the human condition.

These changes pose new problems of adaptation for individuals and the organizations through which their relations are regulated and on which they are dependent. New attitudes and values must be found; old organizations must renew themselves; new organizational forms and behaviors have to be brought into being and tested.

2. One way of attempting to increase adaptive capability under these conditions is to couple the resources of the social sciences with the competences already available in organizations. One way of effecting this coupling is through establishing a collaborative, action-research-type, relationship between social scientists outside and independent of the organization and those inside it who represent its various systems and are directly concerned with its affairs.

In such a relationship joint responsibility is accepted for bringing about organizational change toward agreed ends identified through a search process to which each party makes his own contribution; although all decisions regarding the actual introduction of any change of whatever character remain strictly with members of the client system. Frequent evaluations must be made both of what is experienced and what is done so that on the one hand a process of social learning can be released in the organization and on the other an increase in knowledge be returned to the scientific community.

3. These last two aspects are of central importance, for even if the available social science resources were the only constraint, the number of organizations able and willing to enter into thoroughgoing engagements of this type must be limited. Even if not formally researched, every such engagement should be regarded as a research undertaking in the informal sense, from which an attempt should be made to secure a "multiplier effect."

This effect is beginning to be brought about in a number of ways. For example, with both the organizations and the social scientists concerned, such programs are getting to know each other within and across national boundaries. The overlapping informal sets so composed have the properties of a low-register but higher-order system capable of influencing neighboring sets to which their members also belong.

There are now also many more people inside organizations with varying degrees of social science competence, so that there often exists a third force, an internal as well as an external resource group, whose presence can accelerate the rate at which change can take place. The character of the organization-changing system is itself changing; it is already far more complex than the model of the single change agent working with the single organization.

4. In the United States the mainstream of work concerned with changing organizations derives from the field experiments on various aspects of social change carried out by Kurt Lewin and his associates during the last years of his life (see Cartwright, *Field Theory in Social Science*, 1951). These led to a field-theory formulation of how to bring about social change which has affected areas of work far wider than that which we are here concerned. It also led through the unexpected effect on the members of an experimental workshop on community relations to the discovery of the T-group, the innovation of the laboratory method of training, the concept of the cultural island, and the establishment of a new type of social science institution – the National Training Laboratories (NTL) (Bradford et al. 1964).

This development was premised on the need to abstract the individual from his usual organizational setting in order to learn experientially about small group processes and himself in relation to them in the "here and now." In these respects the method proved to have great power, but the effects on their organizations of the abstracted members when they returned were negligible, while the effects of returning on them were often to undo what had been gained. The original model of the "strangers" human-relations training laboratory was not in itself a method of effecting organizational change. Its transformation into such a method took another ten years to discover.

5.   In Britain the counterpart of the Lewin change experiments was the development in the wartime army by a group, most of whom had been at the prewar Tavistock Clinic, of a form of operational field psychiatry—a sort of psychosocial equivalent of operational research (Rees 1945). As the tasks undertaken became more complex, psychologists, sociologists, and anthropologists were added to the team.

Interdisciplinary collaboration was achieved in an action frame of reference, and a common set of understandings developed based on a shared core-value commitment to the social engagement of social science, both as a strategy for advancing the base of fundamental knowledge and as a way of enabling the social sciences to contribute to "the important practical affairs of men." The value position was the same as Lewin's—although the conceptual background was different: that of psychoanalytically oriented, interdisciplinary social psychiatry rather than of a social psychology based on field theory.

However, as the British group became better acquainted with Lewin's work, its influence on them was far-reaching. Indeed, some mixture of these two heritages may be detected in most of the work on changing organizations that developed in the early postwar year.

6. The method developed by the British group depended in the first place on a free search of the military environment to discover points of relevant engagement. The right had then to be earned to have a problem that could not be met by customary military methods referred to the technical team for investigation and diagnosis. This diagnosis would next be discussed with the appropriate regimental personnel and a likely remedy jointly worked out. The feasibility and acceptability of this remedy as well as its technical efficacy would be tested in a pilot scheme under protected conditions and technical control.

As the pilot proved itself the scheme would become operational, control being handed back to the regimental personnel. The technical team would "retreat" to advisory roles or remove their presence entirely except for purposes of monitoring and follow-up. What was learned was how to take the collaborative role in innovating special-purpose service organizations with built-in social science capability in a large multiorganization—the army— of which the social science professionals were themselves temporary members under conditions of crisis.

7. The second phase in the theme that now unfolds covers the decade that elapsed between Lewin's death in 1947 and the fusion that took place between the training-centered laboratory of NTL and the consulting studies of organizational change demanded in increasing volume toward the end of the 1950s by large-scale science-based industries in the United States.

To illustrate the distinctive contributions of this period, we shall select two well-known studies from the Institute of Social Research at the University of Michigan and two from the Tavistock Institute in London. The first two combine field studies with experimental design, the intention bring to test specific hypotheses. The second two combine field studies with clincal exploration, the intention being to follow the course of a social process. All four depend on a collaborative relationship being maintained between a research team and a client system consisting of a single organization considered as a whole. All four attempt to deal with organizational as distinct from simply group or attitudinal variables, which had been the center of concern in the previous period. All continued over long periods of time, the premature curtailment of one of the Michigan studies serving to underline the need for a long-term basis.

8. The first Michigan study is the Morse–Reimer Experiment (Morse and Reimer 1956–1957), a systematic attempt under conditions of full organizational reality to test a critical hypothesis: that degree of hierarchical control is inversely related both to worker morale and to productivity.

After one year during which contrasting programs were in official operation following a lengthy preparatory period, results in terms of morale were in the expected direction.

Productivity, however, was higher in the more hierarchically controlled group. Analysis of this unpredicted result revealed its conditionality: the character of the tasks produced a constant work flow so that only by having fewer workers could productivity be increased—a result easier to achieve in the more hierarchically controlled group; the character of the workers, young women, for many of whom employment was transitional to marriage, made this also more easily acceptable; the character of the measure of productivity neglected labor turnover, which rose in the hierarchically controlled group; its cost in the longer run could have reversed the trend. The scientific lesson of the experiment was theoretical: the need to advance in studies of organizational change from traditional concepts of discrete functional relationships to a systems approach.

9. The second Michigan study concerns the method of the systematic feedback of survey data for group discussion in "organizational families," developed by Floyd Mann (1957). Data of this kind were fed back to each organizational family beginning with the top in a large company; each level had discretion to consider the implications for itself of the findings; but each level reported the outcome of its meetings up the line.

Repeats were made in some parts of the company, with others omitted as control groups, at intervals that allowed for consequent actions and changes in climate to be realized. Results consistently favored the experimental groups. This research, which lasted some four years, demonstrated the effectiveness of a method that can become self-administering and provide a basis for continuous organizational learning.

10. The next study, formally associated with the Tavistock in its first three years, is the Glacier Project, a continuous collaborative research into the organization and management of a total industrial concern which had been proceeding for fourteen years when Jaques last reported it (1964). This project established a scientific rationale and ethical rules for the "independent role" and developed the method of "social analysis." Discussion with informal groups was abandoned in favor of working with individuals in their executive or representative roles or with formal groups such as managerial commands and committees.

The first phase of the project was dominated by the need to undo the widespread organizational confusion that existed in the company; the next with facilitating the extensive reorganization rendered possible by the insights gained; the third with enabling a consistent set of policies to be formulated that expressed the principles on which reorganization was based and provide a guide for the future.

Since all managers needed to know these, a training school was set up, later opened to members of other companies. The course of the Glacier Project therefore illustrates the opposite trend to that of NTL, which began in the training frame of reference and only later moved into the organizational.

11. A second trend in work at the Tavistock entailed a shift in the unit of analysis from the social system to the sociotechnical system, which in turn required the replacement of a closed-by an open-system approach (Trist and Bamforth 1951; Emery 1959; Trist et al. 1963).

The studies in the British coal industry that provided the first detailed empirical evidence of the superiority of certain forms of work organization over others for the same technological tasks led to the concept of the joint optimization of the technical and social systems as a goal of organizational change and raised the question of the participation of the social scientist in the design process.

An opportunity for such participation arose in collaborative work with the Sarabhai group of companies in India (Rice 1958, 1963). The opening phase of this project was concerned with the sociotechnical reorganization of an automatic weaving shed where Rice became a member of a spontaneously formed design team that included the workers as well as the management and himself.

12. The third phase of collaborative organization research began with the wave of developments released in the United States in 1958 when Esso, through Shepard and Blake, inaugurated a series of laboratory training programs throughout the refineries (Shepard 1960). Other large companies followed suit so that a new pattern was established.

This gave the T group a central position in collaborative projects on organizational change and produced such variations of the original model as "cousin" labs, "diagonal slice" labs, and "family" labs. These innovations turned a number of earlier assumptions inside out and forced a theoretical reappraisal that had to take account of a much wider range of process and phenomena (Schein and Bennis 1965). Little consensus has yet been reached.

13. In the writer's hypothesis (see Emery and Trist 1965; Emery 1967), these developments were occasioned by the mounting need of the science-based industries in the world's most advanced economy—in the face of higher orders of complexity and environmental uncertainty—to evolve organizational forms, climates, and values beyond and different from those of the more customary bureaucratic patterns that were no longer adaptive.

These needs account also for the impact of Theory Y as formulated by McGregor (1960) which, by stating the direction of emergent relevant values, indicated the new type of organizational relationships likely to be required. Theory Y constituted a new "appreciation" in Sir Geoffrey Vickers's sense (1965). Likert (1961, 1967) has brought together research evidence to show that the performance of enterprises managed in terms of "System 4" (direction of Theory Y) is superior to that of those managed in terms of "System 1" (direction of Theory X). The findings of the Glacier Project, on the other hand, favor what might be described as an enlightened form of Theory X.

These differences may be accounted for by the different requirements of largescale enterprises in advanced science-based industries in a society already in transition to postindustrialism (Bell 1967) as compared with those of medium-sized enterprises in less-advanced technologies in a society still centered on the later phase of industrialism.

14. In addition, current research suggests that the various subsystems of complex organizations have their own dynamics, organizational characters and psychosocial climates (Katz and Kahn 1966) and that the capacity to tolerate different subidentities within a given organization contributes significantly to the level of the performance (Lawrence and Lorsch 1967).

Such studies suggest that sociological and environmental context must be taken into account to a greater extent than was evident in earlier versions of the still rudimentary theory and practice of changing organizations.

15. At the present time the practice of leading professionals in the field is guided by an extending repertoire of concepts and techniques, which they combine in "personal styles" difficult to decode. No one knows what a Tannenbaum (Tannenbaum et al. 1961) or an Argyris (1964), in the United States, or a Bridger (1946, 1964) or a Pages (1964), in Europe, in fact does, unless he works with him. Although joint work is increasing, it is not in itself enough to ensure systematic advance.

Much interest therefore has attached to the formulation by Blake (Blake and Mouton 1964) of a depersonalized model capable of independent assessment. This is based on a concept of managerial styles as mixes of concern with "production" and "people" (the managerial grid). A high concern with both, called the "9,9" style, is regarded as optimum, and the objective of an organizational change program is defined as a systematic attempt to induce an overall change in management behavior in this direction throughout the enterprise.

There are six phases: (1) off-site training in "diagonal slice" groups with an emphasis on structured exercises rather than unstructured settings to avoid too high a level of initial anxiety; (2) off-site team training based on "family" groups; (3) on-site intergroup training to achieve better integration between functional groups; (4) discussions with various managerial groups to set goals for the total organization; (5) consultant help in implementing the consequential changes; (6) their consolidation, and withdrawal of the consulting team. The overall program, however, which takes a minimum of four years, has rarely been attempted. First attempts have been made to evaluate its application (Blake et al. 1964), and some positive evidence has been adduced for its effectiveness both in terms of "intervening" and "outcome" variables (Likert op. cit).

Evaluation studies in this whole field have been remarkable by their absence. However difficult, as Bennis (1966) says, "the (evaluation) research effort has somehow to equal all the energy that goes into developing planned change programs themselves." Until this effort is made, the wider body of social scientists is likely to preserve its skepticism as to their worth.

16. Apart from the Tavistock studies and certain projects at the Institute of Preventive Medicine in Leiden (see Hutte 1949, 1969), little work on the introduction of planned change on a collaborative basis had taken place in Europe up to the mid-1950s. Moreover, although Wilfred Bion from a psychoanalytic background had proposed some entirely novel ideas on the nature of group process in relation to task performance (Bion and Rickman 1943; Bion 1946, 1948, 1955, 1961), which created wide theoretical interest, their effect on the practice of those concerned with organizational change in the United States had been negligible.

It is doubtful if even today the differences between the analogs of the T-group that grew out of his work (Trist and Sofer 1959; Rice 1965) and any of the varieties of the NTL tradition are widely realized. But visits to Europe during 1955 and 1956 by a team of American consultants sponsored by the European Productivity Agency triggered widespread developments in a number of countries where a fusion took place between the NTL T-group tradition and collaborative studies of organizational change, much as it had in the United States. By this time the dynamic recovery of the European economics had become evident, and these developments may be regarded as a manifestation of the renewed societal vitality of a number of these countries.

Pointedly, there was little effect on Britain despite the originality and importance of earlier British contributions. Volume of work relative to size of country has been greatest in Holland. So far, however, this has replicated American models rather than created a new tradition (by contrast with much of the Dutch work in social psychiatry).

In France, however, process-centered long-range studies have been proceeding where basic anxieties of "the human condition" are confronted in organizational contexts (Pages 1964) in a way that reflects the influence of Sartre, even if it is not avowedly existentialist as is the current work of Laing at the Tavistock (Laing and Cooper 1964).

By contrast, the work in the Scandinavian countries is task- rather than process-centered. Hjelholt (1963) has initiated a series of studies of the restructuring of roles and relationships in automated tankers. Patterns agreed on in group discussion in Copenhagen were immediately tried out at sea. This work reflects a fusion of a task-centered approach to the T-group with sociotechnical concepts.

Since 1964 a European organization in some ways similar to the NTL network and its Institute of Applied Behavioral Science (there are arrangements for overlapping membership) has developed—the European Institute for Transnational Studies in Group and Organizational Development (EIT).

17. The latest development has been the appearance of collaborative studies concerned with sets of organizations related to the wider social environment as contrasted with the single organization related to its immediate environment. This has come about because the critical problems facing contemporary societies under conditions of complex turbulent environments (Emery and Trist op. cit.) have taken on the character of what Chevalier (1967) has called metaproblems.

These are diffuse social problems affecting major sectors of a society. Moreover, this quality of social extension is becoming perceived so that an existential dimension is added. Such problems are beyond the scope of single organizations to solve. Their solution requires the collaboration of a number of organizations.

18. Such problems appear first to have become accessible to collaborative social research in one or two of the smaller societies of Western Europe. An example is the industrial-democracy project in Norway (Thorsrud and Emery 1966), which has now been proceeding for some five years as a collaborative enterprise between the Norwegian Confederations of Employers and Trade Unions and the Trondheim Institute of Industrial and Social Research and the Human Resources Centre of the Tavistock Institute.

At a later stage the Norwegian government joined the consortium of sponsors while the Trondheim Institute had to set up a new center in Oslo. The problem arose because of a sudden increase in the Norwegian trade unions of a demand for workers' representation on boards of management. What is remarkable is that the two confederations should have requested the assistance of social scientists in order to gain a better understanding of such a problem. The first phase of the project involved a field study of the main enterprises in Norway which included workers' representatives on their boards. The findings, having been reported back to the joint steering committee set up by the sponsors, were widely discussed not only throughout the two confederations but also in the press.

The redefinition of the problem obtained in the first phase set the stage for the second which has been concerned with securing, through sociotechnical experiments, improved conditions for personal participation as "a different and perhaps more important basis for democratization of the work place than the formal systems of representation." The third phase, recently begun, is concerned with the diffusion of organizational learning from these experiments.

19. Projects of this kind involve bringing into existence suitable "institutions" under whose auspices they may be carried out. Such bodies, working intimately with the research team and sanctioned from the highest levels of the sectors of the society concerned are essential if a shared and responsible understanding of what is required is to be created.

On the research side the task is to assemble the relevant resources, which will rarely exist in one center, so that consortia are likely to be brought into existence. Working models of improved systems must not only be established under operational conditions but also possess a cultural congruence that will permit their diffusion throughout the entire societal domain concerned.

20. Work of this kind will extend the interdisciplinary mix of social science professionals to include political scientists and economists and operational research workers and engineers. This extension is already happening in a number of instances. The widened nature of the societal engagement recalls something of the spirit of the pioneering efforts of Lewin and the Tavistock group during World War II, a spirit that was later absent. Everything that has since been learned will be needed, plus more that awaits discovery.

The whole field of collaborative studies in organizational change is undergoing redefinition through the different quality in the pressure on the social scientists to take an active (but professional) role in "the starting conditions" of social innovation (Emery op. cit.). Perlmutter (1965) has suggested a concept of social architecture to express this redefinition. By social architecture he means the process of building, changing, and renewing "indispensable institutions" as distinct from "expendable organizations." By social architects he means the interdisciplinary set of scientific professionals who are beginning to find out how to assist the institution builders—the executive and elected leaders of all kinds—in their task of "building better."

REFERENCES

Argyris, C. 1964. *Integrating the Individual and the Organization.* New York: Wiley.

Bell, D. 1967. "The Year 2000—The Trajectory of an Idea." *Daedalus* (Summer Issue).

Bennis, W. G. 1966. "Theory and Method in Applying Behavioral Science to Planned Organizational Change." In J. R. Lawrence, ed., *Operational Research and the Social Sciences.* London: Tavistock Publications.

Bion, W. R. 1948. "Advances in Group and Individual Therapy." In J. C. Flugel, ed., *International Congress on Mental Health,* vol. 3. London: H. K. Lewis.

Bion, W. R. 1955. "Group Dynamics—A Review." In M. Klein et al., eds., *New Directions in Psychoanalysis*. London: Tavistock Publications.

Bion, W. R., and Rickman, J. 1943. "Intra-Group Tensions in Therapy." *Lancet 2* (November).

Blake, R. R., and Mouton, J. S. 1964. *The Managerial Grid*. Houston, Text.: Gulf.

Blake, R. R.; Mouton, J. S.; Barnes, L. B.; and Greiner, L. E. 1964. "A Managerial Grid Approach to Organization Development: The Theory and Some Research Findings." *Harv. Bus. Rev.* 42.

Bradford, L. P. 1974. *National Training Laboratories, Its History: 1947–1970*. Arlington: NTL.

Bradford, L. P.; Gibb, J. R.; and Benne, K. D. 1964. *T Group Theory and Laboratory Method*. New York: Wiley.

Bridger, H. 1946. "The Northfield Experiment." *Bull. Menninger Clin*. 10.

Boshear, W. C., and Albrecht, K. G. 1977. *Understanding People, Models and Concepts*. La Jolla, Calif.: University Associates.

Chevalier, M. 1967. *Stimulation of Needed Social Science Research for Canadian Water Resource Problems*. Ottawa: Privy Council Science Secretariat.

Emery, F. E. 1959. *Characteristics of Socio-Technical Systems*. London: TIHR, Doc. no. 527.

Emery, F. E. 1967. "The Next Thirty Years: Concepts, Methods and Anticipations." *Hum. Relat*. 20 (3).

Emery, F. E., and Thorsrud, E. 1975. *Democracy at Work*. Canberra: Australian National University, Centre for Continuing Education.

Emery, F. E., and Trist, E. L. 1965. "The Causal Texture of Organizational Environments. *Hum. Relat*. 18 (1).

Emery, F. E., and Trist, E. L. 1972. *Towards a Social Ecology*. London and New York: Plenum Press.

Higgin, G. W., and Bridger, H. 1964. "The Psychodynamics of an Inter-Group Experience. *Hum. Relat*. 17 (4).

Hjelholt, G. 1963. "Training for Reality." Papers of the Department of Industrial Management, Leeds University.

Hutte, H. 1949. "Experiences in Studying Social Psychological Structures in Industry." *Hum. Relat*. 2 (2).

Hutte, H. 1969. *The Sociatry of Work* (English edition). London: Tavistock Publications, forthcoming.

Jaques, E. 1964. "Social-Analysis and the Glacier Project. *Hum. Relat*. 17 (4).

Katz, D., and Kahn, R. L. 1966. *The Social Psychology of Organizations*. New York: Wiley.

Laing, R. D., and Cooper, D. G. 1964. *Reason and Violence. A Decade of Sartre's Philosophy, 1950–60*. London: Tavistock Publications.

Lawrence, P. R., and Lorsch, J. W. 1967. *Organization and Environment*. Boston: Division of Research, Graduate School of Business Administration, Harvard University.

Lewin, K. 1951. *Field Theory in Social Science*, D. Cartwright, ed., New York: Harper.

Likert, R. 1961. *New Patterns of Management*. New York: McGraw-Hill.

Likert, R. 1967. *The Human Organization*. New York: McGraw-Hill.

Mann, F. 1957. "Studying and Creating Change: A Means to Understanding Social Organization." Industrial Relations Research Association, Publication no. 17.

McGregor, D. 1960. *The Human Side of Enterprise*. New York: McGraw-Hill.

Morse, N., and Reimer, E. 1955. "Report on Organizational Change." Survey Research Center, University of Michigan.

Morse, N., and Reimer, E. 1956. "The Experimental Change of a Major Organizational Change." Survey Research Centre, University of Michigan.

Pages, M. 1964. In A.R.I.P., *Pedagogie et Psychologie des Groupes*. Paris: Editions de l'opi.

Perlmutter, H. W. 1965. *Towards a Theory and Practice of Social Architecture*. London: Tavistock Publications.

Rees, J. R. 1945. *The Shaping of Psychiatry by War*. New York: Norton.

Rice, A. K. 1958. *Productivity and Social Organization. The Ahmedabad Experiment*. London: Tavistock Publications.

Rice, A. K. 1963. *The Enterprise and Its Environment*. London: Tavistock Publications.

Rice, A. K. 1965. *Learning for Leadership*. London: Tavistock Publications.

Schein, E. H., and Bennis, W. G. 1965. *Personal and Organizational Change Through Group Methods*. New York: Wiley.

Shepard, H. A. 1960. "Three Management Programs and the Theories Behind Them: In an Action Research Program for Organization Improvement." Foundation for Research on Human Behavior, Ann Arbor, Mich.

Tannenbaum, R.; Wechsler, I. R.; and Massarik, F. 1961. *Leadership and Organization*. New York: McGraw-Hill.

Thorsrud, E., and Emery, F. E. 1966. "Industrial Conflict and 'Industrial Democracy.'" In *Operational Research and the Social Sciences*, J. R. Lawrence, ed. London: Tavistock Publications.

Trist, E. L., and Bamforth, K. W. 1951. "Some Social and Psychological Consequences of the Longwall Method of Coal-Getting." *Hum. Relat.* 4 (3).

Trist, E. L., and Sofer, C. 1959. *Exploration in Group Relations*. Leicester: Leicester University Press.

Trist, E. L.; Higgin, G. W.; Murray, H.; and Pollock, A. B. 1963. *Organizational Choice: Capabilities of Groups at the Coal Face under Changing Technologies*. London: Tavistock Publications.

Vickers, Sir G. 1965. *The Art of Judgement*. London: Chapman & Hall.

Chapter 4

The Scientific Communication Model of Group Dynamics: A New Scientific Approach?

Peter Heintel

THE CONTRADICTION INHERENT IN DIFFERENT LEVELS OF COMMUNICATION

The subject of communication has, in recent decades, become markedly more attractive. This can be seen from the number of publications, from the institutionalization of schools of science and research, from the diverse social practical experiments in "communication training," and from the increasing importance of this subject in all kinds of sciences from information theory via diverse technical sciences to linguistics, philosophy, and theology. Indeed, some of the terminology of this subject has even crept into the vocabulary of "high-brow" colloquial language.

I see the reasons for this increase in importance in one fundamental global contradiction from which many others can be derived. On the one hand the necessity for the survival of our civilization imposes a global organization of all people in the world and communication between them; on the other hand, particular interests and universally developed disparities

This chapter, originally titled "Das Kommunikationswissenschaftliche Modell der Gruppendynamik," was translated from the German by Trygve Johnstad.

seem to forbid equal rights of communication. Even now, I am not talking about specific difficulties in communication within a society, or about the different language and norm systems and the different conditions for thought and action that emerge from them, nor about the technical-organizational problems, and so on. What this is about is essentially a basic contradiction relating to our survival. This contradiction has to be removed as soon as possible if communication by violence is not to be the final solution.

This basic contradiction is expressed on other levels as a contradiction between disciplined "freedom" according to a hierarchical power constellation, and civil constitutional rights of independence according to a democratic model to be organized and sanctioned under international law. Of course, the survival of our civilization presupposes a restriction of freedom: Particular and individual self-interest must naturally be limited or, even better, learn to limit itself. The problem remains as to who will be in charge of the measures to be taken, who will sanction, and for whose benefit? At present, we can hardly expect to see universally organized translations of democratic rights of freedom, and I find it cynical to maintain that this is the case only because the historically underprivileged have never been interested or sufficiently "mature."

Since this contradiction, left unresolved, presents itself in the way described, the communication problem acquires in addition the following contradictory form. On the one hand, a global communication is required to function because people are too dependent on each other and have to live together; on the other hand, it is impossible to solve the simplest problems in a communicative and shared way, and these are problems that are held by individuals and societies alike to be most important. The power constellations in our unequal hierarchical system of the world are certainly primarily interested that communications should take place, but cannot do anything about the application of communication to problem-solving— apparently as a consequence of their very nature, because to do so would imply relinquishing part of their own authority.

The result is that global communication has been reduced to technical and economic information and "exchange" systems that are careful not to jeopardize the existing power structure because they are governed by it. Therefore, they have lost their importance on the world scene just as all the remaining elements of communication have, both directly and indirectly, by making language private and irrational, individual and particular. Here it should in no way be overlooked that the very basis and presupposition of an international law, founded upon a democratic, constitutional right to freedom, has to be built up from totally different communicational conditions than technical-economic ones. If sudden claims for new kinds of communication appear now and then on the world historical scene, the first reaction of the system is to bring them under existing technocratic control, that is, to submit them to the existing power system and the norms underlying it. In this way what freedom and its defense might signify is almost daily beaten into us normatively, in order that we should not get the idea of using it for our own purposes.

These three examples of the basic contradiction in our global "system" have consequences for human communication for every one of us. What has been established here in broad outline extends into distant regions of detail and is there very often overlooked, since the connections are unknown. The global notions with which I began are only meant as a background to reflect the problems within group dynamics with which we are dealing. It is always dangerous to start out with such encompassing and necessarily general notions that the reader suspects, often rightly, an underlying religious motive with group dynamics being used as a salvation-bringing world religion. I hope in what follows to be able to prove my realistic common sense, but without neglecting this background.

To return to the problem of communication. One of the most important theoretical and practical problems of group dynamics, which has reality, is set out as follows:

Universal Communication

Worldwide communication concerning the survival of our civilization is reserved for technology and the powers by which it is controlled. Most people are controlled and organized by these powers and are unable to say or do anything about it. The old fate—the unshakable necessity— has a new shape for the individual; it is now apparently entirely mastered by people. The individuals become world-historic fatalists who moreover have to withdraw from earlier hopes of salvation. What they must now learn is that it is no longer the good God making the world's history, but some selected people; or anyway, these people pretend to do so. There is an aggravating paradox in this situation that can only lead to an unhappy awareness, namely the contradiction between more or less comprehensive information (be it one-sided and partial) and an impossibility of being able to contribute anything of one's own. I leave it to the reader to picture for himself what resigned privatistic attitudes this fact produces in the individual.

Transnational Communication

With insignificant variations and in spite of the worldwide power con-glomeration, our world society is still organized into national states. This leads on the one hand to a contradiction between national autonomy and international dependence (particularly for the smaller countries, which are hardly allowed any trade margins), and on the other hand to a domestic contradiction between the real and the imaginary power of one's own state, one's own nation. It is precisely lack of information about the first contradiction that leads to a domestic idolatry, entailing the formation of emotional identifications long since obsolete. The international power connections have their interests in this, just as the national states and their representatives have theirs, in order not to be looked on as puppets.

Therefore, mostly in the same manner as universal communication, transnational communication is restricted to the economic-technical set of rules, aside from cultural exchanges, sport arrangements, and scientific symposia, which are politically mostly unimportant. How difficult it is to communicate on many levels between nations—even without laying too much stress on the language problem—is something everyone knows who has taken part in group-dynamics seminars with participants from different countries.

National Communication

The national state, as supreme, regulates the public, shared life of the people. The constitution and the judicial system form the basis of this public communication. They cannot uphold individual wishes and opinions just as they please. On the contrary, without this basis individual needs and expectations cannot be realized.

Here again we find the fundamental contradiction, now in another form. Through this public system, communication is for most people in some way determined by fate, so that all individual and even collective demonstrations for or against must be seen as ineffective reasoning. In the course of time, and by relating everything to division of labor and expertise, it is then left to a few to make the decisions that should be taken by the people as a whole. Furthermore, the rights and rules of public life become more and more complicated and confusing, which necessitates special translations and organizations; for example, the bureaucrats of public administration. Special jobs must even be provided, and these organizations are seen to be just as complex and preordained as the motives for having them.

As a result of this contradiction, ascribed to the general division of labor, on the one hand the judicial system is degraded to functional formalism, while on the other hand we find that all kinds of communication and initiatives, which do not occur within this formalism and are not manageable by it, are pushed into private life. Even if this kind of communication (for example the total emotionally defined area) were also naturally real and active in all public domains and their organizations, it would have no right to appear there. It is repressed, expelled, and disqualified as irrational. Naturally, it finally gets its own back on the public systems in informal ways by continuously impeding the proceedings.

Activities in group-dynamics, social interventions in civil service agencies make the disunion and indirect interweaving of these two levels very distinct. It is also true that an extensive insensibility prevails here about the price for "overcoming" this conflict. A particular example of how a decision-making organization in public life communicates is, however, hardly the parliamentarily constituted acts, but rather white papers and standing orders from the ministries, through which it is *really* governed, since often even carefully drafted laws can be distorted so that they almost contradict themselves. Besides, it is still very little known to what extent such orders handed down from above may alter the communal life of the institutions below and may be capable of influencing the emotional situation throughout.

The Formal-Democratic Level of Communication

The contradiction to which I have referred generally appears in a similar way as "formal democracy" in every democratic state. This represents the historical continuation of the basic contradiction we have witnessed in our history when power has been taken over by the people: on the one hand, to speak for all mankind (equality, freedom, brotherhood, democracy, constitution); on the other hand, not to yield any of their own power and not to find any relevant organizational models for the ideal postulates.

Public communication in all national democracies is therefore also marked by these contradictions: The people shall rule, but from lack of information and organization they cannot. "The people" is atomized into individuals who serve only as formal justification for the decisions of interest groups. The mass media, happy to inform as they may be, hardly improve the situation for different reasons. They are themselves partly controlled by interest groups and scarcely to be questioned by anybody, so that their information contribution is more likely to further a growing passivity instead of individual initiatives.

Alongside a democratic constitution, with its fundamental regulatory laws and rights of freedom, and its firm foundation of jurisdiction, the undemocratic powers of hierarchical institutions are still there, well organized. Consequently, we find the old irrationalities in political decision-making procedures furthered by permitting only a few to have the duty to decide for the many. Experiments with direct democracy (initiatives by citizens, and so on) usually prove themselves right from the start to be ridiculous in this situation because they have as their starting point particularism, false information, or indirect political control.

These circumstances have serious consequences for public, democratic communication. The result is an increasing political disinterest observable in "the people"; with a state of political passivity as the most obvious characteristic, while not so easily perceptible political influences indirectly persuade people to play the role of useful objects for manipulation. Even more, this leads to a personal irresponsibility in relation to political power and interest constellations (associations, political parties, unions), whereby people, out of a regard for personal security and individual gratification (for example, appointments), accept a considerable amount of undemocratic practice.

Politics in a democratic sense is not simply a matter of laws and regulations. On the one hand it constantly provides for an opportunity for hidden and concealed power, on the other hand it is positively upheld as providing opportunities for individual and collective education and organization. As the only form of government, democracy demands not just a system of constitution and jurisdiction, it demands in addition an individual attitude; a commitment to and training in the never ending task of reestablishing democracy again and again. Collective forms of organization are demanded that are now short-circuited in functional hierarchies.

Some group-dynamics seminars in political training have clearly demonstrated the great discrepancy between a thoroughly acceptable knowledge of democracy and politics, and a practical attitude to them. Incompetence in practical, political, and democratic behavior was painfully obvious when it came to organizing one's own "policy." This democratic incompetence is more common than is usually believed, and leads directly and indirectly to delegation of responsibility; a return to the old hierarchical system, which can never be dismissed anyway even when, as in so many cases, it has demonstrated itself to be clumsy and ineffective.

Organizational Communication

The most important communication area in our lives (perhaps with the exception of the primary group) is, after all, the publicly organized world of work and business; the institutional, communal area. Here all levels of contradictions are found together. It has immediate reality in our lives and does not let itself be pushed aside into notions of fate and anonymity like the state and world society. Certainly one tries as best one can to get rid of the contradictions mentioned earlier or at least to make them anonymous. But it has never been possible to succeed fully in this.

So it is here that the contradictions really come together: the one between the total political background of the institution and its individual manifestations; another between the official hierarchical structure and the informal communication structure, which is at least as important; yet another between the permitted code of behavior and repressed emotionality; a fourth between the official way of functioning and recurring conflicts that can never be settled because the system forbids it. Here too is found the contradiction inherent in very unequal payment for work often of comparable importance; the contradiction between activity only being seen as work, and passivity in relation to the organization; between an invitation to cooperation that is frequently worth considering and a subsequently rather insignificant scope for action; between latent or open suffering in a situation of dependence and bad organization, and an often striking lack of awareness of its causes and conditions; and so on. These contradictions could be added to and set out in more detail, but what is important for us is, above all, to recognize and to understand their importance for communication as a whole.

Although many critical social scientific analyses have already demonstrated these contradictions, the practical consequences have been mostly left out. Usually the concrete analyses evaporate into general models of society, which are theoretically just as correct as they are practically useless. For example, it must be noted that in these areas of communication every institution and every company is an "individual." Practical changes must make it possible for this to be taken seriously in its own right, particularly because the areas of public policy and informal privacy here cross each other, often very irrationally interwoven. Here group-dynamics work is basically different from the traditional science of communication and organization, but this still remains to be demonstrated.

Indirect Communication

However, our communication is determined not only by the anonymity of functionalistic and technical economy which, simply and without discussion, structures our daily communal life. Here atavisms unite with formal regulations, rituals of interaction, courtesy, etiquette, "body language," defense mechanisms, fixed language form and pattern, and so on.

Communication based on these rules settles to a considerable degree our daily intercourse with people and institutions. Mostly it is an (often taboo) outcome of certain survival systems of societies, to protect their norms, their hierarchies, their institutions, their relations between the sexes, and so on. It is frequently precisely these indirect forms of communication that regulate those important areas of human living together that daily and often must be regulated, and that politically, publicly, and officially are usually very hard to regulate. They are easily concealed or automatically rendered, and are not willingly exposed to public discussion.

Even if we cannot do without these often unconscious regulations, the same contradiction is to be found here as well, consisting of two components: The relativity of these communicational regulations on a world-wide scale (from one culture to another they are often very different in content) and the fact that science and public administration question their natural and self-evident nature. That is to say, it is pretended that all communication can in principal be defined and changed only when the reasons for its existence are understood (for example, in the abolition of taboos) in accordance with the basic democratic idea that everything that has a public existence should be determinable.

Against this we have our ideas, our consciousness and insight into social-communicative survival—so often totally consistent with "atavistic" findings. But this insensibility is furthered by those conventions, in fact democratically carried over, that justify their existence exactly by appealing to the indirect rules of communication. Therefore, an effort to clear away indirect forms of communication is often prevented precisely by those conventions that also expect to be criticized for their constitution-like attitude: the old idea of the empire, the idea of emotional followers, and so on. The rituals and patterns of behavior connected with this continue to survive in institutions and companies. Internal group-dynamics work in institutions deals especially with these often very different systems of indirect communication. But in practice nothing is changed unless the new insights are actually experienced quite apart from a continuous process of absorbing the effects of indirect communication in daily life.

Direct Communication

The last level to be analytically separated and specified is the level of direct communication in small groups. Of course, the distinctions between the seven points enumerated are analytic distinctions only, and in hardly any phase of life or the understanding of it is one level separated from another. They are cut across and influence each other at the same time. However, this last level differs from the others in a particular way: It is open to direct communication. Here dialogue is possible, here norms and agreements can be formed in a rather flexible way, and here no "external" objective need be given within which and according to which people are organized. Direct communication occur principally wherever it is possible for the members of a group to question the regulatory determinants of their communication and where the relations can be renegotiated.

This form of communication is known first of all from the family as the primary group which, at least at first, tries to filter the norms that are imposed from the outside. (It is not possible to raise here the psycho-analytically interesting question of the unconscious life of these primary groups.) It is further familiar from a circle of friends, and finally from smaller committees, youth and other groups, who often pretend to have an external goal to which they can officially refer, but whose real intention is to strive for direct communication.

Tasks and limits of direct communication are easy to elicit from this description: On the one hand, it provides a context where the individual can express his wishes and emotions or explore what is really happening, where the least external control is given. On the other hand, it is limited to small groups and cannot be transferred to organizations and institutions. This is one of the reasons that direct communication in our complex society has ended up as private and informal (the social-historic reasons cannot be given here in detail), while externally controlled communication is the rule in all other areas of life.

The characteristic jargon we often hear today about free and uncontrolled communication seems to me to be mainly the ideal of the small group transferred to the whole society—a late appearance of German-pietistic cordiality. Bearing in mind the contradictions in our societies, one would certainly have to take care in selecting which powers are historically conditioned and which could be made superfluous. Indeed, if one tries to make the claim for freedom from control valid as a postulate in a practical sense, it would be naive to believe that communication can be divorced from authority altogether, taking into consideration all the different levels of communication.

Naturally the contradictions visible elsewhere appear also here, this time in a double way. First, on this very level we have the paradoxical situation that self-realization, recognition, and identity formation are in reality separated from public life. They take place in an atmosphere of freedom and openness, with no consequences for society as a whole because they only occur in *small* groups with a largely private character (in group dynamics often only the character of an experimental laboratory). At the same time the difference between this "real" life and the externally regulated life that can arbitrarily restrict, enlarge, and influence the margin of this "real" life, is experienced very painfully and creates a continuously unhappy awareness, especially in well-functioning small groups examining their own values.

Second, this level is *in itself* in contradiction to the others, because here a communication is possible that seems to be excluded on the other levels. Here we have reached a watershed in the development of our societies. Whereas the economic-functional, technocratic, and global communication organized according to relevant power constellations is prepared to take any communication areas whatsoever into its power and subject them all to an externally controlled allegiance, this level, on the other hand, gives expression to the world-historic ideology of the middle class, and offers a new opportunity to speak further about autonomy, individual self-regulation, and self-realization. In fact, the total democratic idea grew out of this background. Because of the organization of the middle class and its power basis—namely, the process of industrial production—these ideological expectations have so far been successfully established only in areas separated from of public administration, whereby people naturally lose more and more in competence and self-esteem. I cannot pursue here whether these ideas of the middle class, which reflect its organization for its own survival as a class, are to be seen as abstractly idealistic, naive, or simply utopian (indeed, communism belongs here with its class-free society). Nor can I take up whether the survival of our civilization permits autonomy and direct communication at all outside the private sphere. Even when we take into account that, because of advanced automation, the system will make available more and more time off, and we do not pessimistically believe that this has already been taken care of in a way that leaves no place for direct communication; if, moreover, a real reduction in power and privileges can be expected; and if furthermore the realization of democracy were to be a primary task; we are still left with a problem. How can the contradiction between direct and all other kinds of communication be organized so that now and then direct communication will have a chance to break through and assert itself; so that autonomy does not have to be something private; and so that what belongs to public life need not necessarily be decided from outside. Nowadays the institutionalized part of public life demands more and more individual responsibility, personal initiative, even creativity— all qualities definitely not promoted by permanent external regulation.

THE STARTING-POINT OF GROUP DYNAMICS AND HOW IT DEVELOPED: (Group Dynamics as a Dynamic Science of Communication)

Unlike all other sciences of communication until now, which may be described as statically descriptive or technocratically prescriptive, I maintain that group dynamics is the only dynamic science of communication practically consistent with its subject. This is apart from scattered attempts by action research and interaction training as well as the profound psychological and analytic models, which cannot unfortunately be dealt with here. This rather portentous-sounding assertion must now be proved, even if it is already almost derivable from my description of the communication levels and their contradictions.

Science, in particular social science, precisely reflects an institutionalized, indirect level of communication where attempts at self-understanding or self-realization are hardly possible. In fact, this is where the very identity formation can take place for those referred to in a project, who themselves—for the most part—are not scientifically active.

In this manner something alien and externally controlled is usually added to most sciences. Paradoxically, they are expected to form an exact opinion in their own terminology and jargon about those whose language has already been excluded beforehand, namely those affected. This alienated relationship is motivated and justified by reference to a need for division of labor and for professional competence. The still extant and superficial scientific orthodoxy (whose influence, fortunately, is not so weighty) plays its part in maintaining this difference between the subject and the object of science. No one doubts that the result of a sufficiently honest introspection and scientific dialogue would be seen as obviously right and true by everyone, according to the principle that "we are all human beings," but also that there is no harm in the fact that only some can know while the rest have to believe.

This last difference is already exacerbated by the fact that it is not possible for those concerned to act according to their own insight and reason, nor to change themselves or their surroundings so long as they are not able to understand the reasons for and against as a logical argument. It is also exacerbated by the fact that scientific systems that want to express a certain degree of general commitment often have to leave this realism aside, even if it is important to the single individual and his social and institutional surroundings. These systems are therefore frequently seen as unrealistic, unpractical, and purely theoretical, and therefore are often unjustly given a bad reputation. Certainly, even when such general statements, models and explanations are found in the social sciences as well, their specific character will still at times be faced with the concrete reality of groups, institutions, and so on. This is exactly the starting point for practical and individual experience and its change. Only in this way is it possible for those affected to start something.

The institutionally organized character of the sciences to which I have referred has as its condition that science can only be used properly for technical or descriptive purposes related to its practical application. It can be technically applied where the results are simply implemented without asking those who are affected by the outcome for their views. Indeed, very often they cannot be asked because they are unable to discuss how the results are brought about or how they can be related to daily life. Technical sciences of organization and communication work almost exclusively on this basis, whereby they grow even more technical and imperialistic. The larger the organization, the more extensive is the area of communication where regulation is required.

Science is descriptive—tending toward the contemplative—when it is discussing areas where it is mostly obsolete social structures and fields of communication that are being simply and empirically displayed. But recent critical-empirical and dialectic-interpretative scientific work has tried to move away from this ground. This applies to Apel, for instance, with his demand for change and emancipative work that is so forceful that it leaves our ears tingling. But still, as I see it, most of this science remains anchored in theory (also true of Apel's "virtual communication society,") with its regulatory task for all philosophy and social science).

I would prefer not even to mention that science of communication which still deals in a more or less overcomplicated sender-receiver model (and gives rise to doctorates all round) without recognizing its undialectic, individually mechanical character. Likewise I do not believe that we will be carried any further forward by the science of communication, which develops models founded on modern linguistics and fails to recognize the pragmatic nature of language and other media of communication.

As distinct from the static and technical sciences of communication, I have designated group dynamics as a dynamic science of communication. This means primarily two things. In the first place the relation between theory and application is different; and second, as a consequence, the relation between science and those affected by it. Thereby a new and dynamic relationship between theory and practice of communication, and the science of communication can be motivated. I will not describe this in more detail.

Not without reason, group dynamics started out as small-group research. It was still essentially committed to the classical scientific model, which maintains a difference between the object of research (the small group) and the researchers. No research into the communication between these two "groups" took place. Seldom if ever did the experimental "subject" and "groups" experience what was really happening.

The small group appeared to be an ideal object of research. It was surveyable and as a social unit was easily conceivable. In addition, it appeared to be possible to bring about direct communication in small groups, and then, from what happened, perhaps to deduct analogical keys for understanding wider areas of society.

It may be, although certainly not consciously, that in a middle-class autonomy-claiming sense, the idea was rationally to get hold of the smallest and most private entity still available for individual identity formation.

This small—and sometimes large—group research, with a social scientific model analogous to the classical natural scientific one, is still undertaken even today and fills the "strictly" empirical encyclopedia with its observations and research findings. It lends itself to the same objections we have mentioned before. What takes place here is really only an internal scientific dialogue about results if social engineers are given the task of bringing about practical consequences of some of the findings.

In contrast to this, I am talking about that kind of group dynamics that principally dissociates itself from this model and has found a totally new relation to practice. With this it has prepared the way for a new communicative relationship between science and daily life. What originally looked almost like an accident, namely that the individuals and groups taking part in the experience were confronted with the results and then suddenly started to behave differently, was developed into a system.

The approach is no longer to observe social phenomena nor to describe (criticize) in order to deduct generalizations with the pretended character of laws; nor again to aim at effects that can then be offered as results or implemented, often when the only function of this is to falsify the prejudices in the hypothesis.

What we are really concerned to do is *to connect a process of cognition and observation with an educative and communicative process* so that in the course of this process the difference between thought and action, specialist and layman, researcher and those affected, and so on, can possibly be communicated and done away with. Anyone originally of the opinion that what are found in the social field are groups with laws (determinants of communication) that have almost the character of natural laws, would be instructed that this presumption is valid only so long as these groups hardly know anything about themselves and their social life. If, on the other hand, they are told not only what has been but also the assumptions that can be made about which actions, decisions, intentions, and so on cause such and such phenomena to occur, then the effects of this immediately become grounds for review and reconsideration and the planning of change.

To abolish the classical schism between researchers and "researched" resulted in practical models of group dynamics. For here the aim can be said to be to experience directly this difference, to neutralize it, and to make oneself ready for a new social awareness. A parallel and continuous feedback process makes possible a unity between observation, experience, and change, and leads to training in social sensitivity and diagnostic ability. Even if the problem of how communication is settled and structured, which determinants are present, and how they are dealt with on different occasions is observed entirely in the spirit of the classical science of communication; the observation itself emerges directly from a process of communication, is committed to it, is experienced in the present, and is relevant in a very practical sense.

Consequently, what I understand by a dynamic science of communication is that form of group dynamics, in theory and practice, in which science and research can no longer be separated from the process of education (of those affected, of course). It is no longer concerned with the description and explanation of communication in terms of its preconditions, qualifications, and unconscious "laws." Rather it concerns an attempt to develop a model for practical experience of the self and self-examination that invites groups to learn about the conditions in which communication takes place in the first place, in order to enable them to secure their own social-communicative experience later on; and in the second, so that they learn to decide for themselves what conditions and norms they would find acceptable and what it is otherwise up to themselves to change. Without this incorporation of the concerned individuals and groups themselves, every science of communication will be either technical (treating the social field as an object of nature) or ineffectively descriptive in its implementation.

Summing up, this much can be said: Even if at the outset and in its first attempts group dynamics entirely corresponded with the classical scientific model, by abolishing the subject-object relationship in this model it has moved in a direction from which there is no way back. In this way it approached the social sciences, the sciences of human beings, with, traditionally speaking, simultaneously higher and lower expectations. These expectations, which I shall refer to again later, are of central concern to the problem of communication generally, but above all to communication between science and life.

Group dynamics today tries to work on this communication problem, not by working out new models out or new hypotheses, nor by constructing new proceedings and methods, but by maintaining that the problem can be solved only if group dynamics, as a dynamic science of communication, totally changes its scientific character. The claim to solve problems of communication adequately and not analyze them critically in a technical or descriptive way, must produce a change in the shape and character of the science itself as a communicative activity. This change relates to the very core of the science: its methods, its organization, its adaptability to institutionalized settings, the limited validity of the content of its statements, the temporary nature of its models and its readiness to correct them, its relationship to practice, how one can be educated for it, and so on.

These radical consequences were not taken sufficiently seriously earlier by any of the critical "emancipatory" sciences. Therefore their claims to be emancipatory and their appeals for change remained merely as theoretical postulates. Repeatedly, the content of their statements was too general to be related to individual or particular collective social practice.

It is certain that group dynamics will also have a problem with meta-theoretical and scientific justification. It should and must be possible to give information about motives, models, modes of proceeding, goals, and so on. It is precisely the often very scattered and arbitrary practices that make this information necessary. But so is a semantic commitment that must be plausible in itself, independent of what happens in practice. I am aware of the limited reality and impact of this "theory" of group dynamics, as well as of the risks of seeking independence and attempting to justify rationally what is, in itself, a much more complex practice.

The circumstance with self-legitimating practice is naturally not yet sufficiently clear in group-dynamics science either. Radical hostility to theory exists alongside subtle critical theory and justification. This preliminary unresolved and contradictory state cannot be seen only as the uncertain beginnings of a new science, but rather as deriving from the essentially different claims of group dynamics.

The purpose of its theory is not to have statements made *about* an object or a field (analogous with classical, empirical natural sciences). Nor is its purpose to carry over normative content or to anticipate this in order to make proposals for some practice (analogous with the moral and ideological sciences). Neither is the task to give descriptions "free from value judgments" (which is anyhow impossible). Finally, this theory should not be allowed to take the form of a metatheoretical, classical philosophical theory, which can indeed be consistent within itself, but remains, because of language tradition and terminology, limited to likeminded equals with a similar educational background.

In a way we are dealing with a new concept of theory, which in practice attempts to take seriously and to realize traditions for which claims were made a long time ago. But so far those have not had a chance to be put into practice. Let me mention some: the majestic and dialectic character of the philosophy of Plato and its well documented skepticism about the written word; the concept of autonomous collectivity in Christianity; the transcendental change in philosophy when it was recognized and established that a proper theory about human beings could not be worked out in the form of "intentione recta" as knowledge "about," but rather had to face and adapt to the conditions dictated by its own possibilities; and the development of this idea in the great dialectic system of Hegel, with the grand notion of the identity of concept and reality. Other examples are the abolition postulate of Marx where theory is seen as a leader that throws itself away once it has ascended; the somewhat fading request for a "virtual communication society" by Apel, the "dialogue" philosophy of Ebner via Bahner to Habermas. Within all these efforts there is certainly a fundamental awareness of what it is theoretically all about and what risks are attached to it. Nevertheless, these efforts had consequences only for an "elite" (I even count the avant garde of the proletariat in this group, since they try dogmatically to maintain a higher communicational competence than everyone else.)

In group dynamics this relation between theory and practice is in some sense inverted without its becoming excessively practical or pragmatic. Here empirical orientation, practice, and joint reflection on the situation further a commitment to the concept and make it possible to express in language a theory of reconstruction from which generalizations can be made in which different stages and levels are displayed that can be used for different purposes.

The simple self-examination that takes place in small groups, departments, and so on, can already be seen as constituting a theory on a primary level, directed toward a better understanding of oneself. This serves as a guarantee that members have things in common and have differences—in short, that the conditions of communication and of life are present. The content can be particular and individual in a very concrete way. This certainly limits its value for the purpose of making general and comparative statements, but on the other hand immensely increases the understanding and survival of this particular group. This is made feasible by having the details decided in common by the individuals present. In this way, a starting point and basis is also found for changes, where more general appeals for change very often fail to perceive this reality clearly and so lose—not without repercussions—this "individual" aspect of groups.

Naturally there are also theories on other levels, as when institutions, organizations, and finally nations and peoples, societies, and classes provide their own "theory" for themselves. This is no "hierarchy of theories." Only the terms and conditions of communication are changed, and consequently the processes for the formation and validation of the theory. In these gestalts and levels of theory as reconstruction and thoughtful examination of the experience of the self in a practical setting, the empirical orientation—as distinct from the theory of empiricism—is now installed in its own right (Hegel calls this "speculative empirical orientation"). It starts with the living experience as the basis for all theory, which, in turn, it must be possible to communicate. It concerns a unity of experience, life, and theory building that has been forgotten because of the division of labor and the impact from natural sciences and that cannot be given up without serious consequences, especially not when we have the experiences of human beings and their societies in mind.

The aim of group dynamics is therefore to outline majestic explorative models and to allow those affected, those who are living with the situation, to find *their* theory through self-examination and communication. It must apply to all the levels on which theories are formed. This means that the models themselves do not display a methodical character in the classical sense, where conditions, aims and factors are formulated in advance. They are much more models designed to promote self-examination and communication and are models that may well select certain main points for exploration, but at the same time are essentially characterized by there being no decisions or knowledge in advance about the application or the outcome of models and methods.

Group dynamics must be said to have been quite successful on the level of small groups. This field of direct communication is also the first and most important training ground for theory-building, self-examination, and identity-formation. It relates closely to areas important for promoting the expression of individual emotions and "virtual communication society." In my contribution, "The Importance of Group Dynamics for Human Communication," in *This is Group Dynamics* (Munich, 1974), I have tried to analyze this field of training and theory formation in its different dimensions: verbal and nonverbal communication, vertical and horizontal communication, the quantitative and qualitative conditions for communication, and how communication is influenced by time and space.

Today group dynamics addresses itself more and more to the next level: to institutions, organizations, communities, and so on; and there are already models that reject description and analysis from the outside in the same way as they are rejected by the small group. The task is instead defined as helping concerned institutions and organizations with their self-examination, and as initiating and encouraging communication between those working within them. Consequently, the counseling function in group dynamics is limited to knowing the models and thus being able to offer help in the communication process, and possibly to telling about comparable experiences—although this usually has little effect.

In the United States, in schools of anthropology and interaction research, empirical research started long ago with the method of living together with those who were to be studied, since in the first place one experiences more (trust relationship), and, second, one learns to appreciate better what is experienced. This procedure corresponds exactly to the new attempt at communication in the science of human beings. I see the difference from group dynamics in the tendency of this type of research quite inconsequently to hold on to descriptive methods. The scientists record their findings and maybe publish them, without really considering the new communicative situation, which would imply that the observations should be fed back to those affected. They are therefore standing still at a certain level of communication, which finally ends up as exploitative and rightly gives the flat feeling of not having been given anything on the one hand, and on the other of their not being able to convince readers of the generality and transferability of their experiences.

Not only small groups but also larger human associations can be brought to a collective self-examination and communication. It is only this self-examination and self-realization communicated verbally which creates the possibility of self-initiated change. Referring to my prefatory note, I may say that group dynamics has already contributed something and has presented important models that make possible understanding of the last three levels of communication: the organizational, the direct, and the indirect. The other levels can hardly be touched on. Naturally, there will always be difficulties with any metatheory that is not built on the basis of practice and experience alone and yet is expected to expose the total system of motives, models, and proceedings. Here much is left to do in the coming years.

From what I have said it may now be clear what I mean by simultaneously lower and higher expectations. The lower expectation concerns the problem area of traditionally understood criteria of science, while the higher is the real and dynamic incorporation of practice with the abolition of a situation in which people and their associations are mere objects for observation and research.

As to the first, I would say further that group dynamics is repeatedly criticized for not leaving its results, contributions, theories, and assertions open to control in the way that the human sciences have done before. In truth, it has been recently more and more admitted that differentiated and to some extent generalizable results, if they are to pass for anything more than already obsolete phenomena, necessitate highly complex long-term projects. Compared with this methodology, the traditional psychological experiments seem like simple kindergarten games. But even if this were the case, one would still adhere to the classical system of division of labor with the researchers and professionals on one side and on the other the "researched" and the laymen. This clerical institutional model has certainly been important for the natural sciences, as well as for the sciences, which want to regard human beings and human groups and societies as objects of nature. But when our prime concern is people, this "division into classes," which may be unintentional, is unacceptable because it leads to a prede- termined separation between human beings of different categories as if there were no need for any further debate on the choice of models. It can easily be seen that a division of this kind establishes a relationship analo- gous to a "natural state" (this holds true at least in all areas related to this subject).

The advantages of institutionalized separation, brought about by the division of labor, are easy to see. They originate, not by chance, from a time when efforts were being made, through imitation of the natural sciences, to form an exact conception of the human being and his society. By introducing a division of labor between professional and layman, between the subject and object of research, the professional will, as a matter of course, be the only one to decide on the conditions, methods, and procedures of the research.

He defines the experimental constellations, decides about the beginning and end, which variables are to be considered and which not, how an observation situation is ideally to be arranged, who shall have the results and who not (usually not the persons investigated), which subject is interesting, which one is dangerous, and so on.

Concurrent reactions to the research and to the experiments themselves are therefore scarcely wanted, since the additional variables then intro- duced only make the investigation more complex. What is obvious is that this separation, owing to the division of labor, must be a prerequisite and a basis for science if situations are to be provided that can be experienced as "exactly" as possible, by methodically excluding all unwanted and disturb- ing factors. Division of labor (institutionalized even to this extent) is the grounds for turning laymen into objects, and in turn provides the background for a most far-reaching exactness (and for the use of mathematics).

A closer look at this basic communication model leads us to notice that no dialogue, no reciprocal relationship whatsoever, occurs, even though we have to deal with people on both sides. The question is restricted to what the research constellation uncovers about the experiment. All "answers" beyond this question will have to be neglected. Neither are those affected expected to defend themselves, nor to suggest other constellations. It is assumed that they are not educated and not informed. As to communication theory, this is a case of a completely unilateral relationship, where the notorious "exactness" is certainly made possible but where human beings must ultimately be treated as if they were natural phenomena.

Kant, reflecting on the Copernican change in European thought, once said that we can understand nature only after having built our own rational framework. We approach nature "but not as a student who lets himself be told anything that the teacher wants to tell him, but as someone called in to judge, forcing the witnesses to answer the questions he poses" (*Kritik der reinen Vernunft*, vol. 13). A similar relationship obviously seems to have been foreseen in the case of human beings. Until now all classical human sciences seem to have functioned according to this model, but one point has been overlooked, and this, because it is so central, has finally indicated itself.

People, individuals and groups, collectives and organizations, may wish to lay claim for themselves to *one* factor that is derived from nature and therefore makes all investigations problematic that are conducted on the same theoretical basis as the natural sciences, which I have just described. This factor incorporates self-examination, self-conception, conscious motivation—in short, what we call freedom. This human characteristic, this inherent freedom (nature has its concept outside of itself, while human beings have it within themselves) cannot be overlooked with impunity. If, nevertheless, it is overlooked, it will have three consequences, which, as I see it, constitute the whole dilemma of contemporary human sciences.

In order to attain an exactness, in itself questionable, which is either rather meager or too general and determined by a relationship of unilateral communication, an attempt is first made (usually indirectly) to let people continue to live in their naturally or normatively determined unconsciousness. It is not desired that they should learn something about themselves that might enable them to change. Second, the gap between the professionals and the laymen is widened to the disadvantage of both; and third, the implementation of science and its results is left to the implementors' arbitrary discretion. Besides, those not involved in the research process and whose "freedom" has already been "forgotten" during the investigation mostly defend themselves against any application, something that further impedes the relation of science to practice.

The first consequence is clearly apparent in the predominantly conservative character of all traditional human sciences. Just as nature is not allowed any caprices when it is to be exactly comprehended (indeed such an obtrusion would arouse considerable surprise because it would imply that nature can answer for herself), so a human being is not allowed to learn too much about himself, since he would then have the possibility of doing something with this knowledge, which would throw every ideal experimental situation to Jericho. However, this conservative scientific practice may only express a historical social state in the development of mankind where we are not yet ready to let people out of their "self-inflicted state of dependence."

The second consequence is a new division of classes, a new priesthood, which naturally has to adapt itself, theoretically as well as practically, to its own religious world and all the norms and laws operating therein, since they have long ago ceased to live in this earthly world. This leads to the continued rational subjection of laymen who, because they are excluded from any scientific discussion, have to accept simply what is held to be true and right about themselves.

The third consequence exposes the fundamental dilemma. Lack of practice and the totally unilaterally defined communication system backfires when those affected are "urged" to apply the theoretical model. They rightly hesitate when suddenly asked to do something and to develop initiatives that they have earlier been forbidden to do and to undertake. If the goal of science is not only to manage people and to control them rationally, then unilateral communication structures always backfire. Therefore this form of science, if it wants to remain practical, is frequently found to carry through its results in a very dictatorial way, albeit unwillingly. That science thereby very often serves political purposes is a well-known fact, but there are even more subtle and less noticeable ways in which it is used, for example by making advertising "scientific."

Group dynamics has abandoned as unsuitable both the unilateral model of communication and the classical claim to exactness as *the* "object" of research. When a science aims to abolish unilateral communication from professional to layman in its proceedings, its ways of looking for results, and its definitions of interests and goals, then exactness cannot at all be what is required. What is required is much more a will and a wish to incorporate what are the "most radical disturbing factors" (for all classical sciences, namely the incorporation of freedom, self-examination, and self-organization—in short, the autonomous initiatives of those concerned). Then only very few predictions can be made, and groupings, content, and conditions can be changed unexpectedly, whereby again new proceedings have to be brought in. This *incorporation of systematic freedom,* consciously organized and introduced by the groups themselves, is the proper goal of scientific work and research and changes the condition, form, and organization of science radically. Certainly it is no longer possible to preserve claim to an exact science as understood until now, for reasons that are now more easily understandable. However, if this "systematic freedom"—on the individual's conditions—is taken into consideration, then methods, proceedings, findings, and aims of application are released even in this system, and results are reached that are always important for and wanted by this system.

This means that scientific concepts are more individualized and concrete, whereby the broader and broadest generalizations and universal consensus have to be given up, at least in relation to practice. But this cannot be the only meaning of science, in particular when practical consequences are to result. It is certain that the bringing about of a reciprocal relationship in communication involves, above all, a limitation of theories that are generally binding and require commitment. But here as well the expectation of group dynamics is lower: that it is necessary for practical work and "application" to make the concept individual and concrete in conjunction with those who created it. It claims further that generalizing theories can easily come far too close to a technocratic use of science.

Every "systematic free system" has, in accordance with those who live and work within it, its specific gestalt, although they may have structures that are legally and formally similar. This should not be neglected if practice is going to be changed from within and not from without.

General theories and statements generally requiring commitment are not interesting or important unless they say something about the "systematic free system" for all mankind. On this subject, some important general and transcendental statements have naturally already been made.

Substantially they must, as they are concrete in form, limit themselves to a paradigm of conditions (or categories) for this freedom that would make the system capable of surviving. Thus it seems that it is not yet possible to make specific statements, since the system has hardly begun to be organized according to its own concepts.

Against the three consequences mentioned earlier, this attempt of a new science of communication conveys advantages that should not be overlooked. Systematic free systems involved in scientific communication as dialogue partner learn to develop their own conception of themselves and to raise the natural determinants of their communication to a conscious level. In short, they achieve a clarity about themselves that enables them to carry out autonomous changes. The gap between scientists and laymen is abolished. Should it still be necessary to have a division of labor, then the scientist should take up the role of a counselor who, in the course of time, would make himself superfluous. the problem of application will largely fade away because the reciprocal model of communication is really continual analysis and application all in one, since those "affected," by taking part in the science and research, are hardly apt to develop resistance against their own results, as distinct from those that are prescribed from the outside.

Indirectly, no doubt we have already discussed at length the "higher expectation" of group dynamics. If further life and growth is to be allowed —and after all that has been said, it is clear that science has here a gestalt that must be problematic for any political system, or human organization—the aim must be to overcome the classical scientific design and its unilateral model of communication for the benefit of a "subject-adequate" perception of people and social formations.

"Subject-adequate" means in the main nothing else but fulfilling the expectations of the subjects (those "affected"). But people—individuals, groups, societies, and so on—develop expectations different from those elsewhere in nature. They will at times be respected as systematic free systems, in which people make their own decisions and organize themselves. Science should not overlook this fact—the essence of its research material —if its intention is not to become a new religion or a useful eunuch. Therefore, it is more or less forced to change its model of communication, with consequences both for concept building and for processes, as well as for total institutionalization and organization. The new expectation will not be satisfied until radical changes are allowed to take place here.

The term "dynamic science of communication" may have become clearer after this presentation. Group dynamics assumes this title only because its own scientific model is in the process of being changed in this direction, and because group dynamics is preparing itself for the abolition of the unilateral communication of classical scientific models. Since in this way another model of communication is presented, it becomes possible to avoid the static descriptions or the technical objectives of classical sciences of communication, which until now have hardly shown any interest in the practical "systematic free system" of communication units.

This implies that the task for group dynamics is to develop models for all the levels of communication I have mentioned and for their subsystems. These models should be helpful in bringing about adapted systematic free systems and in securing for them the relevant self-awareness. Something has already been contributed to the three levels of communication to which I have been referring that raises hopes that it is essentially possible to follow this road. Determinants of communication for these levels and systems should not only be described and exposed or reorganized from the outside. They should be worked on together by those concerned, who should be made conscious of their deciding function and their role in determining the possibilities for change. Consequently, group dynamics has to offer models of communication that make communication in systematic free systems conscious and manageable.

Finally it must be said that the "higher" expectation not only bears on the problem of communication, but also on the relationship between science and education and upbringing. But I cannot explore this further here. Let me draw attention only to the following. An identification of science with education is reached through the changed gestalt of science with its new reciprocal model of communication, which has until now only been expressed as desiderata in legal prefaces. To be engaged in science and research in the way we have described implies a living and experiential learning that finally reaches its peak in an individual and collective self-examination, which in itself has a natural educative effect. Since one's own practice is not totally abandoned but rather raised to a concept that requires the commitment of those concerned, then to be engaged in science means to surrender to an educative process together with others where the idea is to deal not with distant objects outside of ourselves, but with our own experiential world. In this way it is possible to identify with what is acquired and accepted and not only to acquire knowledge externally.

New assignments will naturally emerge from this identification of science with education. What is lost by way of holy professional authority is regained by way of mission. At any rate, the midwife art will again be honored, and counseling no longer only associated with meddling.

COMMENTS

I realize that this claim I have made against all theoretical and practical efforts within contemporary science of communication has to be argued and discussed openly. This, however, would go decisively beyond the directions I have been given. Therefore, I would like briefly to mark the boundaries in relation to the other approaches so that we do not leave it without any referents. I will follow a designation and classification suggested both by a colleague of mine, Thomas Macho, a researcher on communication theory at our institute, and by D. Baacke in his book (1975).

I know very well that by the use of this method much has to be abbreviated and schematically presented, and that a complete picture cannot be drawn. I can hope only that my intentions will be seen more clearly with the help of the following comments. A few subtle differences between the approaches will have to be passed over. What to me is important is to get hold of the principal differences in relation to group dynamics: those which—seen from the point of view of scientific theory—involve developing a new relationship between model (theory) and communicative reality (practice) and organizing this relationship in practice.

Mathematical Theory of Communication[a]

The kind of model developed here is largely determined by its close connection with the news media. The commercial and technological use of the new signal-transmitting techniques resulted in theories and formulas that aimed to compress and optimize this signal transmission. A system (model) is efficient when the difference between the signs given and the signs received is as small as possible. The idea is to minimize the loss of information.

In spite of its technological merits, this mathematical theory of information and communication is therefore in reality a theory of signal transmission. The meaning of the colloquial and socially determined components of the signs must not be considered. A further development of these theories and the logical deciphering of the syntactic and semantic dimension will certainly continue in the differentiation of the theory, but will be limited to simple, logical sentences.

What is sought is a strictly defined language system that allows only the logical freedom of contradiction or probability. Nothing must be said about real colloquial occurrences—for this, a meta-language would have been necessary—or about the pragmatic dimension by transmission of signs, or about intentions, effects, contradictions, etc., not to mention nonverbal and emotional conditions of communication. Therefore, this approach does not help the understanding of real communication in smaller or larger social units. It remains static and limited to meta-language systems, or serves the technology of the news media, in which the autonomy and activity of the recipient of the news is never really considered or built into the system.

Mechanistic Stimulus-Response Model

Without trying to qualify the stimulus-response model as an independent approach, it nevertheless deserves a special mention because of its comprehensive impact in one sector, relevant to traditional communication theory. It is mainly used to explain mass communication, and in reality it represents a transfer of the mathematical-technological models to the practice of public communication. An example would be the theory of the "two-step flow of communication." Here a distinction is assumed between mass media and recipient, whereby a small group of "opinion leaders" who understand how to use mass media intensively are ascribed an exalted and relevant social impact. In such models, members of the public are purely

[a] Representative literature for each section is given in a separate appendix.

recipients of information to which they are exposed without defense. This is how a person can be manipulated and indoctrinated, as well as trained, educated, and integrated, in a common "democratic" society. Thus did the myth of "omnipotence of the media" rise. Later research could disprove this simple mechanistic theory empirically by the discovery of the importance of the social group and its opinion-forming function, even if the necessary practical consequences have not always been drawn. The stimulus-response model is completely consistent with a formal-democratic, bureaucratic, mainly centralized executive system, in which the important thing is to use information as indoctrination and to minimize as much as possible the resistance of the recipient (the basis). Important in this system is the conscious or unconscious tendency to isolate people from their primary groups and their social environments and thereby to withdraw an influence that otherwise could be expected to have a real impact on the information by changing it. This puts the stimulus-response model in radical opposition to the group-dynamics approach, in which the intention is to build on the recipient's own "systematic freedom" and to bring it to the consciousness of those concerned.

The Cybernetic Approach

A further step is taken with the cybernetic approach, but it is still not quite detached from a closed cause-effect connection. Principally by allowing for a feedback model, the recipient of information is given another dimension than that of the recipient who purely registers information. Yet the often rather complicated range of rules is ultimately limited to a transfer of the stimulus-response scheme. These approaches are certainly possible to apply in areas beyond technology and computer theory, including the organic-biological world. So far, however, they have been of no help in understanding human communication. The sets of rules stay confined in themselves. The model does not lead to a real understanding of disturbances, changes, and new developments, or of contradictions on the whole; rather, it ascribes all these to a complexity connected with the multitude of variables necessary for the comprehension of human communication.

Indeed, group dynamics also works with a feedback system, but there is a basic difference here: feedback does not take place within given sets of rules but rather depends on the intentions, wishes, and limitations of social groups. In the first instance they decide what to do and what not to do with the feedback; however, every feedback immediately changes the social situation again and overrules the content and form characteristic of all previous sets of rules.

Undoubtedly, cybernetic models are useful in the construction of computers and electronic brains. It is problematic, however, when claims creep in unnoticed behind all the presupposed abstractions, as we can see in certain schools of biocybernetics, for instance. In this research area, interest is concentrated on the information process within an organism, on the stimulation of certain nerves and brain processes, and on the perceptions and experiences resulting from the experiments. Even in this short description the reduction of the communication problem is clear. Not only does this mostly experimental abstraction call for a rigid separation between the subject and object of information but also, in fact, the social interaction has to be totally omitted. The cognitive dimension of communication is thereby reduced to organic-biological processes in which it can never really occur.

Linguistic Approaches

The earlier-mentioned theoreticians have undoubtedly recognized the consequences that arise from the dilemma of the meta-linguistic approaches and have seen the formalism and the impossibility of finding a way back to colloquial language. These approaches are also for the greater part unsuited to the understanding of communication that is relevant to group dynamics in the social field. Above all, it is impossible from these approaches to bring about the synthesis of a model with any actual social situation, which is understandable when the analytic descriptive models are considered.

So far, all the linguistic approaches are encumbered with exactly the theory-practice contradiction that has to be avoided in group-dynamics work. In fact, the interaction between the language analyst and the analyzed person is established in a way that prevents any further consequences of the analysis. It is not accidental that an analytic model of this kind ends up in game theory. Since language is irrevocably presupposed by any language analysis, while the analysis in itself has no retroactive effect on this presupposed language, it becomes a game that is correlated with different logical contexts, in which a system of rules sets the limits for what can be done. To break out of this means only to replace one game with another. Even the self-examination in these games is accomplished in a game system and has no effect. From a group-dynamics viewpoint, this linguistic game theory can be seen as a typical consequence of a dualistic theory (analysis), a practice situation in which the causes and the social context underlying the rules of the game must be impossible to reflect. The limitations of the conventions of rules show on the one hand the practical ineffectiveness of the analysis, and on the other hand a picture of the actual communication barriers that so often separate whole worlds. A central task in group-dynamics practice is precisely to overcome this separation through common interaction and reflection. In addition, one can hardly use this approach for the understanding of nonverbal or "unconscious" behavior that takes place without a clear picture of the conventional agreement behind it. Even when the analysis of the act of speaking addresses itself more to the intention, to the actual use of expressions, and to the changes occurring as a result of the intention, to me the objective is still to work with definitions and fixed systems—i.e., analytically and, in the end, formally ineffective. The interest in colloquial language and its casuistics seems to be raised by practical communicative reality, but loses this link with reality either through systematization or through a renewed reminder of its limits in practical situations, since casuistic material cannot be transferred, not even when it is well ordered.

The approaches I have mentioned so far have one thing in common: either they isolate individuals from their social environments or they subject them to a cybernetically or conventionally controlled process that goes over people's heads or exceeds their ability for decision making because of its generality. The only possibilities for ongoing control of the communication are either a pure analysis, whereby the communication is no longer connected with practical colloquial language, or a technology, according to which the idea is to construct and control communicative situations with no allowance made for those affected to defend themselves. With such alternatives these theories give a clear picture of the situation today, with an individualization of communication (destruction of socially active units and opinion-building processes) opposed to a system of communicative rules according to which individuals are disposed in the proper order, often without knowing how the system functions and without being able to do anything about it.

Group dynamics tries to dissolve precisely this polarity between an abstract individual and an anonymous generality. The group is the mediating agency, trying to work on its own self-consciousness. The approaches discussed below demonstrate how the importance of the group and the social environment have been known for a long time, but this has not meant that this importance has been recognized in practice.

Approaches from Learning Theory; The Discovery of the Social Group and Its Importance for Mass Communication

The stimulus-response model had in no way been abolished and the mechanistic input–output scheme was still strictly maintained when the first blow came from learning theory: the presentation of experiences demonstrating different individual reactions to one and the same stimulus. This meant that the individual, the recipient of information, was also influenced by other sources that now had to be harmonized with this information. The concept of the "attitude" was born, so it was possible to take life experiences and additional communicative influences into account in the explanation of individual differences in reactions. In this way it was acknowledged that learning experiences and social relations decide the stimulus-response behavior of individuals. This process does not lose its reality even if it goes on more or less unconsciously.

One impact was that mass communication was now seen as unthinkable without group communication in primary reference groups. Another was the discovery of the importance of the informal group; thus the first step was taken toward research in small groups. However, we shall not here pursue the road to group dynamics. At least it was clear—also in mass communication research—that the recipients of media messages could not be seen as a "mass," but as an audience belonging to many different social groups. Social changes are at this point characterized as changes in the organization of information and no longer unilaterally delegated to "opinion leaders." Yet the group-dynamic consequences were not fully grasped. It was, and still is, agreed that these "new" phenomena should be investigated analytically from the outside and that in this way the difference between researcher and object of research would be strictly maintained. In all events, it is clearly no accident that work started with small groups. The abolition of the difference between researcher and researched naturally made mass communication a great deal more complicated.

The approaches below are different from those above, in that they have rather critically dissociated themselves from positivism, analytics, and abstract individualization, and that they have recognized the reality of indirect and direct social interaction; however, they have not developed beyond the research and description of these facts, even if they claim to have overcome in practice the contradiction emerging from this (for example, K. O. Apel). The transition in terms of models to the group-dynamics approach takes place, as I see it, with the psychoanalytic approach, which will be dealt with as the last in this series.

The Systems Theory Approach

The systems theory approach represents a most remarkable and—because of its differentiation—unique effort to come to grips with communication problems. On the one hand it avoids the abstract individualistic exclusion of the individual (recipient, sender, response, etc.) from the real communicative environment, but on the other hand it does not expose him to an anonymous, inescapable generality subjected to a system of rules. Instead, systems and system differences are introduced, expected to be worked through, and exhausted by the multitude of information. This selection and reduction of social systems of communication keeps the communication in constant motion because the information situation constantly changes, and also because changes take place within the systems. In spite of this reaction and reflection motion, the systems theory approach does not address the communication problems that are of special interest to group dynamics. The dynamics of systems theory resigns before the selection-and-reduction automatism in the system. Social systems (communication systems) are not "necessary" only because they can be comprehended, wanted, and intentionally used and changed by those concerned. Their validity is rather to be seen as an attempt to harmonize the multitude of possibilities available, the existing complexity in experiences and activities, with the limited capacity of the human ability to observe, to handle information, and to act. The building of systems implies selection from this multitude of possibilities, reduction of their complexity, and condensation of the selected possibilities for building structures of expectations for social systems. It is possible to improve both selection and reduction possibilities by applying processes to oneself (reflexivity) and by intensifying the transmission of data and decisions within the total system (communication). In this way society is defined as a structure of functional systems—its history made into a system expressed as a Darwinian process —but with no goal. The content of information is in principle interchangeable, and its value is decided by how well it fits into the system. Even science (the Systems Theory) is subject to this systems-theoretical approach and is made an example of its own existence. This circle illuminates how the theory is caught in itself and has subjected itself to the axiom of a selective functionalism. A communication has already taken place and cannot understand itself by self-help and throw its own mechanisms overboard. In any system, freedom of a group or any available social unity is gone. In reality, freedom belongs to the individual's irrationality and, as such, is incommunicable.

Hermeneutic Approaches

The approaches in this area do not, of course, deal only with communication problems: they also comprehend much of many other considerations. Generally, it is possible to abstract much theoretical equipment from the hermeneutic approaches for the building of group-dynamics theory. In reality, the experiment repeatedly taken on here is to think out theoretically beforehand what group dynamics tries to realize in practice. Exactly here, however, are the limits of these theoretical, scientifically oriented hermeneutics. It is not possible to think out beforehand anything that has no practical reality and is not dealt with by the communicable systematic freedom of those concerned. Of course, it is possible to think something out beforehand, but this leads to an unmanageable contradiction in relation to the empirical reality and remains a theoretical idea about the right things to do (ideal communication society, free and uncontrolled discussion, etc.). The problem of communication is rather clearly understood even if it is too much limited to verbal communication and even without the possibility of taking into account the reality and activity of institutions and organizations. The understanding is based on a historical, critical process and follows the principles of dialectic truth-finding earlier demonstrated by Plato. Even so, the final and consequent step is missing, namely, to allow actual communication its role in the reconstruction and determination of theory and model-building. Real communication is limited to a discussion among those who control it. This to me seems to be the final paradox of a theoretical blind alley where all the critical and analytical material as well as its dialectic elaboration can be used only on itself. An inability to turn to the communication problems of daily life, of the world around us, and of practice, and at the same time an adherence to an "ideal" communication model, leads to a further insoluble dichotomy. In fact, communication is not really tried (i.e., discussion is not really allowed) but rather only described, respectively demanded. Since the demand will get lost in an arrangement that is theoretically meager, its presupposed basis will be either a just as meager postulate or, again, historical empirical material, which can then be described (universal pragmatics, transcendental pragmatics). In this way, the real basis for communication, its precondition, whereby the ideal would have been made concrete, is not cleared off by those who are concerned. The basis here is still related only to the guiding demands.

As I said earlier, however, much material in the hermeneutic approaches can be used to describe group-dynamics theory. Above all, it is interesting to observe the attempt, to see how far it is possible to develop theoretical insight—which paradoxically recognizes the limits of this theory—and once again to try to theoretically master even these thoughts of insight or recognition. Surely, a certain scholasticism of a differentiated jargon often emerges that is hardly possible to use to communicate any longer, that has reservations established, and that no longer has anything to do with real communication. It seems as if it describes the historical fate of a classical philosophy that has ended up as pure theory crammed with critique and tradition, knowing a great deal—if not everything, even its own limits— but unable to take a step out of itself. The mass-communication theory building on the critical theory seems to be encumbered with the same irrelevance. Concepts such as counterpublicity, "spontaneity," or the use of the aesthetic analysis of the commodity on communication fail because of the lack of an organizational model to compensate the certainly appropriate analysis. A too tempting final way out is offered by Adorno, who here and there in his writings epitomizes a prerehearsed apocalyptic resignation in the face of an intrusive misfortune, which can hardly any longer be denied an unhistorical and metaphysical quality.

Sociolinguistic Approaches

These approaches start with the reality and difficulty of the communication specific to social levels. This reality is not set against a postulate. There is an attempt to explain the different language games and communication levels sociohistorically, and thereby to make them transparent. However much merit each of these explanations may have, they usually capitulate when facing two difficulties: in the first place, they are very firmly attached to their differentiating concepts (the level theory, the role theory, the code theory, etc.). These attachments are at times so heavily emphasized that one feels obliged to ask if people from different levels and with different roles can still, after all, talk to one another. In this case I still see no models developed that have been able to abolish these sociohistorical pretenses. Even if this approach has brought about quite a few changes within pedagogics (especially the model of compensatory language training), its adherents still miss successful, practical models to implement their insights. So once again those concerned are excluded, together with the sociolinguistic approaches to describe language differences. (The area of nonverbal transmission, which is especially important here, will anyway come off as a loser). Those who work group-dynamically within organizations and institutions (social intervention) are constantly confronted with these problems and cannot accept a pure descriptive assessment as satisfying, or try to work only within single levels or roles. And here the compensatory approach does not help either. It suggests that restricted codes should be pedagogically compensated, but it presupposes at the same time a certain amount of elaborate code that is likely to have been the result of previous communication. Instead, the origins of the codes brought along by those concerned should have been taken seriously, and exactly this transmission should have been the starting point. In turn, those concerned should determine their own code and not finally and formally be included in a general principle of existing differences by seeking a linguistically accidental formal equality, which is already the main result of unmanaged communication differences.

Marxist Approaches

Even though the two last-mentioned approaches are undoubtedly influenced by Marxism, I have still preferred to mention them separately.

Marxist approaches generally avoid abstract individualistic, as well as mechanistic, models. It is possible to extract motives and areas germane to group dynamics that are missing in the other theoretical approaches to communication, even if the word "reciprocity" (between infrastructure and superstructure) often remains rather obscure and is used only in a very mystical way to master real dialectic problems, and even if the reflection theory often ends up pretty close to a mechanistic view, as can be seen in popular Marxist publications. Issues relevant to group dynamics are the social inquiry into nature, the meaning of work and production processes, the political dimension and commitment of thought and science, and the organizational and institutional derivations of scientifically based practical strategies. The motives and approaches to which I have referred are still relevant to group dynamics, even when the "scientific view of the world" as presented in the existing representative compendia and textbooks often cannot compete with Marxist self-criticism (criticism of the isolation and emancipation of superstructures), and when new classes, élites, and cliques tend to dogmatize communication strategies. It would be natural here to make a distinction between theoretical approaches and presentations in "East" and "West," which as far as content is concerned can give much guidance for social and political-economic understanding of communication phenomena, and of the actual political organization of Marxism in socialist countries. The latter, however, is certainly too extensive to be taken as one topic. But it seems at least fair to say that research into the Chinese cultural revolution and its consequences, intentions, results, and difficulties can give important clues to what publicly and politically engaged group dynamics is dealing with.

With the approaches mentioned here we have now in principle left the more theoretically constructed and descriptive communication theory. Even if many Marxist approaches exist only in a theoretical form (especially those following the critical theory), the principal claim—that theory and practice must go together and that communication theories must entail political and social strategies—is valid also for them. These postulates lead communication theory to an irrevocable claim that is undoubtedly akin to the dynamic principle in group dynamics. Another point is that the postulates partly emerge in very alienated and cynical forms, as when social practice is decided simply out of an anticipated theory, in which no one is asked and in which the executive power takes the obedience of people as an indication of the verification of the theory. What group dynamics has so far been able to offer small groups—at best, minor organizations and institutions—is here claiming its right on a comprehensive social and worldwide scale. For obvious reasons, this implementation is not easy to bring about. However, all communication theoreticians are now obliged to be concerned with the practicability of their concepts, and to reflect on and experiment with their general and practical organization.

Separately, this much can be summed up: Communication is defined in orthodox Marxism as understanding for the purpose of letting socially connected individuals deal cooperatively with nature. The goal is to secure the material basis for individual and social existence. There are two forms of social communication in this basic supposition: on the one hand communication is the medium for exchange of material goods between man (society) and nature, and on the other hand it is the medium for internal social discussion and understanding. This implies that the social production process as a primary sector of social life and the use of systems of symbols are linked together genetically and functionally. Insight and communication are the two sides of the process that regulates the socially organized exchange with nature and internal social discussion. The consistent social movement of individuals makes it possible to explain interpersonal communication as a consequence of the given social situation. The exchange of comprehensible information and intelligible meanings can be secured only on a foundation of joint concerns based on the individuals' social movement.

In this way, verbal communication is also directly connected with the concept of work. Words—as basic elements of a language—can be seen as products of linguistic work.

In this connection, the uncritical transfer of categories from the political economy to linguistics seems problematic. Since the end of the antiauthoritarian movement, discussion of the problems relating to conditions for communication and organization has again intensified. Contrary to a rigid party model borrowed from Leninism (Kader and avant-garde) and used in Eastern Communist countries and in popular Marxism, the question of the subjective factor in the genesis of prerevolutionary situations is allotted greater importance.

To speak of independent approaches here seems rather dubious because of the fragmentary area where they are supposed to be valid and the unsatisfactory control of such theoretical attempts.

To recapitulate: Marxist approaches to communications theory—in spite of some short cuts with respect to actual dialectics of individual and the collective—have the following starting points for group dynamic work. In the first place, it is possible to derive strategies for work in institutions and organizations. Second, Marxist approaches offer a clear picture of the connection between economics and communication—almost contrary to the division Habermas makes between instrumental and communication action. Third, they present the obligation that every theory of communication should have actual political relevance. What is missing in the traditional Marxist approaches—namely, a developed theory of the psychology of the individual—seems to be possible to procure through group dynamics. It may be that political group dynamics can open perspectives for a termination of the old dispute about the instrumentality of psychoanalysis and Marxism.

Interactionist Approaches

For two reasons the approaches within this area, which have expanded into entire schools, are of great interest for group dynamics: first because their starting point is the world of everyday life, and second because of the research strategies connected with this. The former is seen as a system of immediate action-promoting orientations. Husserl, from whom the orientation toward the world of everyday life originates, builds his concepts on one isolated subject, seen as a pure unit of comprehension confronting an unhistoric general system of the world as a comprehending object. Symbolic interactionism goes farther and sees the subject trying to orient himself in the world as already a member of society, and the world as already a world for all members of society. The relation between this socially connected individual and the world is presented as a task that takes a lifetime and all an individual's existential energy. This task is possible to realize only in social interactions ordinarily taking place within the routine practices of daily life. In this world of everyday life, every subject, every ego, experiences "significant others." The concept of significant others is the most general formula for all important interaction partners, such as family, friends, and colleagues. The individual is now seen as having a clear conception, beyond the immediate interaction processes, of how these important reference groups, these significant others, experience and interpret the crucial social-problem areas and the possible ways to handle them, ways that in turn influence daily, practical life. A member of society in this orientation will have no chance to eliminate the condition that experiences and interpretations of the world are perspectives developed by more or less imaginary subjects outside of the individual, and that as such they offer an "outsider's" picture of the world's interaction field. And it is just as important that this imaginary subject (the significant other) is composed of the generalized abstraction we find in an interaction partner relevant to the world of daily life. The significant others can now be universalized and seen as representing society as a whole. The essence of knowledge of everyday life is that the individual's expectations lead him to believe that the significant others are focusing on his behavior. For instance, in speech, the speaker listens to himself and through this listening raises the importance of his intentions, since at the same time the interaction partner presumably finds them important too.

With scientific analysis of interaction structures, the interactionists have made this briefly outlined approach into a complicated system. There is, for instance, the concept of basic rules: rules to activate information (socially distributed knowledge) stored for shorter or longer periods. This socially distributed knowledge makes it possible for the actor to combine general normative rules with actually occurring, interactional scenes.

These basic rules regulate the conclusive interpretations, constitute the foundation of social order, and provide conditions for the assessment and procurement of behavioral manifestations that the researcher can describe as appropriate status or role attributes or as corresponding behavior. Only an exploration of these basic rules permits a definition of concepts such as status, role, or norm.

To illustrate the concept of the common action, an analysis of symbolic communication will be given as an example. Symbolic communication is defined as a presentation of gestures and a reaction to the meaning of such gestures. The gestures have a meaning for the person who uses them as well as for the person to whom they are directed. When the gestures have the same meaning for both, the two people understand each other. Thus the full meaning of a gesture is reached via three channels: by indicating what the person to whom it is directed will do, by indicating the intentions of the person who uses it, and finally by indicating the common action that results from a combination of the actions of both people involved. The level of abstraction in this conceptual definition of an interaction structure (and even a symbolic one) is shown by the fact that even an assault can be included within this concept of "common" action (cf. one of Blumer's examples).

Farther connections are specified in a thorough analysis of interaction rituals in daily life. Society is seen to be organized according to the principle that every individual with certain social criteria has a moral right to expect that others will evaluate and treat him in a correct and relevant way. When an individual has thrown out a definition of the situation and thus implicitly or explicitly claims to be a person of a certain kind, he automatically also lays a moral claim on the others, committing them to evaluate and treat him in a way a person of his kind could expect. Analysis of techniques of image building, of embarrassment, of respect, and so on, are derived from this.

In this context there is a great deal of analytical material of importance to group dynamics, even if we are here more concerned with concrete analysis of interaction situations from daily life than with an elaborate scientific theory of these structures.

Also, when a difficult analysis of the world of everyday life reaches a level of abstraction in its definitions apparently ending up far away from daily life, the world of everyday life is nevertheless the ultimate point of reference. This "humility" in relation to practical communication that has occurred necessitates research categories deviating a step from the classical ones, and in the direction of group dynamics. Researchers are ready to live in these areas of everyday life, to observe them, and to be active there in order to observe authentically.

Mostly researchers omit giving their observations and analyses directly back to those concerned, and therefore they seldom initiate change processes in the communication structure. On the contrary, they want to be recognized as little as possible in order to perceive the everyday life as it is, with all its automatic and unconscious processes. Still it is realized in this approach that many structures, details, rituals, and symbols from the world of everyday life can be "understood" in their full meaning only through direct participation. To include one's own emotional reactions in the research work is something interactionist approaches have in common with group dynamics.

Psychoanalytic Approaches

These approaches are the last to be mentioned because I find they come closest to group-dynamic approaches in method, theory, practice, and model. Here, too, we are dealing with a dynamic science of communication. Here, too, the idea is not simply, as in the classic dyad situation, to observe communication phenomena or disturbances, in order finally to introduce therapies on patients based on a generalizing differential diagnosis. Where a communication process is started, it is not simply seen as necessary for the recovery of a subject from an illness but as a condition for healing. The course of a communication of this kind cannot be set by the "scientist" alone. Even if he has certain theories and ideas about his case (as relatively the "better" partner) based on experience and models, the important thing is not to verify the theories by selecting the dialogue forms; rather, it is for his partner to find an independent relationship with the reasons for his disturbances, reflecting on his memories in an emotional way. The only way to do this is to enter autonomously into the released communication process. Even when only individuals are considered here, we are nonetheless dealing with a dynamic science of communication because it starts out by accepting and developing the partner's individual systematic freedom. The objection that we are now dealing with unfree, sick people who have lost their egos is not conclusive in psychoanalysis. In the first place, the ego cannot be totally lost, except through death (naturally, there are limits to how far treatment can succeed, but this is for other reasons). Second, the only way to handle a disturbed communication and avoid the process of transferring the symptoms is to let the ego take its own stand on the reasons independently. Thus even when it is highly possible that the analyst's diagnosis is correct, it is not of very much help to him. His job, without putting himself into the foreground, is to induce the kind of communication that activates the partner's own resources. The helplessness and incompleteness of theoretical insight is never seen more clearly than here. The theory is not correct until the partner can accept it himself, and in that very moment it has already substantially changed. This basically necessary acceptance of the other (in fact, the "research object" in the classic sense) as a communication partner, in individual system freedom, demands—from psychoanalysis as well as from group dynamics—a completely new theoretical scientific approach, because of a thoroughly altered relationship between theory and practice. The effects of this are not yet fully accomplished and clarified. There are still sufficient meta-theories of psychoanalytic therapy that try to reduce the dichotomy between theory and practice (the science and art of curing) as favored by classical theoretical science. (A classical conception of science could be morally based on the superego.) In addition, psychoanalysis cannot be separated from its specific practice, which means that all theory is limited in its content to some degree. The limits of its practice are certainly related to the isolation of the dyad, which, as I see it, excludes some ways of handling specific reasons for the disturbances, and does not really get hold of them emotionally. Therefore various expanding alternatives to this dyad have been developed. A great deal of experimentation takes place, and the closeness to group dynamics becomes more and more clear. In my view, dyads are necessary instruments, but expansion is taking a wrong direction when it is still caught in an individualistic approach and uses the other partner only to support this.

This criticism of an abstract theoretical meta-theory does not mean that psychoanalytic group dynamic theory should be totally dissolved in the practice and art of curing. It is necessary, however, to have its specific form changed and to understand fully both its insufficiency and its intersubjective necessity. This will make it possible to deduce a new understanding of theory from the specific relationship between theory and practice in the frame of dynamic communication. Theories are not truths, nor are they models of social realities to which they must be conveyed. They have themselves come into existence out of a necessity for social survival: different system freedoms, not directly communicating, must coexist. A coming task for a dynamic science of communication that is unable both to neutralize its theory building in its practice and to assign a founding place for this practice in its theory building would be to regard theory from this angle: to pursue it from the particular single-hypothesis and daily-life conception to the most difficult metatheory.

REFERENCES

Introduction
Baacke, D. *Kommunikation und Kompetenz: Grundlegung einer Didaktik der Komunikation und ihrer Medien.* Munich, 1975.

Mathematical Theory of Communication

Bar Hillel, Y. *Language and Information*. Reading, Mass., 1964.

Carnap, R. *Der Logische Aufbau der Sprache*. Vienna, 1934

———. *Der Logische Aufbau der Welt*. Hamburg, 1961.

Cherry, E. C. *Information Theory*. London, 1956.

———. *Kommunikationsforschung—Eine neue Wissenschaft*. Frankfurt on Main, 1963.

Fey, P. *Informationstheorie*. Berlin, 1963.

Meyer-Eppler, W. *Grundlagen und Anwendunger der Informationstheorie*. Berlin/Göttingen/Heidelberg, 1959.

Shannon, C. E., and W. Weaver. *The Mathematical Theory of Communication*. Urbana, Ill., 1949.

Mechanistic Stimulus-Response Model

Aufermann, J. *Kommunikation und Modernisierung*. Berlin, 1971.

Lazarsfeld, P. *The People's Choice—How the Voter Makes up His Mind in a Presidential Campaign*. New York, 1948.

The Cybernetic Approach

Deutsch, K. W. *Politische Kybernetik—Modelle und Perspektiven*. Freiburg, 1969.

Frank, H. *Kybernetik und Philosophie*. Berlin, 1966.

Moles, A. *Informationstheorie und ästgetuscge Wahrnehmung*. Cologne, 1971.

Moser, S. (ed.). *Information und Kommunikation*. Munich and Vienna, 1968.

Steinbuch, K. *Automat und Mensch*. Berlin/Göttingen/Heidelberg, 1961.

– – –. *Die informierte Gesellschaft*. Munich, 1966.

———. *Falsch programmiert*. Munich, 1969.

Wiener, N. *Kybernetik—Regelung und Nachrichten—übertragung im Lebewesen und in der Maschine*. Düsseldorf and Vienna, 1963.

Linguistic Approaches

Austin, J. L. *Zur Theorie der Sprechakte*. Stuttgart, 1972.

Searle, J. R. *Sprechakte*. Frankfurt, 1971.

Strawson, P. F. *Logik und Linguistik*. Miunich, 1974.

Wittgenstein, L. *Gesammelte Schriften*. Frankfurt on Main, 1969/70.

Wunderlich, D. *Studien zur Sprechakttheorie*. Frankfurt on Main, 1977.

Approaches from Learning Theory; The Discovery of the Social Group and Its Importance for Mass Communication

DeFleur, M. L. *Theories of Mass Communication*. New York, 1966.

Dröge, F. *Wissen ohne Bewusstein—Materialien zur Medienanalyse*. Frankfurt on Main, 1972.

Ronneberger, F. (ed.). *Sozialisation durch Massenkommunikation*. Stuttgart, 1971.

Schramm, W. *Mass Communication*. Urbana, Ill., 1949.

The Systems Theory Approach

Habermas, J., and N. Luhmann. *Theorie der Gesellschaft oder Sozialtechnologie— Was leistet die Systemforschung.* Frankfurt on Main, 1971.

Luhmann, N. *Soziologische Aufklärung.* Cologne and Opladen, 1970.

———. *Zweckbegriff und Systemrationalit2t.* Frankfurt on Main, 1973.

Thome, H. *Der Versuch die "Welt" zu begriefen. Fragezeichen zur Systemtheorie von Niklas Luhmann.* Frankfurt on Main, 1973.

Hermeneutic Approaches

Apel, K. O. *Die Transformation der Philosophie.* Frankfurt on Main, 1973.

Gadamer, H. G. *Wahrheit und Methode. Grundzüge einer philosophischen Hermeneutik.* Tübingen, 1965.

Habermas, J. *Erkenntnis und Interesse.* Frankfurt on Main, 1968.

———. *Legitimationsprobleme im Spätkapitalismus.* Frankfurt on Main, 1973.

———. *Technik und Wissenschaft als "Ideologie."* Frankfurt on Main, 1968.

———. *Theorie und Praxis.* Neuwied, 1963.

———. *Zur Logik der Sozialwissenschaften.* Frankfurt on Main, 1970.

Kluge, A., and O. Negt. *Öffentlichkeit und Erfahrung. Zur Organisationsanalyse von bürgerlicher und proletarischer Öffentlichkeit.* Frankfurt on Main, 1973

Prokop, D. *Massenkultur und Spontaneität.* Frankfurt on Main, 1974.

Ricoeur, P. *Die Interpretation.* Frankfurt on Main, 1975.

Sociolinguistic Approaches

Bernstein, B. *Soziale Struktur, Sozialisation und Sprachverhalten.* Amsterdam, 1970.

———. *Studien zur Sprachlichen Sozialisation.* Düsseldorf, 1971.

Klein, W., and D. Wunderlich (eds.). *Aspekte der Sociolinguistik.* Frankfurt on Main, 1971.

Oevermann, U. *Sprache und soziale Herkunft.* Berlin, 1970.

Marxist Approaches

Duhm, D. *Warenstruktur und zerstörte Zwischernmenschlichkeit. Cologne, 1975.*

Erckenbrecht, U. *Marx' Materialistische Sprachtheorie.* Kronberg, 1973.

Hahn, E. *Historischer Materialismus und marxistische Soziologie.* Berlin, 1968.

Holzer, H. *Kommunikationssoziologie.* Reinbek, 1973.

Rossi-Landi, F. *Sprache als Arbeit und als Markt.* Munich, 1972.

Wygotski, L. S. *Denken und Sprechen.* Frankfurt on Main, 1971.

Interactionist Approaches

Blumer, H. *Symbolic Interactionism.* Englewood Cliffs, N.J., 1969.

Cicourel, A. *Methode und Messung in der Soziologie.* Frankfurt on Main, 1970.

———. *The Social Organization of Juvenile Justice.* New York, 1968.

Garfinkel, H. *Studies in Ethnomethodology.* Englewood Cliffs, N.J., 1967.

Goffmann, E. *Interaktionsrituale.* Frankfurt on Main, 1971.

Laing, R. D. *Das Selbst und die Anderen.* Cologne, 1974.

———. *Knoten.* Reinbek, 1972 (London, 1970).

Matthes, J., and F. Schütze (eds.). *Alltagswissen, Interaktion und gesellschaft-liche Wirklichkeit.* Reinbek, 1973.
Mead, G. H. *Geist, Identität und Gesellschaft.* Frankfurt on Main, 1968.
———. *Philosophie der Sozialität.* Frankfurt on Main, 1969.
Sudnow, D. *Organisiertes Sterben.* Frankfurt on Main, 1973.

Psychoanalytic Approaches
Ammon, G. *Dynamische Psychiatrie.* Neuwied, 1973.
Freud, S. *Collected Works.* London, 1971.
Pirella, A. (ed.). *Sozialisation der Ausgeschlossenen.* Reinbek, 1975.

Chapter 5

Group Dynamics and Patriarchal Hierarchy

Gerhard Schwarz

It is certainly not accidental that nowadays, among those qualifying as trainers in group dynamics, quite a number are women. Part of the reason may be that the men's "holy order" (Greek: hierarchy) has been somewhat reevaluated by group dynamics.

This order will never perish, because it is based on the division of labor and represents one of man's greatest cultural achievements. Nevertheless, the question is raised today whether, and in what way, this hierarchy should be modified.

A question like this usually causes perceptible uncertainty in a communication structure, as considerations that question the establishment always do. In my experience it often helps reduce this uncertainty somewhat to offer a rational model in order to understand what it is all about. Especially when working in group-dynamics laboratories, such a model can be of great help for the "back-home" application of what has been learned.

This chapter, originally titled "Gruppendynamik und Patriarchalische Hierarchie," was translated from the German by Trygve Johnstad.

A rational understanding of hierarchic structure is most easily attained by way of a historical reconstruction. Today historians assume that at some time in our history the matriarchal tribe culture was replaced by the patriarchal hierarchy. The principle of achievement is then applied by the males, whereas the females (the mothers) tend to distribute existing resources more according to need. A mother will give more care to the child who needs it (like the sick or newborn). The boss promotes the one who achieves more.

Group dynamics incorporates a little of the mothers' system. In addition to group members' achievements their needs are also considered, since only then can the picture be complete. Occasionally the achievement principle, with its tendency toward comparison and fighting, is neglected for a while.

This implies that the rational, fact-oriented components are thrown somewhat into the shade by feelings. Logic is set aside for the benefit of existing differences. Psychologically, anyone is right when he says he feels himself attacked, even when the "aggressor" asserts that he did not mean to attack. It was felt that way, and why it was felt that way can thereafter be examined.

Many trainers feel somehow that a female element is introduced into male society in this way—by means of the group process in group dynamics. The group often behaves "like a woman"—emotional and capricious, illogical and irrational. In order to understand this, it is quite interesting to examine how the logical patriarchal "holy order" of men really came into existence.

We know that in primitive times, before the first economic revolution brought cattle breeding and agriculture, people lived in hunting and collecting tribes. At that time there was no communication on a large scale between the tribes, and no anonymous organization either.

Not until they developed exchange and barter and a storage system, with domestic animals and agriculture, could people who had settled make a surplus that could be exchanged. This exchange was carried out at so-called "central places."[1] (See Figure 5–1.)

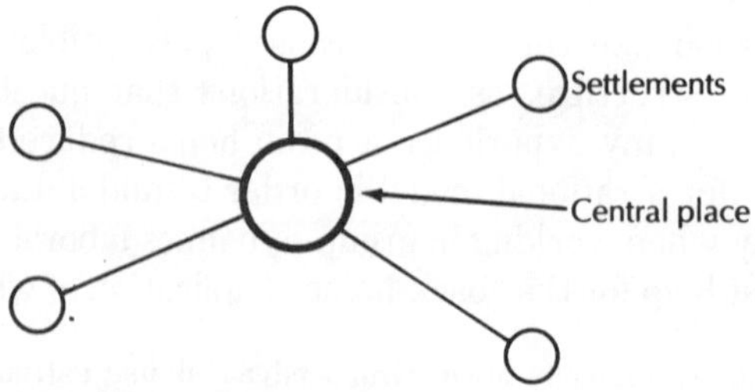

Figure 5–1.

At a point of intersection of natural lines of communication—like the mouths of rivers and valleys—people met to exchange their goods. Soon a division of labor emerged: (1) the production of different products to be exchanged (for example, animals for agricultural products), and (2) the functon of effecting and protecting the exchange.

"The main task of a town is to be the centre of its rural surroundings."[2] When several villages united, market places were created, which already catered to the centralized functions of the villages (Figure 5–2).

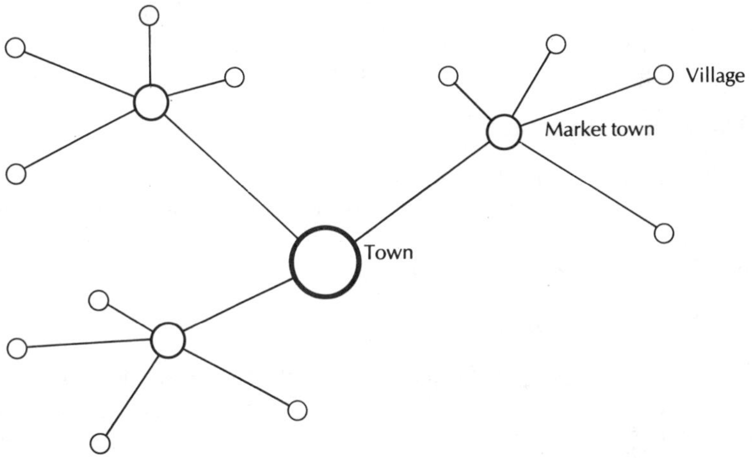

Figure 5–2.

One of the most important centralized functions was certainly to protect this whole arrangement against intruders from the outside. As excavations in Mesopotamia show,[3] the first towns seem to have been destroyed over and over again under pressure from nomads, until they succeeded in discovering a new kind of organization and a new social structure. If Figure 5–2 is drawn in a section, we see the classic picture of a hierarchy (Figure 5–3).

The efficiency of this new kind of organization is based on four principles, which can be said to represent the "axioms of hierarchy" today.[4]

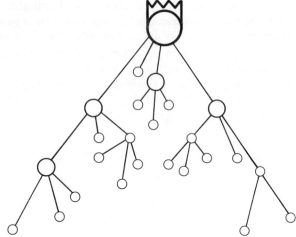

Figure 5–3.

The Truth Continuum

Only centrally located authorities have access to the information necessary for making decisions. By a process of accumulation, persons with higher and therefore more central positions have more information at their disposal. They come closer to the truth.

The Wisdom Continuum

When contradictory information or conflicts arise, the relevant central authorities have to make a decision. In order to do so, at all times they are also attributed the appropriate wisdom, as the old saying goes: "Wem Gott ein Amt gegeben, dem gibt er auch Verstand" ("Whomever God installs in an office will also be given wisdom").

The Dependence Continuum

Decisions made by the more central and therefore higher authorities must be carried out by people in lower, peripheral positions in order that the system may function. To guarantee this all these people have to live in a permanent state of dependence.[5]

Only when all four continua appear together, when the one in power has all the wisdom and truth, and the subordinates—those with less power—are ready under compulsion to carry out the decisions of the ruler—only then can this model function. Today the concept of superiors and subordinates, of masters and servants, seems to be a more recent description of this same relationship. For a long while—especially during feudal times—the master was seen as a necessary protector and not as an oppressor. It was consistent with the needs of the servant to have a master. If he lost him, he would have to find another to serve.

Even if this model is still correct as a formal description of the big organizations of today, on some points it does not hold true any longer. The classic principles of hierarchy are not absolutely valid in business and administration any longer.

1. The decision continuum is no longer completely continual. Here and there one who is "higher" is no longer in a better position than a subordinate to find solutions. Specialists on lower levels often represent an inversion of competence and expose thereby the inferior quality of the decisions of incompetent superiors.
2. The truth continuum is no longer stable. Very often a subordinate has information and more professional knowledge at his disposal than a superior. But the superior still has to make the decisions, since theoretically he is closer to the truth. The breakdown of the truth continuum may not be so extreme in other places as it is in business, where the superior is occasionally unable to understand information from his subordinate (for example, in the computer field). Nevertheless, with more and more specialization, this tendency becomes visible within other hierarchical formations as well (such as administration and the army, church, and school).
3. For some time now there have been difficulties associated with the wisdom continuum. The higher one ascends in a hierarchy, the wiser and more capable superiors should appear to be. In practice, inconsistencies become apparent here as well, which—particularly when dealing with conflicts—again and again lead subordinates to question the wisdom of their superiors. To believe that a higher "third party" is better at resolving a conflict between two views than the parties to the conflict themselves is a prejudice derived from a fact-oriented notion of communication. The myth that maintains that it can be ascertained unambiguously which opinion is right and which is wrong, according to a logical system, begins to break down. It is precisely the content of the superior's wisdom that is used as the criterion to discriminate in this case. But it is possible to make an unquestionable decision only when dealing with so-called "facts." Whenever the case is emotionally loaded, particularly when it is about purely emotional problems, then "critical" power to discriminate will often appear as irrelevant when exercised by a third party not involved in the conflict, in this case a superior.

To formulate this in a radical way: Only material things and not people can be managed by a strict hierarchy. The reactionary bureaucracies of the East demonstrate clearly the limit of this "people management." Hierarchies in the West will in the future have to deal with more and more powerful citizens and officials. One can take for granted that the high professional and intellectual level of the manager has not yet been sufficiently used in the cultivation of self-government. On the one hand here are some unused resources for the future, including rich potential for reform; on the other, however, this is also explosive stuff for all too "materialist" (authoritarian) managements and organizational structures.

INTERPERSONAL RELATIONSHIPS— A SUBJECT FOR THE NATURAL SCIENCES?

My way of explaining the stability of the hierarchical model is to see it not just as an organizational model but also as a model for thinking. The basic principle of hierarchy looks like this: Order equals super- and subordination. But this is one of the principles of logic as well. However, in the European tradition not only logic but nature itself is often (as in the sciences) seen as an order of superordinated and subordinated universalities. The animal order and the botanic system of Linné are both formal hierarchical systems.

This thinking had great importance in the Middle Ages. Thomas Aquinas wrote: "By the precepts of the devine law the human mind is subordinated to God, and all the rest of man is subordinated to reason. But this is just what natural order requires that the inferior be subject to the superior. Therefore what is commanded by the devine law is in itself naturally right."[6]

This abstract model illustrates the historical breakthrough in the natural sciences at the beginning of modern history. When they succeeded in constructing models where motivation and human communication could be ignored, an application of formal structures (such as mathematics) was possible. Galileo is said to have addressed this statement to the Grand Inquisitor: "It is your problem how people move towards heaven. My problem is how heaven moves."[7]

In the history of science abstraction takes on an important role.[8] Only some aspects are selected from a phenomenon for further investigation while the rest are left outside. By only choosing some aspects—for example, just objects in time and space—an abstract method can be used, for example, mathematics. If "heaven" is examined only in an "abstract" way, as movements of the stars, then naturally any other meaning this concept might have (such as is found in the Bible) is ignored. But it is no longer possible to draw conclusions from abstract models (that is, concerning only some aspects) to those dimensions of life that have been ignored. This self-evident consequence of abstraction was often forgotten. Thus many physicists made statements on theology, many biologists on philosophy, even though biology and physics had achieved their results only by ignoring the problems of human beings—their sufferings and joys, conflicts and anxieties, motives and needs.

The methodology of the natural sciences proved to be successful, and very soon other sciences tried to imitate it. As the latest one to take up this recipe for success, the social sciences of today are looking for results using the logical principle of abstraction from the natural sciences. Organizational models are constructed mathematically. Screening processes are used in personnel selection, which are analogous to the testing of material. In business games executives learn abstract decision models on a computer. Organization consulting firms are selling computerized communication and information systems. The method of Galileo with respect to the movement of the heavens makes its entry into the scientific analysis of hierarchies.

As these methods were arrived at and further developed in importance because they ignored human problems and limited themselves to the relation between objects, it can hardly be argued that they can be proved suitable for handling the problems of human relations. There is no joy or sorrow among atoms and molecules. There are no crises or conflicts between fixed stars and the solar system. There is no self-determination for the objects of the natural sciences. They remain objects.

As if this were not enough, the social sciences have still more problems. Social sciences today are careful to see to it that their method does not "fit."[9] The more people start to reflect on the "lawfulness" in human coexistence, the more grounds they have to manipulate with the aid of this lawfulness. But only very seldom does an analysis of this kind result in the stabilization of an authoritarian structure. More often this sort of examination provides an impulse to make some changes in the structure.

In the classical hierarchies the system of super- and subordinates functioned without anyone making a great fuss about it. In the Middle Ages the social system was natural and God-given. With scientific analysis came a desire to bring about some changes in the structure.

We know today that groups and organizations are neither natural nor God-given, and that it is perfectly possible to change them.

But change according to which laws? Even nature is manipulatable, but only with the help of stable natural laws. We can depend on "free fall" or rectilinear light, but are there similar "safe" laws for human beings to live together? Are there abstract, objective, exact rules, or maybe even models, or at least general concepts that can be used to describe social organizations? They are nowhere to be found!

Social scientists have not even reached agreement regarding basic concepts like group, class, society, authority, freedom, and so on; nor will they succeed in doing so since every definition of a concept in the human area—unlike in nature—is a matter of opinion and is guided by sectional interests. An authoritarian situation must now and then be perceived in a totally different way by the authority and by the subordinates. The position of an outsider is seen very differently by the outsider and by the group itself. An "objective," "neutral," "exact," "scientific" standpoint is not in evidence here! Many rulers—political power centers—still hope that by sticking to their own "court sociologists," they can have their standpoint confirmed as the only scientific one. However, it is only a question of time before this hope must disappear.

THE SIGNIFICANCE OF GROUP DYNAMICS

As long as there are no general, objective, exact methods for the understanding of hierarchies and problems of human relations, how can a science deal with them? A science of this kind would obviously have to change its method at important points away from our concept of science until now. These points are to be found where difficulties appeared in the earlier method.

These difficulties arose when the focus was on people and not on objects. People are in a position to be further motivated by the so-called laws set up for them, so that on occasions the content of the theory has to be changed again.

Thus when it seems to have been agreed (for example, by means of an inquiry) that one person in the group—let us call him Mr. Smith—ranks first in prestige; and another person—let us call her Mrs. Jones—is at the bottom of the list; then the announcement of this "scientific" insight together with the group process that follows may have the effect that Mr. Smith loses his top position and Mrs. Jones moves upward in the group's order of precedence. It can further happen that during the process of a group like this, order of rank ends up as totally unimportant. Does the theory about group positions fit this or not?

Here it is obvious that a scientific theory that is based not only on observation but also on authentic statements of their motives by the participants themselves can only be verified or falsified by further developments in the group process; and even then this is not universal or perpetually valid, but only for this particular population and for this one time. For another group or for the same group at another time, still other relations may be relevant.

Now the question arises: Why not make a virtue of necessity? When, as a result of the feedback of perceptions, a change process is initiated to which no exact method can be applied, why not let these very processes be the foundation for a science? This understanding—and this is our thesis—

offers an entirely new horizon to the social sciences. The science of people living in communities is the science of changes brought about by eating from the tree of knowledge of human relations.

Reflection on a situation lets people discover new motives that will often change that situation. Our new method with feedback from abstract models is therefore not only a new method of understanding but also a method of intervention—a method for changing group and organizational structures. That is the reason why this method is called "group dynamics" and not "group statics."

The drawbacks described earlier that arise when transferring the methods of the natural sciences to the social sciences do not hold true for group dynamics. In group dynamics motives are not ignored and thus a certain self-determination of the groups and their participants always takes place. Changes happen in any situation where those concerned think that change is appropriate. But who guarantees that the situation will change for the better and not for the worse?

The answer is simple: those taking part in the group process. It might happen that the newly procured situation of more independence is less acceptable to the participants than the old authoritarian situation. In this case it is up to them to reestablish an authority. By the continuous feedback process a sensitive instrument is created, making it possible to judge whether the quality of the new situation meets the requirements of the participants. If no external circumstances obstruct it, this group process will in any case be a step forward for those taking part.

THE GUIDANCE OF GROUP PROCESSES

We must now define what kind of progress takes place within group-dynamics processes. They are processes of understanding that are for the most part directed toward the emotional occurrences in the group. They are the give and take of feedback, the process of seeing through and overcoming expectations about role, of recognizing and changing positions, and so on. These processes always have an emotional character. Such affective processes become conscious and manageable through the feedback of observations and their interpretation. The progress that occurs in group dynamics is represented by learning to manage group processes and personal behavior. Whenever a group has been through this process, it has at its disposal a greater variety of interdependent ways of behaving. For every participant as well as for the whole group, this makes available new opportunities for freedom and self-determination that did not previously arise in group processes.[10]

In the guidance of such a process, the rule of thumb of trainer interventions is to intervene whenever the process is in danger of being discontinued. This procedure can be roughly divided into five steps:

1. Managing the situation. If the group ceases to reflect on the situation any more, then the development of an analytic group process in a group-dynamics sense will not take place. In this case the trainer must

2. observe and feed back his observations. For example: "I have noticed that in this conference Mr. K always speaks after Mr. F. I have also registered that Mr. K always disagrees with Mr. F." If no one reacts to an observation like this, the process will come to a standstill right from the beginning, and will have to be started again on the next occasion, at best with a new observation. If the group accepts this observation, it must be

3. interpreted and controlled. Why is Mr. K fighting with Mr. F? Is there personal dislike between them, do they come from antagonistic departments, or does Mr. K today accidentally always take an opposite viewpoint? The group will now present a series of assumptions in order to interpret the observation. There will be many wrong ones but also, when everything works well, some correct ones. If there is a consensus on one of them, and this consensus must necessarily include those concerned, then the right interpretation is found, and one can from this

4. draw consequences for further action. Either Mr. K and Mr. F can discuss their problem between themselves, or the group can work on this competition directly, or they can simply take note of the two positions and look at them while the two parties attempt to present their "objective" arguments—or some other solution. Dependent on the consequences, the next step will be

5. to manage the new situation which in turn has to be observed, interpreted, and so on. The trainer's task (among others) is to intervene whenever the process is in danger of coming to a standstill, and to do that long enough for the participants to develop their own competence in handling group processes. When a group already observes well, he will give interpretations of the observations or stimulate the use of them. If a group already gives interpretations, he will try to describe consequences, etc. Such a group process could also be called "reform from within."

For those who work professionally with group dynamics the role of the trainer is primarily seen as only a short initial phase. Beyond that it is a matter of leadership functions, which can be taken care of by some other participant.[11]

THE ROLE OF THE SCIENTIST

If you see this role of the social scientist in the light of traditional scientific work, some troubling differences emerge. The scientist is at the same time actor and observer in a process that can no longer be described by means of natural scientific methods.

This is because learning about and verbalization of the "laws" found in human communities does not leave those concerned as "cold" as, for instance, the stones in the "discovery" of the law of gravity. Moreover, stones cannot develop motives for action from the laws made up to describe them. This is another matter where human beings are concerned.

When the outsider role of a member is being discussed, in the course of the discussion this very often leads to an integration of that outsider. The group has changed as a result of the process of reflection and thereby released ability to handle a problem.

This fact is of far-reaching significance, as much for the role of the scientist engaged in a social scientific inquiry as for the subject of his investigation. Certainly, no one can be quite sure that reflection on the position of an outsider will lead to an integration of the member concerned. It might also happen that his role is consolidated, which will give him still less chance to become an ordinary group member again within a conceivable time.

Many "laws" that can be formulated here hold good, or then again they do not, since the reverse can now and then also be valid.

Consequently, group dynamics dismissed the strict subject-object separation as a postulate for scientific work. For a social scientist it is impossible to examine his objects, so to speak, from the "outside," as an aquarium. The scientist himself has a role that must appear in the methodology in a meaningful way. Every scientific investigation within group dynamics has for that reason the character of an intervention. But every intervention also has scientific aspects. The scientist plays his part. This is connected with the process of emancipation: "Every enlightenment is self-enlightenment. Therefore in a process of enlightenment there are only participants."[12]

Thus group dynamics works with processes in which the scientist takes part, and where indeed he is not the only one to take care of the scientific goals of understanding and emancipation. This leads to a new way not only of looking at the criteria for verification and falsification but also of examining authority problems, work, decision making, and so on. For example it is very difficult to assume that a theoretically correct organizational structure could possibly be accepted as correct independent of the developmental process going on within the organization; or that an unresolved power conflict between the object of investigation (a certain group) and the subject (the searching scientist) will not necessarily falsify the results.

The old philosophic argument—that we always need a "we" in order to establish an "I," is in group dynamics given a new and, so to speak, practical actuality for every member. Conversely, the "we" of a group exists, of course, only as an "I," or else the "we" would have no identity. So there comes a time when somebody in a training group (T group) realizes that

1. He learns more and is more integrated the more he gives of himself and takes part in the communication.
2. He receives "feedback" only when he gives something himself.
3. When another uses this insight in the group, he feels that even negative emotions (rejection, doubt, aggression, etc.)when talked about, can result in integration into the groups.
4. Finally somebody in surprise formulates the sentence: "It's really a funny thing, this acknowledgment business; the more I acknowledge someone else, the better I feel myself."

Then the group has developed an important aspect of what in the philosophic tradition is called the problem of freedom.

Again, in connection with this, the question can be raised whether or not the object "man," also called an individual, exists essentially in the form of an individual at all? Can the individual really be the key to the understanding of man? Or does not the group have to be considered the smallest entity? Is not the individual the result of an abstraction of a false ideology?

> Majesty of human nature,
> Thee shall I seek in the crowd.
> Few only dwelt in your halls,
> While all the rest are blind ciphers,
> Their emptiness enfolding the elect.
> *(Schiller)*

But then, is it not questionable anyway to ally the concept of equality to the concept of liberty? I propose the following thesis: Equality is unnecessary in a group. On the contrary, the differences are useful prerequisites of communication in any self-governing group. Only the differences that are not communicated and not resolved in the self-governing process, that is, the unaccepted differences, lead to alienation.

By renunciation of the methodical separation of subject and object, by the new way of looking at the concept of authority, and by the idea of the group as a starting point, group dynamics also obtained access to the actual "here and now" of social organization. But to reflect upon the immediate situation is an organizational taboo for many people, even for social scientists. For although they do reflect upon social processes, preferably and if possible those related to authority, they rarely reflect upon their own roles.

Many social scientists are still of the opinion that the scientist can only describe the object of his research "objectively" when he himself is kept outside the structures and procedures examined by him and thereby keeps his authority intact. Many scientists even refuse to see how this attitude helps to maintain an authoritarian position. The thought of entering into communication with oneself as a person—with all its unpredictable consequences—is repugnant to them.

These scientists are rightly scoffed at in their ivory towers. Within the group it quickly becomes evident that no one is in possession of an objective truth, but nevertheless they communicate consistently. Again and again I experience in myself a wish to run away when the group starts to talk about my role, or when I become aware of the vanity of "scientific truth," or when it becomes apparent that my interpretations were wrong.

The group-dynamics dimension of the situation entails the abolition of another prejudice: that an ideal society is theoretically possible. Is it possible to formulate theoretically how a social structure should be organized? Experience from group dynamics tells us that this is impossible to accomplish in practice. Even when an organization—for instance a company—has precisely defined goals, the relevant ideal organization is not the one made up by theorists according to some organizational-sociological principles (scientific management)—ingenious though it may be—but rather the one sought after as the appropriate one by the people who are part of the organization.

What the organization achieves cannot be separated from the motives that participants have for achieving something. This is at the same time also the principle behind the learning in group dynamics.

Thus the importance of the matriarchal "need culture" to a patriarchal society, which I mentioned at the beginning of this chapter, has become evident. It may be that group dynamics is only one way for the patriarchal hierarchy to become conscious of this problem. Is this the reason that men and women are so fascinated by group dynamics today?

REFERENCES

1. Michael Mitterauer. "Das Problem der zentralen Orte als sozial- und wirtschaftshistorische Forschungsaufgabe." In *Vierteljahresschrift für Sozial- und Wirtschaftsgeschichte* 58, No. 4 (1971): 433–467.

2. Robert Gradmann. "Schwäbische Städte." *Zeitschrift der Gesellschaft für Erdkunde* (1916): 427.
3. Rushtion Coulborn. "Der Ursprung der Hochkulturen." *University Library*, 65, p. 19ff.
4. G. Schwarz. "Die Problematik der Gruppe." In *Das ist Gruppendynamik*, Peter Heintel, ed. Heyne-Kompaktwissen, no. 37, pp. 60–129.
5. T. Lindner. "Das monarchisch-aristokratische Organisationsmodell." *Gruppendynamik*, no. 1 (1971), pp. 1–11.
6. "Summa contra gentiles," Book III, ch. 129, sect. 1, transl. J. Rickaby; S. J. London: Burns & Oates, 1905.
7. Ludwig Biberach. *Galilei und die Inquisition*. München, 1942.
8. Erhard Oeser. *Begriff und Systematik der Abstraktion*. Oldenburg, 1969.
9. Jürgen Habermas. "Zur Logik der Sozialwissenschaften." Suhrkamp (1971): 125ff.
10. Jack Gibb. "Sensitivitätstraining als Mittel zur Förderung individueller Bildungsprozesse und Verbesserung zwischenmenschlicher Beziehungen." In *Gruppendynamik und der subjektive Faktor*, Klaus Horn, ed., Suhrkamp, 1972, pp. 139–181.
11. Gerhard Schwarz. "Die Gruppenfunktionen." In *Das ist Gruppendynamik*, Peter Heintel, ed. Heyne-Kompaktwissen, no. 37, pp. 117–127.
12. Jürgen Habermas. "Theorie und Praxis." *Suhrkamp* 9: 45.

Chapter 6

Group Dynamics and Analytic
Group Therapy

Kurt Buchinger

As the title indicates, this chapter is an inquiring one that deals with problems of group therapy raised by the intimate relationship between group-therapeutic and group-dynamics processes.

The scope of the chapter is limited for three reasons. First, because its deliberations (however valid for other kinds of group therapy) concentrate on those psychoanalytically oriented group psychotherapies most familiar to the author.

Second, it does not analyze and differentiate among the curative factors and curative powers specific to group-therapeutic treatment. Neither does it say anything about when a patient should participate in group therapy instead of individual therapy. The chapter only deals with some problems for the patient as well as for the therapist that arise out of their participation in a group-therapy situation.

The third limitation of the article is its failure to mention group-dynamics and psychoanalytic research and practice. Independently of each other, both have had a tremendous influence on the development and widespread acceptance of group therapy. The article does not focus on the great importance psychoanalytic thinking has had for the clinical acceptance of group therapy, concerning:

This chapter, originally titled "Analytische Gruppentherapie und Gruppendynamik," was translated from the German by Trygve Johnstad.

1. the new concept of so-called mental illness as a result of an early disturbed social interaction;
2. the relation between therapist and client and its development in a complicated process of interaction;
3. the hic-and-nunc aspect of therapy. The importance of this is evident in psychoanalysis where the therapist must be concerned with transference and countertransference reactions.

The article does, however, deal with some problems that arise when psychoanalytic concepts and techniques are transferred to group therapy. It tries to point out obstacles to a meaningful acceptance and application of group therapy—obstacles often hidden behind an assessment of group-therapeutic techniques that is only superficial. If you are not aware of this your approval may become a subtle form of disqualification, which is in fact worse than open rejection.

In the first part of the chapter I will mention some forms of this disqualifying approval of group therapy. The second part will look at some consequences for practical work.

DIFFICULTIES OF AN ADOPTION

Many serious and successful attempts are being made to establish group therapy as an original kind of therapy, rather than a modification of any sort of individual therapy. These attempts can be associated with names like Foulkes, Kemper, Heigl, and Heigl-Evers, Pohlen, Yalom. Other therapists have adopted the group as a fashionable or advantageous therapeutic instrument, understood in terms of rules and techniques of the individual therapy that they have been practicing.

Insecurities of the therapist about the differences in procedures and his feelings when he is confronted with a situation where his techniques fail, mobilize defense mechanisms:

1. We are all familiar with the mechanism of giving too much *ambivalent attention* to an adopted but really unloved child, so as not to let him know that he is not wanted.
2. The case of adoption for an *economic advantage* is also not uncommon.
3. One can also express neglect by being *benevolently careless*.

Sometimes group therapy seems to be an adopted child suffering from this kind of upbringing.

The Ambivalent Attention

The creation of "new" group techniques has become such a fad that it is difficult to distinguish therapeutic or paratherapeutic value from market value [6, chapters 5, 20, 30, 31]. Yalom and two of his colleagues [40, p. 341] convey a picture of the group scene in the Palo Alto, California area, where the group subculture has spread most explosively and unscrupulously.

They found about 200 groups currently operating in an area of approximately 100,000 inhabitants. "Esalen, an Institute in Big Sur, California, has had over 50,000 participants in various programs and has a mailing list of 21,500 individuals to whom it distributes a massive catalogue of group activities including non-verbal groups, experiential groups, gestalt therapy groups, body dynamic groups, breathing and awareness groups, sensory awakening groups, etc." [40, p. 34]. In 1969, 75 other growth centers were operating throughout the country.

The wish to take part in this subculture has become almost too fashionable, and is surely economically exploited. Yet this group-experience movement, which C. Rogers calls the most significant social invention of this century [40, p. 342], seems to represent more than a fashion: It signals a deeper individual and social need. According to H. E. Richter, the universal problem from which it promises to free or at least to relieve us is Western individualism, thereby creating a new expectation of salvation: "To us psychoanalysts it seems as if this big yearning for fulfillment in a community *(Wir-Gemeinschaft)* reveals much more than a need for therapy in a conventional medical sense. It is as if it were the search for a new generalized form of existence to take the place of the old concept of individual self-realization" [28, p. 41, translated by the author]. This seems to be the power behind the new group movement and behind the tendency to apply group techniques in various areas of organized social interaction. Therapy is but one of them.

The group promises a fulfillment of the need for a new form of existence. However, a considerable part of the group movement organizes and destroys needs in a way Marcuse called repressive tolerance [23]. Needs are exploited and endlessly recreated instead of being met in a truly satisfying way.

In addition a lot of laboratories and weekend marathon sessions—whatever kind of group experience they promise to convey—are so highly attractive because they remove one from the social structures of everyday life and provide an artificial environment in their place. There one may learn to. build a microcosm without repression, where one can really communicate with others—for two days of a week. But one does not learn how to bridge the gap between the laboratory culture and the real-life situation. The experience of the gap only deepens the feeling of contrast [29, p. 240]. The revitalizing vacation gives one new energy to get through one's daily sufferings: social isolation, socially and emotionally frustrating working conditions, stereotyped relations. But the group experience might also make daily life seem intolerable. However, one now has the opportunity to escape from it more often—by attending more laboratories and trying out the whole variety of group experiences available. And so one becomes a group addict.

Thus the group culture subtly supports the stability of those alienating social structures to which it was thought to be an alternative. This may be the reason that laboratories are not only tolerated but also supported, above all by the economic establishment. The potential of the group as an instrument for social and emotional change can only remain a potential in this isolated playground. There one can act out everything one must suppress in everyday life. One can change and free one's behavior on the group stage. In real life, however, this behavior is rejected. This kind of tolerance toward groups is an attempt to pervert the movement into a "group amusement industry," selling its product to a "middle-class party culture" [29, p. 212].

This is also where K. Horn [17, pp. 17-116] sees the danger of the group-dynamics laboratory culture: Organized capitalism uses group-dynamics for a pseudomediation between individual communicational needs and the structures of societies. These needs are not satisfied. They are allowed expression only in irrelevant forms like group dynamics. The increased presence of such *entpolitisierte Bereiche* ("nonpolitical areas") is of political interest to capitalism in its policy of reducing the political involvement of the majority of the population.

Group therapy sometimes suffers from a comparable kind of ambivalent attention. In 1951 M. Rosenbaum [30] questioned a group of thirty-nine psychotherapists about their attitude toward group therapy. The twenty-one psychoanalysts who returned the questionnaire spoke more or less in favor of group therapy. All thirty-nine, however, showed considerable resistance in recommending it to patients. "Is it possible that these analysts, in writing an answer to a questionnaire, must fulfill a self-concept of the permissive, accepting therapist?" [30, p. 51].

Today, twenty-five years later, this attitude is still prevalent. Not that psychoanalysts would not send patients to group therapy, but often these are either the patients with whom the therapists do not know what else to do, or the patients who are diagnosed as more or less "sane and healthy." They are sent to group therapy to be given the opportunity for what I call a therapeutic chat.

The therapeutic aim of the group is, in this case, not to change the behavior or attitudes of a patient in order to make his everyday life less neurotic or painful. His everyday life situation is not altered, nor is the subjective component of his behavior. The group simply grants him something that everyday life does not: continuous, personal contact with a group of people. It may be very helpful to offer people a forum for meaningful communication. However, if this is to be the main task of group therapy, then the group is deprived of a therapeutic function. Let us, for instance, take the case of a patient who suffers from a lack of meaningful communication during most of his working hours, but who is otherwise healthy. His symptom may just as well be an additional sign of his sanity, for his problems might be caused by the social structure of his work situation and not by his individual background. Therapy would hardly be of any use in this case, for what should the man be changed into—a neurotic who is not suffering any more from severe shortcomings in his life situation?

Therapists may realize that social structures can be reasons for the individual's cry for therapeutic help: alienating working and learning conditions; pretended equality in a situation with real inequality, such as career prospects for people from different social classes; and so on. Yet therapists cannot be forced to think it is their task to initiate changes in neurotic and neurosis-inducing social structures. So they treat these suffering people in group therapy, which, under these circumstances, becomes a kind of psychosocial waiting room, helping people to tolerate the intolerable until others who are not so tolerant change social conditions in such a way as to make these groups unnecessary.

It is obvious that in this way group therapy gets disregarded as do all the other methods of the laboratory culture. It does not improve the patients' real communication and is [22] integrated into everyday life on only one level. Thus it becomes part of a "middle-class group-movement party culture." This misuse of group therapy gives it a socially stabilizing rather than a therapeutic function. In this context it does not matter if one criticizes group therapy for a considerable lack of depth [30], a criticism that is often made. In this case it is almost an advantage.

Another kind of ambivalent appreciation of group therapy, which is also a way to disregard its therapeutic qualities, lies in the selection of patients. We often take social isolation, inhibitions, social fear, and the like as indications of a need for group therapy. The group seems the best place to get rid of such difficulties. This may well be so, but what are the ramifications of accepting only such patients for group-therapeutic treatment? Does this not limit the main therapeutic value to the nascent group, with an increased risk that the group will not realize its full potential? It will lack the therapeutic potential of a reasonably functioning group that has already reached its first state of cohesion.

With the exclusive selection of the kind of patients I have mentioned, the group could end the moment these initial insecurities were dealt with. The group would then terminate at the very point when it could start to mobilize all the therapeutic elements of a working group.

In contrast to this we should be aware of the fact that only in the working group can the sick individual make any progress, and that the task of the therapist is not only to make the group prepared to work, but also to *keep* it capable of working [35, p. 23].

Economic Advantage as a Reason for the Adoption of Group Therapy

Economically, group therapy combines several advantages. First, more patients can be treated without increasing the number of therapists. Second, although the patient has to pay less than for individual therapy, the therapist earns more money without investing more time. Third, because it is cheaper and because of the special setting of communication, group therapy is also more available to the lower classes than any other kind of therapy. All these advantages, however, are at the same time reasons that group therapy is often considered a second-class treatment.

As to the increased number of patients, it is obvious that group therapy substantially contributes to the supply of sufficient psychotherapeutic resources. There were never enough well-trained therapists for the number of patients desiring treatment. Historically this was (and surely still is) one important reason for the rapid development of group therapy and its ambiguous popularity as a crisis solution. This attitude justifies reservations for its use in less serious cases or for patients who might not benefit from individual treatment (which certainly does not mean that they are easy cases—quite the contrary sometimes). In such a situation or for that very reason a patient might well suspect that he is being given second-class treatment.

The aim of traditional therapy—if we do not take into account the late development of family therapy—is to help the single individual. The therapist's attention and training is therefore directed toward a diligent and differentiated understanding of the individual's psychic dynamics: his traumas, fantasies, wishes, defense mechanisms, symptoms.

Now, if group therapy is understood and judged according to these standards, then it must be perceived as a superficial treatment: The attention of the therapist is always distracted from the individual too quickly; there are other nonprofessional helpers (the other patients) who lack the well-trained understanding and intervention techniques of the therapist. Yet they too intervene therapeutically. In a group it is not possible to reach the depth of individual therapy. The advantage in quantity seems to be paid for by a loss in quality.

This is only the case, however, if one does not see how a group is confronting one with a situation that calls for a different therapeutic activity. Such a situation will cause difficulties for a therapist who is not familiar both with a differentiated theory of interaction and with the sociological problems underlying the dynamics of the development of this social microorganization. Psychoanalytic understanding in the traditional sense is not sufficient.

Even though the psychotherapeutic scene has changed and group therapy is no longer considered only as a crisis solution, the prejudices I have described still exist behind the praise for its value. Some examples: "The character of the therapeutic situation is no more that once-in-a-life, removed-from-the-world experience" [25, p. 88]. And: "There is no doubt that in group therapeutic treatment you cannot develop such a deep insight into the unconscious uncertainties as you can in individual therapy. Slavson has pointed out that the acting out in the group of fits of anger, hostile feelings, of rejection, and other sudden emotions, reduces the intrapsychic tensions by a cathartic reaction. Thus access to a deeper layer of the unconscious is blocked. From this the conclusion has to be drawn that a fully developed psychoneurosis can only be treated in a profound psychoanalysis" [25, p. 87].

The subtitle of the work from which these quotes were taken is "Group Therapy Versus Individual Therapy" [25]. This article was published in 1966, and even though most group therapists today have a different understanding of group therapy, many patients do still consider group therapy a second-class treatment. This is a result of the economic advantages it offers and the ambivalent consequences thereof. In addition, if the therapist's attention is more individually centered, the patient is justified in thinking he has bought second-class goods at a discount.

Even in the United States this prejudice seems to be widespread today, although this is the country where group therapy, for various reasons, has been more readily and more widely accepted than in Europe [21, chapter 2]. The prejudice seems so deeply rooted there that Yalom finds it necessary to tell his patients that the attraction of group therapy today does not lie in its economic advantage but in its therapeutically unique offer. He thereby hopes to increase the patients' confidence and to destroy the image of group therapy as second-rate treatment [41, p. 248].

Financially, group therapy offers a two-fold advantage, that is, for the therapist as well as for the clients. For the unspoken financial moral code of a responsible therapist this advantage could be problematic if not subconsciously or openly condemnable. It seems to contradict the moral argument often used in individual therapy that the fee should not only support the therapist but should also be equivalent to the value of the therapy. The client pays for what he gets; the therapist gets paid for what he offers or makes possible.

Whatever may be our estimation of the value of group therapy, this formula does not apply. If the value of the group therapy is high and the therapist gets his commensurate fee, each individual client is in fact paying only a part of the total price because the fee is paid jointly by the group. Each client is, in a sense, receiving a gift from the therapist.

If, on the other hand, each has to pay the actual worth of the therapy, the therapist gets his fee six or eight times over. This means either that he is exploiting the clients or that he is receiving a gift from them.

Inequity also occurs if the estimated value of the therapy is low and each patient pays his share for a treatment that the therapist considers unworthy of the fee. Again he receives his fee six or eight times over, but in this case it is for something with no value. Whatever way you look at it, the whole thing takes on a commercial nature with one side always making a profit. Of course it is not difficult in this situation to reach an agreement whereby both parties benefit; but the fact remains that the proper psychoanalytic working contract seems to be perverted into a profit-oriented bargain.

Yet this is only true if the group therapists maintain the individualistic concept of therapy and the ideal of the autonomous personality. If this were the case, then the financial problem would be just one more reason for giving group threapy only ambivalent attention: openly being in favor of the new method, at the same time as secretly condemning it by maintaining the individual therapeutic approach and conscience. This is hardly a good start for a therapeutic enterprise.

THE AVAILABILITY OF GROUP THERAPY FOR THE LOWER CLASSES

Individual psychotherapy has always been a privilege of the upper middle class [13, pp. 60, 66ff]. People of the lower classes could neither afford treatment nor could they meet its mental demands: intelligence, ability to verbalize and tolerance of frustration, that is, the capacity to intellectualize rather than act out the tensions of emotional difficulties.

For most schools of therapy these qualities are both requirements for and aims of the treatment. Yet these requirements are actually values of the middle class—to which the subculture of therapists belongs. Members of the lower class could hardly adapt themselves to these standards, mainly owing to their restricted code of language [4].

Group therapy, on the other hand, presents a different situation. It is not only financially accessible to the lower-class population but also much more attractive, since it is no longer the therapist alone who is setting standards of communication (from above), but also the patients, who are setting them together with the therapist. The coming into being as well as the further existence of the group is determined by the ability of the members to communicate with each other. Thus the group offers members of the lower classes access to psychotherapy. This does not mean that it was invented for them. It is surprising, however, that for a long time it was not considered suitable for anyone else: "When Hollingshead and Redlich,

1958 published their big investigation . . . group therapy in America played a role only—if at all—for the lowest social class" [14, p. 307; the quoted investigation, 18]. Can it be that this was part of the reason for turning group therapy into a second-class therapy?

The Benevolent Carelessness

Usually people and institutions that promote group therapy as a really new therapeutic instrument require a specific knowledge of and experience in handling the constituents of a group. Group dynamics and sociology have to be added to the theoretical framework of therapeutic concepts derived from individual therapy [2, p. 136ff; 19; 17, p. 67ff]. In addition to experience in individual therapy, training in group dynamics and group therapy is suggested [3, p. 136ff; 39, p. 312ff].

Yet there is a tendency to think that a psychoanalyst, or any therapist with a traditional training, is already well prepared for group therapy. Even a classic and otherwise very instructive book on psychoanalytic group therapy says that "anyone who has worked with single patients as a psychoanalyst . . . is fundamentally prepared for the task of a group therapist" [19, p. 74].

Certainly it is necessary for a group therapist to be well-trained in pychoanalysis or in any other traditional technique of psychotherapy, as well as in psychiatry. He has to have a knowledge of the different neurotic and psychotic manifestations. He has to recognize them and be able to distinguish one from the other, and he has to have experience in treating them. It is especially important to emphasize this as a counterbalance against a growing group ideology, which sees the group-dynamic potential as a general remedy for any kind of psychic troubles. Yet a psychoanalytic background alone is not sufficient training for a group therapist. If that were the case, the advantage of group therapy would be reduced to the rather problematic economic one. Also there would be the risk of actualizing one of the two fundamental and well-known misunderstandings about group therapy: The group would either be seen as consisting of six or eight cotherapists all treating one patient—that is, as a single therapy or analysis in the group: or as one big individual patient treated by the group therapist —that is, as a therapy of the group as a whole.

The first misunderstanding cannot really be called a concept of group therapy. It simply ignores the therapeutic or curative factors specific to a group: altruism, the universality of problems, group cohesiveness, interpersonal or social learning experience, and so on [41]. In this situation, if these factors are considered at all, it is only to create an atmosphere favorable either to the concentration of everybody's attention on the one patient treated at the moment, or to the patient's willingness to "produce material" and to accept the therapeutic interventions directed toward him.

These interventions are only directed toward the individual, interpreting his statements and behavior in the group. They never focus on a sequence of interactions between the members of the therapeutic group to interpret them in terms of different aspects of the present situation—its prevailing group standards, the distribution of roles and functions, its present phase in its development, its dependence on the leader, the building up of subgroups, the acceptance of different sexes, and so on.

Group therapy thus really does become a second-rate treatment, since an individual cannot be analyzed as profoundly in a group (where there are six or eight individuals all trying to attract the others' attention) as in single therapy. But it is simply not the therapeutic task of a group to function in this manner.

The second misunderstanding, that of analysis of the group as a whole, arises from a conceptual and technical orientation also derived from a concept of therapy of the single individual. However, in this situation it is not quite so obvious that the therapy is misdirected, since the focus is not on a single patient but on the group as a whole. For it is reasonable to accept the group as a distinct entity that functions according to social laws that are not simply a collection of psychic mechanisms of the individual members.

Now where is the mistake? This organic concept of the group as a whole easily leads to a concept of the group as one big person, with different and dependent functions put together into an independent unity. Therapeutic attention is then directed only toward the development of this unity and the influence the therapist can have on it [5]. Individual members are relevant only to the extent that their functions in the whole organism are of interest. Their psychopathology loses importance, and the specific individual ways in which each plays his role when interacting with others become more or less irrelevant. It is easy to make this mistake because of a superficial similarity between the dynamic context of the functions of a group and the dynamics of an individual. The psychoanalytic personality model, in particular, can easily be used or misused in describing groups [7]: "The similar nature of the unconscious gives the group the effect of a person, because one patient's statements represent and reflect everybody's inner events. Thus the interpretations have an effect on everybody" [26, p. 22].

Some analysts therefore think that the group situation can be treated in the same way as a real psychoanalytic situation [1, p. 72]. As in Pohlen's important statement [27, p. 60]: In this context the Freudian structural model of the individual is transferred to the group in a linear way and the single members are seen as its partial egos. In R. Schindler's group concept [33] the position of the leader (alpha) would incorporate the ideal ego, the expert (beta) would represent the reality-principle of the group-ego, "better the superego," and so on [27, p. 60].

This concept of the group as one big person analyzed and treated by the therapist creates new problems for the patients as well as for the therapist. If the patients are nothing but dependent functions, it will be difficult to encourage their relative independence, above all in situations where the group produces a strong inner pressure on everyone—for example, to conform to each other.

If the therapist tries to conceptualize the group in terms of a personality model, he will have difficulty understanding fully certain phases in the development of the first phase of dependence when the pressure for uniformity among members is especially strong, or the phase of pairing. As R. Schindler says: "It seems to me impossible to analyze the group as a whole, since it . . . only exists as the conceptualization of a process of interaction" [34, p. 234].

The therapist will furthermore have difficulty sticking to the role he is accustomed to play in single therapy, where he is the only object of transference as well as the only interpreter. In the group situation he must also be a member [2, p. 259], and his partial integration is necessary for the group's functioning [30, p. 368]. He will have to express his own feelings and impressions concerning the correct situation of the group as well as giving his analytic interpretations.

In addition to these difficulties, an attempt to view and handle the group as an integral person helps to spread the following popular misunderstanding about psychoanalysis: As this kind of group therapy applies the psychoanalytic personality model to the group, and in particular the concepts of id, ego, and super-ego as represented by different group members, these concepts become hypostasized and turned into visible realities in the philosophic sense of conceptual or ideal realism.

This reification of concepts increases the suspicion that psychoanalysis has always been an idealistic system of metaphysics that transforms mental processes into real substances. Yet the Freudian personality model never presented the id, ego, and super-ego as self-sufficient substances of which the person was somehow composed. They are an attempt to conceptualize the different determinants of our behavior and their interdependence [36, p. 280ff]. The names they have been given, which somehow substantiate them, are symbols for conscious and unconscious motivational forces, nothing more.

Finally, let me present an illustration of the subtle way this psychoanalytic reduction of the group—turning it into a two-person situation—is carried through. This quotation, which is taken from a reasonable book on group psychotherapy, suggests an attempt to acknowledge the group as a specifically new therapeutic setting, yet ends up identifying it with a classical psychoanalytic situation.

The working hypothesis from which we start reads as follows: A group meeting continuously under specified conditions over a longer period of several years develops its specific structure insofar as the individual actions of single group members have their roots in the unconscious motive common to all the participants. Insofar, the group follows one line of development (so much for the acceptance of the group as specific gestalt—now he takes it back) just like the sequence of a single patient's diverse statements in the classical two-person situation [1, p. 77ff].

SOME REASONS FOR THE AMBIVALENCE TOWARD GROUP THERAPY

The Single Individual as the Object of Treatment

Moreno [24] suggests that the reason group psychiatry and group psychotherapy have appeared so late on the therapeutic scene is that modern psychiatry in general descended from somatic medicine. And one may add that this is also the reason for the *ambivalent acceptance* of group therapy.

The somatic illness of a single person does not usually necessitate the treatment of his relatives or other persons of reference. One person's appendectomy does not affect the appendixes of his family members [24]. The reasons for his illness will not be sought for in the organisms of other people, nor will it be treated there, but rather in the patient himself. The relation of the functions and forces in the system of *his* organism will be therapeutically influenced.

Similarly, in organic psychiatry the exogenic factors of mental illness play a secondary role compared to the endogenic factors, which are actually medically treated. These important distinctions are mirrored in the professions devoted to the care of the mentally ill: The social worker, institutionally less important, is in charge of the exogenic side of the illness. He helps to find reasonable solutions for the real-life problems of the patient— his family situation, work, and general social situation, all of which contribute to the illness, accelerate its onset, and influence its course. Although social workers are sometimes the only ones giving the patients any sort of psychotherapeutic treatment, their work is considered to be only preparation for an efficient traditional somatic psychiatric treatment, performed by the doctors. During treatment all other influences besides those necessary for therapy are reduced to a minimum. The patient should be relieved of the excitement caused by his family or his job. Social isolation is, and in organic medicine always was, part of the therapy.

Psychoanalysis above all has helped us toward a new understanding of mental illness. Freud found that neurotic symptoms have a psychological meaning, being a compromise between two contradictory motivational forces. They have their origin in the mental experience of the patient. Thus mental illness has become the object of a method of treatment other than the somatic. The "drug" or better "antidrug" of psychoanalysis is *meaningful verbal interaction* intended to make it possible for the patient to relive and gain insight into the traumatic experiences that caused the patient to be ill.

Yet in its early development psychoanalysis could not help borrowing from somatic medical science and art some characteristic features of the concept of illness and its therapy, features that contradict the specific therapeutic method of group therapy. Psychoanalytic theory holds the specific organism as the "locus of pyschic ailment," and—according to Moreno—even celebrates as such "its most triumphant confirmation" [24]. The intrapsychic dynamics are essentials. Even though the importance of social interaction centered around the early childhood relations of the individual to his parents and siblings is accepted, they appear within the therapy only as intrapsychic forces rather than as actual social interactions.

There have always been psychoanalytic concepts based more heavily on the social aspect of the individual's mental existence, pointing out that the individual is nothing but the result of interpersonal processes [4]. But only lately has psychoanalytic family therapy been developed as a therapeutic instrument based on this knowledge. Traditional psychoanalysis, however, with its focus on the individual rather than on a system of social interactions, still tends to concentrate on the single mental system of the individual.

A similar difficulty appears in the psychoanalytic—or more generally in the psychotherapeutic—relationship between therapist and patient. This relationship itself now plays a curative role unlike that between the doctor and patient in somatic medicine. In the latter, the doctor uses the relationship simply to find out what kind of therapy is required and to control the therapeutic effects of his prescriptions. The therapy itself, while guided and controlled by the doctor, actually occurs outside the interaction between doctor and patient.

In psychoanalytic psychotherapy the deeply personal interaction process and its development is the therapeutic or curing process itself. Yet the psychoanalytic working alliance does not represent an attempt to cure illness by what in everyday life is understood as "an interpersonal relationship." This relationship, which has to develop deeply and therapeutically, has a particular structure and dynamic process known as the working through of transference neurosis and of the countertransference reactions.

Thus the personal therapeutic relationship, although essential and powerfully evoked by the therapeutic setting, can finally be seen as a necessary stimulation for the patient's production of therapeutic material. The therapist should be simply a screen for the patient's unconscious conflicts. The personal relationship and the social interaction is therefore a direct manifestation of the intrapsychic processes of the patient. The individual patient and his desire for a relationship with the therapist remain objects of treatment.

For a long period in the development of psychoanalysis, Ackermann's considerations were correct; that the psychoanalytic method, although originating in a bipolar situation is, in its techniques, almost exclusively directed toward the experience of only one of the two people, namely the patient.

External conflicts with the analyst are translated into terms of the patient's internal conflicts with himself [2, p. 255]. Only very cautiously has psychoanalysis begun to pay more attention to the importance of some aspects of the personal relationship between therapist and patient, aspects that exceed the bounds of what is called transference or countertransference [13, p. 65ff]. This may help to explain the ambivalence of psychoanalysis toward the concept of group therapy, where analytic tools and insights are used, but only in conjunction with acceptance of the importance of specific group-dynamics factors to the development and work of the group. These factors represent the main curative potential of the group and cannot be fully explained by referring exclusively to individual psychodynamics.

The ambivalence is embedded within psychoanalysis itself. On the one hand this treatment considered (the early) social interactions and the individual's internal reactions to them, which are responsible for the individual person's mental constitution. It also founded its method of treatment on the power of the social interaction between two people where the hic et nunc of the therapeutic process, called transference neurosis, is central.

On the other hand, psychoanalysis requires the therapeutic interaction to be subject to the individual's intrapsychic processes, which also function as the source for explanations and interpretations. Thus it should not easily accept the consequences of what it had conceptually helped to establish, namely the group as a social and therapeutic instrument that cannot be fully understood simply as one big individual, or as a collection of individual intrapsychic processes.

Freud, however, seems to support this last view when he talks about mass phenomena. He presents them as sufficiently explicable within the psychoanalytic conceptual framework, and says that the profound changes of mental activity that a single person has to undergo as participant in a bigger group [12, p. 27] become objects of research only insofar as they provoke quasineurotic reactions in the individual [12, chapters 7, 8, 9].

It is not certain whether Freud claims his analysis of the large group to be valid for the small therapeutic group as well (Freud at least does not make any distinction). If, however, this is the case, then Moreno is right when he says that Freud's view of the group is that of an epiphenomenon of the individual's psychodynamics [24], an epiphenomenon that causes regression of the mental activity to an earlier phase of development—something we might observe in the savage and the child [12, p. 56].

The Therapist's Position

When I dealt with the relation between therapist and patient, I already touched on the problem in group therapy posed by the traditional psychoanalytically oriented psychotherapist's position in the therapeutic process. This problem has to be separately examined now, since it leads us to further difficulties with which group therapy is confronted.

I have suggested that the psychoanalytic understanding of mental illness led to a psychotherapeutic relationship between doctor and patient different from the traditional pattern of this relationship. The interaction between the two is now the curative process. The doctor does not give prescriptions for treatment to take place mainly outside the interaction. Yet on the other hand, the psychoanalytic relation is still influenced by the traditional concept of illness as something happening in the isolated biological or mental system of the patient. The psychoanalytic interaction is subject to the internal processes of the client. Certainly, one of the two reasons for this lies in what was the dominant interest of research at the time when psychoanalytic science began to develop. The internal dynamics of the individual were investigated much earlier than the dynamics of social interaction. The isolated individual, his drives and mental forces were the objects of psychological research. Freud's step beyond this could not really break the individualistic framework, nor did it intend to do so. His new psychological view of the individual's social dimension was later developed further by social psychology and communications theory. Recently it has come to the systematic attention of psychotherapy.

The traditional image and social position of the doctor and the therapist is another cause for the late interest in the interaction process and its use as a therapeutic instrument. With the patient (as a more or less closed system of forces) as the focus of therapeutic attention, the doctor's position is self-evident. He is the investigator who does not himself have to become the object of investigation. He must possess enough knowledge to cure people and must be in a position to use this resource in the interest of his patients. His personal interests and personal relationship with the patient must not interfere with the correct application of his knowledge, and should be separated from his professional activity.

But psychoanalysis has introduced a change. The psychoanalyst must constantly reflect on his own position. It is part of his professional activity to analyze his own reactions toward the patient. He has to find out where his objectivity risks becoming trapped by uncontrolled feelings toward the patient. Moreover, he himself must have been the patient at some point during his training.

Yet this continuous self-reflection of the doctor, the relative nature of his position, requiring the analysis of his countertransference, actually supports the traditional position of the therapist. By working through his subjectivity the therapist can purify himself of outside forces in dealing with the patient, thereby securing his function as a screen on which the inner struggles of the patient are reflected. At the same time the patient must realize that the therapist is not the figure of his fantasies, but the object of his transferences. Thus the self-reflective activity of the therapist is solitary, and not intended to be part of a direct relationship. On the contrary, all the patient's attempts to include this dimension have to be seen as the patient's struggle, not with a real person—the therapist—but with his own inner conflicts. The real person of the therapist remains exterritorial. This interaction between doctor and patient is unique to psychoanalysis, but in the recognition and acceptance of the specific roles in this interaction, the objectivity of the traditional doctor-patient relationship is achieved.

It is obvious that this thorough, methodically purified objectivity of the therapist, and the permanently purified "unimportance" of the therapist's real personality in a therapeutic interaction, in effect invests the therapist with singular power over the patient, power in the interest of the patient's mental health.

The doctor/therapist is supposed to be in control of the situation. He sets the rules of communication, he subtly determines what is going to be worked through, he proposes new and often surprising connections between different parts of the therapeutic material the patient produces. He and his relationship with the patient are, so to speak, transcendental elements of the therapeutic experience. They are the a priori conditions for the therapeutic process, the material for which is presented by the patient. They never become visible parts of this process. Even the patient's reference to them is important only for the inner mental system of the patient, not of the doctor. Nor do they become important for the real interaction between the two. All the remarks of the patient concerning the person of the doctor, or concerning the process of interaction, are interpreted only insofar as the mental dynamics of the patient are concerned. Rightly understood, this is not a criticism of the therapist's power and exterritoriality, which are indeed necessary for a successful psychoanalysis. I want to emphasize them simply because they differ from the resources of the therapists in group therapy. An analytically trained therapist working with groups has to modify his therapeutic identity. He has to give up the analyst's safe, defined position if he does not want to treat the group as one big individual, or to treat the individuals in the group. In both these cases, as we know, he would ignore the specific group-dynamics therapeutic potential.

The difficulty in modifying one's role is increased by the fact that the traditional analytic role is closer to the professional role of a somatic medical doctor than to that of a group therapist. There is no appropriate model for a group therapist in the traditional academic helping professions.

How does the group therapist's professional role differ from that of the analyst? Owing to the different therapeutic situations presented in a group, the way the therapist becomes a participant-observer is different from that of the analyst. In individual therapy, as I have mentioned, the rules of interaction are set by the therapist alone. All the rules the patient tries to establish, even though they may be intended to destroy the analytic situation, are interpreted within the given interactional framework as different forms of transference and acting out. It is the therapist's task not to act out himself, but simply to interpret all the patient's attempts to do so.

In group therapy the whole group establishes the rules of interaction as its social norms. The whole group agrees on a distribution of roles, obliging everybody to act out his real function within this microcosm. The therapist's special function and initial authority in the group lies in his ability to help establish, as a metanorm, that the rules of interaction and the distribution of roles are not final but must always be the object of therapeutic analysis in which he will guide the group. To function in this way the therapist has to become a member of the group. He has to become integrated in the group without losing his therapeutic function, part of which lies in not hindering but helping the patients to share this with him. This is made possible by the multipersonal situation in the group. Here, unlike in individual therapy, the therapist's actual behavior and person hic et nunc can be compared with the behavior of the other participants in the group. In and through the multipersonal interaction process, the therapist's person becomes comparable to the others, which means that he becomes integrated. In individual therapy he can be compared only with persons outside the therapy situation—figures in the patient's fantasies.

In the group the comparison between him and the other members makes him much more visible as a person. Therefore, the struggle against authority is also a real one in which he must not only intervene analytically, provoke transference reactions and analyze them; but must also intervene as a real, though especially distinguished, member of the group. He, too, has to act out.

His position in the group is not only determined and changed by the multiple transference, but also by the actual phase of development of the group and his behavior as an especially distinguished member. "In this system of transference and countertransference reactions the therapist is included in the group as a special person. He is "prominent" only insofar as his (emphatically determined) functions as interpreter places him a bit ahead of the others—but only for the moment of the interpretation. Otherwise the therapist should be "equally situated" with the others in order to give the individual members of the group an opportunity to take over therapeutic functions themselves. In this way everybody can act as a cotherapist for the others. And this is a condition for the development of the therapeutic potential of a group. Through developing attention to the reaction of others to one's own behavior (including projective and introjective mechanisms) the patient can gain a better understanding of himself and also get some insights into unconscious motivations [21, p. 65]. Thus it becomes possible and necessary for the therapist to speak at times about his very personal emotions and difficulties concerning the situation of the group, but not about those concerning his own psychic problems outside the group.

The special kind of professional help in group therapy is characterized by including nonprofessional help as well, a fact that is easily taken as an excuse for a lack of group therapeutic training and often for a neglect of such training. This combination of professional with nonprofessional help requires, on the contrary, an especially careful and elaborate training of a group therapist. The therapist's, as well as the patient's, changed and changing positions in a multipersonal process require "new steps in the widening of the understanding of the socialization process of the participant"; and, which is even more difficult, "a systematic analysis of the analytical attitude and analytical theory with the aids of psychoanalysis" [27, p. 13ff]. This concerns not only the therapist's position in the group but also his professional identity, as well as the identity of the organization for which he is working.

The Natural Sciences as a Point of Reference for Medical and Psychotherapeutic Science and Art

The last two sections have dealt with two interrelated factors behind the ambivalent acceptance of psychoanalytically oriented group therapy: the single individual as the object of traditional treatment, and the extraterritorial objectivity of the traditional therapist. If the curative process involves a change in the organic or psychological system known as "the patient," then the initiation and administration of this change must be executed by a doctor whose objectivity is unaffected by the process. The significant variables of the interaction process effecting the change must also remain constant. All the patient's desires, for instance for a relationship with the doctor, remain transferential and are hardly ever analyzed within the "real" relationship between patient and doctor. The process ends when the desired change has occurred.

This therapeutic setting is analogous to that of traditional medical research, a branch of the natural sciences. The object of such research is the isolated human organism, which is scientifically dissected and analyzed in order to determine the laws governing it. In pure medical research it is important that the researcher is objective and does not exert any influence on the organism that will in any way distort it. (Yet interestingly enough, our knowledge of anatomy has been gained from distorted, dead parts of the body.)

Since Kant, scientific theory has maintained that every object is influenced and determined by the circumstances through which we know it: The process of discovery and our participation in that process determine the result. One of these circumstances is a clear practical interest and aim. In medical science this aim is healing. But this aim lies beyond objectivity. It is a very subjective human aim that, however, can only be reached by the use of scientific method. Practical interest and application precede and follow this scientific method but cannot be derived from it. In fact, practical interest is not at all objective, but implies rather a power over the object of research. The aim is to influence and change the object as if it were a human construction following the laws of planned constructions. In traditional medicine and psychiatry, the somatic and psychic system has become just such a natural, causally determined object.

However limited it may be, the claim for objectivity is as impressive as it is because its authority is based on the results of its application: the technical achievements of the modern world. And only because this is so impressive can the nonobjective practical interest in gaining more technical power be hidden behind the cloak of fascination for the system of necessary scientific connections. Scientists pretend that this desire for more "useful" power is derived from objective scientific laws, particularly when the object of research and change is the human being. What is actually happening, however, is that a case is being made for the control of one human being over another.

In medical science and its application this takes the form of the subordination of patient to doctor. When the interest of the doctor to cure is identical with the interest of the patient to be cured, then this subordination is acceptable. But when we examine the practical organization in society of this type of power, the apparent scientific justification for it reveals dangerous ambiguities. In medicine, the object of research is the patient. The technical relationship between researcher and object should, however, become a human one when technical methods are being applied to ease the sufferings of a human being. But more often than not the object of research has simply been transformed into an object of treatment. The so-called objectivity of the researcher turns into the real social power of the doctor. He swears an oath, gains membership in a powerful organization that protects his interests, and enjoys a prestigious social position. No one doubts the position of the doctor because of his image of unselfish objectivity. The patient, on the other hand, not only possesses none of the social benefits enjoyed by the doctor, but is completely at his mercy.

If we relate this position of the doctor to what was said in the last section, it becomes clear that the therapists' position in group therapy cannot be derived from the medical model: It has other roots.

The Organizational Texture: Hierarchy

The situation just described is particularly noticeable in hospitals. Here the relationship between the doctor and the patient, parallel to that of the scientist and his object of research, is institutionalized in a closed social organization, namely the hierarchy of the hospital in which the patient appears at the bottom. He must accept the doctor's orders without questioning them. Furthermore, he has no insight into the objective conditions of his treatment as administrated by the doctors. If the patient does not behave suitably as an object of treatment, the success of the therapy can be seriously endangered. The social isolation of the patient corresponds to the methodic isolation of an object of research. The transformation of the scientist's power over his object into the social power of the doctor over the patient is especially obvious in psychiatry. The patient can legally be forced to enter a psychiatric hospital, and to stay there.

Today the understanding of scientific objectivity, on which the relationship between doctor and patient seems to be based, has changed. The fascination of technically applied scientific objectivity is well analyzed, and we understand the social conditions that underlie the special kinds of objectivity in which we believe. We also know that the relationship between the patient and the doctor is not merely scientific, but social as well. The interaction between them is not like that of a scientist and his object of research, but it is that of two human beings with different social positions. Yet the power bestowed on the social organization of medical treatment through the claim to objectivity has undergone practically no change, and it will surely remain resistant to any such attempt so long as it adequately reflects the structure of the organization of our society.

The doctor's relationship with the patient (upon which the psychotherapeutic interaction is based) mirrors the social structures of its surroundings in which all organizations, of whatever kind, are hierarchically structured for ostensibly objective reasons. But these objective claims are very often only rationalizations of pragmatic interests, which are couched in terms of the laws of formal logic and the structure of scientific thinking. The objectivity of this thinking, however, begins to sound strange when used to justify a claim for power and control.

Let me give some examples: A higher and more general concept embraces many lower ones. It represents what they have in common. It represents what beyond their individuality is general in their reality, without which we do not even get all the species under it. Similarly, the claim is that a person with higher hierarchical status embraces many persons of lower status, who are therefore dependent on him. The higher his position, the more he represents the so-called common interests, and the greater is his responsibility for his subordinates and for those common interests. Obviously his control over both is greater as well.

Again, single, empirical examples belonging to a conceptually analyzed and comprehended case are connected with each other only insofar as they are embraced by the general concept. The single species of a genus are only comparable to each other insofar as they belong to this genus. In the logical hierarchy, therefore, they are placed on a lower level than the genus, just as in the hierarchies in reality, which are also governed by this formal logic. Here the superior, or boss, represents the institutional homogeneity of his otherwise independent subordinates or assistants. The official and usually also the informal relations among the subordinates are mediated and defined by the primary relation of each of them to the boss.

The differentia specifica determines the relationship of the single species to its genus, without which it is nothing (whereas each species can easily exist independently of another). At the same time it automatically determines the differences and distinctions amongst these species. Similarly the contact of each subordinate to his boss and the differences among the subordinates are determined by each one's specific function and job. For the most part colleagues can exist without each other, but not without their boss.

The hierarchical bipolar relationship of superiority and subordination is the basis for the functioning of most of the organizations where we do our work. It provides a guarantee of stability in social systems (such as the hospital). The strict delineation of role distribution seems necessary for the most efficient flow in the work process. It leads to a stable social structure where direct communication among subordinates would disrupt the order of the system. Any cooperation that is not mediated by a superior introduces a risk of a breakdown in the system. Thus a well-functioning group within this system would be an annoyance, since it could endanger the stable structure of the whole. The organizational and emotional problems it would raise and the emerging requests for a different form of communication, could distract the energy of the people from their work. Thus the social potential of a group, both for conflict and for conflict solution, has been restricted for the sake of efficient performance, and directed instead into the official, hierarchically accepted channels. Group therapy, on the other hand, makes abundant use of this social potential, which is elsewhere systematically limited. The therapeutic efforts of the group are based on the free development of this potential.

CONSEQUENCES

Contradictions Between Group and Everyday Life

The structuring principles according to which a therapeutic group functions are very different from those of a department in an organization. The therapeutic group (at least in the sense of analytic group therapy) is only minimally structured at the outset.

Heigl and Heigl-Evers speak about an "insignificant regulation of behavior (minimal structuring)" [16, p. 239]. As in no other kind of organization, the participants in a therapy group are not confronted with a specific, rational task with the necessary roles distributed in advance, and with the possibilities of human interaction limited once and for all.

Like free association in individual psychoanalysis, the principle of communication in the group is that of free interaction [16]. (In this analogy it is important to emphasize the concept of interaction. Otherwise, if we talk about group association in the way that Foulkes does [8, p. 25], it is highly probable that we will support the analytic misconception of the group as one big individual.)

The preliminary structure of the group and its role distribution grow out of the dynamics of the interaction. The aim of the group is to change this structure and thus develop further. The therapeutic interventions are therefore directed toward the variables of the current hic-et-nunc process: the modes of interaction, the different roles that participants take on or are pushed into, the emotional dynamics of interaction, and the unconscious wishes and fantasies according to which issues are selected and roles distributed. All this is analyzed and worked through.

Thus the group is provided with the possibility of continuously changing and revising its structure in the course of its development. Greenberg, Langer, and Rodrigue [19, p. 158] even say that therapeutic groups, whose "dynamic collective constellation" does not change over a certain period of time, have a bad prognosis. It is part of the curative process that the distribution of roles and functions in the group changes again and again. The stability of the therapeutic group should be guaranteed by its flexible emotional cohesiveness and not by a fixed, predetermined internal organization.

The principles of interaction in therapeutic groups that are functioning constructively and those in official groups in institutions elsewhere are contradictory. In therapeutic groups a desire for a rigid organization, prescribed role distribution, and a structure of fixed authority would be regarded as regressive and its fulfillment by the therapist as a technical mistake. On the contrary, he should help to have these desires explored and worked through. In a department in business, a college, a hospital, or another institution, any attempt to achieve a new, more flexible, theme-centered communication and some emotional cohesion in a group through an inquiry into the processes of interaction and a questioning of the distribution of roles and authority is what would be regarded as regressive. Members would persistently avoid such practices as a disturbance in the work situation.

This contrast does not seem to be at all surprising. Even when the doctor-patient relationship is determined by the socially accepted hierarchical principles of organization, what happens in psychotherapy is contrary to the norms of communication in everyday life. The two-person relation of the therapeutic situation is paradoxical enough and a provocation to the patient even without the applications of Frankl's or Watzlawick's method of a "paradoxical intention" [39, chapters 6, 7, 14; also chapter 8]. The contrast between this individual-therapy situation and communication in everyday life is obvious: a boss will never analyze the unconscious of his subordinates, work through their transferences, or wait silently for thoughts to occur to them.

But the contrast between the group-therapy situation and everyday life is not quite so self-evident. The integration of the therapist in the group and its partially nonprofessional character are first attempts at a practical application of the scientific insight that the circumstances of the investigation and the influence of the researched object should be considered when analyzing results. What was formerly the power of researcher over object, doctor over patient becomes, for the group therapist, the power of doctor among patients, that is, power through participation.

This new nonhierarchical understanding of the subject-object relationship in scientific practice is now being applied to the therapeutic micro-organization, introducing a new social dimension partly opposed to the hierarchical order. This could be the beginning of an organizational redefinition of the scientific hierarchy, practically applied to the structure of a hospital.

The differences between the principles of interaction in the therapeutic group and in the groups in a hospital department, which are organized in other ways, is not immediately so obvious or self-evident. Patients and therapists experience this difference in a way that raises doubts about some aspects of it. The goal of group thrapy for the patients is to give them relief from their sufferings and not to deepen their knowledge about the functioning of groups, as is done in group-dynamics training sessions [9, p. 446]. However, the therapeutic theme concentration and concern with structures of interaction make it impossible to avoid an increase in sensitivity toward group processes. The attempts to establish defense mechanisms and the power relationships, the hidden signs of competition, the mechanisms used to exclude someone from the group—all these become more easily recognized by the patients. They are then able to apply this insight to daily-life situations, thereby recognizing some of the causes of their difficulties. It is the goal of the group to find solutions to these problems as they arise in the group.

In official work groups these problems not only remain unresolved but are sometimes even institutionalized. In the same way it is possible that group therapy, while decreasing individual pathological suffering, can at the same time increase general suffering in work situations and in private life. The explosive material of group therapy cannot be limited to the relatively isolated framework of the therapeutic group, just as the symptoms or troubles of the patients are not to be cured only within the group, but outside as well.

Consequences for the Therapeutic Institution

Effects Within a Department. Let us take a look at the situation in a traditional, psychiatric department. A patient is there for treatment, and part of his treatment will be group therapy. But the patient is immediately faced with a problem, for his behavior in the group and his behavior as an individual patient in the hospital when he is not in the group are mutually exclusive patterns. He will be reprimanded if he behaves in the same way in the hospital hierarchy as he behaves in the therapeutic group. In order to avoid this confusion he must either leave the group altogether, or function in it as in a two-person relationship. Thus the special therapeutic, group-dynamic potential is repressed and the group has adapted itself to the structure of the department.

Another alternative that is much more difficult and usually produces more resistance is to include the structure of the department in the group-therapeutic process. In this way the therapeutic integration of the therapist in the group would take on an organizational dimension. Then at the very least one would have to raise the question posed by Pohlen [27, p. 83]: "But aren't these considerations also valid for the hospital personnel: that they only repeat their own, unresolved conflicts in their dealings with the patients, instead of bringing their internalized conflicts out in self-examination? And is it not possible, as we know from observations of families, that certain tensions in the personnel group can be discharged through the structuring of the patients into certain role positions, so that a suitable patient (as categorical figure of projection) takes over a certain function?" Again and again we might observe how the patient's "independence" and "ability," just like "helplessness" and "inability" for the personnel, could be made a "point of attack," and thereby "made" a case of disease according to the dominant unconscious anxieties and tensions in the total group.

Such structuring of the patients into projection figures occurs, in our experience, in periodic sequences and seems to lend balance and stability to the clinical system, as in the families described by Vogel and Bell [42].

Stanton and Schwartz [35] presented similar group phenomena in their analysis of a therapeutic institution: the unconscious differences in the personnel group were reflected in the symptoms of the patients. They could further observe that the symptoms of the patients disappeared as soon as the personnel were able to deal with their conflicts in the open.

Effects on the Training of Group Therapists. The integration of the institution into the therapeutic process, which then becomes a process of self-examination, creates problems even in the group-therapeutic training situation. (Analogous to the training analysis required for individual therapists, there are training standards in the institutions of group and family therapy involving the self-analysis of an organization or a group). A dilemma might arise similar to what we have seen with inpatient group therapy within a department—a dilemma certainly more important for the candidates and trainers in the institution than for the patients, although the patients will certainly be affected detrimentally if this dilemma is not resolved.

Again, the persons in question must work in two mutually contradictory systems of interaction and reflection. On the one hand, they are more or less committed to a fixed distribution of roles and to acting as candidates and members of the organization with the usual, established hierarchical structure. On the other hand, the same persons interact in the training group according to the principles of group therapy: minimal structuring, free interaction, formulation of emotional conflicts, thrashing out of authority problems, flexibility in role distribution, and concentration on unconscious fantasies. To remain in any given fixed group structure means to accept regressive wishes, and this must also be worked through. It is certain that the organization will be influenced here as well by the free interaction of the group. Once started, it is not possible to limit the working out of these problems to the fixed framework of the group-therapy sessions. The very differences experienced in the structures of interaction in the job situation on the one hand and in the group on the other make these structures the actual objects of therapeutic work. The unmentioned difficulties experienced with group members in the job situation have to be worked through, in order that the group can establish a situation in which the two people concerned can communicate effectively. The full and proper resolution of this difficulty, if it takes place, will then influence interaction in the job situation.

Suggestions and Reflections. Just as in the previous example of the psychiatric department, an institution would have to accept the task that is so frightening for every organization with a rational orientation: reflection on the emotional, interactional, and social conditions of work and cooperation. Transcendental reflection would no longer be the exclusive domain of theoretical social psychology. Instead, reflection would be part of the empirical work. The knowledge, already relevant for scientific theory, that the researcher and his activities influence the objective results, would have to be applied organizationally by wider use of the principles of a therapeutic group.

It has not yet been empirically proved that this feared consequence of group-therapy training and activity, from which a temporary decline in productivity is expected, will not be advantageous in the long run. It has already been pointed out that it certainly benefits the patients.

To try to avoid a priori a possible effect of this kind for the institution, and still to wish to work in a group-therapeutic way, implies a risk of developing a new double standard. The candidates of the institution in which they get their training would have to deal, like the patients mentioned before, with the accepted norms of behavior within the group, as well as those outside the group. The same people would interact with each other in two social situations on contradictory levels of interaction. They would have to pretend that there was no connection between the two social settings. This double standard would undoubtedly have an effect on their work in therapeutic groups. A countertransference would easily arise that would be untreatable in this social context. For how is it possible, as therapist, to contribute within the group to the promotion of a basic interaction-oriented attitude when this attitude is rejected in work outside the group. Will not the patients in the group have to be socialized to the same double standard?

This double standard, or rather this double standard coupled with an uneasiness about it, is actually an advantage in this situation, in which there is an established contradiction between mutually exclusive systems of interaction. At least it serves as a guarantee against the possibility that therapy will turn into an insignificant barren ritual of freedom by simply creating new nonalienating social structures, for example by promoting the new "group-party" culture.

In this article I have set down some deliberations founded on the attempt to articulate a feeling which, although just a feeling, need not be without effect on science and its application. These speculations are still only hypothetical, and therefore unscientific. They will remain that way until a group decides to do "action research" using itself as object. This is the challenge put forward by Foulkes [8, p. 76] when he says: "As we see it, we need a dynamic science open to the revolutionary idea that in this area therapy is science and science, therapy."

BIBLIOGRAPHY

1. Argelander, H. *Gruppenprozesse, Wege zur Anwendung der Psychoanalyse in Lehre und Forschung*. Rororo, Hamburg, 1970.
2. Ackermann, N. W. "Psychoanalysis and Group-Psychotherapy." In M. Rosenbaum and M. Berger, eds., *Group-Psychotherapy and Group Function*. Basic Books, New York, 1963.
3. Battegay, R. "Ausbildungsmethoden in Gruppenpsychotherapie." In A. Heigl-Evers, ed., *Psychoanalyse und Gruppe*. Vandenhoek, Göttingen, 1971.
4. Bernstein, B. "Soziale Struktur, Sozialisation und Sprachverhalten: Aufsätze von 1958–1970" *Schwarze Reihe*, no. 8. De Munter, Amsterdam, 1970.
5. Bion, W. R. *Erfahrungen in Gruppen*. Klett, Stuttgart, 1970.
6. Däumling, A. M., J. Fengler, and S. Nellessen. *Angewandte Gruppendynamik*. Klett, Stuttgart, 1974.
7. Ezriell, H. "Übertragung und psychoanalytische Deutung in der Einzel- und Gruppen-Psychotherapie." *Psyche* 14 (1960): 496–523.
8. Foulkes, S. H. *Gruppenanalytische Psychotherapie*. Kindler, Munich, 1974.
9. Frank, J. W. "Training and Therapy." In L. P. Bradford, J. R. Gibb, and K. D. Benne, eds., *T-Group Theory and Laboratory Method*. Wiley, New York, 1967.
10. Freud, S. *Vorlesungen zur Einführung in die Psychoanalyse*. Fischer, Frankfurt, 1969.
11. Freud, S. *Massenpsychologie und Ich-Analyse*. Fischer, Frankfurt, 1972.
12. Graupe, S. R. "Ergebnisse und Probleme der quantitativen Erforschung traditioneller Psychotherapie verfahren." In H. Strotzka, ed., *Psychotherapie, Grundlagen, Verfahren and Indikationen*. Urban & Schwarzenberg, Munich, 1975.
13. Greenson, R. R., and M. Wexler. "Die Übertragungsfreie Beziehung in der psychoanalytischen Situation." *Psyche* 25 (1971): 206–230.
14. Grumiller, I. "Therapeutische Gruppenkonzepten." In H. Strotzka, ed., *Psychotherapie, Grundlagen, Verfahren und Indikationen*. Urban & Schwarzenberg, Munich, 1975.
15. Haley, J. *Strategies of Psychotherapy*. Grune & Stratton, New York, 1972.
16. Heigl-Evers, A., and F. Heigel. "Zur tiefenpsychologisch fundierten oder analytisch orientierten Gruppenpsychotherapie des Göttinger Modells." *Gruppenpsychotherapie und Gruppendynamik* 9, no. 3 (December 1975).
17. Horn, K. ed. *Gruppendynamik und der subjektive Faktor*. Suhrkamp, Frankfurt, 1972.

18. Hollingshead, A. B., and F. C. Redlich. *Social Class and Mental Illness.* Wiley, New York, 1958.
19. Kemper, ed. *Psychoanalytische Gruppentherapie.* Kindler, Munich.
20. Liebermann, A. M., M. Labin, and D. Stock Whitaker. "Probleme und Perspektiven psychoanalytischer Theorien für die Gruppentherapie." In Klaus Horn, ed. *Gruppendynamik und der subjektive Faktor.* Suhrkamp, Frankfurt, 1972.
21. Liebermann, A. M., I. D. Yalom, and M. P. Miles. *Encounter Groups: First Facts.* Basic Books, New York, 1973.
22. Marcuse, H. *One-Dimensional Man.* Beacon Press, Boston, 1968.
23. Marcuse, H. "Repressive Tolerance." In R. P. Wolf, B. More, and H. Marcuse, eds., *A Critique of Pure Tolerance.* Beacon Press, Boston, 1965.
24. Moreno, J. L. "Scientific Foundations of Group Psychotherapy." In J. L. Moreno, ed., *Group Psychotherapy.* Beatson House, New York, 1945.
25. Preuss, H. G. "Wirkungs- und Indikationsbereich der analytischen Gruppenpsychotherapie (Gruppentherapie versus Einzeltherapie)." In H. G. Preuss, ed., *Analytische Gruppenpsychotherapie, Grundlagen und Praxis.* Urban & Schwarzenberg, Munich, 1966.
26. Preuss, H. G. "Die psychotherapeutische Gruppe (zur Einführung in analytische Gruppenpsychotherapie)." In H. G. Preuss, ed., *Analytische Gruppenpsychotherapie, Grundlagen und Praxis.* Urban & Schwarzenberg, Munich, 1966.
27. Pohlen, M. *Gruppenanalyse.* Vandenhoek, Göttingen, 1972.
28. Richter, H. E. *Die Gruppe.* Rowohlt, Reinbeck bei Hamburg, 1972.
29. Richter, H. E. *Lernziel Solidarität.* Rowohlt, Reinbeck bei Hamburg, 1974.
30. Rosenbaum, M. "The Challenge of Group Psychoanalysis." *Psychoanalysis: Journal of Psychoanalytic Psychology* 1, no. 2: 50–58.
31. Ruitenbeck, H. B. *Die neuen Gruppentherapien.* Klett, Stuttgart, 1974.
32. Sager, C. J., and H. Singer-Kaplan (ed.). *Handbuch der Ehe-, Familien- und Gruppentherapie.* Kindler, Munich, 1972.
33. Schindler, R. "Grundprinzipien der Psychodynamik in der Gruppe." *Psyche* 11 (1957).
34. Schindler, W. "Gruppenanalytische Psychotherapie und das Selbst." In *Gruppenpsychotherapie und Gruppendynamik* 9, no. 3 (December 1975): 227–236.
35. Stanton, A. H., and N. S. Schwarz. The Mental Hospital. Basic Books, New York, 1954.
36. Stierlin, H. "Gruppendynamische Prozesse I: Übertragung und Widerstand." In H. G. Preuss, ed., *Analytische Gruppenpsychotherapie, Grundlagen und Praxis.* Urban & Schwarzenberg, Munich, 1966.
37. Strotzka, H., and K. Buchinger. "Freiheit und Neurose." In A. Pauss, ed., *Freiheit des Menschen.* Styria, Graz, 1974.
38. Schwarz, G. "Von der indirekten zur direkten Pädagogik." In *Gruppendynamik für die Schule.* Jugend und Volk, Vienna and Munich, 1974.
39. Watzlawick, P., H. H. Seavin, and P. D. Jackson. *Menschliche Kommunikation.* Huber, Bern, 1971.
40. Wolf, A. "The Psychoanalysis of Groups." In M. Rosenbaum and M. Berger,

eds., *Group-Psychotherapy and Group Functions*. Basic Books, New York, 1963.
41. Wolf, A., and B. K. Schwartz. *Psychoanalysis in Groups*. Grune & Stratton, New York, 1962.
42. Wynne, Lidz, Vogel, and Bell. *Schizophrenie und Familie*. Suhrkamp, Frankfurt, 1970.
43. Yalom, I. D. *Gruppenpsychotherapie*. Kindler, Munich, 1974.
44. Yalom, I. D., and A. M. Liebermann. "Eine Studie über negative Auswirkungen bei Encountergruppen." In C. J. Sager and H. Singer-Kaplan, *Handbuch der Ehe- und Familientherapie*. Kindler, Munich, 1972, pp. 273–308.

Chapter 7

Group Dynamics and Marxism

Bernhard F. Pesendorfer

THE QUESTION

Group dynamics and Marxism have in common that they were both born out of a need to provide helpful alternatives in new and still unmanageable times. However, there is a very wide range of differences between them. Whereas Marxism considers the largest social unit—from the class society to mankind—as the subject of world history, group dynamics concentrates on face-to-face primary communication. Yet, as the historical nemesis among other things has shown, the one can forget about the other only at the cost of its own extinction.

This chapter sets out to show, first, that some of the elements of Marxist theory can only be understood from what we are doing in group dynamics, and second, that experiences in group dynamics confirm and supplement the social scientific statements of Marxism.

GROUP AND ORGANIZATION

Group dynamics has undertaken the task of inquiring into and improving relations between people in groups. Both of these aims are easier to achieve the more actively those concerned are engaged as much in

This chapter, originally titled "Gruppendynamik und Marxismus," was translated from the German by Trygve Johnstad and Ulla Ernst.

the study of themselves as in the planning and construction of their social structure. But although the participation of all those concerned (like the family, a company, or a city) is getting more and more necessary, at the same time it is increasingly difficult to organize. Social formations in which everyone can join in the discussion about anything that concerns them and take part in the decision-making process are small and demand strong emotional participation. On the other hand, they are of limited range, complexity, and flexibility. All energy is invested in the narrow family circle or the tribe, or some such group that is of easy compass. Nothing is left for the nearby village, or company, or country. The tighter the reference group, the more threatening is felt to be the confrontation with those who are different and alien. Only by crossing group and tribe borders— with all the conflicts involved—will more far-reaching communication be possible for organizations, as well as division of labor, specialization, exchange of people and goods. The small social unit is then incorporated in a comprehensive structure of economic, political, and cultural interdependencies. Essential functions, such as defense, trade, and science, are taken over by the next most central unit. This protects and guarantees the fertile one-sidedness of divided labor and the exchange of surplus goods whose production is made possible by this one-sidedness. The price for enjoying this organized division of labor and differentiated consumption is dependence on the central coordination of this variety. (For further exploration of this problem, see the chapters by T. A. Lindner and G. Schwarz in this book.) A group can no longer define for itself its system of needs; it can no longer decide for itself how its members shall think or act or how they want to die. Instead the organization fixes the norms, regulates the ideology, defeats the enemy, makes the laws, and limits the area of freedom of the subsystems.

THE HISTORICAL FRAMEWORK

With the industrial and world-trade revolution, the bourgeoisie succeeded for the first time in introducing a really universal economic and political system that surpassed every previous system in its complexity, range, and flexibility. Thus, whether he wanted to or not, man became a world citizen, certainly protected by international law but almost totally anonymous, emancipated by force from all his former ties: from the patriarchical family structure, from the security of the village church and community, from his local vernacular to a national standard language and from this to a (foreign) world language, and so on. F. Kafka called this total isolation and alienation "sea-sickness on dry land." There were a number of more or less unsuccessful attempts to find a new protective unit. While the Holy Alliance thought that they were saving the old monarchies, the aspiring bourgeoisie collapsed totally in the meantime and left behind class differences deeper and more universal than ever before.

In old Austria for instance it was the military that kept together the aging monarchs, the aristocracy, the sparse bourgeoisie, the many nationalities, and the vast number of the proletariat who flocked into Vienna. For this reason some still see the military as a model for cooperative leadership that can bridge class differences.

Mass society has become a fact today. And these mass societies even pretend to be democracies. But do an election and voting formalities alone make for a democracy? To insist on the necessity of representation, and to doubt this as a way to use power legitimately, are today almost one and the same.

In addition there is the impossibility of administering the needs of the masses in any other than an institutionalized way—through bureaucracies. Therefore, many conservatives say: When so many entrepreneurs in the economic field desperately defend the right secured by civil law to capitalize and dispose of property and in this way try to keep politics out of the self-regulating economic circle, who knows, after all, if this isn't better than to throw property into the maw of a disinterested bureaucracy? Within these alternatives there is no longer a place for democracy.

THE INFRA-SUPERSTRUCTURE THEOREM I: MOBILE AND CONSOLIDATED FREEDOM: FREEDOM AND ORDER RESPECTIVELY

It is the peculiar characteristic of man that he can act freely. But this freedom is no fixed dimension available at any time and independent of all other circumstances. The question is rather: How can we guarantee that progress made in the field of technology or the realm of human relations is not lost but continues through time and commands general support within the social order? We have learned to recognize what goes beyond the day and beyond the area of direct communication that exists in the family or tribe. This we know as the standard, the norm, law, custom, contract, and so on. This superstructure reflects at best the variety of social life and provides us with a secure framework without which nothing would develop beyond a savage free-for-all. The superstructure is therefore always conservative: congealed experience, preservation of that which has been tried and proved, truth delivered from the past and preserved for the present. Pragmatically, the superstructure is the means whereby the number of conflicts threatening the individual, groups, and maybe the state may be reduced to a minimum. People who hate each other will nevertheless greet each other, wish each other a happy birthday, give way to each other politely. In prehistoric times they would already have killed, poisoned, mutilated, or enslaved each other. Today they do so in a substantially more temperate manner.

But what happens when social antagonisms occur and a satisfactory solution can no longer be found by holding onto the established norms? When the old armor no longer protects but rather restricts and stifles? Then—says Marx—the social and contradictory aspects of life will always take precedence over the corset of the past. Then the superstructure must accept that it will be examined, without regard for its dignity, as to how it can justify itself in the face of this new situation. But—as history has shown again and again—it is only that part of the superstructure involved in the actual conflict that is questioned. The majority of norms and standards quietly continue their influence without anyone being aware of them. Peace is not restored until the conflict has been resolved and new norms and agreements for a new law have been established, a law that is accepted and considered binding by all those concerned. Thus every step forward needs the firm ground of preserved freedom. The old ground is, however, rendered superfluous as soon as the new ground has become firm enough. There is a historical example of this. No sooner had the modern national state emerged from the struggle between the churches and confessional creeds than the differences between creeds shrank to an unimportant game; thus also the anachronistic rituals around a possible ecumenism end up in a trifle. (See Karl Rahner, S.J. Experiment Mensch, *Schriften zur Theologie*, Band 8, Benziger Verlag, 1967, pp. 260–285.)

THE INFRA-SUPERSTRUCTURE THEOREM I (FREEDOM AND ORDER) AND GROUP DYNAMICS

When a department in a company is not functioning well, it is customary in hierarchical thinking to hold the head of that department responsible. When the situation does not improve in spite of disciplinary measures, this person is replaced. In some companies up to five different departmental heads have been fired for such reasons before anyone got the idea that perhaps the reason for the failure was to be found in the structure or objectives of the department.

In group dynamics, which, as we practice it, goes far beyond sensitivity training, the participants get a clear idea of the interdependency of the behavior of individuals and the norms and standards that the group consciously or unconsciously promptly installs. Since the others, the strangers, are threatening in their strangeness, the individual borrows extremely creatively from all possible generally accepted patterns of behavior, introduces them into the group, and thus succeeds in getting safely through the new situation—in fact by playing an old game over again. Here the old analytic finding is proved correct in that many prefer to repeat a familiar misfortune rather than to venture on an unknown fortune. With the help of constant analytic attention to the social process, the following become evident to the participants:

1. That a social process conforms to its own laws, which are only marginally influenced by the intentions and wishes of the participants.
2. That the participants can more easily differentiate between what is their own responsibility and where there is a role allotted by the group that is to be taken into account. Usually this is accompanied by considerable relief, as it reduces many anxieties and feelings of guilt and leaves the way open to new creative energies. We must certainly not forget that either consciously or unconsciously we often seduce a group into giving us a role we have already played with success somewhere else. When we are refused our old roles and are expected to play new ones, it is a painful way to learn; but it does enable our ego to grow and develop.
3. That insight into the group process is possible only when those concerned are actively involved in gaining it. This experience of group dynamics has totally upset the old system of the social sciences. The picture drawn by the natural sciences of a finished reality that is to be described, measured, and cast in moulds is no longer acceptable. Man considers as real and essential so much more than the dry categories of natural science can possibly comprehend.

It can be said that people define reality by the way they live together. As mentioned previously, we mostly subject ourselves to the logic of currently accepted norms. This logic only very rarely becomes conscious, in fact only where it ceases to be logical, where it collides with other logical structures, or where it no longer helps to solve problems in an old, established way. In such cases we are forced by the social infrastructure to leave the superstructure of fixed behavior patterns and go back to the infrastructure to examine the problem all over again. But in most cases the infrastructure, when faced with these new conflicts, lacks language to express them. The new conflict must first "find expression."

It is said that metabolic change from social infrastructure to institutional superstructure could, in former times, take much longer. All we know is that today it must take place more often and more effectively than we are capable of handling. The misery of fossilized bureaucracies demonstrate this very well. The methods of group dynamics are resources to accelerate this change from a life of antagonism to a secure and stable situation. This applies as much to the compass of a small group as to an organization. Consider what we are doing when we give advice to an organization: We make a structural analysis based on the statements of those concerned with the help of depth psychology and sociometric and other methods, and compare this analysis with the official objectives of the employer, investor, employees, the market, or whoever it may be; and mirror this analysis back to all those involved. When antagonistic interests and groups come to light, which is to be expected, we provide catalytic discussion situations in order to give those concerned a chance to grasp how to compare the actual with the desired situation and draw out the contradictions. This helps the organization to design and realize for themselves the conceptual structure that is most appropriate to their particular goals and capabilities.

THE INFRA-SUPERSTRUCTURE THEOREM II: THEORY AND PRACTICE

This theorem states that *the way we live* defines *the way we think*. "It is not the consciousness of men that determines their being, but, on the contrary, their social being that determines their consciousness." "Does it require deep intuition to comprehend that man's ideas, views and conceptions, in a word, man's consciousness, changes with every change in the conditions of his material existence, in his social relations and in his social life?" (K. Marx, Preface to the *Critique of Political Economy; Manifesto of the Communist Party*; in K. Marx and F. Engels, *Selected Works in One Volume*, Moscow, 1968, pp. 181.51.)

Art, religion, philosophy, and all sciences follow the established social circumstances and justify them as beautiful, divine, rational, and true. In so doing, they are always right to a certain extent, as long as the institutional and normative power, sanctioned in this way, can in fact manage the central contradictions for a time. When it can no longer do so, the superstructure phenomena that legitimize this power will become an impediment to development.

Societies or sociocultural systems serve the reproduction of social life. Definitions of life are, of course, changing insofar as they depend on structural systems. What is accepted as social life is culturally defined in terms of world pictures which represent the reference system relevant to the interpretation of compelling needs. . . . Repression (as the renunciation of desires in order to achieve something in the larger community) is continuously exercised in the shape of institutionally established normative power. The exercise of normative power is in constant need of justification, either through a power-legitimizing world picture, the validity of which is linked to the condition of systematic restriction of volition-forming communication, or through unconstrained and unrestricted practical discussion. (J. Habermas, "Exkurs über Grundannahmen des Historischen Materialismus, 1970," in J. Habermas and N. Luhmann, *Theorie der Gessellschaft oder Sozialtechnologie*, Suhrkamp, 1971).

THE INFRA-SUPERSTRUCTURE THEOREM II (THEORY AND PRACTICE) IN GROUP DYNAMICS

Social truth can only be attained as the result of free discussion between individuals and groups challenging each other. There is no theoretical access to social truth, only the consensus of those concerned. If this is nevertheless pretended, we may simply describe this as an illegitimate exercise of power. Have we not again and again heard somebody in a group say: "But we all agreed that . . ." even before all of them had had a chance to speak? There is of course truth that is known before we act. Nevertheless, its confirmation does not go beyond applying past practice to the future.

With group dynamics the twentieth century has found an instrument whereby the origins and effects of social interdependencies in small groups can simultaneously be experienced and analyzed. The question of authority in a group may serve as an example.

Whereas in the middle ages, in the final analysis, authority was derived from God—who assigned everybody his place *in ordo mundi* and made it every man's task and duty to fill this place—in more recent times quite a different principle was discovered: that an individual's freedom, achievement, and work should determine his place in society and before men (see John Locke's *Second Treatise of Government*, 1689). With World War I the old divinely ordained empires collapsed. Thereafter a leading personality had to have as an individual all those qualities for which in former times an office or selection *praedestinatio* were required: charisma, wisdom, talent, farsightedness, decisiveness, and so on. When we look at our management-training centers in Europe, we often find that it is exactly these qualities of leadership that are held out to a manager today as the final goal of training. Modern history is full of examples that show where the close link between authority and the individual leader personality leads: fascism and the cult of personality.

In group dynamics the old question about the qualities of a leader was finally settled. The key emerged from the new question: "Which functions must be taken care of by a group to attain its ends?" Now it suddenly became clear why the same person could be accepted as an authority in one situation, while in another he would be without any influence. Personality characteristics could hardly have changed so quickly, but the needs of a group do.

Authority could now be redefined as the total potential of problem-solving energy at a group's disposal, which might be administered by one or more group members as an explicit or unconscious task. This new method of group dynamics of involving those concerned in the analysis of the social structure made it possible to question naturally evolved or constructed power structures in a group as to their functional capacity on the one hand, and their acceptability on the other. Often group members see the underlying collective needs of a group only when they notice this seemingly accidental distribution of power. Naturally there has always been misuse of power. It can be defined as "private exploitation of public communication energy." But continuous analysis quickly reveals such misuse. This also explains why the analysis of situations exposes dominance and at the same time rejects it, why analytic procedure is often equated with destruction. When the distribution of power and roles is accepted in a group, the accumulation of pressure motivating the analysis of a situation will not occur. Furthermore, it is easy to see that this pressure more often occurs among the underprivileged members of a group or of a society. They feel they are insufficiently represented or considered in the "prevailing opinion," which is always also the "opinion of those who prevail." However, a group will only seldom try to change a situation before its possibilities are fully exhausted. (Compare K. Marx: "No social order ever perishes before all the productive forces which are available within it have developed; nor do new, better conditions of production appear before the material conditions for their existence have matured in the womb of the old society itself (Marx and Engels, *Selected Works in One Volume*, p. 182).

Only when the homeostatis of the existing situation is considerably disturbed and can no longer be maintained by any compensatory sacrifice will social asymmetries or power structures become the subject first of analysis, then of action. Social analysis, when it is carried out by those concerned, urged on by growing dissatisfaction with the situation as it is, is always emancipatory. Even when the traditional forms of discussion come very close to the reproduction of this social asymmetry in the discussion itself, a real antagonism will always run through the language and the conversation.

Seen in this way, every social analysis of group dynamics and organizational psychology provides bricks to build the foundations for an adequate theoretical superstructure. This should offer us patterns of thinking and talking that will facilitate and not hinder us in the understanding of our time.

THE INFRA-SUPERSTRUCTURE THEOREM III
ECONOMY AND POLITICS

It is certainly one of the most eminent achievements of the bourgeoisie to have procured for us in the industrial type of production and the corresponding organization of capital the most effective instrument to eliminate scarcity in the history of man.

First, two concept explanations: The mode of production is determined by:

1. productive forces
    a. the work strength of the producers
    b. technically useful and applicable knowledge and production techniques
    c. organizational knowledge, coordination, and so on;
2. conditions of production. These form the social structure which decides on the disposal and utilization of resources, labor power, and acquired wealth.

Marx assumes that the capitalist mode of production constantly increases its achievements as a result of continuously revolutionizing the productive forces, while the conditions of production constantly lag behind. Obsolete information systems, decision-making systems, and systems of property and law prevent an adequate revolutionization of the total area of social life. Thus the Social-Democratic Minister of Finance once asked a group of Austrian entrepreneurs: "Which is my primary task when I want to further the economy in a purely capitalist spirit:—to protect private ownership of the means of production by whatever means as it is the basis of private capital? or to keep the capital flow mobile enough to enable it to be directed quickly to where the greatest profits can be expected?" (The polemical short version of this runs: Where there is wit, there is also capital, but where there is capital there is not always wit.)

The social structures in the economic world, that is, the conditions of production, are today as in the past under constant pressure to adapt. This is definitely one of the sources of the demand for group-dynamics methods in the economy. The traditional, hierarchical decision making by one person no longer produces the necessary quality. It requires well-functioning groups, organizations, and institutions to utilize all the resources of information, imagination, creativity, and identification. Thus far group dynamics, like any other management techniques, simply serves the improvement of capitalism.

However, the unavoidable distribution of decisions to lower levels in the hierarchy, the necessity of having far-reaching planning decisions made by groups (perhaps even in expensive consensus proceedings) has a very significant side effect. It is not possible to limit the distribution of the power to make decisions simply to one particular area; it has far-reaching effects on the disciplinary situation throughout the company. A person who is listened to on technical questions, who is, in fact, used to carry the weight of the decision, will no longer accept being treated as a child in questions concerning the social order of the company. In short: The delegation and widening of responsibility for decision making implies not only greater efficiency but also increased sensitivity toward and a desire to question the social structure, the decision-making procedure, and the capital structure of the company as a whole. The hitherto established scaled distribution of authority would be flattened out by economic pressure, thus bringing about a substantially higher degree of political cooperation. This is one view of the socialization of the means of production in the way it was intended by Marx—as not simply a formal nationalization leaving the structures unchanged and only replacing an egotistical management with a stupid bureaucracy. Therefore, the postulate of necessary socialization is valid not only for the means of production but also for the bureaucracies of the state—of countries, cities, and communities. The council system which Marx so admired in the Paris Commune of 1871 included in its program decentralization, constant renewal and replacement of the representative bodies, far-reaching federalism, self-government of firms, and so on.

This is perhaps the right place to do away with an old misunderstanding, that is, that in Marxism economic conditions constitute the very center of life. The mode of production is, of course, a powerful factor in the entire social life of people, but in no case its objective. Economy and the management of it is a means to live and of organization for survival. But the purpose of life is not sheer survival; it is the "good life" as the political organization of the coexistence of men. In other words, the goals of coexistence cannot be derived from economic necessity—to which we submit ourselves in order to be able to banish it. Paradoxically, the only ones to believe in that today are old liberals, pragmatic managers, and vulgar-materialistic political functionaries, who all invest exclusively in economic conditions. In the management of the economy we are dealing with objects, even when these objects happen to be people. We need and use each other, no matter whether we respect or despise each other. As beings who eat, drink, live, breed, and die, we cannot avoid this estrangement. Furthermore, work in the meaning of "necessary work" has no value beyond this. It is simply a necessary evil to acquire what we need. The conclusion that "we have clearly much more than we need, therefore we work meaninglessly and too hard," is absolutely right. But obviously to many people work represents a minor evil compared with the difficulties of self-discovery and of communication that a family, girlfriends, or political activity in the community and state bring with them. (Necessary) work or labor does not make one free, as can be read on the door of Auschwitz; it simply leads away from life.

Marx therefore differentiates between *necessary* work and *creative* work. In the field of necessary work or labor I use myself and others as objects and means to live, and must accept being used as such myself—in the most rational, wise, and subtle way possible. "Labor . . . is restrained desire . . . it shapes and forms." (Hegel). Labor shapes and forms the object as well as the laborer. In creative work, however, I see myself and others as human beings and ends in themselves, and want to be seen by others in this way. Injustice is not generally the outcome of necessary work that is part and parcel of the life of any being who is mortal and in need. It is the result of the social and political conditions under which this work has to be carried out. Injustice prevails when the burden of necessary work is not distributed equally among the different social groups. And the key to distribution is not to be found in the hard logic of economics, but rather in the prevailing social and political conditions. Whether someone may take part in discussion about the organization of society, the distribution of necessary work, his own place in that society, and his opportunities for development within it, or about his share in the realm of freedom, is a political issue. This is seen in the fact that in our hemisphere the current issue is not the amount of work one has to contribute in order to survive physically. This would presumably be rather little. Today the issue is much more: What does each one of us have to do in order to remain a member of our society? This is certainly not a problem that can be finally answered with commodities.

In fact, the realm of freedom actually begins only where labour which is determined by necessity and other expedients ceases; thus in the very nature of things it lies beyond the sphere of actual material production. Just as the savage must wrestle with Nature to satisfy his wants, to keep himself alive and to reproduce, so must civilised man, and he must do so in all kinds of societies and under all possible modes of production. As civilised man develops this realm of physical necessity expands as a result of his needs; but, at the same time, the forces of production which satisfy these needs also increase. Freedom in this field can only consist that socialized man—the producers in cooperation with one another—regulate their material change in accordance with the laws of Nature, bring it under their common control, instead of being ruled by it as by a blind force, and achieve this with the least expenditure of energy and under conditions most favourable to, and worthy of, their human nature. But it will always remain a realm of necessity. Beyond it begins that development of human energy which is an end in itself, the true realm of freedom, which however can blossom forth only with this realm of necessity as its foundation. (K. Marx, *Capital*, vol. 3, Moscow, 1974, chapter 48, p. 820)

The immediate conclusion drawn by Marx from these considerations, that "the shortening of the working-day is its basic prerequisite," was at that time fully justified. But it remains as only a first and negative postulate—like the claim for the abolition of private ownership of the means of production: "Reduce the necessary time of labour for the benefit of creative and political life!" and "Do away with the ownership conditions which are suffocating further economic as well as political development!" Beyond this, Marx deserves high credit for not being carried away and depicting a utopia; but, faithful to the materialist-dialectic way of thinking, he leaves the whole process from the sharpening of contradictions to the formulation of the qualitatively new to evolution itself. However, quantitative shortening of the working day does, of course, not abolish alienation or estrangement, neither during the working day nor during subsequent spare time, which is spent just as meaninglessly.

When, after a hundred years of struggle, the unions have not gone beyond demands for old privileges, higher wages, and a shorter working-day, they have become anachronistic impediments. They are certainly right in saying that redistribution is in no way completed, and that a worker solidarity that extends beyond individual companies is required more strongly than ever before; but the hierarchic, bureaucratic manner in which these interests are defended often perverts the original intention into quite its contrary. To a large extent the trade unions have migrated into the superstructure, and here they support the other just as fragile hierarchies of entrepreneurs and state, instead of introducing the unrest of the infrastructure into these hierarchies. For just as the proprietors under liberalism kept the state as an official servant to defend their property, the "social partners" today keep the state for the same purpose. Consequently the corresponding governments are social-liberal, and in no way social-democratic. Thus the old basic evil is again visible: that the meaning of life is defined by the means of life and not the other way round.

THE INFRA-SUPERSTRUCTURE THEOREM III (ECONOMICS AND POLITICS) IN GROUP DYNAMICS

The socialization not only of the ownership conditions and the mode of production but first and foremost of the bureaucratic state, demands ways of communication that we simply have not yet at our command. Since this task can be delegated neither to the hard logic of economics nor to the most clever communication science, there remains only one way: to support the attempts of those concerned to organize themselves with all the refinements of the social sciences and social technology, so that the organizational principle of representation (representation of the absent by the present) once again deserves its name. This can be illustrated by an example from group dynamics:

It has again and again been discussed how "deep" one should or could go in the work of group dynamics: for example, where to draw the line between group dynamics and group therapy; to what extent individual and private history should or should not be included; whether the private sphere has to be dealt with in order to understand the social process; and so on. If we take as an example a one-week T group whose participants do not know each other and are most probably not going to work together afterwards, then this sets clear boundaries. It is not very sensible when the group turns the week into a ritual feast of intimate decompensation. So-called "group addicts" have doubts about the possibility of a satisfactory common life "out there," and therefore allow themselves every now and then the one-week or weekend illusion that somehow it could be possible. The hangover gets worse every time. And it is certainly an illusion to think that people really get closer in this way. It is only that the boundaries are more easily denied.

Nor will the participants learn anything if they go to the other extreme and totally hide behind prescribed rules of behavior or subordinate the variety and multiplicity of different connections, all happening at the same time, to one central task, and thereby run away from each other. In the first case privacy would be totally wiped out, in the second absolutely untouched. Communication—which on every occasion is an act of crossing over a boundary—will not take place in either case.

What can take place in groups and can contribute to social learning is that someone from time to time can announce freely in open discussion what he thinks about the other participants and about the situation, and his own feelings about being in that situation.

Not everything can be brought out in this way, partly because the participant is not aware of it himself, or the others are unable to see it, but also because any participant is always a member of other groups as well—groups that necessarily will be partly "private," that is, out of bounds. This privacy is protection of the member's identity from the collective pressure of one single reference group. For if the only alternative to his sole reference group is total isolation, then the group can force him to do almost anything. However, there is another form of privacy that kills any communication, which occurs when a member keeps his observations to himself and does not say how he is being influenced by the other members and by the atmosphere in the group. He then keeps private and secret what the group needs to know in order to decide its own policy. Then it can never be tested whether the group structure is accepted or rejected; whether decisions are supported by everyone, by a few, or by just one person; and so on. The general competitive situation that forces us to feel dissatisfied with the present and to wish to be *more*, stands in massive opposition to public discussion. If this discussion does not take place for some reason, then individuals and groups are totally subjected to the hard logic of economics. The inquiry into its social impact does not take place; the management of the political situation at work is surrendered to seemingly unpolitical economic necessity.

Those who are familiar with how the phases of a group-dynamic process develop will know what an enormous struggle it is for a group to pave the way for any solidarity between its members. The common flight into introduction rituals, external topics, and prescribed role playing is often followed by an even more vigorous struggle for leadership and influence. The group will often allow influence only to the official leader or trainer, but to none of the members, as this influence is immediately interpreted as dominance and authority. There is a fantasy that unconditional equality, equal validity, and equal estimation of all members will provide protection against differences and conflicts and that this protection will be guaranteed by authority. This is the "cling" effect, which gives warmth and comfort to the group members but at the same time prevents any confrontation among the members of the group. They are all so close to each other that they cannot (and will not) see those around them, nor how they are seen themselves by these others. The sworn faithfulness of shy young lovers shows in this context the same characteristics of attempting to avoid conflicts that can be seen in the oath of loyalty of fascist organizations. Both of them prefer maintained internal harmony to any confrontation and conflict. Any cause, any structure, any leader is good enough to guarantee such pseudo-unity, as long as the members' equality is secured and absolutely safe group membership is guaranteed to all.

This blind security, however, can only be guaranteed when the drive and energy to communicate is perceived as coming from a central position of power. No one will ever deny that division of labor and variety of needs can only blossom where there is a concentration of knowledge, power, labor, and capital all at the same time. But the bigger and the more complex the economic space, the harder it is to carry through the primary goal (the political) against the means (the economy). As is proved by multinational concerns everywhere, international economic communication functions according to the law of the jungle better than according to international law—stuck fast in the wrangling of the individual national states. Without international laws, however, the primary goal of world politics as against world economy will always be an illusion, because the multinational companies must otherwise operate in a lawless field, almost in spite of themselves. The same holds true in the microcosm of the group. When the differences of its members are not accepted and the conflicts caused by these differences are not mastered, a situation will never arrive that allows for complexity of relations adequate to the needs of group members and of the entire group, whereby influence would be possible through mutual communication and understanding and through supporting and being supported. Then it becomes obvious that equality cannot consist of uniformity, but of accepting the differences between rather different people, the different relations in their lives or—if you like—their inequalities. Democracy is therefore that way of living together in which the security of the system lies in permanent alert insecurity in the face of new contradictions and conflicts and the interchange between infrastructure and superstructure takes place faster than in any other system.

What has this to do with the relation between economy and politics, between group dynamics and Marxism?

The decisive point is that situations of dominance stop people from influencing each other and from learning from one another. Dominance is private possession of what is public, private use of common libido, private consumption of social transference-, conflict-, and solidarity-creating energy. Every doctor, trainer, teacher, and manager is familiar with this temptation of power and has certainly been trapped by it, too. Economics, in particular capitalist economics, is considered by its adherents to be an effective and rational means of overcoming scarcity; and they want to regulate the entire life process of the civil democratic world according to this pattern. The defense of private ownership of capital and the means of production is only one facet. Today the main problem is that economic objectivity administers private ownership of groups, organizations, institutions, bureaucracies, and management power.

Socialization of the means of production and capital is, therefore, not a problem of simple dispossession of the one and the forceful takeover of power by the others, even if this may perhaps have been necessary in many places in the beginning; it is rather joint control of resources acquired by joint labor. State ownership, public stocks, cooperative models that are limited to participation in turnover or profit, and so on, have not changed the authoritarian social structure of companies. Nor has the sudden transfer of trade unionists onto the boards of directors altered anything either. There is no one in Austria today who treats union people on the boards of nationalized industry more brutally and cynically than the avowed socialist manager. In union-owned companies there are, for safety's sake, no shopstewards at all. There is, certainly a need for the strongest possible workers' and employers' organizations, but progressive impulses to change the system are sooner to be found in the systematic build-up of democracy within companies. As long as those concerned do not particpate in the decision-making process but are directed by the decisions of others, the lack of meaning in labor and its organization will continue.

History will prove again and again that political life and political will lay behind economic conditions, the development of the productive forces, and economic practice. Whether the "realm of freedom" expands or not will depend on the rate at which those who are affected—at first unconsciously, responding sporadically and to different laws—recognize a common interest and join forces to acknowledge the contradiction in the infrastructure and bring it back to the superstructure, which seems in itself so harmonious, and thereby change it. (Marx speaks in this context of the class in itself that has to become a class conscious of itself in order to build a classless society.) In this context it seems a simple but nevertheless effective idea to start with a T group and to experience and understand, if possible simultaneously, the social life of a group, by talking as openly as possible about what is going on. In this way a group as a social unit can very often understand more promptly and talk about and control what is really going on and explore whether that is, indeed, what they want to do.

If we may, by rough rule of thumb, describe what could be called "socialist" in a society by saying that such a society is investing in the permanent revolutionization and improvement of the political and social relations as much time, energy, money, and power, as in the permanent revolutionization and improvement of productivity and the relations of production, then group dynamics can contribute substantially to this process. In the beginning group-dynamics methods are purchased for purposes of improving productivity and profits; under the surface and in the long run, however, they will lead to a sharpening of political questions about the meaning of and justice in the way we live and work together.

Finally, another example from a training group: A participant came up with the question as to whether this dealing with the emotions, relations, and social structures of the here and now were not only a "game" in relation to the earnest of the real constraints, rational decisions, and economic facts "of the real world." Another questioned in reply whether we were not so entirely led by the rules of the game, the norms, the daily work load, and the prescribed patterns of behavior that we did not even have time to raise the question about the meaning of it all (that is the reality). "But where does that lead us?" the first one asked, "Things would possibly come to mind which I would rather not think about!" Then the thought of a decreasing economic growth, followed by less work, and thereby fewer socially accepted ways of diversion really must imply something horrible.

Work is a distraction, but what does one do, if this distraction does not work any more?

Chapter 8

Conflict Resolution as a Process

Gerhard Schwarz

INTRODUCTION

One of the greatest weaknesses of our educational system is that we do not learn how to deal with conflicts. Within the family, at school, and above all in hierarchically structured institutions, conflicts are often traced back to mistakes that "should really have been avoided." The avoidance of conflicts is suggested both by the system of religious and moral standards and by the logical and legal forms of the organization. Exploring this in more detail, we find this poor treatment of a most important aspect of interpersonal communication to be one of the constituent principles of our social order: Conflict avoidance inhibits the too rapid development of individuals and structures and is thus one of the axioms of hierarchical structures.

At a time when it is just this stable state of order in terms of superordination and subordination that has become a problem, the question of the significance of conflict and the advantages and disadvantages of particular ways of resolving conflicts must come to the forefront of public discussion of the further development of our way of living together. The possibilities for meaningful conflict management are increasingly becoming the "daily

This chapter, originally titled "Konfliktlösung als Prozess," was translated from the German by the author.

bread" of the coordination functions fulfilled by leaders in the economy and the administration, the church and the army, in schools and international organizations,. Conflict situations are therefore often the reason for calling in an organization consultant, since traditional patterns of behavior are no longer sufficient to solve the problem. The following basic material for an analysis of the meaning of conflicts in interpersonal communication has been derived from such consulting situations, as well as from seminars held under the auspices of the Hernstein Institut für Unternehmensführung (the Hernstein Management Institute) in Vienna and from several research projects on this subject conducted by the consulting firm of Intermanagement Sozialforschung und Organisationsberatung (Intermanagement Social Research and Organization Consultancy), also in Vienna.

From the pragmatic angle, the significance of conflicts is easily defined: if there are too many and too extensive conflicts within a social entity, the security necessary for any kind of coexistence is absent. Work and recreation are impossible without a minimum of stability and emotional security. On the other hand, if conflicts are perceived simply as a disturbance, then the opportunity for advance that is inherent in any conflict situation cannot be appreciated.

DEFINITION OF "CONFLICT"

Logically speaking, a conflict is a dispute in which people or groups identify themselves with mutually exclusive contradictory statements. Frequently, differing interests are behind a conflict, which only comes into being when people persist in considering only one side of the argument to be true or practicable. In a borderline case, such a conflict is settled in only one person's mind when he is obliged to assimilate both sides of the argument; thus a workers' council often has to represent the employees' interests before management and those of the total enterprise before the work force. More often than not, however, such conflicts cannot be solved by one person alone.

DIFFERENT METHODS OF RESOLVING CONFLICTS

Examining the behavior patterns that people employ in solving conflicts, we find that an interesting classification emerges: The solutions to conflicts most frequently quoted or observed by us can be subsumed under five different general terms: flight, fight, delegation, compromise, and consensus. A more detailed analysis shows these five categories to be a useful systematic classification because historically:

1. These categories can be perceived as stages in a historical process of development.

2. They describe the maturing process of an individual, a group or an institution.
3. They can represent the stages of any particular conflict.

Flight

Flight is presumably the original and most natural pattern of behavior adopted when a conflict arises. Behavioral science defines primates, which of course includes *homo sapiens*, as animals that would rather flee than fight. In any hazardous situation, when he lacks specific weapons man first seeks refuge in flight. It is only at a later stage in hominid evolution that the collective aggression of a hunting team was added as a behavior pattern to the flight reaction. The aggression between different groups is frequently only the reason for attempts to flee.

For many hundreds of thousands of years, groups of human beings on an earth only thinly populated by *homo sapiens* can be assumed to have given each other a wide berth, as is still the case with native hunters today (for example, in the Amazon).

Modern civilized man can still be assumed to resort frequently to this type of problem solving when putting off, ignoring, repressing, or denying a problem, or when disregarding the essentials. If a conflict situation can in fact be resolved by flight, which must frequently have been the case with our forebears, then this strategy is certainly the best one. More often than not, however, fleeing from conflict seems to create even greater difficulties than does facing the problem.

Psychoanalysts are all too aware of the symptoms that can be attributed to repressed or denied conflicts. Presumably in conjunction with man's adoption of a sedentary life, the number of problems that can no longer be resolved by flight is growing apace. Conflicts arise that the individual and society must face at some time. In this situation, it usually comes to a fight.

Fight

(a) destruction   (b) subordination

Conflict can be resolved by fighting if it is possible either to destroy the opponent (a) or subjugate him (b). in both cases the first premise is that one of the two contradictory statements is false and the other is true. The second premise is that he who holds the truth is the victor and remains victorious. If these premises are wrong or only partialy correct, fighting does not provide the solution to the conflict. Destroying the opponent either physically, socially, economically, or psychologically certainly is—as was stated in a working group at a congress—the "cleanest" solution, but it removes the opponent simultaneously with the conflict. If the opponent is right in any way (be it only the "right" to survival or because he is useful for something), the superior and victorious party must become poorer because of this "right."

Prehistoric finds prove that the struggle for life and death between groups of human beings is not a recent discovery of civilization, but can be assumed to have been a daily happening since the dawn of man. In any event, up to and into historical time, groups of humans have often been annihilated by other groups.

Somewhere, at some point in the transition from fight (a) to fight (b), slavery was invented. The victor spares the life of the vanquished and makes him work for him, thus introducing dependence as the basic structure for the interaction relationship. Conflict solving by subjugation or subordination still plays a significant role in hierarchical forms of organization. This not only includes all forms of pressure on the opponent, but also "convincing" and "persuading," even to the inclusion of "yielding" and "bribing," "surrendering" and "manipulating."

The defeated, subjugated, vanquished, or convinced person, by the very act of subordinating himself, does lose his self-determination, but in exchange achieves the security that his master (boss, superior, mother, father, marriage partner) can provide. "Will exchange freedom and self-determination for security and subordination" is the motto for this type of conflict solving, but this solution itself contains the seeds of new conflict. To this very day, the few nomads remaining on earth despise the peasants (fellaheen) and townsmen for being less "free," yet envy them for having acquired security and culture in exchange.

However, cultural development has only been possible because the way in which conflicts are handled has progressed beyond the subjugation level. Subjugation is an extremely unstable form of conflict solving, since the subjugated not infrequently use their "survival" to renew the struggle. Only after another principle had been added to this "infantilizing" pattern, did the social entity prove to be stable. This principle is centralization of functions, which thereby, makes possible the delegation of conflicts.

Delegation

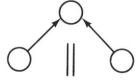

Delegation means that communication between two or among several people is arranged by a third, central person. For this central person can also be substituted anonymous structures (rules, laws). Presumably, large-scale cooperation between people has been made possible only by the system of delegation.

The socioeconomic basis for the system of delegation was the division of labor based on stockpiling. Domestication of animals and arable farming provided a surplus that could be exchanged. The exchange took place at central points occurring at the intersection of natural lines of communication, at the junction of two or more valleys, on estuaries, and so on.

The division of labor worked in two ways, horizontally and vertically: horizontally among those who bartered sheep for goats and the goats in turn for farm produce, and vertically among those who had items for barter and those organizing the trade, that is, the masters of the points of exchange and later of the modes of exchange. We call them holders of central functions (central functionaries). The most important task for those fulfilling central functions at central points was to safeguard the whole structure of anonymous communication.

In the early days of this development, this protection must have failed at times, since the game of "nomads against tillers of the soil" can be assumed to have led again and again, for thousands of years, to the extinction of the first cultures and cooperative efforts. The central functionaries had first to make a series of communication "discoveries" before the social entity, characterized by the division of labor, was able to hold its own against aggressive nomadic tribes.

These discoveries included (this list is by no means exhaustive) systems of anonymous communication (writing); systems of standards indicating the priority of overriding and "more general" points of view; the associated power and dependence system; and conflict delegation. This delegation represents a step forward when human beings are essentially unable to achieve cooperation by direct communication, but can "get along" via "third parties." This third party likes to see the other two engaged in combat and unable to settle the fight, because it vests in him a function that he would not otherwise have, that is, authority. Conversely, authority suggests delegation in the case of conflict. Children delegate to parents, pupils to teachers, subordinates to superiors, football teams to referees.

The great advance brought about by this system of dealing with conflicts is, however, gained at the expense of creating a situation of alienation: He who delegates to an authority wants his problem to be solved by somebody who basically does not have anything to do with it. In the legal context the judge's "impartiality" is an essential precondition to delegation; only where the judge is not involved in any way in either side of the conflict is he allowed to administer justice. "Justice" in this sense means removing the conflict situation into a realm in which the conflict no longer exists, thus making it easier to resolve.

This principle of transforming a problem (difference, dispute), removing it to a "higher plane" on which the conflict vanishes, is one of the greatest communication discoveries in the history of cultures. The ascent to ever higher, more general planes is simply the expression of the general principle of order as the centralization of functions or as superordination and subordination. The communication structure of the bartering society can be drawn in the following way using the familiar pyramid model:

The pyramid results when the particular central function is drawn as the higher position. Historically, the central person in a particular group must also have become an external representative, which, conversely must have reinforced the person's authority in the particular group. Idols are created, thus probably making a connection between individual and authority for the very first time. The authorities demand of man that he should orient himself to more general principles (Moses' tablets). This type of order ties into group-induced factors of instinct renunciation because it demands that direct communication, and in certain circumstances also direct needs, be subordinated to general, "higher" needs. It is this very principle that has made the model so powerful in history: the handing over of functions and hence power to central positions that were able to use the asymmetrical power distribution for their own benefit. "All power goes out from the people," states Article 1 of the Austrian constitution—"never to return," added a cynic.

This type of order had to be enforced and supported by a normative system with stable sanctions, since it always ran counter to the needs and nearly always to the insights of the peripheral positions. Handing over part of the produce obtained—usually the best part—to the central function only works if this levy is related to the highest agencies establishing political, legal, and religious standards. Thus animals or crops handed over in this way were regarded as sacred animals or crops.

Even in bad years, there was no reduction in the levy. It is obvious that this type of order could only be maintained in the long run by some form of "policing." From early times, it was designated as a holy order—in Greek, "hierarchy." The Greek term *arché* also means "rule" in addition to "order." The Greek language, like some present-day managers, does not yet differentiate between order and rule. To be able to conceptualize order only in the shape of the "holy rule" (hierarchy) means not being able to deal with conflicts, only being able to delegate them.

This method of solving conflicts between two persons or groups by delegation to a higher agency (which may sometimes be "nature," chance, or a formal scheme) presupposes the same premises as fight (b), namely:

1. that to the conflict in question there is a correct and an incorrect solution;
2. that the higher agency invoked will be able to find the correct solution.

If one of the two premises does not apply, conflicts cannot be solved by delegation. The question of whether it is at all possible and permissible to doubt the universality of these premises is difficult to formulate, because it is one of the postulates of the holy order.

Examining the functional conditions for hierarchical systems, we find that there are four ultimate conditions that jointly dictate the workings of this holy order (be it said that cultural development has come with this order).

1. The identity of any hierarchical position is defined by superordination and subordination. This determines competence to make decisions (degree of generality). Higher positions make more general and more important decisions. The holder of the uppermost, central position makes the most important, final decisions. In logic this axiom states that the position of a human being has to be identical with the person. The proposition of identity (formally, $A = A$) argues that everything is identical to itself. The duality of human existence, in which someone is able to stand in relationship to himself, is made a unity. In this proposition "someone" and "to himself" are used. The two are different, but must be a unity, "someone" being the position fulfilled, generally defined by name, age, descent, and so on, "himself" being the person, which may well differ from this definition. Both must be identical in the hierarchy.
2. The second axiom of "holy order" follows directly from the first, stating that there can be no contradiction: $(A \neq \text{non-}A)$. Something cannot be its opposite as well. The proposition of avoidance of contra-

diction is a constituent element in an organization based on anonymous communication. Contradictions that are permanently present on the emotional level of direct communication are avoided by abstracting to anonymous communication. Without this axiom, the construction of an organization would be difficult. Although it is possible for somebody both to love and to hate, for his feelings of belonging to a group to be ambivalent, it is definitely not possible for him to have paid a bookseller's invoice and not to have paid it. The bookseller's organization must exclude this case. However, this means that the competence to resolve conflict must not be vested in the litigant parties. The truth lies in abstraction from the conflict. Identity and contradiction avoidance means that the hierarchy determines what might and might not be; what someone is and is not; what he is competent to do and what he is not competent to do. The holy order relieves man of ambivalence by this generalization. There is an unequivocal Good and an unequivocal Bad, as provided for by the normative system.

If everything is identical to itself, then one must determine how the truth is to be arrived at when contradictions nevertheless arise; by delegation to the next higher agency, which must not be involved in the contradiction.

3. Everything is A or non-A. The decision has to be in favor of one of these alternatives. The third party, excluded from the ambivalence, has to decide between A and non-A. He is impartial and possesses the wisdom to do so. At the higher level of generality, contradictions become differences, thus making it possible for order to be restored as superordination and subordination.

4. This higher general level of decision must, in terms of the centralization of functions, simultaneously represent be the reason for the lower levels: There is sufficient reason for everything, and this reason is vested in the particular superior. Central agencies make decisions for the peripheral functions, which have to be dependent on these decisions for the organization of the holy order to function.

The four axioms of hierarchy constitute a closed organizational system, within which competences can be subdivided continuously. The establishment of identity constitutes a decision continuum. Where one man's competence stops, that of the next agency begins.

The avoidance of contradiction constitutes a truth continuum. Either one or the other is right. Determination of the truth in each case is incumbent on the person acting at the central position, because he alone has access to the information context. A continuum of wisdom is thus constituted. The person who is not involved in a conflict is essentially wiser than the two litigant partners (*audiatur et altera pars*). To make this system operational, however, the subordinates in each case must be dependent on the superordinates, thus creating a dependence continuum. This is sufficient reason for a subordinate to do something his superior has ordered him to do. Special hierarchies even hold that the only possible and sufficient reason for a subject to implement an act is that it has been ordered from above.

The principle of holy order in terms of superordination and subordination in Western civilization has gained precedence over other possible order systems. For example, totemistic order, in which human beings group themselves in terms of animals—some living like birds, others like rabbits—has been overcome. Admittedly, when applying the hierarchical principle to many social aspects, all needs that cannot be met either by superordination or subordination must be suppressed or neglected: for example, conflicts. The hierarchical principle with its system of delegation has in fact undergone a remarkable degree of generalization in many sectors of cultural differentiation. Thus natural science was for a long time based on the use of the hierarchical principle of order to explain natural contexts.

In the Middle Ages, St. Thomas Aquinas expressed this as follows (*Summa contra Gentiles* 129, 1): "It is by the precepts of divine law that the spirit of man is subordinated to God, and everything else that is in man is subordinated to reason. It follows from natural order that the inferior be subordinated to the superior. Thus that which is prescribed by divine law is right in nature, i.e. moral, good and binding."

In this respect, natural science in modern times has consistently followed St. Thomas' thinking, arranging everything according to the principle of superordination and subordination.

The action of delegating to more central, more general agencies (induction) and the consequent reversal of power relationships, so that the more central agencies become the actual determinative reason (deduction), is repeated in the explanatory context of natural science. Different objects falling to the ground lead to the (central) assumption that gravity is responsible for the free fall of a body. Once "found," this general term is at once regarded as the reason or cause for the fall of a body; gravity itself, on the other hand, is simply a specific case of general mass attraction, and so on.

The regular constitution of nature by ever more general laws has also been constructed by science in accordance with the model of holy order in terms of superordination and subordination. A similar thing is done in classifying animals. Different dachshunds are grouped into the general term "dachshund," while they in turn belong, together with poodles and others, to the group "dogs," and so on. That an individual dachshund has particular eating habits is explained by saying that this is just the way dogs eat. The "reason" lies in the superior (preassumed) generality. A similar procedure is followed in classifying plants—in fact, nature in its entirety.

on *helping to liberate the energetic and expression potential of the whole group.* In this sense the exercises, body expression, bioenergetics, and gestalt therapy are, in my opinion, more harmful than useful in practice because they restrict the spontaneity that should have been developed and often isolate individuals from one another. I prefer to be on the watch for spontaneous movements and actions in the group, which are often very tentative in the beginning, and to give a spontaneous response by involving myself; looking for the echoes, connections, breaks in the rhythms; going from one language to another; helping the group to produce its cacophony and its symphony. In this respect dance seems to me one of the most effective tools. I do not know whether this is because of my personal preference, or if it really is of greater efficacy than other instruments.

Group Myths and the Mythical Group

In the course of their work, groups develop all kinds of illusions and myths, as has been pointed out by several authors.[21]

In my opinion the central myth concerns the idea of the group itself. The picture of a group that so often haunts groups is that of the members forming a distinct entity that is above any one of the members and that also dominates them.

Such a group is at the same time a protection and a threat. It is a haven, a benevolent God and a Good Mother; but also a Janus, a Moloch, the Devil—a whole pantheon, good and terrifying at the same time. Within the idea of the family, it takes up the functions of a mother figure, nursing but also devouring; and a father figure, protecting and at the same time castrating.

The picture of the group and its more or less conscious emotional life is accompanied by an ideology of devotion and sacrifice. It is implicitly or explicitly accepted that one has to dedicate oneself to "the group," to sacrifice oneself for it so that *it* will survive. Group members talk to other members "in the name of the group," reminding them of their duty to the group, appealing to ideas of devotion and sacrifice and making a display of their own—then using this as blackmail.

It is also "in the name of the group" that members are excluded for deviation and for betraying the collective ideals, and that other members who agree with the ideals are admitted; because "the group" is closed by definition. It is a sect with a religion, whether secular or no, with its banner, its scriptures, its ministers, its high priest, its classes, and its commoners.[22] These beliefs and these practices previously depended on the ideologies of established institutions like the state, the church, the family, the army, the school, and the business, and used to some extent the same language.

finally inorganic nature. All subunits are also arranged in hierarchical order; thus every family has a head, every abbey an abbot, every group a boss.

The question now arises: What about those problems that cannot be subordinated by holy order as the universal principle? Does this order not do violence to reality every now and then? Is it really possible to explain everything in this way or might there also be possibilities for advancing this system?

Are the possibilities for treating conflict exhausted by flight, struggle, and delegation? Are these two postulates—"in a case of conflict there is a right and a wrong solution," and "powers of discrimination always reside in the superordinated agency" (as it were, as an eschatological hope: to whomsoever God has given an office He has also given wisdom)—unshakably correct? Is it not possible to solve conflicts by means other than fighting or destruction? Can there never be a case in which both parties are right? Logically this case cannot arise, psycho-logically it arises in every conflict. Emotionally, the conflicting parties hold their views to be right and those of their adversary to be wrong. If this feeling includes but a grain of truth, then the methods discussed so far are inadequate.

When pursuing this thought, the first thing to do is to question the universality of the four axioms. Why should everything always be identical to itself? Can life and development not be described as a "differing-from-oneself"? Doesn't man continuously rewrite his past by surviving the present? Doesn't identity perish in any genuine interpersonal communication, to find itself renewed and different?

These doubts become stronger still if one looks at the practical aspects of the continua of decision and truth: Does one's superior really know better nowadays? The hypothesis that there is only one truth and that this is (if possible exclusively) possessed by the superior often no longer applies with regard to centralized factual contexts. Can emotions also be centralized? Can emotional competence be handed over at all?

There are a number of quite simple experiments to test this. Let an assembly crew decide for itself on the distribution of work; let an office team decide on space allocation; let any group decide on a subject that is not complex but is emotionally controversial. In most cases such groups will come to a decision that is different from the one the superior would have taken. Even where the superior, as it were gifted with clairvoyance, could have anticipated the final result and would have given his orders accordingly, the groups would not muster the same degree of emotional agreement. A person's real wishes only evolve in the course of a communication and decision process. There is no previously fixed, correct result in the emotional field which is, as it were, independent of the process by which the result is arrived at. Emotional competence can only be transferred at a very infantile stage of development.

This serves to explain the emphasis put on the factual, logical element in all hierarchical orders. "Objectivizing" a conflict—which besides triggers very strong emotional processes in all involved—is a method of delegation that rarely satisfies those concerned.

What is to be done when the opponents not only feel emotionally that they are right, but are in fact right in the matter itself? Suppose the second axiom of holy order does not apply: "of two contradicting statements one at least is false"? How can conflicts be resolved when both parties are right? What is to be done if even the wisest superior does not know the solution? What is to be done if there are no superiors at all? An umpire simply cannot be found for all conflicts. What is to be done when people refuse to find the reason for their actions in a superior's order? What is to be done when they choose self-determination? when parties to a conflict do not want to delegate their conflict? In this case they must try to find for themselves a compromise or a consensus.

Compromise and Consensus

The search for a compromise or a consensus is meaningful only at the moment when the methods listed so far (flight, fight, and delegation) are unsuccessful—when the controversy is contradictory to the axioms of logic not only emotionally but also on the factual level. In this case we speak of an *aporia*, which in English approximates to "logical impasse."

So long as the situation does not change, there is no way out. An aporia is characterized by three properties:

1. two mutually contradictory statements;
2. both are true;
3. both are dependent on one another. Only if one statement is true can the other be so, and vice versa.

A classical example for such an aporia is the dialectic of power and law. The statement "law takes precedence over power" is certainly a true one, for power not legitimized by law would certainly not be of long duration. However, the converse is equally true: Power takes precedence over law, for a law not supported by power would not be of long duration either.

A conflict arises when different people or groups of persons see their interests embodied in either of the two parts of the aporia. Conversely, it might be said: The interests of groups opposing one another in a conflict can often be formulated aporetically. A typical example of such an aporia is an employee's independence. On the one hand, increasingly independent employees are required because of the increasingly complex organization and decision structure of modern enterprises. There is less demand for employees who have to be told what to do or even be shown how to do it, who need information on the slightest details, for, given a certain degree of complexity of the organization, this must of necessity lead to excessive strain on their superiors. But by recruiting more independent employees, most enterprises often jump from the frying pan into the fire because independent employees are less inclined to follow instructions, quite apart from the fact that "obedience" is a more or less foreign word to them, otherwise they would not be able to work independently. However, industrial production, with its very sensitive interlinking structures, requires increasingly fine correlation of individual decisions (such as network technique), which, conversely, is only possible with increased centralization of functions. The two are contradictory. Progress can only be achieved when employees are increasingly independent, and progress can only be achieved when employees are increasingly less independent in fulfilling their functions. How can this conflict be resolved?

The aporia described here is a special case of the aporia between freedom and order. They are opposites: Order destroys freedom, freedom destroys order. Both are true, and both are dependent on each other. Only when order limits freedom is it order; only when freedom modifies order is it freedom.

The solution of such an aporetical conflict by means of flight, fight, or delegation is not feasible. It is useless to have one of the two win, since the other is also true. It is impossible to decide between the alternatives, since both are dependent on one another. The ruin of every type of order would ruin freedom; eliminating every freedom would make order meaningless. To resolve it, it is first necessary to diagnose the nature of this conflict correctly as aporetical and to appreciate that the solutions of flight, fight, and delegation are not feasible. This means, however, that the opponents will have to enter into a dialectical development process, as a result of which a solution is found that takes into account both opposing positions without destroying either or both or subordinating one to the other.

This development process, which might be said to comprise "liquidating" and reshaping both positions into a common synthesis, passes through several stages, in our experience of conflict management. First of all the logical solutions have to be tried one after the other. Only their failure will finally illustrate the aporetical nature of the conflict.

First phase: the conflict arises.

The start of an aporetical conflict, as in all conflicts, is accompanied by flight reactions on the part of one or both parties. Sometimes it will take a very long time before the conflict is accepted as such and is dealt with. For many people, for example in a marriage (a classical field for aporetical conflicts, since the opposition of the sexes in any case is constructive), conflicts are still regarded as a failure on the part of one or both partners. The fact that many marriage conflicts could be resolved through an evolutionary process is only slowly dawning on marriage guidance counsellors.

Once the conflict has arisen and can no longer be ignored, we reach the second phase: fight.

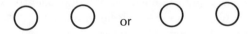

Both parties try to prove they are right and to put the other in the wrong, that is, they try to kill each other. In our example of order and freedom, the conflict may arise from the introduction of a more varied order, against which either freedom will defend itself or the need for emancipation will lead to a rejection of the order. If this is an aporetical conflict, then struggle cannot lead to the desired goal; on the contrary, when the other party is destroyed or subjugated, if only for a short time, then the victor will also suffer from this. If freedom succeeds in actually destroying order (which is often not nearly as difficult as restoring it again), then soon there will no longer be any freedom at all. In the general chaos, freedom also perishes, having achieved more than it wanted to achieve.

If, conversely, it were possible to set up such a rigid system of order that there was no longer any margin for freedom (a thought sometimes brought to its logical conclusion in utopian novels), then this abstract puppet-style order would not in the end be an order for human beings, but rather for machines: *reductio ad absurdum*.

Third phase: compromise.

Very often it is not necessary to continue the fight to the bitter end. Fighting only needs to go on until *both* parties appreciate that they are unable to destroy or subjugate one another. Both parties are now ready to make a compromise. They are prepared to soften elements of their contrasting points of view before reaching agreement. Depending on how important these elements are and how essential the points of conflict thus excluded, the conflict may arise again. There will then be renewed fighting and renewed realization of the impossibility of killing one another. In a labor conflict, for instance, a fight of this kind could mean either a strike or a lockout. Most labor conflicts are of an aporetical nature, since both parties are right and are dependent on each other. Striking can never be intended to destroy the enterprise, just as locking out does not mean that the company wishes to get rid of employees. The only aim is to enhance willingness to compromise.

The compromise phase can last a very long time and can be repeatedly interrupted by fighting. Though compromise in itself involves direct inter-

interrupted by fighting. Though compromise in itself involves direct inter-action of the litigant parties—requiring a third party at most as a mediator, but not as a decision maker—it is still not the best solution to aporetic conflicts. At a certain point this seesawing back and forth between fight and compromise initiates a new phase.

Fourth phase: Conflict arises within the two opposing parties.

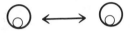

The opponents per se, who accept the compromise, notice—often with dismay—that the other opponent has slipped into their own ranks. Conflict arises within the litigant parties. In our example of freedom and order, some representatives of freedom would, in the face of imminent chaos, call for order; representatives of order, faced with total regimentation of action, would demand that laws be of a voluntary nature. "Laws are to be obeyed through acceptance, not coercion" might be approximately their argument. This phase, too, usually lasts a long time, while the possibility of fighting the opponent diminishes more and more. A state that is not able to wage war outside its boundaries without risking civil war inside would find itself in such a phase. This is why an attempt is often made to keep internal dissi-dents loyal by making war externally. It might be interesting to analyze the transition from cold war to detente with reference to this scheme.

Fifth phase: synthesis.

If the number of dissidents is growing in both opposing camps, the point will eventually be reached where the opponents discover that they are no longer all that different. In our examples, if the striving for order has grown to just the same extent in the representatives of freedom as has the need for the exercise of free will in the upholders of order, then the dialectal solution to this conflict is already at hand: A type of order desired by freedom will be installed. Thus both have been proved right; something new has been created, representing progress without destruction of the opponents. Voluntarily recognized order must of course be open to examination by freedom, to see whether it is still compatible with freedom. Freedom is freer than before, when it had to fight order. The order is a better order than before, when unrecognized order had to be imposed by force. What we have described here is the dialectal development toward democracy. It has now become so general that even this synthesis leads into aporia, thereby making further developments necessary.

A synthesis such as the result of a dialectic process that opposing points of view have gone through, but in such a way that both were proved right and both have gained something, can also be called a genuine consensus. This type of consensus is the best solution to a conflict at the present time.

PRACTICAL IMPLICATIONS FOR MANAGERS

With regard to conflict management: Assuming that top managers today, and their counterparts in the future even more so, will be expected to have less expert knowledge and more management expertise, it follows that this dialectical process can be accelerated or slowed down.

Depending on the phase the dispute has reached at a given moment, other actions have to be taken. In phase 1 care has to be taken to ensure that the conflict is not swept under the carpet again (for the umpteenth time?). In phase 2 there is the danger that support given to one party will make it appear that the conflict might be resolved by fighting. For instance, neutralizing or sacking the representative of a group within an organization that is making a justified demand simply slows down the process. However, the greatest danger in phase 2 is to give in to the *temptation of letting the conflict be resolved by delegation*. Where there is an aporia, this only retards the process.

In phases 3 and 4, on the other hand, it is not uniformity but variation in the points of view of a group that must be supported, so that useful compromises can be found. It is still better, however, to point out the short-lived nature of compromises in general, and to work toward a consensus. The rather longer duration of the dispute is easily compensated for by the better durability of the consensus compared with the compromise. Finally, in phase 5 one must be wary of offering a *formula for synthesis at too early a moment*. The opposing parties should always be allowed to go through this phase alone.

Rather different rules derive from this conflict model when one is involved in such a conflict oneself. Here, the general rule is to force oneself and the opponent to endure the individual phases and *not to give up* prematurely. The most difficult problem in this case is making the right diagnosis. It will often be useful to bring in an advisor. Someone in whom one places one's confidence, who is in a position to interpret the different elements of diagnosis and use them as feedback, will often be better than a professional consultant. In diagnosing a social entity, however, professional help will be essential as long as management training on the one hand and the position of authority of the superior on the other remain oriented toward the traditional hierarchy (holy order), because the superior who has authority essentially *only receives "colored information"* and this in itself makes a correct diagnosis of the situation impossible. Here, however, the question of conflict management passes into that of management style, a subject with which I do not intend to deal here.

Chapter 9

The Collective Unconscious and Social Change

Max Pagès

I was delighted to be offered an opportunity to make a statement on the theme about which I wrote an article some 10 years ago,[1] and a few years later a more extensive book.[2]

However, my pleasure was not without some apprehension. This area of activity has since then actually developed and split up in all directions. To quote only the most important, I would refer to the California school of bioenergetics, gestalt therapy, and encounter groups,[3] and above all the European trends in antipsychiatry and institutional analysis, and more recently in schizoanalysis,[4] as well as to the French work with groups inspired by psychoanalysis.[5]

At the same time the number of techniques began to multiply: The T-group—the basic or classic diagnostic group—is dead in the Lewinian version of the analysis of the processes within authority, influence, and participation. In his version of the verbal expression and analysis of the feelings in a group situation, it is dying. It only survives in an archaic form, particularly in France, or as a prop for commercial undertakings. Sometimes it revives, restored or transformed—whatever you like to call it—by psychoanalysis, and is used as a tool for psychoanalysis in group situations.

This chapter, originally titled "Inconscient Collectif et Changement Social," was translated from the French by Inge Hagen and Trygve Johnstad.

In place of the T-group we now have encounter groups, groups for gestalt therapy and for bioenergetics; body expression; psychological expression in dance, massage, music, and painting; autonomous groups, or institutional analysis in training or "natural" settings; seminars with a flexible structure,[6] and "analytical" training seminars.

From the masseur, the dancer, and the artist to the political agitator, by way of the psychoanalyst, we no longer know what a psychosociologist is today, and the temptation is great to predict the breakup of such a heterogeneous field. On the other hand, one can also choose, as I have done, to work toward a new integration within this diversity.

As I see it, in this respect the two most important aspects of group theory and practice during this last decade are:

1. the massive invasion of nonverbal techniques and body techniques;
2. the introduction of a political-economic-cultural dimension.

The simultaneous mastery of these two dimensions, sometimes divergent or mutually exclusive, sometimes convergent or combined, depending on the approach, creates the biggest problem—I feel—in psychosociology today. Perhaps I should add the integration of the psychoanalysis of groups, conceived as the analysis of collective systems of defense.[7] Finally and above all, the profound social, political, and cultural changes in recent years, particularly in France since May 1968, demand an elaborate reexamination of theoretical systems and methods and the ideological functions of both.

Within the framework of this short chapter, I will limit myself to a few suggestions in the form of outlined plans, drawn from my recent experiences in both training and "natural" groups. They are no more than incomplete syntheses and do not pretend to any kind of dogmatic formulation, which I would find premature at this point.

GROUP PHENOMENA ARE LOCATED IN A MULTIDIMENSIONAL FIELD

No group is isolated, whether it is a training group or a group in everyday life related to work, leisure, or the community; or whether it is formal or informal. Groups are totally accessible to and influenced by macrosociological reality, which runs them through with contradictory restraints and alternative structures. They are open systems.

On the other hand, the structures of groups, both internal and external, are multidimensional. They have political, economic, psychological, biological, and cultural aspects. In short, we could call them *socioaffective structures*. For instance, political and economic domination rests on a system of belief, on an affective system that sets up privileged individuals or groups, and on unconscious feelings of identification with, dependence on, and/or hostility to these groups.

Nor can the forces of change be reduced to one dimension. They have libidinal aspects as well. They invade the social field, as was clearly seen by Deleuze and Guattari, and they tend to provoke political, economic, and cultural change.

This, of course, applies to the relation between trainers and trainees in a training group. The training directs itself toward one or, more often, contradictory aims (of the trainers, the trainees, or the authorities that directly or indirectly "sponsor" the training), which are supported by the ideological and affective systems.

It seems unnecessary to recall how often, particularly in practice, research workers and trainers treat groups as closed systems, even one-dimensional. The choice of variables available to the research worker or the trainer (for example the psychological, economic, or political variables) is one of the most efficient, because the most concealed, means by which he can gain control—and, through this, the control of the social aims and of the groups with which he identifies himself.

GROUP PHENOMENA ARE REVEALED THROUGH AN EXPERIENCE OF CHANGE

There is no neutral behavior face to face with a group, only conscious or unconscious aims on several levels. "Acknowledgment" of group phenomena exposes these aims and the conflict between them, and releases consciousness of the true aims of the self.[8]

The more clearly the research worker or the trainer has defined his aims for himself, the less selective his behavior and the less he conceals the phenomena that he is examining, the better he will understand and expose the aims of the others.

This is why the training group and the intervention group present an exceptionally good means—although not the only one—for the study of groups in general, in spite of the narrow field of observation they offer at the moment.

THE COLLECTIVE ORGANIZATION OF FEELINGS

Here is one of the few points on which the various schools mentioned above will undoubtedly agree: There exists a *transversal* dimension of feelings, not only one that is longitudinal or historical, particularly on the unconscious level. Impulses and defense systems are *shared* by the group members at different times in the group's history and in a different way for everyone, depending on each member's individual history. The unconscious and its defenses are of a collective order.[9] Le Bon,[10] in spite of some criticizable aspects of his thought, has some recognition of this in his "law of the mental unity of crowds." Thus he was right compared with Freud, who in his "Group Psychology and the Analysis of the Ego"[11] makes the group's links derive from the group leader.

Later Bion[12] talked about "valency" as a momentary combination of feelings in a group, organized according to several possible "basic assumptions"; and the particular link with the leader, far from bringing these valencies about, was for him the result of them.

With regard to the "protomental system," an obscure concept used by Bion to describe the deepest level of the unconscious, underlying that of these basic assumptions, this is a collective level that entirely transcends all individual personality. I propose to distinguish two levels of collective organization of group feelings:

1. One is the unconscious defense system that generally corresponds with Bion's basic assumptions; this is the level of structures of feeling that joins with other structures (political, economic, cultural) in order to maintain a certain framework for living and social organization.
2. The other is the repressed and controlled collective desires and aims that carry the germ of a global reorganization of human relations.

THE EXISTENCE OF UNCONSCIOUS GROUP AIMS

This is undoubtedly my central hypothesis. In many a group situation I thought I could ascertain the manifestation of unconscious aims to reorganize the life of the group. These very indirect and, in the beginning, hidden manifestations were sometimes clarified as the defense systems were elucidated and the political-economic structures changed. For example, a group of participants in a seminar organized what they called a *tam-tam* in a session without trainers, using various pieces of furniture.

This tam-tam, which they later could only talk about with reluctance to their trainers, was meant, according to them, as an *invitation* to the other participants (in neighboring rooms) to *protest* against the trainers and against the noise in the seminar. This was a noise designed to stop the noise in which they heard confused and covered-up aggression, and the satisfaction of talking about oneself before the trainers and for them, instead of getting down to work. It was a *struggle against suffocation* (by the trainers, by the other participants, and by themselves); a *desire for life*, for *influence*, for *action*—individual or collective—to take the *initiative* in the seminar instead of always being led by trainers: an experience of joy, happiness, and fun, mixed with anxiety. This seminar aimed to experiment with spontaneous developments of forms of organization among a collection of people.

At this moment in the life of the seminar, the plan made by the trainers with the complicity of the group was to follow the feudal-patriarchal model of organization (which is the usual model for this type of seminar). Later, after many vicissitudes, and particularly after a phase of trade-union-type organization in between the patriarchal and the common-property phases, the aim of the group could be expressed clearly. The participants decided unanimously to take over the responsibility for the aims and the organization of the seminar. Still later individual aims could be expressed, at first in a chaotic and contradictory way, but later coherently. They had until then been camouflaged by the collective aims and by the exigencies of the struggle against the trainers and the "trade unionists," and equally by internal psychological conflicts as well as by the anxiety caused by giving up the protection of the trainers.[13]

How should we characterize this unconscious aim of groups? It is the aim of the group to take over responsibility for all aspects of its own life. In my opinion there is an *unconscious autonomous aim* in all groups, independent of their ideological or social membership; and I think I have found it even in groups with the most conservative framework. On the other hand, the aim is at the same time *individual* and *interactional*. It has in view tackling the contradiction between the expressions of *individual* desires without repression or inhibition, and the effect of this on relationships with others. It is also the *aim of a group without boundaries*, an open group— Deleuze and Guattari would say "molecular and not molar"—where the group structures that trap individuals disintegrate, to be replaced by incidental and flexible ties between individuals and free personal associations between people (which is never the case with so-called associations).

In this respect the aim opposes all our known forms of organization, which are segmental, molar, and imposed by one fraction of the group. It is an *anti-organizational* aim. We could also say that it is the aim of a *production group* in the Marxist sense of the term, where the forces of production operate freely, without being limited by group structures or superstructures, by systems of property and social control, by ideological justifications, or by constellations of psychological defenses that increase the group's viscosity.[14]

This also means that the *group aim is simultaneously of a libidinal-sexual order and a political-economic-cultural order*. Its energy is that of desire, and it manifests itself as desire and pleasure. But it involves the entire social field and proposes a system of human relations, goals, and methods of production, and changes of the existing social relations, at first in limited and repressed forms.

Another way of saying this is that groups *exist* in reality and not only as dreams or fantasies. They exist as a place to organize individual defenses against desire, which is conceived as an individual force itself; as a place for camouflage, flight, and protection against desires and their disguises.

They are this, but they are also something else: *a place to share and to declare desires, an active association in the pursuit of an unconscious collective goal,* although this may be most often hidden, repressed by all sorts of systems of social control and overlaid with layers of psychological defenses that are just so many masks.

In my book La Vie Affective des Groups (The Emotional Life of Groups), I have tried to express this fundamental idea by formulating a "hypothesis of a collective unconscious, situated in the present, which occurs in the emotional experience of interaction, and manages the phenomena of the group";[15] and by adding that this experience, which tends to be universal, is the one that brings the group together. My mistake was then to deny the libidinal-sexual character of the collective unconscious, its biological and energetic aspects, and to confuse the *movement* of the collective unconscious, found in all interactions, with its *consequences*, described as an unconscious feeling of contact. Moreover, this feeling, being always partial, is just produced by the movement of the unconscious to form a contact, one of the lateral connections that is being established constantly. My description, which certain people have called pan-psychological,[16] had also the inconvenience of only emphasizing the movement that goes from the collective unconscious to social institutions, without clearly recognizing the movement in the opposite direction, namely the repression of the unconscious by the institutions.

Also it had the appearance of—and undoubtedly was to some degree—a mystifying idealism, minimizing the *work* of the unconscious, its struggle against the already existing repressive structures and its own changes during this struggle.[17]

But however confused and distorted they may have been, this book contains ideas that I do not want to disown. One is the existence of groups, in the sense in which I have just spoken of them, with active, joint, and unconscious aims, at first pursued secretly before they can be openly recognized.

Another is the creation of social structures by unconscious defensive behavior and the central role of these structures in maintaining a defense sytem. And finally—and I will come back to this later—the necessary tie between self-assertion (today I would call it assertion of desire), anxiety about death, and the recognition of desire in others.

It is the first of these, the existence of groups as a real place for change, and not only as a defense system, which the psychoanalysts could never accept (not even Bion, who was prepared to go furthest in this respect), and which constitutes the real dividing line between us.

However relevant the analysis of defense systems, if it does not recognize the collective and social nature of desire, which is always *actually* involved in a situation of change, but ascribes it to family history, group history, or social history, which means to its own defense system, then it is in my opinion misleading and plays a major role in the maintenance of existing political, economic, cultural, and psychological structures.

SOCIAL FANTASY AND NONVERBAL LANGUAGE

Prehistory of Groups

I would like to refer here to an aspect of the tam-tam mentioned above: the spontaneous resort to nonverbal communication. We feel undoubtedly that nonverbal communication gives more direct access to repressed impulses. On the other hand, the nonverbal fulfills a double function of protection and of conflict. Of protection, because it allows us to escape from the accepted rules; we can always say "it was only a game." Of conflict, because it expresses a rebuttal of the socially accepted language, which is felt as alienating. In that seminar it was quite clear that the language spoken was the official language; it was the language of the trainers, which the participants wanted to avoid even when they talked.

So when they wanted to talk about the sessions where all the participants would be present, they avoided in a comical way the expression "plenary session," which had been introduced by the trainers in the opening program. In the Baleine group, which I studied some time ago, English, rather than French, was the trainer's language, and one could observe this in that interaction with him showed the same ambiguity. *Recourse to the nonverbal represents a movement to reconstruct and adapt language.*

In recent years in sessions and seminars, and particularly in their early stages, I have been struck many times by the group resorting to nonverbal communication to express their unconscious social goals.

During an intervention seminar in an educational center, where the director as well as some twenty of his colleagues were participants, the first afternoon was sluggish and silent. There were no interventions about the purpose of the session, nor on the problems with which they should have been dealing. However, I knew from private conversations that the most real and strongly felt conflicts were those that existed between the director and the teachers and among the teachers themselves. An earlier meeting, where the same people had met in order to agree on the aims of my intervention seminar, had developed in the same way. After a time, while the conversation still languished, two of my neighbors set up a rhythm by tapping their fingers on a piece of furniture. I picked up the rhythm and before long five or six others joined us. After two or three false starts a rhythm developed, gained strength, and spread through the group, supported by various instruments: flute, guitar, tambourine,[18] until at certain times one could believe that the group would start to dance. Then it collapsed.

After that we did some verbal and nonverbal communication exercises, which I had suggested in the beginning and which the group now demanded. After dinner the same game started again, but this time everybody began to dance, wildly and uncontrolledly. Thereafter, within a very short period of time, an extremely rich and complex sequence of events took place as a sort of happening, of which I cannot report all the details here.

At one moment all the group members took off their socks, removing them by force from those few who were reluctant. The last whom they approached, after a little hesitation, were myself and the director. Out of the socks they made a sort of a long rope with which they played, surrounding the group, catching some, and jumping over the rope two, three, or four at a time. Then there were some separation and conflict games: splitting up bearded and nonbearded men, women and men, titled and not titled, directors and nondirectors, psychologists and sociologists; with phases of fight, removal, some overwhelming others, huddling together, change of group (symbolizing treason), reunion—all very speedy and almost without a word being exchanged.

The following morning, after some fruitless attempts at conversation, in a few minutes and wihout being given any instructions everybody found himself painting or designing individually or in small groups. The designs were full of violent and contrasting colors, and here and there one could recognize symbols of the institution, treated with derision. At the end of the morning we danced. They made a kind of suit out of several designs in which they dressed one of the participants very solemnly until he looked like a ridiculous king, sad and degraded. (Later, when we talked about it, a participant used the expression "galley-slave king," and in the end the group was drawn as a galley.)

In the afternoon several people said they had had enough of the nonverbal and would like to try to express themselves verbally. A group was quickly formed in the center of the room with their heads together, and they soon went off. This left five people, among whom were the director and myself. One hour later they came back and started a difficult dialogue with the director about his role, his decisions, his philosophy, his contradictions, as well as the contradictions existing in the group between their objectives and practice—in short, about the purpose of the session.

I will not analyze this example in detail: the institutional aggression shown by the director, the aggressive feelings directed toward him, toward the institution, and toward myself; the individual or subgroup feelings of being overwhelmed; the division of the group, rivalry, competition, desire for unity, desire for the group's supremacy, and bitterness that this would be ridiculed or impossible. The example shows well enough, to my mind, the riches of nonverbal communication and its mobilizing value. Certain of the feelings expressed were known by certain participants, others very probably were not. It seems to me that nonverbal games permitted the participants to express themselves finally, and in every case in a clear manner, more precisely and with more commitment.

The point I would like to stress above all is the sociopolitical character of this entire fantasy. I think it would make no sense to interpret it only in individual terms. Rather it is about the *hidden expression of the goal of a social group*. Here I like to talk about a *prehistory of groups*, earlier than the moment when the group goal becomes conscious and is expressed verbally, when the group and its members make themselves the subjects of the story. During this period the group's autonomous production is mainly imaginative, using means of body expression, artistic production, and social imagery. This is a sign of a suppressed and repressed production, without any direct access to the structure of social relationships. It is also the moment when the contrast is greatest between the group's verbal and official talk, which is serious, conformist, alienated, and subject to social institutions; and its autonomous production, which is wild, delirious, funny, violent, and poetic. Furthermore, groups often return later to nonverbal expression, when they come up against new obstructions.[19]

The prehistory of groups in the sense in which we understand it here, the study of the obscure pathways taken by the social goal in the fields of imagination and fantasy, the study of the *relations* between the fantasy activity and this goal, is in my opinion a major field for research. It has been all too little explored, but is accessible to study just as well in real groups as in training groups. Through a better understanding of this field, *techniques for the mobilization of groups* toward their sociopolitical goals are able to develop, using the resources of a psychosociology of the unconscious.[20]

Indeed, far too often the techniques of political agitation are only rudimentary and are also authoritarian, since they mainly use rational tools. The fascists, as Reich clearly saw, have been among the first to use the unconscious effectively, but evidently by using the repressive and suppressive aspects of it.

Here I will limit myself to indicating the essential role that can be played by nonverbal techniques: dance, music, painting, drawing, body expression, mime, the use of masks, and so on. It is important to make sure they are not focused on the single individual, as the Californians tend to do, but on *helping to liberate the energetic and expression potential of the whole group.* In this sense the exercises, body expression, bioenergetics, and gestalt therapy are, in my opinion, more harmful than useful in practice because they restrict the spontaneity that should have been developed and often isolate individuals from one another. I prefer to be on the watch for spontaneous movements and actions in the group, which are often very tentative in the beginning, and to give a spontaneous response by involving myself; looking for the echoes, connections, breaks in the rhythms; going from one language to another; helping the group to produce its cacophony and its symphony. In this respect dance seems to me one of the most effective tools. I do not know whether this is because of my personal preference, or if it really is of greater efficacy than other instruments.

Group Myths and the Mythical Group

In the course of their work, groups develop all kinds of illusions and myths, as has been pointed out by several authors.[21]

In my opinion the central myth concerns the idea of the group itself. The picture of a group that so often haunts groups is that of the members forming a distinct entity that is above any one of the members and that also dominates them.

Such a group is at the same time a protection and a threat. It is a haven, a benevolent God and a Good Mother; but also a Janus, a Moloch, the Devil—a whole pantheon, good and terrifying at the same time. Within the idea of the family, it takes up the functions of a mother figure, nursing but also devouring; and a father figure, protecting and at the same time castrating.

The picture of the group and its more or less conscious emotional life is accompanied by an ideology of devotion and sacrifice. It is implicitly or explicitly accepted that one has to dedicate oneself to "the group," to sacrifice oneself for it so that *it* will survive. Group members talk to other members "in the name of the group," reminding them of their duty to the group, appealing to ideas of devotion and sacrifice and making a display of their own—then using this as blackmail.

It is also "in the name of the group" that members are excluded for deviation and for betraying the collective ideals, and that other members who agree with the ideals are admitted; because "the group" is closed by definition. It is a sect with a religion, whether secular or not, with its banner, its scriptures, its ministers, its high priest, its classes, and its commoners.[22] These beliefs and these practices previously depended on the ideologies of established institutions like the state, the church, the family, the army, the school, and the business, and used to some extent the same language.

Some people draw the conclusion from these statements that the group attaches itself to these myths.[23] I cannot go along with this, for *the myth of a group is a product of that group. The myth of a closed group is a product of the open group.* This is the combined result of the internal action of the defense systems operating in the collective unconscious, and of the external action of the social repression that channels, limits, and fragments unconscious drives. It must be recognized, however, that by talking in this way we radically transform the concept of the group. *All the known expressions of the concept of the group refer to the myths* and belong to the universe of closed, punishing, protecting, and castrating concepts. It is only when we try to get rid of this concept that we can, with difficulty, begin to imagine the concept of a group that identifies itself with its members at any one time without established borders, without fixed structures, without dogma, without banners, and without leaders, and that is consistent with the productive drives of the unconscious.[24]

It is also necessary to distinguish between the myths of the group and its creative fantasy mentioned in the paragraph above. It is another type of unconscious or semiconscious group training. Group myths are on the same side as defense systems. They form a very well-integrated structural unity with the political, economic, and cultural structures in the group. This socioaffective structure, which is opposed to change, will be overturned by the creative fantasies of the group.

Desire and Anxiety about Death

The affirmation of desire implies a confrontation with anxiety about death. Any demonstration of desire involves the risk of destruction. It survives as if in an uncaring or hostile universe. But it is *quite otherwise* with the desire that this universe is going to change or overturn. It is neither able to respond to nor reject this and will consequently be killed, which corresponds very precisely with the experience of death. Even when shared, desire is always that of an individual or of a part of an individual; it is alone and isolated from the world, cutting itself off in an effort to establish new ties, introducing simultaneously the experience of *uniqueness* and of *change*, which is experienced as potentially destructive.

It is fashionable to relate anxiety about death to fears of castration or of being devoured and to the fantasies of the destructive father or mother figures, or, more generally, to the fear induced by repressive social forces. Certainly these fears dominate the unconscious, particularly in a situation where desire is strongly suppressed and repressed. But as far as I can see, they are already secondary and are part of the defense system. They are the result of social conditioning, of a desire that sets itself precise targets and focuses on privileged figures in society, to channel and organize according to a system of reward and punishment.

At the deepest level, anxiety about death is *generalized* and not localized; it views the *world* as hostile or indifferent, and not this or that privileged individual. Concentrating on other fears in this way diverts our attention from anxiety about death. We must also distinguish between anxiety about death, the desire for death (submitted to or inflicted), and the fear of death. At its deepest level, anxiety about death is neither desire for nor fear of death, but a "consciousness" or feeling of death, a consciousness of the risk of death implied by the desire for and facing of this risk. It is only later, as a result of a refusal to face anxiety about death, that the desire for and fear of death take shape and form part of the defenses against this anxiety. Anxiety that is not faced is transformed into terror and into terrorism. The original combination of desire and anxiety splits apart; the rejected anxiety, when projected into the outer world, creates the terrifying objects, which we try to terrify in return. The original unity of the present and absent object in the unity of anxiety-loaded desire, is split up into a good object that we wish to possess—and by which we are possessed—and a bad, destructive object that we want to destroy. Thus the possessive-hostile love couple is constituted.[26]

This is why the *concept of a death wish* seems to me inadequate, since desires for and fears of death are not the beginning, even if they were the first to appear in an observable form. They are part of a very primitive defense against a more unconscious anxiety about death that is indissolubly bound up with desire.

This primitive defense system consists of a double process: on the one hand of splitting and projection, which produces the love-hate couples and the good-bad object, and is a process of repression and transformation of desire and of anxiety; and on the other hand a focus that concentrates the feelings thus transformed into ambivalent ones of love and hate, onto privileged figures, individuals or groups. So there is an *endogenous* origin of this defense system, produced by the repression and transformation of desire and anxiety. But it has an *exogenous* origin as well, which is the result of social structures that offer us privileged figures, parents, and social forces, which are remarkably well equipped with the power to punish and reward, and support this by training emotional behavior with a possessive-aggressive focus. It is in this sense that the defense system, as a joint product of internal and external action, functions as intermediary between the libido and the social system. This explains at least in part the individual's atachment to repressive and alienating social structures.

Finally, one can establish a connection between the affirmation of one's own desire, the confrontation with the anxiety about death, and the recognition of the desires of others—that is, human relationships in the full sense of the word. Anxiety about death, if it has not already fled and been transformed into the terror system of the terrorists, is an awareness of the desire of others as constituting the limits—albeit unknown—of one's own desire. It is a simultaneous awareness of uniqueness and of change, and implies recognition of the desire of others. *Awareness of desire is simultaneously the awareness of its denial and its limit which is the desire of others.* And it is the recognition of one's own desire and its manifestations that makes it possible to establish genuine contact with others, which is neither possessive nor destructive and which allows for the simultaneous existence of different desires, even contradictory ones.

It is as well to recognize, however, that these speculations about the deepest level of the unconscious, like other speculations about the same topic, have a metapsychological character and are difficult to prove. They are only of interest, as are all the most abstract scientific constructs, if they allow us to explain in a more satisfactory way phenomena that are more directly observable. One of the difficulties arising out of the ideas I have just presented, as I have explained elsewhere,[27] is that they make a distinction between an ontological origin and that which is primary chronologically. Thus the fears and desires of a small child or of a group in its early stages will be different from a fear that is of an unconscious ontological origin, and that already constitutes a defense system against this. In support of my theory I have introduced the argument that social structures already interfere in the establishment of a primary defense system, and that the latter cannot be described as some sort of "raw unconscious." On the other hand, I think I have observed in my work with groups the existence of a level underlying the focus of fear-desire, which is, as I will discuss later, that of *generalized* paranoia. Ultimately, paranoia and terror seem well able to cover up an unconscious aim of a group (which I have already described as autonomous and interactional) where the fear of death could dissolve into an awareness of the finite and the desire to produce with others.

Evidently my hypotheis implies that these formations, which appear very slowly in a manifest form, are already present at the unconscious level earlier on; and one could assert with Freud and orthodox psychoanalysis that they result from socialization and not from a liberation of the unconscious. But clinically we can show the relationship between generalized paranoia and the unconscious aim from the earliest stages, through nonverbal manifestations, for example, where they find essential expression. On the other hand, the step that I am proposing can only clarify and push a little further the classical psychoanalytic position, by claiming that the deepest levels of the unconscious manifest themselves extremely slowly. And isn't the work of the unconscious exactly this: to mold and remold social structures and defense systems in order that they will appear each time in a clearer and more exposed way?

Paranoia, Terror, and Chaos

During the seminar that I described at the beginning of this article, an interesting phenomenon came up at the start of the third session, after the group had confirmed its collective aim to take over responsibility for the seminar. Very quickly the participants—until then unanimous as to this common aim, which was common but empty with regard to content— rushed forward with a multiplicity of individual aims, which they expressed with force in a most aggressive manner. Everybody, or almost everybody, talked at the same time, ignoring everyone else. The paradox was that each aim required the cooperation of others—or of everybody—but resisted this at the same time. So Gérard hit the table with his fist and demanded a plenary session to answer three essential questions: Where are decisions made? Who makes decisions? What is the role of the trainers?

But if someone had said: "But Gérard, in order for you to have a *plenary* session, it is necessary that everybody is present and that the others agree to it," he would have begun again: "I want the plenary sessions in order to answer three questions," and so on.

The astonishing thing about these sessions that lasted close to twenty-four hours was the vitality, the commitment, the involvement, the assertion of individual aims, and the almost absolute impossibility of connecting them all with each other. It seemed as if everybody felt that his aim was unacceptable to the others, and *that everyone was seen as a potential enemy of everyone else.*

It is this state of feeling that I propose to describe as *chaos* and *generalized paranoia.* In generalized paranoia the threatening figures and the targets for aggression are no longer the traditional authorities or counterauthorities (here the trainers or the trade unionist leaders). Everybody else is to a certain degree a potential aggressor, whom one attacks and against whom one defends oneself. There are no longer any norms, no authorities that are recognized or attacked by the whole group, nor even by subgroups. Power breaks up into a multitude of separate centers, none of which is able to dominate, although they try unsuccessfully to impose their influence on others in the most laborious and exhaustive way.

At the same time there is a state of activity and intense creativity, where the original goals come together and where concepts and attitudes clash. Without doubt this is a state of the group where possibilities for individual and group change are at their greatest and most available.

Generalized paranoia follows the *institutional violence* and the *terror* of earlier stages. Repression exercised by traditional authorities, or by counterauthorities who want to displace them, reveals itself, as has often been said, in concealed violence that is not recognized as such by the authorities, nor even by the subjects, even if it results in war, famine, limits to freedom of speech and initiative, and various other frustrations. In this case the paranoia of the leaders, who are confused by the manifestations of desire and initiative among those whom they lead, replaces and covers up the generalized paranoia of the group, against which it protects them.

This may help to explain why revolutionary leaders, placed in a situation where the desires of the group are expressed more openly, tend to become more openly repressive than traditional leaders. The eternal argument of all authorities is that they must protect society against chaos. Certainly they are also defending themselves, their class privileges, and their emotional structures. But the argument points to a reality that makes it impossible for the group to face its paranoia, to face its own defense systems against the risks of generalized aggression, and this makes them accomplices of the leaders.

Institutional violence has a counterpart in the unconscious *terror* and *terrorism* of the group. And this is strengthened the more the group is submissive and conforms, not only in behavior but consciously as well. In my work with groups I am more and more astonished to see how much the prehistory of the groups, which I have just mentioned, is truly reflected in this terror and terrorism.

It is a history full of sound and fury, full of plans for murder and suicidal fantasies, and of feelings of loneliness and distress, which come out particularly in the group's nonverbal and artistic output. And the unconscious group aim, which now already shows itself in a sketchy way, exists alongside this terror and terrorism.

The conceptual difference between terror and generalized paranoia is found in the fact that terror is focused on the authorities, traditional or not, and the generalized paranoia is not. Terror is on the other hand more violent in its fantasy than is paranoia. It is the unconscious fear of and desire for murder, which is a desperate denial of the risk of death; while generalized paranoia comes closer to a consciousness of death that is more lucid and more serene.

Generalized paranoia and chaos also constitute a definite step forward in the sense that they are the beginning of group work on a common goal. Objectively, they are accompanied by less violence and devastation, because the devastation caused by institutional violence is effectively blocked at this stage by individuals. These are the productive, creative stages where goals that take into account individual desires are formulated in outline. Subjectively, these are the active and dynamic stages, expressed in excitement and joy. We are invited by an awareness of others and the possibility of relationships with them, within a conflicting awareness of the desires of others.

Chaos and generalized paranoia are seldom seen in training groups, and even more seldom in intervention groups, and even then in very restricted forms. They are forbidden or bound by the castrating and limiting interventions of the trainers and the power structures they maintain. In a more general way, society may by its structure be understood as a defense against chaos, which, however, is a condition of its progress. And I think that progress in the human sciences, of a finally reconciled and articulated psycho-sociopolitical type, can be understood as showing the way to develop strategies that combine biological, psychological, economic, political, and cultural aspects in order to liberate latent and repressed social chaos, which is a necessary phase in social reorganization.

REMARKS ABOUT GROUP WORK

This means, in my opinion, that group work necessarily opens up a theory of, and methodology, for social change. In conclusion I will limit myself to a few general remarks on this subject.

The work of a psychosociologist is work with and within contradictions. And the greatest problem of psychosociology is how to treat these contradictions dialectically, and not to eliminate one concept in favor of another or one contradiction in favor of another.[28] I will quote some of these contradictions without putting them in any particular order.

The contradiction between the biopsychological and the social-political (including the economic, cultural, and so on). Certain theories and techniques rightly accentuate the release of repressed and suppressed libidinal energy. I am thinking particularly of the California schools of bioenergetics, gestalt therapy, and encounter groups, most of all of the first. They have made possible a considerable progress in techniques —for instance, it is possible in a few hours to enable an individual to relive intensely and accurately earlier infantile conflicts that only come to the surface in a blurred and confused way (if at all) after several years of classical analysis. But they do so from a strictly individualistic "therapeutic" point of view (therapy for the normal), which does not allow the energy of the group to manifest itself and even less to be applied to an external social action. They are often accompanied by a "back to nature" ideology, by an oriental mysticism of equilibrium and wisdom, by a flight from and not a confrontation with industrial society—all of which have evident mystical aspects. They do not "attack" the everyday reality of urban life, of industrial workers, of the dispossessed class, or of the Third World. They are easily recruited by an efficient leisure industry into training that is often nothing other than the organized leisure, to work with a clientele who are depressed and alienated by their work. In fact, their chances of spreading throughout industry, even French industry, are far from negligible.[29]

In contrast to this, others develop techniques that aim at revealing social conflicts, the struggle against institutions and sometimes against the internalization of repressive institutions. I am thinking here of institutional analysis and, even more, of the practices employed by political movements of the extreme left. But they often underestimate the psychobiological dimensions, which are excluded as reactionary, and thus short-circuit both the sexual-political unconscious and the defense systems.

An urgent and immense task awaits the psychosociologist, which is just emerging here and there. It involves integrating instead of splitting up these two requirements. These two types of stimulus, the libidinal and the sociopolitical, are in reality a single unity, which only the "experts" have divided. Here I cannot elaborate further on this subject, but will only return to what I said earlier about the use of nonverbal language to express the unconscious social goals of groups. It is obvious, however, that this task implies a collaboration instead of the usual dissension between practitioners of bioenergetics, institutional analysts, psychosociologists, adherents of antipsychiatry, schizoanalysts, sociologists, economists, ethnologists, and so on.

The contradiction between action and analysis. Here we meet again a simplified dichotomy by mutual exclusion of the contradictory terms. On the one hand, orthodox psychoanalysis defines action within the framework of the analysis, as acting out. Either it is prohibited (but this tends to be out of date) or it is not encouraged, and the psychoanalyst on his part maintains his holy and comfortable neutrality (should I add, benevolent or guilty?). And the acting out is patiently reduced by the analysis. The result is highly effective castration of the client on the level of social action, and even on the level of internal psychological change, from which come these sad analyses of the analysis of the absence of drives, at best with the loss of an incredible amount of time. But the drives and transferences are present and immediately available for those who do not want systematically to prevent their activity.

On the other hand, modern extremists, whether biopsychologists or political extremists, go so far in their pure form as to outlaw analysis ("intellectual bullshit," as certain Americans call it), in favor of any action in the form that suits them. Action is this time considered the analyzer. This is the opposite of acting out and of a flight from analysis. And the "analyzer" replaces an analysis that is perceived as inhibiting.[30]

To my mind the inconvenience of this position is the prevention of a clear and conscious grasp of the structures: individual mental structures, internalized social structures, and defense systems, which are precisely what it is the first effect of action to reveal.

For instance, a group that is moving away from alienation will never

enter a new world that by magic will eliminate its history. Its first discovery is of the structures that alienate and within which it alienated itself,
the socioaffective power systems and the conflicting dependence on
authority. This discovery already transforms the group. It presupposes
possibilities of expression and communication and a power structure that is
already seen as different from the one they have established. *Action and
analysis do not exclude each other in a change process, but mutually
support each other and keep each other in a circular relation.* Otherwise
action is truly a flight, a flight into an imaginary world contradicted by the
real life of the group.

This analysis is certainly not only the task of the change agent,[31] but the
group does the main part of it, and nothing is more dreadful than these
analytical lectures stuck onto a living process. But let us not get carried
away: The change agent is an important and necessary part of the analysis.
This is because not only is he the symbol of social authority, but also in a
very real way he is society's agent in the group by virtue of the power he
wields, the institutions he represents and defends, the ideology he supports, the attitudes he encourages and the affective systems he tends to
focus around himself. *It is the change agent who mainly represents social
forces in the group at the level of reality and not only of fantasy. And it is to
the extent to which he assumes this repressive role that an analysis and
eventually a transformation of the real power phenomena in the group will
be possible.*

The demands for analysis introduced by the change agent rest then on
his power. (His presence alone is enough; it is better to have the analysis
actually carried out by others.) This means that the demands of science, at
least partially and by their very nature, have a repressive character.
Today it is of course trite to proclaim the repressive character of science.
But we do not draw the conclusion that science should be thrown to the
winds, or that a science should be invented magically free from repression;
but that the researcher-practitioner of change must face the contradictions
of his own role. The result is then, as we have just mentioned, that the
*change agent is necessarily caught in a contradiction between a subversive
and a repressive role.* While he is an agent of social forces, supporting to
the hilt the established structures (with his conceptual and methodological
tools), his aim is to transform them. He is unable to renounce either side of
this contradiction. By denial of the second, he becomes an affective and
political organizer and renounces all change. By denial of the first, he
mystifies the group about his real role, encourages mystification and
escape into idealization, refuses to let the group take over, and so neutral-
izes his own effect.

Confrontation with this contradiction constitutes an essential field of
research and experimentation for the change agent. In my opinion—a

humble conclusion compared with the extent of the problem—*the change agent can only confront this contradiction by confronting those who demonstrate his own real transformation (in his role, in his personality) during the process of change.* This means for instance that he should no longer give way to the group unconditionally, follow it, or go along with it; but should instead frustrate it systematically, and in both cases (paternal leader or neutral analyst) keep outside the area of change activity. What is at stake is a real change in his status, his power, his theories, his methods, his attitudes, and not a protected analytical game or some subversive gimmick. This contradiction reveals another.

The need for security and the need for change. We already touched on this when we talked about the problem of institutionalization. Neither defense systems nor social structures can at any time be totally eliminated. But changing balances, which are more or less stable, are established between them and the unconscious drives under the influence of the work of the unconscious; and this corresponds simultaneously with the possibilities of change and the limits of security.

Consciously or unconsciously, individually or collectively, the group members fix these more or less precise limits, which change with the work of the group. The difficulty of recognizing these limits precisely is undoubtedly the major problem of change. To overestimate or underestimate their own desire for change or their own need for security leads in both cases to individual or group stagnation. My hypothesis that the most efficient contribution from the change agent to this problem is to be conscious of his own security limits in a situation, and how the change in these limits changes the situation. I do not mean to say that the limits for the change agent are the same as for the members of the group; the latter can be found on either one side or the other. The group may go further than the change agent or vice versa, but in both cases the change agent will help the group most by showing in his behavior what is possible and what is impossible for him, that is, by informing them in a valid way (verbally or nonverbally) about his own position and his own conflicts.

Here too we start from the hypothesis that the change agent is a real part of the situation and not only a simple symbolic screen, who brings about change through his repressed impulses and at the same time represses change. Any denial of this conflictual reality, either at the emotional or the political level, is an obstacle in the way of change. It is the work of change agent to reduce his own tendency to denial with the help of the group, and to help the group to do the same. I will limit myself to pointing out two contradictions in connection with the above.

The contradiction between work on the level of the small group and work on the level of much larger groups (organizations, global societies,

unorganized gatherings, classes, special minority groups). The possibilities of work for the change agent are always at the heart of restricted groups that are more or less large and complex. The temptation is certainly great to depersonalize these groups (which are only, so far as we can see, temporary defense systems limiting the transversal organizational pressures of the social unconscious), and to cut off in this way the possibility of connections, of action, and of analysis of the greater social unities, by which they are penetrated throughout and on which these groups tend to work.

The opposite temptation is to break up the small groups and lead them in a military way to an attack on the "social system," breaking down at the same time their energy and the possibility of action on their own. As I see it, the change agent should open doors and windows in closed groups and particularly enter through those opened by the group itself. He should accept the fragmenting and restructuring of the groups with which he works (which are not idols but provisional tools of the unconscious, good to take and to leave without regret) without going so far on his own as to pass the limits of security found by the individuals in the more or less protective functioning of "their" group. And finally:

The contradiction between training and intervention in the field. It is evident that training serves as an alibi for nonintervention in the field when it is concerned with definite problems posed to particular populations that are at odds with organized power. But it is also a useful distance and protection, which allows work to take place. It would undoubtedly be a good idea to rethink the whole problem of training while facing this contradiction.

The training groups that we are actually offered by the change agents, particularly the psychological, psychosociological, sociopsychoanalytical, and bioenergetic factions, constitute a kind of general methodology (of interaction, of communication, of formal education, of the perception of the group—its organization, its self-generative character—that might lead us to wonder if it does not have an abstract and mystical character compared with social reality. However sophisticated the techniques may be, and however widespread, are they really going to change significantly—or at all—any of the urban problems, work problems, or problems of political power? Perhaps it is about time to extend this method, of which the value is beyond doubt, much more directly toward definite social problems, and to focus training on preparation for action regarding these problems in conjunction with the population concerned.

I will conclude by applying the frame of reference that I have described to work with groups in order to propose a simple system—maybe too simple, with three factors that may be helpful in locating the different currents present. One factor is *biopsychological extremism*, characterized by an endeavor to release sexual drives; by the intensive or exclusive use of nonverbal and body techniques; by encouragement to fulfill desires in interpersonal situations; by the reduction—even prohibition—of analysis; by the psychologist's emotional and libidinal involvement; by the limitation of work to the individual level; by keeping secret the political, economic, and cultural dimensions of the group; and sometimes by certain mystical (especially oriental) trends.

Another factor we find is *political-economic-cultural extremism*, which is exclusively focused on or gives prerogative to the idea of changing the social structure. It encourages action and reduces or prohibits analytical activity just as in the previous case, but this time at the level of the social-political structures. It promotes work on the collective level, especially in the very big institutionalized groups. It fosters the political involvement of the change agent and eliminates or covers up the psychobiological factors.

A third dimension reveals a *sociopsychoanalytical* orientation, characterized by the analysis of individual and collective fantasies and defense

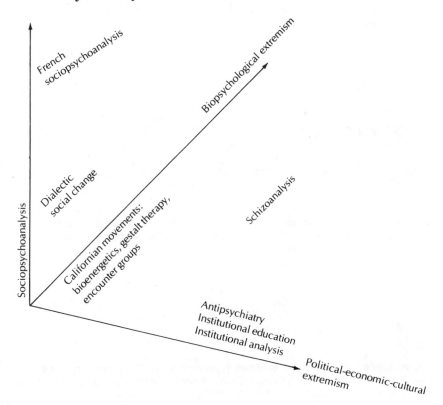

Figure 9–1.

systems, and by the prohibition or nonencouragement of action of whatever kind within the framework of the analysis, which is always interpreted as acting out. It is further characterized by a predominance of rational control of psychic organization, by the denial of the liberating role of drives insofar as they are not permanently controlled, by the maintenance of a clear demarcation line betwen analyst and analyzed and of a stable power structure between them, and by the noninvolvement or controlled emotional and political involvement of the analyst.

These, of course, are the pure types, while the real schools and and movements are located on a three-dimensional continuum, as shown in Figure 9–1.

My own approach, which I provisionally describe as *dialectic or multidimensional social change* is located on a vector clearly parallel to schizo-analysis but on a level closer to sociopsychoanalysis in the sense that on the one hand it admits and tries to promote the liberating role of a collective unconscious, which is at the same time sexual and political, and on the other hand recognizes the importance of analysis of the defensive and repressive socioaffective structures and for that reason allows a certain analytical constraint to be put on the group, thus accepting the necessity of some repressive socialization of the unconscious.

NOTES

1. M. Pagès, "Note on the Emotional Life of Groups," *Bull. Psych.* 214, XVI, 6–7 (1963).
2. M. Pagès, *La vie Affective des Groupes, Esquisse d'une Théorie de la Relation Humaine (The Emotional Life of Groups, an Outline of a Theory on Human Relations)* (Paris: Dunod, 1968).
3. Cf. F., Perls, *Gestalt Therapy* (New York: Delta, 1951); F. Perls, *Ego, Hunger and Aggression* (New York: Random House, 1969); and W. Schutz, *Joy* (New York: Grove Press, 1967).
4. D. Cooper, *Psychiatrie et Antipsychiatrie (Psychiatry and Antipsychiatry)* (Paris: Seuil, 1972); R. Laing and A. Esterson, *Sanity, Madness and the Family: Families of Schizophrenics* (London: Tavistock, 1964); F. Basaglia, *Institution en Négation (The Negative Institution)* (Paris: Seuil, 1970); G. Lapassade, *Groupes, Organisations et Institutions (Groups, Organizations and Institutions)* (Paris: Gauthier-Villars, 1967); G. Lapassade, *L'analyseur et L'analyste (The Analyzer and the Analyst)* (Paris: Gauthier-Villars, 1971); G. Lapassade, *L'autogestion Pédagogique (Pedagogic Autonomy)* (Paris: Gauthier-Villars, 1971); R. Lourau, *L'analyse Institutionelle (Institutional Analysis)* (Paris: Minuit, 1970); G. Deleuze and F. Guattari, *L'anti-Oedipe (The Anti-Oedipus)* (Paris: Minuit, 1972).
5. Compare D. Anzieu, *Le Travail Psychoanalytique dans les Groupes (Psychoanalysis in Groups)* (Paris: Dunod, 1972).
6. M. Pagès, "An Experiment in Human Relations Training: The Laboratory with Flexible Structures," In *T-Group Theory and the Laboratory Method,* a collective work (new ed., New York: Holt, 1974).

7. My hesitance, indicated by the word "perhaps," comes from my feeling that the psychoanalytic tools applied in group situations are very often useful to describe collective defense systems. At the same time they reinforce these systems in the same way as the structures of social control that accompany them, because they deny the existence of a collective sexual and political unconscious with freedom as its aim. I will come back to this later.

8. Talking about institutions, René Lourau develops a distinction between the real objective and the conscious one (*Institutional Analysis*, pp. 17–18, 53, 77).

9. This is why psychoanalysis of groups is radically different from individual psychoanalysis, even if the latter is done in a group.

10. G. Le Bon, *Psychologie des Foules (Psychology of Crowds)* (Paris: Alcan, 1895; new ed., Paris: P.U.F., 1963).

11. S. Freud, (French ed. 1948), "Group Psychology and the Analysis of the Ego," in *Essays on Psychoanalysis (Essais de Psychoanalyse)* (Paris: Payot, 1921; French ed., 1948).

12. W. R. Bion, *Experiences in Groups* (London: Tavistock, 1961), French transl., Mme. Herbert, *Recherches sur les Petites Groupes* (Paris: P.U.F., 1965).

13. For analysis of this seminar, compare Pagès, "An Experiment in Human Relations Training."

14. The mobility of these groups is astonishing, just as is their apparent capacity to produce change at all levels among the participants.

15. Pagès, *The Emotional Life of Groups*, p. 300.

16. Jean Maisonneuve, private conversation.

17. This description of the unconscious aim is doubtless still too static, as it presents as a formulated and formulatable aim what is really only an outline, a tam-tam, a vague struggle against suffocation, a plan for living against external and internal death.

18. I had brought with me some material for making music, painting, drawing, and had asked the participants to do the same, having informed them that we were also able to express ourselves in this way. Three people had previously participated in a seminar with me in which we had made considerable use of these materials. Perhaps one may think that I had introduced this means of expression; my feeling is rather that I had made it possible.

19. Compare Pagès, *Emotional Life of Groups*, p. 431 ("Progression Contrapuntique des Groupes").

20. The new style adopted by certain left-wing newspapers (strip cartoons, sketches) follows this idea.

21. D. Anzieu, "Etude Psychoanalytique des Groupes Réels" ("Psychoanalytic Study of Real Groups"), *Temps Moderne* 242, pp. 56–73; D. Anzieu, "L'illusion Groupale" ("The Group Myth"), *Nouvelle Revue de Psychoanalyse*, no. 4. In Pagès, *Emotional Life of Groups*, pp. 365, 376–381, I take up Anzieu's ideas and examine them.

22. I have not met any group, including the more "modern," where these same archaic models are not evident, at least in the beginning, and where analyses of them would not be beneficial. But I do not believe that it is possible to explain this only in terms of survivals from a now outdated way of life or in terms of cultural influences. I believe rather that the groups themselves produce these models as defense systems against the collective unconscious and use the available cultural models to create them.

23. Anzieu, *Psychoanalysis in Groups*.

24. I do not by any means pretend that any such "group" exists in reality, although some come more or less close to it. My aim here is to design a concept to show a *process* that operates at the heart of any real group.

25. In the same way, Deleuze and Guattari distinguish between two kinds of group fantasies, those that concern the invasion of the existing social field by the libido, and those that concern the spread of revolutionary desire throughout the social field (*Anti-Oedipus*, p. 38).

26. Compare Pagès, *Emotional Life of Groups*, chaps. 8, 9.

27. Ibid., particularly pp. 79–82, 202, 304–307.

28. Compare Pagès, "Pour un Laboratoire de Changement Social" ("Toward a Laboratory of Social Change"), in *Bull. Psych.*

29. In France the training schools inspired by this approach are to be found under the wing of the Ministry of Commerce.

30. G. Lapassade suggests the concept of "the analyzer" *(The Analyzer and the Analyst)*. He underlines by this title the contradiction between the analyzer and the analyst, which is what we are pointing out here. But it seems to me that he tends toward a suppression of one of the contradictory terms.

31. By this expression we characterize the multidisciplinary group of psychosociologists, sociologists, politicians, biologists, and so on working with change.

Chapter 10

Some Ethical Considerations in Consultation and So-Called Training Activities

Ronald Markillie

INTRODUCTION

It is difficult to write about a dynamic system, for where does one start? Every point under examination is the result of a balance of forces operating, and consulting is no exception to this. But it is also a component of larger systems and can only be considered within its setting. I regret that the larger and far from unimportant matter that such systems themselves operate in an environment, a causal texture, that has profound bearing on them, is one that I am unable to consider in any effective detail here. The ethical issues discussed later which arise in consultation are just one parameter within such a system, for they determine a mode of operation within it. Attending to them, assessing them, and being conditioned by them can have as its aim an optimally effective functioning of the system. Anyone currently practicing as a consultant or trainer must already have taken some position vis-/a-vis these facts, and will have done so, I suspect, more unconsciously than consciously. Therefore, to each one of us already practicing, an overriding question must be: Is my present position and practice the most efficacious one for me and for my clients? If not, to what extent am I free to change it? To begin to answer those questions necessitates looking at how I arrived in that position, how I am operating in it now, and what predictions can be made about the future, both mine and my clients'.

Hence, I aim to present in a pragmatic way some of the ethical issues of consulting, so that ethical or moral behavior can be seen to be justified, not because it is thought to be a good thing, but justified by being operationally valid, because it fits and arises naturally within the job in hand. In metaphoric terms, I wish to present them as something that minimizes friction and encourages the maximum effective output. I hope to present them as principles that have a general application to almost any task and not as doctrinal issues belonging to a system of belief. They are neither creed nor catechism. But since skill, expertise, and sensitivity are involved, quantitative and qualitative assessments of our position and performance in terms of standards cannot be avoided, nor should they be avoided, for they should be a shared experience of our professional development. The aim of these assessments could be to develop and improve an inbuilt quality: distinctive competence. In other words, I hope they will be seen to be professional behavior in its best sense, for their influence is a working definition of "professional" as I understand the term.

THE STARTING POINT

This outline is determined by attitudes that have now become second nature to me. I started a medical career forty years ago. As my chief formative experience, that career has given me a depth of human encounters, although its breadth is more limited. Those of you who have come from different disciplines and by different routes may not find that my assumptions carry the same weight or significance for you. But that does not diminish the need for all of us to ask questions. How do we come to be in our present position? In what direction, if any, do we wish to move? How can we best fit our behavior to our circumstances?

That a direct transposition from medicine is inappropriate is shown by the fact that in medicine in the U.K. nowadays one most commonly slips into an existing and prescribed consulting post, which is likely to carry restraints and fetters that may not suit the new incumbent. Calling him a consultant raises many questions about what a consultant really is; for example, most of his activities may turn out to be those of an executive or a specialist. How he gets clients is no problem under these circumstances. Either they will be queuing up already or else the provision of the new service will rapidly create demand. Before the National Health Service started, surgeons, for example, put up with many years of menial and unpaid or underpaid tasks because such tasks put them in the running for access to a lucrative clientele. As was true of the guilds of the past, medical intake is strictly controlled—so is advertising—and strong defenses are erected against competition; any threats of supersession evoke an enormously powerful conservative response. This may not yet apply to the world of the consultant in management issues, or in organizational development, for I doubt if many so-called O.D. consultants have yet progressed beyond the stage of barber-surgeons. It will, I believe, inevitably develop over time as supply begins to exceed demand, as science overtakes art, and most important of all, as the need develops for professional indemnity against actions for negligence.

But by saying this I lay myself open to even more indignant criticism that I present everything within a medical model (a term that is invariably unspecified when the argument is being rejected or attacked). My hope is that one professional experience may inform another. The mode of operation can be shared. The setting, as well as some of the tasks, may clearly be different, but if it can be specified then dialogue is possible. To facilitate that dialogue, I must define my use of terms and my positions as clearly as I can. As stated, they without doubt reflect a medical point of view, but in the ensuing discussion I shall try to illustrate their general application because the principles involved in consultancy in all its forms are shared in common and can therefore be established from it.

SOME DEFINITIONS

In any consulting relationship a minimum of two parties are to be satisfied. They operate within, and are bound by, a contract, which is either explicit or implicit. Although it is easier as a consultant to focus on things that belong to the client, the consultant's own satisfactions must not be ignored because many ethical issues arise from within that area. (The behavior of both parties will be studied in what follows.) When mishandled, ethical issues lead to contamination, so within any contract the aim should be to produce the maximum required effect with the minimum contamination. The things pertaining to achieving maximum effect need just as much study and emphasis as do those pertaining to contamination. Synonyms for the latter would be unnecessary disturbance, trauma, and pollution. Maximum effect, on the other hand, is often not achieved from want of effort for a variety of reasons, but not from want of skill. Sins of omission are no less important than sins of commission.

A consultant—and therefore a consulting organization—in practice operates a cluster of roles that are not always clearly distinguished from each other. He may make no attempt to do so, but a predictable consequence of this is likely to be future trouble, some forms of which may be classed as ethical issues. I use the term "consulting" for a particular role and will distinguish others by suitable names. More than one role may be appropriately occupied during the course of any contract; possibly only rarely will one be solely a consultant. It is of first-rank importance to know which role is the right one for the immediate task, the right one for a given moment.

The consultant's role is a service function: he is not an executive. He can exercise his role only by invitation. Hence how to get invited may be an issue. It may be offered but not imposed, which provides peculiar limitations and frustrations. If something is imposed, then a different role and different sanctions are in operation. Obviously, a consultant brings with him a whole range of ideas and wishes of his own, and he develops more of them as he is working. He may wish to be a missionary, a prophet; his gospel may be truly good news to his client. The client may receive and act on it, but the consultant is not a consultant in such action.

After the diagnostic phase, in the action or treatment phase, a specialist is often needed. Although this role is usually an executive one, it may be a training function. The specialist is an operator. It is important to be able to distinguish these roles and to recognize which one is most fitting. You may be sought out for your specialist skills because the client thinks that these will help, whereas you know that this cannot be taken for granted. They must be put to the test so that enquiry is by far the most important first step. It is no less important to recognize in which role you are cast at any given time, for it may be far from obvious. A match between role and task will do more than anything else to reduce the risk of undesirable side effects arising from your activities.

An expert is someone who is experienced in a particular matter. To be an expert is a quality you may have that enhances your carrying out of a task. Experience or special skills can be an impediment, for they can cause us to look for solutions prematurely if things are processed too exclusively in terms of that expert knowledge. That you are an expert will probably be an expectation held about you on the part of your client, deserved or not, because the client is likely to have heard of you or to have had you recommended to him. Hence your expertise and your client's fantasies about it are not the same thing, and one early task is to attempt to reconcile the two, almost as one might calibrate an instrument before using it. "You are the expert" must be one of the commonest opening gambits of an attempt to seduce you out of a proper consulting role into an inappropriate and ill-timed executive one—the first move in your eclipse. It succeeds so often because we are proud of our expertise, and pride precedes a fall. The term *specialist* is virtually synonymous with expert, but I shall try to use it to refer to someone practicing his skills in an appropriate executive way.

The term *trainer* is one that I abominate because I can never get out of my mind "trainer" used in the sense of lion tamer. Hence my misgivings, for that usage would indicate some highly questionable role activities. By derivation the word implies an executive role, and I shall try to restrict its use to a teaching function where teaching means managing, or facilitating learning.

A totally pervasive assumption on my part is the existence of unconscious behavior in persons, groups, and organizations. This requires as much investigation as any other form of behavior. It needs particular skills for the purpose and should be taken into consideration as much as any other factor in deciding on a course of action. Many of the things that I shall present as if they are consciously felt issues, are not so. While I cannot speak of them as being totally repressed, they will only be laid bare and possibly eliminated from the generation of conflict as the consultant is able to bring that which is hidden out into the open.

There are two bipolar pairs of things to be considered and balanced as you work within a contract. Your ethical position will influence how you do this. The first pair is the satisfaction of your needs and the satisfaction of the clients' needs, and the second pair is the achieving of maximum effect at minimum cost. Professional behavior in its best sense and what I am calling ethical behavior is that behavior that will lead to an optimal balance of these things. I repeat, optimal balance, because it can never be more than that. There is neither standard nor ideal. A consultant is responsible for his actions, and he is professional in that he is willing to be so. Neither does he seek to avoid being accountable for what he does in the contract.

THE CONTRACT—THE CONSULTANT'S PART

Let us begin by considering the satisfaction of our needs, for the balance is the basis of the contract between us. Inappropriate or undeclared aims or needs on our part, or of course on his, will either distort the contract or create two of them—a formal and declared one and a hidden and undeclared one, which may in fact be overriding. This is probably the most potent source of difficulty or failure.

A consultant's needs can only be understood in terms of his history. They will change as the phases of his history unfold. His personal needs must change with the development of his career and his personal life. Immediate pressures from his environment must assert themselves, even overwhelmingly so at times, but one measure of professional behavior lies in the degree to which he can operate appropriately, exercise his skills, regardless of these pressures.

Since one has to start somehow, an initial problem must be to get known. I suspect that we most easily get ourselves known through specialist or expert roles. The role of consultant is more likely to follow later. Hence it is by advertising, however covertly it is done, a specialist package, that work and recognition may be sought. Many clients like packages, just as many people like nostrums or patent medicines, and many consultants are in reality vendors of the same. But this need carries with it pitfalls that must be bypassed if survival is to be assured.

The ethical point involved here is not that these processes can be or should be totally avoided, but that each one of us has choice points at which we have to decide how they shall be met. Since one of the questions invariably to be asked is "Why have I been asked to help?" there must be some tension between my asking it, whatever the consequence is, and my need to have work, hence to have been asked in the first place. The consultant then not only needs to live but will also have his personal career and learning goals, and possibly his power and political ones as well. He needs fee-paying contracts to live. If ruin stares him in the face, he is at least tempted to take on work at any price simply because it pays. If he has an office and a staff dependent on his income the temptation must be stronger still. Some also need to feel wanted, for this gives some purpose to their lives. Although to have potential clients may seem to help this, any engagement undertaken with this need operating in chief may only really deceive in the end. A consultant's actual abilities and freedom may be compromised by undertaking an ill-considered task; the task itself may turn out to be a pseudo one or to have no real existence. Either a pseudo-solution is being sought by the client, which can be or will be used as a defense against something else, or the consultant may well be used as an instrument for someone else's undeclared policy, as a kind of camouflage for it or in an attempt to give it greater respectability. Pure consultation should lead to the laying bare of such issues, not to the world but to your client and to yourself. It will emerge anyhow in time, but most suitably it should come out in the inquiry phase, in the contract-making phase. But if you are desperate for work there is an enormous temptation to take short cuts through this. You are unlikely to make a friend if you expose his pseudotask; indeed, you may make an active enemy. With luck you may earn a grudging respect that could be useful in a really difficult spot later on. If it is custom that you need you will not be thinking in terms of enemies. A consultant who is starting up and wanting to be known is likely to be in this position and therefore subject to different pressures than is one whose diary is full. The first is more vulnerable to a kind of seduction from which he may come to the painful realization of being on the hook, of being involved in something very different from what he had expected. The second, because he is successful is at risk of living on a reputation that can tarnish with time, on means which become outmoded. For the busier he is the less time he has to be in touch with recent developments. So a further operational requirement of the professional is the need to maintain a continuing process of self-education by self-review and by sharing with and exposing himself to the scrutiny of his colleagues. In reverse this is a further definition of a professional and a criterion by which a judgment can be made about him. But our personal goals may include political ones, power ones as well. It should be easy to see that however legitimate they may be for the individual concerned, there is likely to be a fundamental conflict between them and operating in a true consultant role.

If a legitimate need of mine is to earn enough to live in the way that I like, then that need should be satisfied in full by my fee and my decision about my fee. Around this clusters a whole host of professional issues, because quite often other needs or other satisfactions are allowed to invade, with troublesome consequences. I sell a service, the client buys, although professional behavior serves the purpose of introducing human concern in a controlled and usable way. The fee also provides a self-respect base, a measure against which to balance our exploitation and other people's entirely human wish to get something for nothing. In a positive way it enables me to work with clients that I may dislike, in circumstances that I hate, but with whom I can do a professional job if I am not otherwise compromised. However hostile a client may be, if he is also paying, then there is direct evidence of an ambivalence of which the positive side can provide the means for effective work. Although commonest in neurotic patients, hostility can occur in any client relationship. A major task in consulting is to be able to handle negative feelings constructively.

A consultant service is likely to be if not a one-time thing, then a short-term one, while living is a long-term matter. You are likely to be anxious and insecure about the future from time to time unless you have continuing work to do. Hence fees in consulting and training, because the work is short-term, are high relative to those for other professional jobs. This creates an incentive to climb on the bandwagon and promotes jealousy of those already on, while it also encourages short cuts and inadequate preparation before starting the work. Since, however, the wise client will be assessing the value for money of the service he is receiving, especially in adverse times, or more importantly, in any negative phase that the relationship must go through, it is sensible to assess your own value realistically. However, one's fee should reflect that realistic self-assessment. If you ask for too little the client may rightly think that you don't think you are worth much.

A consultant's need to survive may imperil his real ability in a number of ways. Too much time may have to be spent looking for work. He may have to tout and at worst prostitute himself. Since it is whores and their keepers who make money, especially the latter, he is tempted by whoredom. That can be defined as taking on work that is profitable in cash terms but in no others—work that in fact compromises him, accepting work that offends against his own value systems. Riches, individual or corporate, enable a client to pay, but worse still to buy, servants. Among the jobs most worth doing are those with persons or institutions who are in no position to pay you adequately, which creates yet another conflict. It is possibly right to allow the rich to pay for the poor, but since you will be the arbiter of this you must therefore be prepared to defend your actions if they are discovered and challenged by either party, as they are very likely to be. There are also jobs in which we shall be working for our own elimination, which therefore postulates our future unemployment if nothing fresh turns up. A consultant working on a task but operating at the same time a covert secondary task either of keeping himself retained by his client, or of creating new work, is not only in dereliction of his role; but what he is doing will become obvious enough before long to those on whom he tries it, even if he is convinced of the subtlety of his methods. Our actions can wittingly or unwittingly create dependence in the client rather than encouraging autonomy and independence. Dependence created in the service of making us needed is sad indeed for the victim.

Problems arise through mixing business with pleasure, but specifically ethical ones come from seeking to gratify our personal needs, which are right enough in their place, through some agency of the client. That is a very different thing from getting pleasure and satisfaction from your work. To avoid this personal gratification may involve you in considerable forbearance and sacrifice. You may be in a position to make a fast buck because of information you have about a business. Your client may have something, or privileged access to something, in which you would very much like to share. There is only one decision required here. How much will your freedom of action, your objectivity, be compromised either in your own eyes if your client knows nothing of it, or in his eyes if he does? He may think you a fool if at first you don't yield to an offer that he makes. It may not be a conscious attempt to buy you or seduce you at first, but a well-meant offer. He may only think differently at the first appearance of negative feelings and then begin to use it differently.[a]

a. At the time of revising this paper (February 1976), this is exemplified by an ugly example slowly being uncovered to public gaze. In a very large land deal a few years earlier, the vendor's agent, adviser, and consultant arranged for himself to have 20 percent of the proceeds of the sale because it is said that the vendor wished to reward him for his services. That turned out to amount to three-quarters of a million pounds, enough to incite envy in others and possibly ideas of taking revenge, which are now materializing.

The principals involved have resigned from their partnership, may have to repay their gain, and are under police investigation. Their temporary gain may thus prove very bitter indeed, and whatever else happens they could well be disbarred from future practice by their professional association. The case has provoked a large correspondence in the *Times*, and I include a quotation from one letter, which outlines some of the points that I have already made.

In my opinion, the integrity of the stewardship that a professional estate agent owes to his client from the moment of his appointment is breached by any departure from the definitive rule, universally understood by the public, that the professional will use his skill and experience solely on his client's

The enormous and pragmatic value of uncontaminated professional behavior lies in the freedom that it gives you to operate easily when the going gets rough. It is precisely then that you need your full freedom of maneuverability, which you do not have if the client recognizes your hidden contract. Unfortunately, it may also only be then that you first realize that you were unwittingly bought earlier on. In reverse, if you employ a client to carry out some task you need, for example repairing your car, because he does it cheaply or for nothing, then if he does it badly or slowly and angers or disappoints you, your objectivity will be imperiled, for you are neither free to complain, nor can you demand the attention that you otherwise might.

Another area of our needs concerns interest and job satisfaction. This is as legitimate a wish for us as it is for the client with whom we may be working on work structuring, or job enrichment, or identifying more desirable and less fraught sociotechnical systems. I find my job so satisfying just because of the degree of interest that it constantly supplies, and even that is overshadowed by the occasions for personal learning and growth that it regularly gives. I am no longer the same person that I was before. I have been enriched in some way by the experience that I have been through. I am enormously grateful for having this opportunity. The fact that we get a great deal of satisfaction from our work should pay off well for the client, for the quality and impact of our work is likely to be enhanced by it. But that satisfaction is always a matter of balance. If it swings too far in the direction of a need to be satisfied, the need to be flattered, that need for flattery will begin to show in an attempt to put on a virtuoso performance. Because my personality is defective I can deny it by reassuring myself, by showing my prowess and having it recognized. There is certainly not much virtuoso possibility in an uncontaminated consultant role, for it is self-effacing. There is more opportunity as a specialist if I can make a virtuoso performance of my technique. There is always a conflict between a need to purvey packages, which primarily enable us to appear especially knowledgeable and efficient, and the effective meeting of our client's needs. Purveying packages is so often a defense on our part against anxiety and

---

behalf and will expect no greater reward than the recognised scale fee for the job. Conversely, if an individual practitioner wishes to change his role from that of a steward to that of a principal he should do so openly and permanently, so that it becomes a matter of public knowledge and removes any possibility of deception as to what his true motives have become.

Apart from the obvious need, both in the public interest and in the interests of my profession as a whole, to ensure that this dutiful relationship remains intact in every way, its preservation in unmistakable terms is also necessary in order to avoid the least possibility of actual harm being done to the interests of a client. Thus, in the case in point, from the very instant at which, as Mr. Guthrie alleges, the agent was promised participation in the profit of the transaction, it was in that agent's interest—even though he did not recognise it—to see that same profit enlarged as much as possible, and the most immediate step towards that end would have been a sale of his first client's interest at as low a price as possible.

uncertainty, a collusion into which the client's anxiety so easily pushes us. A virtuoso performance temporarily reassures him, but possibly denies reality.

There are other unhealthy gratifications that are therefore less desirable still. They belong almost exclusively to the role of group trainer, where the opportunity for their expression is only too open. I call unhealthy gratification that which meets a need of mine at the expense of the client. Some of its forms are unquestionably neurotic, but that is more a matter of degree than quality. I can parody George Bernard Shaw, who said: "He who can, does. He who cannot, teaches," by substituting "he who cannot, trains" and, although I hope not, "or consults." Is this activity a compensation for failure? I am always reminded of the question posed by those books that tell you how to become a millionaire, or how to win on the horses. Why then is the author writing it, rather than doing it? Training motives do need to be evaluated, and an opportunity for this should be part of a professional training program.

I can be what is in effect a voyeur by getting delight and satisfaction from the exposure of others whom I therefore encourage into further exposure by my questions, suggestions, and actions. Although a doctor has a particular opportunity to indulge this in the guise of doing his job, the wish to enter into therapeutic relations, or ones that are therapeutic in essence, crops up again and again in my experience with both consultants and managers. Our curiosity and the client's needs are not always in balance.

I may try to work out my own unresolved problems of sex role and gender identity, identifying too much with some aspects of either one sex or the other as they present in conflict or tension within a group. By that I have in mind, say, emphasizing or playing maternal or paternal roles when there is no real occasion for it, as well as showing inappropriate reactions to male or female attitudes, especially in the gender sense.

I may be so schizoid that I try to operate vicariously through the activities of others. Because I am dependent for my sense of purpose in that way, I have to have clients through whom to live.

Sadistic needs and behavior can be worked off on the client, especially in groups.[b] There is a special tension here between doing this and what I shall discuss shortly, the willingness to disturb and upset if it is truly in the client's interest.

Some of those things listed will be present in all of us, behind the reaction formation involved in our choice of this sort of work. It is neither wrong nor unethical if they are present; that only arises when they are dominant and

b. If you doubt this read the accounts of trainer behavior in Lieberman, Yalom and Miles, *Encounter Groups: First Facts*, 1973.

the client suffers. It becomes unethical if I am unprepared to do anything on my part to examine it and if need be to remedy it. However, it does not make sense to speak of the client in an unqualified way. His freedom is relative to his position. There is a difference between a hardboiled board of directors and a dependent training group (at times one is driven to say "not much"). The one ought to be less captive than the other; the one has more freedom to reject and should be less likely to idealize than is the other. The captive audience that we may have, especially in human-growth group work, needs the protection of our professional behavior from its own vulnerability. That should be a governing principle.

This must be true of sexual behavior, and I wish to consider it in just the same terms except that I particularly want to introduce sensitivity as well. This area is another that is relevant to a trainer role in particular, because in it propinquity operates in a way that is unlikely in consulting. Added to this, in one form of group activity of doubtful philosophy, whose alleged aim is human growth, sexual confrontations are more likely and may even be provoked so that both the opportunity and temptation are increased.

The sexual needs and maturity of a staff will vary from person to person and may vary in intensity at different times. We are also likely to operate in settings where we are more susceptible because we have to cope with our own feelings of loneliness and personal need when we are away from our usual personal environment. There will be different phases of activity and maturity in participants. We may be exposed to seduction pressures serving particular ends, be they to capture us for a particular advantage, to neutralize us, or to control us. Another manifestation may be rivalry or jealousy over us within the group or organization where the working out of infantile sexual conflicts occurs as a contaminant of the primary task. As trainers we are working with a captive audience, one that is dependently expectant and therefore vulnerable. It is not only those whom we may choose sexually who are vulnerable; an even greater vulnerability may be the lot of those not chosen, through their jealousy or their feelings of rejection.

I believe that what is sauce for the goose is sauce for the gander. What goes for staff-participant behavior is relevant for interstaff behavior. The same considerations apply to both. This is not handled any better when a staff lives in a kind of ivory tower, because that only encourages authority and superiority problems. The humanness and the peccadilloes of a staff are possibly the best corrective against the overidealization of it which exists. There will be fantasies galore about its sexual behavior. For these to be realistically worked through can only be hindered by behavior that encourages them. Here my beliefs about the existence of unconscious processes are evident. If you disagree then you are quite likely to deny the existence of unconscious sexual fantasies occurring in groups and of their being focused on staff behavior. This has a particular significance in therapeutic groups, but it is neither absent nor irrelevant in study groups or whatever you call them, especially if they have a pair of staff members attached to them. Our openness and the freedom to discuss such fantasies and to test them against reality provide one of the learning opportunities.

· I can only report second-hand on an aspect of this problem that illustrates a want of sensitivity. A mixed staff arrived to run a program, and an undeclared expectation was that they would share rooms, especially since it was easier to do so because of the sparse accommodation. A fuss was made because this exposure was objected to by the only woman staff member. This strikes me as pointing to a considerable insensitivity behind the whole plan. In its own context it doesn't matter a hoot, because a staff should be able to look after itself. But that same insensitivity is likely to operate for ill in much more important directions for the participants. Someone who cannot see, or who prefers not to see, that such a sharing may be an invasion of privacy, that it could stir up disturbing degrees of longing in the other, even if he repudiates its existence in himself, wants more than just a degree of sensitivity and can hardly be more sensitive in matters concerning the participants. There are problems for us in being sensitive to others' points of view, especially when they are more primitive, less enlightened than we believe ours to be; but it is precisely this that we are paid for and are accountable for.

All of this sounds like a pretty formidable and possibly daunting list, but our professional stance does not consist in being impeccable on all points. We ought at least to have considered them for ourselves and worked them over until we have achieved our own proper balance. Those negative factors are ones that we look to have exposed in a training program for consultants and trainers, not exposed to senior judges who scrutinize and weed out unworthy participants. It would be wrong to deny that they do form impressions and make judgments, but the exposure that counts is a self-disclosure, one that is to me the participant. That exposure should come through interacting with my peers who can spot, react to, and take up with me some of the problem areas and vice versa. The possibility of learning and of changing follows self-disclosure. The success of a training program and especially of its apprenticeship phase will be measured by its capacity to allow for the recognition and working through of defensive processes that might otherwise be projected onto the client in a less desirable way, and by its capacity to provide settings in which the widest range of exposures can occur.

THE CONTRACT—THE CLIENT'S PART

Even within strictly medical relationships the identification—who is the client and who is the patient—is not the obvious thing that it may seem. Even there the so-called patient may be presented by a third party, often a party with a vested interest who wishes you to intervene in the life and affairs of the alleged patient. Clearly this is a more usual state of affairs in business consulting. The true patient may be the person talking with you; the client is the person consulting you. Therefore, in whatever context he is operating, an identification of who is the client, who is the person or system toward which his attention and skill should be directed and for what purpose, is an essential feature of a consultant's assessment. There are therefore at least two ethical considerations. How does my behavior look to the client as meeting his needs, and, what may the client be trying to get me to do and is it right for me to do so?

A model of operation is this: that in exchange for a fee a consultant undertakes to lend his skill to assist in diagnosing some issue, and then possibly in exchange for an extended fee, lends his skill in initiating, implementing, and providing training for a particular task or operation—a role change. Hence in the terms of an English proverb which must be echoed in other tongues: "He who pays the piper calls the tune." The preponderant influence may reside with the source of your fee, to the possible hurt of the person/persons or work system to which your attention is called. Ethical issues may obviously arise if you are paid to be an agent of your paymaster's policy, or to help him sharpen his tools. You may be in total agreement with that policy, you may become convinced that in terms of fit, of its suitability to all the needs of the organization, it is right, and yet there will still remain the question of your relationship with those subordinates on whom you may depend for information and who will be affected by any ensuing changes from your work.

It hardly needs to be mentioned that if you are to get some consultative process going, to use some form of group-discussion technique, sanction for it has to be given. Real sanction may be given if it is thought that you can be trusted, but sanction that is more apparent than real is a sign that your trustworthiness is questioned. Consensus is a vogue word at the moment; therefore a consultant's question must always be: Is consensus really agreement and commitment, or is it a front effected under duress, which will fragment rapidly afterward and lead to conflict and loss of purpose?

Let us consider the first of these ethical points: How does my behavior look to the client as meeting his needs? For ethical standards are only one side of the same medal of which professional behavior is the other. I remember discovering that the best professional behavior for the client requires that you are at least prepared to go to the limit of your skill to achieve what he needs. I do not say, "thou shalt go to the limit" and even beyond. I do say that a client who chooses, or who ends up with, a consultant or specialist who is either unwilling to go to the limit, or who is unequipped to do so, will possibly get no more than a second-rate job done.

This will also depend on whether the task is simple or complex, straightforward or difficult. If it belongs to the complex/difficult category, then he will certainly get an inferior job done. The unequipped and the anxious can get away with a simple, straightforward job.

I discovered as a medical student that what distinguished the top specialist, the expert in a particular field, was that he examined the patient, not that he was a genius or a magician. Not only did he do it more carefully but he went on doing it, asking questions of himself when others had given up and had either expressed more cursory opinions, therefore much more likely to be wrong, or had begun to use plain uninformed guesswork. The surgeons, for example, who have left the most mark have done so by being heroic quite often, through trying out their skill to its anatomical limits, not by seeing how much battering a human being will stand, but by seeing how much can be achieved consistent with the maximum benefit for the patient.

In our appliance-dominated society you must have had the experience of a mechanic or serviceman who says at the first hurdle, "It can't be done." I prefer one who argues to himself that if something can be put together then it can be taken apart and so tries to do it; who argues that if it goes wrong then there must be a cause and systematically hunts for it and does not give up until he has found it. I may look as if I am saying that moral issues like sloth and avarice operate against the best work, and I suppose they do. But there is one particular negative influence, anxiety, which also does. If I trim my work and my counsel to avoid either my experiencing anxiety, or the client becoming anxious, to avoid situations in which I may be totally unsure and in the dark, then the client suffers. I am not advocating that the blind should lead the blind. I do advocate that we learn to navigate in the dark as a professional skill. No one is likely to be called into a genuine consultation unless the client is in a state of uncertainty. Things about which he is certain he can handle himself. Indeed, the absence of uncertainty might well lead one to question the motives of one's being involved. But if uncertainty is an integral part of the problem, then living with it and handling it is an issue for the consultant himself.

Anxiety should not be regarded as undesirable in itself. It has its value as an indicator and as an alerting mechanism. I have quite often seen in labs marked levels of anxiety operating at first in experienced colleagues in the same way that some actors and performers invariably have stage fright before they appear, no matter how experienced they are. Such anxiety usually makes the planning phase more tense and explosive. Insufficient time is allowed for this even if it usually subsides soon after work begins.

It is your misfortune if anxiety is enough to cripple you and leads to breakdown. It is the client's misfortune also if he has a consultant who breaks down. But that at least would be an observable event and one that could probably be rectified, although it might lead him to say, "Never again." It is a much greater misfortune for him if his consultant's avoidance of anxiety—in other words, of work that should have been done—if his avoidance of uncharted areas that are difficult, have led him to become a trimmer, because he, the client, may not realize that this has happened until it is too late. He may not be in a position at first to recognize a second-rate job.

There are many forms that this defensive avoidance takes. Most commonly it results in collusion, the collusion of presenting a package, prescribing a technique like management by objectives. The important point is not that these techniques are wrong. They are wrong when prematurely or inappropriately applied. They can lead to foreclosure so that adequate assessment and diagnosis are not made. They are also applied as universal remedies, so that diseases are made to fit treatments and not treatment made to fit a disease. In a lab it leads to the use of inappropriate gimmicks when the dynamics are crying out for interpretation. Games and exercises are easier to run than sweating out hostility that may be fully justified, dealing with flight, or tolerating the confusion that belongs to real unknowns. It leads to selection of totally inappropriate lab designs, or using inappropriate structures, as when things are done to fill out a program, to have an event, but are not carefully thought out or designed to achieve specific tasks. One example that I have commonly met with is an unwillingness on the part of an anxious staff to deal with intergroup or large-group problems, to relate events to an institutional context. Anxiety, fear, and embarrassment lead to compromise. Compromise invariably leads to missing something.

I have not mentioned confidentiality, which must be implicit. In training groups always, and in consulting to a lesser extent, one is in a very strong position to make recommendations to others about a member's suitability for a position, or some matter of selection. But if your clients are to be free to be open so that they may learn, there is an absolute conflict between these two things. Persecutory anxieties are a common enough cause of organizational difficulties, strife, and inefficiency. They are hardly to be discovered when the means used provokes them. Any intervention as a trainer or consultant will provoke them, and a major professional task is to resolve them. That we respect confidences and will not be used to the hurt of those with whom we deal becomes one of the chief means that we have to carry out that task. Of course, selection can be a valid specialist task if the victims know that they are being selected from. The same is true of any consultancy where consent and confidentiality are always to be considered. In group-training procedures we go to great lengths (sometimes probably to unnecessary lengths) to respect confidentiality by separating indviduals who know and work with each other. In in-company work this is likely to be impossible, yet it usually seems to go just as well. But for the consultant in these conditions, and for an internal one, the pressures to breach confidence will be greater.

I am often appalled at the indiscretion of medical doctors who speak about their patients when they should not. If you need to boast, it is hard if the only thing you have to boast about is your patients; but consultants in general cannot be totally immune from this hazard, for our clients are in a sense our product. Even when you legitimately want to translate an example from a past experience into a new investigation, it may be difficult to do so without disclosing identities. Obviously the context determines the issue. If you are called in to help a firm or an organization with its long-standing bad labor relations, that fact is likely to be public knowledge already, but if the chairman consults you because he is impotent, that is unlikely to be. But boasting belongs to getting known and to advertising, which were mentioned earlier. It may be a narrow point of view, but I am unhappy with those lists of clients put out on so many brochures. It does not seem to matter if it was only the office boy who was sent to the program; it is the name that counts. Evidently it is also hoped that you will believe that they were all satisfied customers. But the longer the lists, presumably the less often representatives of a client firm can participate, so that it seems that there must be many unsatisfied customers.

I need not specify other things that relate to a client's needs, for it is all summed up in the one concept that he requires their maximum satisfaction with the minimum of pollution in the process. This is not the same thing as it being painless. He may well have needed to look at things that embarrass and even hurt. But if I have used him to satisfy my desires, then I have exploited him. If I have done a clumsy job, then I have damaged him more than necessary. If I have left undone that which I ought to have done, then I have failed him. Fortunately, in human encounters there is a wide band of behavior that can be called good enough. One does not have to be blameless, nor perfect in technique. Errors do not necessarily cause irreversible results, especially when the error and its causes can be used for mutual learning, although it must be remembered that some errors will be lethal. However, lack of integrity may well lead to irreversible results, for that precludes my being open, and hence the opportunity for mutual learning.

Let us now consider the second type of relationship, where the client calls the tune. This is something much more likely to be met with in business consultations than medical ones, although less so than you might think. A doctor might be consulted by a wife who is at her wits end because her husband is alcoholic. "You must see him, doctor; he needs help; he will kill himself if you don't." When you are confronted with something that is so manifestly wrong it is so easy to step out of role and take up another one. You can call a husband and ask to see him, or drop in and then, at the most, perhaps get a lukewarm reception if not outright rejection. Certainly you will hear another side of the story. The true patient, however, may be the wife in front of you. She says that she is powerless to do anything to bring any influence to bear on him, but this needs to be examined. It will possibly be much harder to get her to see and accept what her role is in influencing, perhaps quite unconsciously, her husband's drinking. An example that sounds too ludicrous to be true if it were not so, was of a consultant who was offered a large sum of money by his client to persuade his wife that he wanted to, and was going to, divorce her and to tell her of the extremely generous settlement that he was making on her. But what was the real problem here? One certainly was why he couldn't do it himself, and to find himself confronted with his responsibility is unlikely to endear his consultant to him—at least at first.

Rather than becoming his agent, a consultant should help his client to define that area of operation for which he is responsible, in which he has freedom of movement, that area in which he is free to determine events and in which it is chiefly his actions that would influence their course. In a sense this is work within the here and now. You may seem to have to isolate him from a wider environment in order to focus on his area of action and responsibility and to avoid being manipulated into being an agent. Nevertheless, the consequences of your joint actions on the total organization, especially if misperceived by it, cannot be overlooked; and there must be awkward decisions to take and to live with. There are some medical circumstances in which doctors are ethically empowered to deprive persons of their liberty, but almost always only when called in by someone else to help. These are on two counts: (1) to initiate a process of treatment where the patient's reason is so impaired because of his mental state that it is believed he cannot decide rightly for himself; (2) to remove the patient as an agent of society where the patient is thought to be a danger, or at least a grave disturbance to society. Lassa fever is a current example where statutory powers have just been granted to compel suspected persons into isolation. An intermediate area is where he is thought to be a danger to himself, hence in need of protection. One is not only dealing with impulsive, violent, or self-destructive behavior, but with, for example, denying people the right to drive a car and even more an airplane if they suffer from epilepsy or some other condition that could impair their consciousness. What must be noted is the existence of two contractual relationships that may be in conflict; that between doctor and patient, and that between doctor and society. Hence, then, also consultant and employer, and consultant and employee. The ethical issue is most sensitive if the doctor in such a case is unwilling to stand by his actions and decisions in face of resentment, rage, or litigation on the part of the injured party, and uses his status to stay remote and not allow himself to be challenged. If you are approached with problems of this kind, the professional issue is to do justice as far as it can be done to both, or to all, parties involved in it.

Consultancy will very likely at times involve conflicts over what rights an individual has over a group, or a part over the whole, in any setting. Consulting when client-centered does focus on the part's needs regardless of the whole. In a way this tends to split you as a consultant into that part occupying a role, and that part of you—the citizen or member of another group—who may be affected by the results. You can vote with your feet if you are aware of issues before you begin. A colleague refused a consultancy with a pet-food firm because he had very strong feelings about the morality of such a business in the face of world hunger. However, things may only emerge clearly after you have become engaged in the work. The blood is on your head if you accept an engagement for a specific task, the value of which you question beforehand. Whereas your professional disengagement, or your redefinition of a task and your getting sanction to work on that, may lead to more opportunity for learning on the client's part than much else that happens.

The first paid consultancy in which I was engaged was with the owner of a group of companies who had a therapeutic bee in his bonnet. Therapy groups and individual sessions ranged throughout the organization. There was a metaphoric if not an actual couch in the managing director's office, as well as its proper accoutrements. Needless to say, it had turned out like this, and was operated like this, through a charitable and enlightened idea on the owner's part—a wish to help and not just to exploit. For the employees, fear and dependence on him created apparently willing victims —victims who were in need, because they were victims of his behavior as well as having entirely independent problems of their own. I was hired to participate in this and to replace a misguided colleague who had died in the midst of, and possibly partly because of, being involved in total role confusion. It was brought to an end because the owner was an enlightened man who could see the role confusion that he was creating when it was pointed out to him. Its ending did not signal the end of my services. It led to my being consultant within the organization, on its organizational problems of which the persons were a part; not with personal therapy, through which it was hoped that people at screaming point would be able to endure the most cockeyed organizational structure and the highly impulsive but even more highly profitable actions of the owner, who knew no role boundaries. The victims certainly needed protecting, but that never arose as something requiring a moral challenge to the boss but could be handled entirely through defining the primary task and testing the consequences of the role confusion. Therapy, if that is the word, could legitimately be applied to the organizational meetings but not to individuals in nonspecifically therapeutic settings.

It was a salutary lesson in other ways. The term "change agent" is strangely persistent, even though "plus ça change, plus c'est la même chose" has a much more respectable ancestry. Presumably it is persistent because it represents omnipotent fantasies that are in the constitution of all of us. There was much "change" in terms of new business organization and new reporting structures, but there was even more "même chose" in the owner's behavior where his entrepreneurial talents exceeded those of anyone else around him. When at last it came to selling the business for a very enviable profit, the conflict of interests was manifest and inescapable.

The story has another good side, which by no means always happens. Obviously, you hope that you have been engaged to carry out a work task, but you may be engaged to legitimate a ploy of the client's. You may be engaged to take the blame if things go wrong. You may be engaged as a defense against action. A semblance of intention and of action can be well masked within the operation. Best of all is to be engaged in a real work task of the client who does seek for help with what he does not yet understand. The client that I have described had the integrity to see some of the things that he was doing and then desist. In terms of the surreptitious tasks in that list, if you fail to discover their existence you do a bad job. If you do discover them and point them out, you may be hated for your pains. For as Jesus said of the world that hated Him: "Now they have no excuse for their sin."[c] In group training in particular, the strongest resistance you ever meet is caused by this.

This story does illustrate another feature. I was involved first because I was a psychoanalyst and these skills were dear to the owner's heart and relevant to the task as he saw it. He was in fact a therapist *manqué* and I realized as time went on that for my part perhaps I was a manager *manqué*. He engaged other consultants who were close colleagues of mine to work in the area of his operation on his management structure. The boundaries of my operation as he saw them were not the boundaries that I, or we for that matter, thought were the right ones as the work developed. I moved out of, indeed had never entered into, a therapeutic role and into management consultation; but the fact remains that I was engaged because of a known skill that he thought he needed. It could just as well have been because I belonged to a known or recognized consulting organization that was thought to have the answer. There must be a critical task for the consultant of matching the client's expectations, and more especially any misguided preconceptions both with his actual abilities and with those that are needed for the assignment. To be hired as a wizard is asking for trouble, for magic can never be repeated twice, whereas sound work can.

c. John 15.22, Revised Standard Version.

Consulting in industry is therefore very likely to involve your being hired by someone to act, maybe within his territory, but upon others who are in a dependent relationship to him. Mishandling of some ethical problems is likely to arise if you do not even think that there may be painful consequences for some of them in such a course of action. Handling them will involve, not denying the issues, but recognizing them, weighing the possibilities, and choosing the course that minimizes unnecessary conflict and pain for all who are involved.

RECAPITULATION

As a consultant, I am used by the client. My activities are designed to facilitate his self-discovery.

This carries problems over my gratification because I am an enabler—catalyst rather than agent. It is a self-denying role, hence implicitly insecure. Ideally it carries no kudos. Indeed, the client may neither wish to acknowledge my help nor my existence afterwards. When you see problems and possible solutions, it can be frustrating that no one either asks you to help or takes up the ideas you express, especially if you work internally.

As a specialist I work on the client, or in his systems using my expert knowledge to assist in effecting the change that he needs. A particular hazard to avoid is the temptation to try to impose what I think he needs rather than what he needs.

As a trainer I regard myself as trying to teach through experiencing, and as both providing and possibly managing an opportunity to learn about both these roles for the group with whom I am operating.

These roles are carried out in the fulfillment of tasks that take place within a contract between the client and the agent. Although this contract may be more undefined than defined, an essential feature of sound consultancy does consist of trying to identify it, examining it, and making it operationally fitting. Forces on both sides can distort the contract, and the most effective and expeditious work cannot take place within a defective one.

CONCLUSIONS

I wish ethical behavior to be seen to be apt to one's freedom and effectiveness in filling these roles. By analogy, I regard a car as a good one not if it is luxurious, handmade, and expensive, but if it goes in the direction I put it and holds the road under adverse conditions, if it has power enough to accelerate out of trouble and brakes good enough to stop it quickly and in a straight line, if it does all these things while enclosing me in a comfortable and unobtrusive way, and not least if it does all these things at the least cost to me. You will agree that that is a tall order for a car and that such a car probably does not exist, but if one should fulfill those conditions then it will have earned the right for me to put my trust in it.

Let me apply that operational approach to these various roles. As a consultant you need a mind as unencumbered as possible—and even more so if the work you do is sensitive and complex—for you to be free to follow where the client is leading. At the same time, the fuller it is with experience, of hypotheses about action within systems, the more you will be able to link what you hear with what you contain and so bring forth new ideas. You are likely to be required to be sensitive to subtle political pressures and to operate in areas of uncertainty in which things only just begin to take shape. Your freedom and maneuverability will be hopelessly compromised if you become entangled in personal relationships or in the pursuit of personal advantages. You must therefore decide if freedom and maneuverability are desirable or even essential to your work.

Equally as a specialist the client needs to have found out enough about me, and for me to have given him the chance to do so, for his cooperation and trust to be actual and real, rather than based on idealization or on overdependence. In many training activities, the word *trust* is loosely bandied about like a commodity. In fact, I have to earn the right to be trusted. Trust cannot be bought by the gallon.

Chapter 11

Group Dynamics in Germany: Cooling the Marks Glamorously and Leaving the Structures Untouched

Hubertus Hüppauff

Any attempt to discuss West Germany as a working field for group dynamics elicits an ambivalent reaction from me. With my colleagues I have worked in this country for many years, and sheer self-respect forbids me to say that it has all come to nothing. But concrete successes in this field are difficult to pinpoint because everything is possible, just as in other fields like gastronomy, electronics, technical aphrodisiacs, industrial-refinery techniques, neoimperialistic finance policy, and so forth.

West Germany long ago achieved its most urgent post-war dreams, even its desire "to be just as great as the United States." Nevertheless, a sense of lagging behind remains. A glance at the advertisements in psychosocial journals makes it clear that any affluent person with unsatisfied needs for social contacts can easily find a solution, whether the desire is for sensory extension, curing of enuresis, group sex or therapy for married couples, intensive massage, experience-based learning, or simply a vacation on a sailboat. The interest in such offers gives group dynamics in West Germany its best opportunity to compete with other social events like dancing, movies, and gambling.

This chapter, originally titled "Gruppendynamik in Deutschland: Trosthandwerk innerhalb unangetasteter Konfliktstrukturen," was translated from the German by Trygve Johnstad. The title refers to an article by Erving Goffman, "On Cooling the Mark Out—Some Aspects of Adaptation to Failure," in *Human Behavior and Social Processes*, edited by Arnold M. Rose (Boston, 1962), pp. 482–505.

It is doubtful, of course, that this glamorous scene was really what the first group-dynamics initiatives were heading for, especially if one considers oneself, as I do, a conservative EIT representative of group dynamics, trained by one of the pioneers in our field who got to know Germany as a reeducation officer deeply engaged in the "denazifying of the common citizen." But we can meet even this kind of skepticism by referring to the considerable scientific reputation attached to our field of work. Some colleagues have university chairs or are working as lecturers or researchers. There is an endless amount of group-dynamics literature—some of it of very sophisticated scientific design. Special volumes of the basic series of psychological handbooks are dedicated to group dynamics, its pioneers, and its development. And the professional associations and representatives of other disciplines who sponsor the official scientific banquets invariably invite "their" group-dynamics people.

Thus even the conservative skeptic, dissatisfied with the fashionable "touch-and-feel" group dynamics of California origin (or even worse, with its plagiarism), finds that we have an excellent assortment of recognized scientific work at our disposal.

In this chapter we will explore the relationship between, on the one hand the scientific and consumer market for group dynamics, and, on the other hand, the real dynamics of West Germany—the dynamics of its social development and the problems inherent in this development.

SOME GERMAN HISTORY WITH ITS RECURRENT STRUCTURES

In the period of modern German history that immediately preceded its present society, the varying governments have all confirmed the principle of the state and its representatives as the authorities and the citizens as their subordinates. This obvious distinguishing mark of the empire went unchanged during the Weimar Republic, established as it was by the propertied classes. It found its perversion in the Fascist Third Reich and is also evident in the construction of today's republic.

Attempts to put a stop to this tendency for social power to increase, and to introduce a more free and open type of social organization, failed because of restoring alliances that were similar in structure. In 1830 and 1848 the aroused citizenry, strengthened by the development of commerce, were suppressed in their attempts to claim political rights by the powerful princelets and by massive military activity in the name of "representatives of law and order." Although the citizens never conquered this alliance, the management of the national states of the grand dukes permitted the commercial power of the citizens to work in their interests, leading to the foundation of the German Empire in 1871.

At the end of this first empire, the revolutionary movement, exhausted by wars and disappointed in the monarchy, once again saw its political claims overthrown by an alliance between conservative attitudes and military power. Faced with the threat of a democratic movement, the social-democratic leader, President Ebert, entered into a coalition with the openly politically reactionary defenders of the empire—the old monarchistic clique—that ultimately led to the official repression of all independent impulses from the people.

In 1945–1949, after the destruction of the Nazi state, something very similar happened. The liberation from the yoke of Fascist despotism nourished strong tendencies toward a far-reaching liberation from officially based authoritarian traditions. In this anti-Fascist postwar atmosphere, the excitement of realizing that the Nazi rule was over and that one was safe mingled with the political ideas of members of the Resistance who had survived the concentration camps, and also with the traumatic memories the workers and wage earners still retained of the disputes between their political organizations, the Social Democratic Party and the Christian Democratic Party, shortly before the Nazis seized power.

For many people these memories led to pangs of conscience that they hoped to eliminate by the development of agreement and solidarity. But this common wish for renewal had no real chance to succeed. Even before it had been organized into a political power, it was actually bought off by an alliance between liberal and conservative German politicians and American capital (the Marshall Plan). The victorious soldiers' distrust of the defeated ones and their resulting inability, immediately after the war, to distinguish Nazis from anti-Fascists led them to rely on well-known, established professional politicians. This psychosocial management of a social situation incomprehensible to the victor was soon connected with the Allies' interest in using their capital that was no longer tied up in war production. The sudden material blessings of the Marshall Plan were irresistibly seductive for many Germans tired of the miserable living conditions in their bombed-out country.

In the eagerness of the Allies to finance the reconstruction of Germany in this way, the consequences for social reconstruction were forgotten; and the beginning of the Cold War permitted the diversion of critical deliberation and the resecuring of the old modes of authority. This time the authority, instead of the emperor or the propertied middle class, was the Americans—democratic models from the "free world." The focus of this model was that of keeping down Beelzebub, the Stalinist system of the "communist world." The exceedingly rapid change in Germany's status from conquered enemy to esteemed ally offered legitimation through success and blurred the fact that the division of the world into good and bad only stimulated the use of the traditional authority scheme as a domestic-organization model for the development of the republic. The political union desired by the SPD and KPD could now be disavowed as a hazardous illusion by pointing to the Stalinist policies of the zone occupied by the USSR.

This domestic propaganda, even today denounced by the SPD, did something unnecessary in order to repress the hopes of anti-Fascists for a better society and to let the old middle-class conservatives have their will in the restoration of a society based on the authority of the state. What the Marshall Plan and the Allies' decisions—determined by the Cold War— meant for the state's thinking, Lucky Strikes and nylon stockings meant for the restoration of the everyday culture. Ever since the falsely exuberant 1920s the Germans had been unaccustomed to living with the consumer goods now suddenly offered by the occupiers. Soon the level of immediate-need satisfaction was passed, and the goods became gadgets and innovations in a status-oriented culture. Instead of developing a distinct social structure, a distinct culture, and proper social values, the Germans imported American patterns in the form of a "democratic model" and overlaid these on residual monarchist and Nazi elements. The same thing happened in the Eastern zone, except that there political and cultural patterns imported from the USSR were used as anti-Fascist models.

In the second half of the 1940s the politics of the occupiers, the development of the Cold War between them, and the construction of a divided Germany as the arena for this Cold War, were decisive factors in precluding a distinct political and cultural development. Instad, structures representing the various outside interests were restored. In the original Western zone and later Bundesrepublik, the only structures accepted were those built on the principles of individual contribution and profit, the values of the propertied middle class. Thus the common people, who had to accomplish the practical work of the reconstruction, once again had no margin for alternative developments based on anti-Fascist principles.

This policy, although indisputably successful from a commercial point of view, was directly responsible for the lack of a unique German identity, which became evident when the Cold War ended. In addition a political unconsciousness and an indifference to psychosocial needs developed to a degree that was fatal for democratic claims and that led to a social crisis in the second half of the 1960s, a crisis whose impact is still felt today.

These developments can be better understood when we compare them with similar kinds of development that have taken place in small groups and social systems with which we have worked as consultants or interaction trainers. The structure-related view that is central to group dynamics offers a paradigm for understanding and interpreting social developments of this kind. Studies of small groups and organizations reveal how sensitive and vulnerable the constitutional process is—how easily groups can be diverted from the strain of developing their own goals, norms, values, and distribution of functions and roles, through the acceptance of outside models or through the pressure that stems from the competition with others. But we also know that one consequence of such diversion and acceptance of alien models is the creation of a potential for dissatisfaction and latent conflicts. This is expressed in tensions that are often difficult to understand, in irritability, and in all kinds of flight behavior that eventually hinders the development of integration and cohesivness in the group. "Common interests" come to be defined as being against a common enemy or competitor. And when the presure of the task or the threat of the common enemy decreases, this discussion with others is soon replaced by a fight among the group members.

This type of group experience characterizes the development process of German postwar society. Interference with its attempts to reconstitute itself, and with the elaboration of diverse efforts to come up with something new and better, was carried out in the form of a series of influences from the victors—always understandable and further caused by internal tensions and by the search for allies and for outposts in developing the front lines. One might say that the real German contribution to restoration was to permit the front line between the formerly allied, now hostile, victors to be placed in the conquered land, and to let both sides develop their occupied zones into fortresses. The Cold War slogans were well suited to this purpose, with West Germany as the "show case of the free world" and East Germany as the "first socialist state on German land." And this scene was repeated in miniature in the divided city of Berlin, with its western half as the "bulwark of the free world" while the East was declared the "capital of East Germany."

This historical situation caused many difficulties in the development of West German society. First, there was the political and cultural "peace of the grave" that characterized the 1950s. At that time the dominant idea was that of reconstruction. All forces were engaged in this difficult task— so thoroughly that no time was left for the reunion of the family when father came home from prison or a family member moved from East to West Germany. Nor was there time for the integration of refugees in new communities or for the upbringing and emotional protection of one's own children. The results have been seen since the end of the 1960s in an increasing number of young addicts as well as in an increasing number of "dropouts" whose own structure is so poorly developed that they are incapable of an independent discussion with their parents or any other independent development.

At this time one could already see clearly how the emphasis on material restoration and the concomitant neglect of the dynamics of social processes had their negative consequences. The considerable social upheaval caused by the migration of millions of people soon led to isolated political interest groups—isolated because of their intrusion into old regional cultures and their attempts to bring with them parts of their home cultures. These interest groups were, however so efficiently manipulated by the establishment that they either got lost in the mass parties (in the name of "integration") or turned into right-wing sects led by vindictive politicians. Their annual appearance in national reunions heavily reinforced the Cold War atmosphere and simultaneously freed the ruling politicians from formulating similar claims. Thus the interest groups were offered the possibility of acting as mediators between the different social powers. The hostility of the old inhabitants toward the refugees still has not been overcome. It was only in the concentrated urban centers with their especially rapid development in all areas of society that the mistrust of the workers emigrating from Yugoslavia, Greece, Turkey, Italy, Spain, and Portugal could vanish.

THE LEGITIMATION CRISIS OF
THE POSTWAR SOCIETY: THE INHERITORS
AS SCAPEGOATS

In the early 1960s we saw the first gradual changes, starting with clear signs of weakness in the "Christian-democratic states" established under the rigorous leadership of Adenauer. The first indications of structural change in the society were technologically conditioned and were seen against the background of the new prosperity. Traditional middle-class behavior patterns were first attacked at the universities by young intellectuals, and this developed into a massive accusation against the entire generation of the "restoring fathers." This sharp debate was also expressed in demonstrations and in the first confrontations with the police. But for the most part it was a dignified intellectual discussion, its quality demonstrated by the influence of the "Frankfurter School" (Adorno, Horkheimer, Marcuse, Habermas) in German universities at the time.

Cracks in the structure of postwar German society were revealed by the different processes of change in the political-economic, technological, and ideological spheres. In the mid-1960s these fissures enlarged, and the economic crisis of 1966–1967 (one of the cyclical crises of overproduction and exploitation that had recurred every three to five years since the beginning of the restoration) became the central point around which this development crystallized. This movement introduced the idea of the bankruptcy of Christian Democratic policies and their claims of state power. It led to the entry of the Social Democrats into the government (under circumstances comparable to those that gave rise to the "historic compromise" in Italy in the 1970s). It thereby made public the vacuum that had long existed in the opposition and the legitimation crisis of the groups then in power. The leaders of the postwar society were seen as ridiculous followers of the morally bankrupt "free-world" ideology of the Americans. During the Vietnam War, even at the point when neoimperialism and the murder of a people could no longer be overlooked, the reports in the Germman mass media were second to none in their cynical acclamation of American policy. Heretofore these negative aspects of middle-class society had been dealt with primarily in intellectual analyses, but now the immediate confrontation extended and made concrete the protest of the youth into a broad movement of opposition that already, in its name and its obvious extraparliamentary opposition, expressed its defiance of authority. The opposition never became an organization in the true sense of the word, but was rather a broad movement where the tone was no longer set by the generous differentiations of the earlier academic critique, but rather was characterized by a search for alternatives, for a way out of the social system. The official anticommunist doctrines of the Cold War became more offensive as the Marxist way of thinking was revived and introduced in the universities. This was done, however, in a way that reflected not the strictness of this science but rather an omnipresent outrage at the established system expressed through provocative caricatures of its rituals. The predominant word was "disclose." The uncertainty inherent in this departure for a destination still unknown (for no one was so presumptuous as to concretize the goal, apart from —naturally—the orthodox communists, whose attempts to do so met only with resistance), and the frustrations encountered in the search were acted out in angry attacks on the badges of postwar middle-class society.

The extension of this rebellion to a generalized youth movement took place with breathtaking rapidity. The more dramatic occurrences developed—as always in processes of this kind—from the inadequate reactions demonstrated by those under attack, combined with their inability to take part in a productive discussion. Events like the death of a demonstrator against the shah of Iran, who was shot by a policeman, and the near-fatal wounding of a student leader, Rudi Dutschke, who was shot by a youth with nationalistic delusions, led to the growth of a dynamic force, totally out of the hands of the intellectual leaders, who could no longer even catch up with, let alone control, what was going on. The gates were opened that had contained all the psychic impoverishment of these youths who had been brought up with unusually little warmth and attention from parents preoccupied either with the restoration of society or with the related struggle for "success." These youngsters had been brought up and educated in obsolete, hierarchically structured institutions, educated for entrance into a technologically emancipated world of consumption. The discrepancy between the norms of a "youth market" on the one hand (Coca-Cola, Elvis Presley, mopeds, petting), and the rigid mores of the parents on the other, was reflected in the subculture created by the young people. They were preoccupied with all kinds of protests, "countercultures," and models for active opposition against the adult world, perceived as their own dubious —and empty—future.

This mass movement among the youth soon developed a consciousness of its own internationalism. Its impetus toward resistance also gave it an intoxicating productivity—of experimental communities; antiuniversities; "liberation" of students and apprentices who left their families to join collectives; demonstrations; and hectic but intensive reading and political discussion, in which even the most remote examples of both successful and miscarried revolutions were excavated from the history of the labor movement and discussed. Everything nourished the hope that progress in understanding would correspond to a real revolutionary change in the surrounding society.

But the events of May 1968 in France provided the unequivocal lesson that there was no foundation for a revolutionary change in other social groups, and that the hope of seeing the uprising extend to the workers and the petty bourgeoisie was unfounded (or seemed so immediately after May 1968). The overwhelming majority of members of these classes paid large monthly installments for their various acquisitions. And the prospect of a serious crisis in the capitalist system was poor, because constantly increasing automation of plants made capitalism more and more flexible and because the neocolonialism characterized by transfer of production to countries with cheap labor was more subtle than that demonstrated by the United States in Vietnam.

The understanding that there would be no revolutionary changes or renewals in the immediate future penetrated only very slowly. The reaction to this fact and the resistance against it led to a collective inversion, with extraordinarily destructive consequences for social development in Germany. The degree of depression and alarm within the "official society" against which the revolt had been directed is probably impossible to counterfeit experimentally, although abortive struggles for power and their repercussions in the form of dull counterdependence in group-dynamics laboratories can reach a level of tension that is no longer bearable for many participants (and for many trainers as well). But the social reality I am talking about here is worse than the collective depressions and abreactions found in experimental settings. This may be the reason that there seems to be so little chance for a rational discussion with opponents or minorities who feel themselves shunted aside and left with only self-assigned tasks or terror, as in Germany today. Obviously, the escalation of the dispute and the simultaneous disguise of the real power potential in these fights around class, generation, or even belief should not be brought to the point at which the opponents no longer have a chance to see that their position at least has some validity even though they are not winning.

In postwar Germany there has been a strong managerial ideology of avoiding, insofar as possible, any discussion with society's critics, and instead have them treated pragmatically—as tasks for the administration. This reaction from the established society and its administration to the uproar of the late 1960s and early 1970s revealed an overtaxation of the ideology and led to a basic shaking up of the democratic pretensions of the administration. In the mid-1970s we find that Germany's social problems have long since passed the stage of a legitimation crisis and now represent a full-blown socioeconomic crisis. The old reproach that the purely psychological interpretation of the uproar as a generational conflict failed to recognize the seriousness of the resistance now becomes justified in a new sense. The postwar leaders, who made room only for commercial initiatives and who tried to buy themselves free from social problems by raising the budget (according to the model of "reparation payments" to concentration-camp survivors or their dependents), who sought to reduce infrastructure development to what was technically possible, are no longer successful but instead create new problems constantly. Such procedures are in need of urgent revision. Instead of provoking the implacable resistance of nuclear-power opponents, protectors of nature, regional autonomists, socialists, and so forth, those in leadership should make use of the constructive alternative solutions proposed by these groups. Otherwise, shaken by the structural crisis and in real need of such outside help, the leadership may become choked in technocratic centralism, thereby redeeming Orwell's prophecy in *1984*.

As a potential culturalrevolutionary mass movement, the extraparliamentary opposition could have been of substantial aid in the shaping of the social future, which, as it has developed, now appears unpromising and formless. But the leadership erred in relying on the managerial ideology: "We will soon bring that under control." This ideology, imported as part of the "democratic" model, demanded reactions to any social task as free from emotion and as rational as possible. In retrospect this attitude appears to be the fulfillment of Mitscherlich's diagnosis made in the late 1950s: that Germany was a "fatherless society" in which one could no longer find immediate confrontations or personal discussions and in which, consequently, responsibility could never be handed over from person to person. Today we can recognize how the leadership hid, when under attack, behind a technologically based control, and how the "fathers" denied their personal responsibility by referring to technocratic necessities—the modern form of the old belief in authority.

Thus the potentially productive dialogue between the youthful subculture, on the one hand, and on the other the dominant culture of the parents, was thwarted, leading to a disintegration of the subculture into a variety of groups of various sizes and extremely different natures, having in common only a growing tendency toward sectarianism and isolation. The most complex and disturbing variant of this was the development of a conspiratorial underground inspired by the South American model of guerrilla warfare. Aided by the clumsiness and rigidity of police reactions, these groups embarked on a criminal career, leading to the "terrorism problem" of today. The militant ideological sects of the different communist parties and groups, although by no means criminal, are hardly less self-destructive and dangerous. These groups, numbering in the hundreds or even thousands, are in constant rivalry with one another over the supposed "correct line" of the political avant-garde; their political practice, meanwhile, has regressed from their former attempts at political agitation around crucial social problems, to their current role as the bugaboo of the middle class—a role consistent with the earliest patterns of the Cold War. What all these groups have in common is their gradual decline into social isolation, which has come about partly because they wanted to separate themselves and partly because no one listened to them any more. In this situation, most of the victims remain anonymous. They are disillusioned and disoriented young people who form—together with a number of adults—a kind of subcultural domestic emigration. They are seen to be counterdependent and hampered by severe depressive neuroses. They test out one underground movement after another and build a special pseudointellectual subproletariat with no connection to the actual economic situation. They have transformed their earlier impulse toward protest into a chronic turning against everything—ultimately, against themselves.

THE MATERIAL CRISIS OF THE SYSTEM AND THE IDEOLOGICAL REPETITIVE COMPULSION

The period of this development, from the beginning of the uproar to its decline, was characterized in Germany by an unusual economic boom. The recovery from the serious economic recession of 1966–1967 already showed some of the symptoms that illustrated how very different the development was in different parts of the society. The importance of the workers and the petty bourgeoisie threatened by proletarianization was evident in the discussions and the strategies of the extraparliamentary opposition. On the one hand, this had to do with the distinct orientation of the opposition toward Marxist positions and Leninist revolutionary theory. On the other hand, a strong moral motive also played a role for those who talked about the Marxist idea of "alienation." They felt obliged to help and support the proletariat in freeing itself from the yoke of capitalist criteria for action. In connection with the annual wage negotiations in 1968–1969 there was a strange stirring among workers, never before seen in the Federal Republic. In large numbers they suddenly turned back the usual unreasonable demand from the employers that the workers should secure the economic upswing by accepting modest wage increases, thereby enlarging investment capital. The workers even attacked the utterly bureaucratic process of negotiation and, for example, made their union leaders responsible for the uneven distribution of the fruits of the restoration. The extraparliamentary opposition at best declared verbally its solidarity with this development, but it did not take any active part in the very large strikes that followed. Naturally, there were groups who tried. For example, there was a conspiratorial idea that intellectuals should secretly take jobs as industrial workers in order to be able to act from the floor. There was, however, no coalition between the workers and the extraparliamentary opposition that could provide a model for collective action. Struggle for higher wages and protest against the system were such different lines of interest that it was impossible to follow up protestations of solidarity and intellectual understanding with any kind of practical mutual support.

Instead, it was the so-called structural area, that is, the institutions giving structure and constitutional reality to society, that became the arena for practical consequences of the uproar. In these institutions there were and still are numerous liberal intellectuals, business people, journalists, politicians, and educators who welcomed the renewing impulses of the uproar and tried to follow them up. With the adversity that followed the economic boom and the strong call for sociopolitical reforms and innovations in all areas that came about with the change to a Social Democratic government, and especially with Willi Brandt's integration efforts, the opposition was stimulated to take initiatives that would have been unthinkable in the former Christian Democratic state. In this way many critical impulses were translated into efforts toward reform carried out by those who shared the revolutionary impulse but did not actually tend toward revolution; their backgrounds in institutions and professions made them supporters of evolutionary change. Previously introduced reforms, for instance in education, were now accelerated and enforced. Areas that had previously been untouched were now brought up in public—health care, the doctor-patient relationship (especially in psychiatry), the structure of the small family and its mode of childrearing, the construction of homes and towns, the relationship between industrialization and the environment, and others. It was a time for concrete criticism and search for change.

This "long march through the institutions," as the slogan went, was the real outcome of those years; but for success it required cooperation from all institutions. On the one hand it was necessary to adapt sufficiently to the established enterprise to be able to change it from within, and on the other hand it was important to have enough flexibility and clarity about one's aims not be swallowed up by the institution. Only a few were capable of a task that imposed such burdens. Most found themselves alone on their outposts and could not make their protest concrete in real discussions. The most differentiated arena in which the revolution could be put into practice continued to be the universities. All the other battlefields never developed confrontations that could lead to lasting changes. Thus what would have been necessary, namely, successors to those who initiated change, were still missing shortly before the "long march." They should have come from the ranks of young people stimulated by the protest movement, but these young people instead became disillusioned and eventually slipped off into a socially ineffectual underground of depression, militance, and sectarianism. This made it easy for the hard-pressed politicians to put an end to the reforms, something they desired as they often felt overtaxed at the end of the economic boom in 1973–1974.

This represents not only a relapse to the previously described tradition of the authoritarian state, but also the helplessness of the "responsible" people who can see how a changed situation requires creative intervention, but who also see how the old management no longer intervenes. They are confronted not only with one of the well-known recessions but with a structural crisis in socioeconomic development as well, at a time when they are scarcely halfway along in preparing the necessary reforms for the situation. There were also serious personnel problems, since the most brilliant members of the young generation were either active in the years of most heated conflict and therefore considered suspect and threatened with suspension (Berufsverbot), or else withdrew to the niches of an intellectual existence in the cultural area or went on fighting an embittered defensive war as members of one of the many groups and committees, inside or outside the political parties, struggling against a growing excavation of the democratic spirit of the constitution. Only a few could endure the often depressing milieu of professional politicians. And even these individuals have ultimately been just as helpless in their political posts, vis-à-vis the total social situation, as have the outside critics and victims of this development.

Many components come together in the current economic crisis. First, there is unemployment, unknown for a long period and seriously depressing. It is becoming increasingly clear that the system can operate with a number of people out of work for an incalculable number of years. One to two million people will be affected, and the situation will particularly affect those with poor education and training—those who are in any case the stepchildren of the prosperity. At the same time the established administrative system turns out to be so rigid and so controlled by powerful groups that smaller changes fail because of official law, federal disputes about competence, and conservative training programs. This happened, for instance, to the large-scale socioeducational-advancement programs that were provided to disadvantaged groups by social scientists, who likewise were unemployed in appreciable numbers. It was impossible, for instance, to activate university departments to participate even for a short time; instead, their energy was used to hamper private initiatives. Professors also participated in this pedantic administrative chicanery.

Added to this are the financial problems of the state, again resulting from many separate developments. The most important ones are the increased prices of raw materials (like oil), the large-scale tax flight by the multinational concerns, the considerably higher expenses for social security caused by high unemployment and connected with decreased taxable income, the expenses resulting from luxuriously developed infrastructural organization, and the absurd nationalization of all social tasks (thus 35 percent of all employees are engaged in public service, receiving not only good income and social security but also a multitude of expensive privileges). Accordingly, there is a constant lack of money for investment in innovation and planning for the future within the social arena; and all economic resources are put into questionable programs to raise the "investment trust of the industry," which means that they must guarantee prompt return (nuclear power plants, superhighways, investment aids, and so forth).

Another factor is the change in the distribution of the population, with a growing number of old, retired people, with fewer people able to work and to finance pensions through their taxes, and with the large numbers born during the years of high birth rates now reaching apprentice or high school age and having great difficulty in finding adequate educational possibilities. The resultant unemployment rate among young people is alarmingly high and leads for many to an unavoidable proletarian career, since they do not learn the skills needed to obtain good jobs in industry. Modern German industry is characterized by large, automated production plants, made technically possible by developments in electronics, and in many cases made even cheaper because they avoid the higher costs associated with larger numbers of employees, who receive not only salaries but also a considerable amount of money in benefits. This means that in handicraft work the cost of manpower is actually double the cost of salaries, which has led to an enormous increase in price for handicraft workmanship and thus to a tendency to reduce costs through mass production and to attempt to increase production further with the use of automation. In this way more and more craft skills are downgraded. Unemployment increases, affecting all those who keep trying unsuccessfully to retrain for new jobs and thus make themselves employable again. Yet public reports continue to state that investments will further reduce the number of jobs, while it is unequivocally perceptible that expanding and modernizing production generally means automation.

These circumstances create an atmosphere of anxiety and pessimism about the future. The years of reform caused anxiety for many people who saw changes taking place in what they knew and trusted, and eventually a reaction set in. Today, general existential anxiety increases this tendency to want to return to the beautiful past when everything was "in order." In a situation that particularly calls for public interchange, the formation of diverse opinions, and cooperation, instead we find privatistic behavior; weariness in the political parties; nostalgia for the Nazi reign; an inclination toward violent solutions ("foreigners out," "terrorists' heads off"); hysterical witch hunts for radicals; suppression of left-wing activists; and striving for more government control through creation of further red tape in many vital areas. The slogan, "March through the institutions," has been reversed for many liberal intellectuals, now worn out and deprived of their impetus toward reform. The objects of their efforts, the counseling institutions, suffered growing impediments to their work as they perceived themselves as being eroded, infiltrated, and deprived of their identity. As one participant said: "The march through the institutions is over, now the institutions are marching on us."

Formerly constructive attempts at creating sociopolitical alternatives have in many cases turned into nostalgic private undertakings (collectives, rural communities, schools, various local initiatives). The justified criticism of technocratic independence has been degraded from a cooperative project to a defensive battle in which everybody tries to save himself.

This compendium of negatives may appear unduly pessimistic, especially since in this period there were important positive developments that have, at least, demonstrated that the Federal Republic need have no fear of comparison with other countries—just as the official propaganda proudly proclaims. But we are not concerned here with balanced reporting, but rather with a representation of the compulsive behavior that always comes into play in Germany when a situation of upheaval opens up the possibility of giving serious attention to the stated goals of the constitution and to the needs of the underprivileged. At this point there is always much talk of a crisis in the existing order, and the government steps in to manage the conflict and smooth over the emerging discrepancies. Thus, in the situation described in this chapter, the failure to bring about solutions to the multitude of social problems facing Germany was followed by yet another strengthening of the belief in authority.

The middle class, which profits by the established system; the petty bourgeoisie, their blind and loyal followers; and the terrorists who pervert opposition into criminal private action—all these groups aid in the desperate maintenance of something very wrong. The same situation existed after World War II, but the tensions then were transferred to the struggle against a common enemy. This is happening again today: Perceived problems and attempts to find alternatives are no longer dealt with, but are repressed while a fixation on the common enemy is encouraged. After the war, when the spirit of renewal was choked with American capital that hindered the growing independent initiatives, the common enemy was communism, at that time described as "Soviet aspirations to supremacy." In the face of this external threat, all dissent was silenced. Long after the more recent uproar was brought to an end in the mid-1970s, its impulses still have many effects. Now the "common enemy" is the terror acted out by revolutionaries, in the face of which all criticism must once again keep silent. The frightened man in the street, shaken up by evident social difficulties, now has a scapegoat for all his inconvenient reflections about inconsistent values, illegitimate power structures, and the consequences of his own attitudes toward prosperity. He can lean back self-righteously and watch the spectacle enacted by the terrorists and the police. As unforgivable as terrorist acts are from a moral standpoint, their most serious consequences lie in the fact that the problems presented in this exaggerated manner can now be ignored, or answered defensively with infantile gestures: "It's their own fault; it comes from too much criticizing."

The well-controlled and strategically successful liberation of the aircraft in Mogadishu has broken this fascination with violence. It was one of the first examples of a meaningful use of social-scientific advice in solving social conflicts. It also made clear what our working conditions as group-dynamics advisors to social processes were going to be. The social-scientific advice in the Mogadishu incident definitely facilitated the liberation of the hostages, so it is all the more annoying to learn that the advisor was permitted to come in only at the height of the crisis, rather than being used "prophylactically." The situation was permitted to escalate to a dramatic showdown, after which the world would again be set to rights. There was no word about the social misery that destroyed these terrorists—how they were drawn into the whirlwind of criminal activity that promised emancipation, partly as a result of social conscience, partly of unconscious anomie; no understanding of how the terrorists were elevated to "superenemy" by a lascivious press and the initially clumsy reactions of state authorities. The terrorists' actions were political and moral madness, but the way in which this madness was depicted resembled the depiction of witches in the middle ages: Anything their accusers might have done was attributed to them. They were made responsible for recognized problems, held up as examples so that everyone could see in them the consequences of wanting to criticize and change too much. Those on the other side were seen as the "responsible ones": policemen, politicians, planners. Once again the citizenry could hide in an identification with authority.

TASKS FOR THE INTERACTION CONSULTANT

The kind of consultation required in the situation described here should be one that deals with the unhappy relationship between the citizens, who according to the constitution are sovereign, and the state, represented by the administration and seen by the individual citizen as if it were the sovereign, in such a way that the compulsive and repetitive national pattern would be revealed. The compulsion represents an over-identification with and a loss of critical distance from the existing social order and its administration, accomplished through fixation on a common enemy. It is a compulsion actualized precisely at the moment when the signs of a resurgence of political activity and social engagement can be observed in the segments of the population traditionally oriented toward established authority. Declining support for the parties (results of recent polls show that about 45 percent of eligible voters do not see themselves as represented by the established parties), and the rapid expansion of local activities into an unofficial "green party" devoted to protection of the environment and opposition to nuclear power, threaten the established power relationships, the idea that production criteria are the only valid ones, and the pretensions to "responsibility" of the professional politicians. The restoration of the establishment will certainly not result from dictatorial coercion but rather from a nationalized program of conflict management that will thwart any attempts at independent political development.

It would be wrong to assume that the politicians and administrators directly responsible for this situation have a reactionary intention or a special manipulative ability. Rather, they are often victims of their own functions. They are confronted with problems for which their professional knowledge provides no answers, yet they still must deal with the problems. Since their actions must be based on their own experiences, they are just as uncertain and afraid of conflict as anyone else. But it is characteristic of the problem we are discussing that the functionary does not perceive his limits himself. Politicians visit public meetings to introduce themselves and thereby get more votes in coming elections. They do not ask the public for advice on how to tackle this problem or that. The old proverb, "To whom God gives an office he also gives the necessary understanding," characterizes the monarchic heritage of the "democratic" functionaries, who think their authority comes directly from God; and it also explains why a belief in the competence of authority rather than responsible participation in public matters is the dominant pattern. The citizens are not seen by officers and authorities as their mandators—at best, as their customers. Thus citizens see no reason to run the risks of striving actively and responsibly. On the reverse side, the administration nevertheless sees every criticism either as an individual psychiatric case, or as hostility to the system that must be fought.

Our work in applied social science permits us to contribute to the explanation and solution of such connections and their antidemocratic consequences. Group-dynamics methods not only allow the cognition of structural connections, but also call for action-oriented consequences. It therefore seems even more striking that almost no one within German group dynamics is occupied with this kind of sociostructural development. On the contrary, they are almost exclusively occupied with epiphenomena of these social structures. This situation seems in itself to be a symptom of the tenacity of the authoritarian-state orientation. In the next section we will examine this aspect of the problem and ask why group dynamics, with its professional focus on German social structures, has not taken any visibly creative role, and why those who work in the field remain within an established group providing the trivial scientific and psychosocial services mentioned at the beginning of this chapter.

REACTIONS TO THE INTRODUCTION OF GROUP DYNAMICS IN GERMANY

Discussion of the use of group-dynamics techniques and cognitive methods started in Germany in the mid-1960s. At that time group dynamics was an intellectual import, mainly addressing itself to a vague antitraditional trend among social scientists. It was little more than a fashionable variation in the ongoing dispute with rigid academic traditions. The significance of a concrete implementation of social-scientific results on practical problems could not be seen at that time, partly because the potentially interested people were preoccupied with investigating social reality, using the highly refined cognitive methods of the "critical theory" (the Frankfurt School), and combining their results with patterns of action learned from the history of the labor movement, including the Russian Revolution. Another problem was that group-dynamics cognitive methods in the Lewinian tradition seemed simplistic. This led to the idea that group dynamics was a kind of reformed method of manipulation for enlightened and cooperatively inclined employers and managers. In fact, discussions of this kind went on far into the 1970s. Although they were only peripheral to intellectual daily life, they nevertheless influenced the reception of group dynamics by that group of social scientists who themselves were politically engaged and on the outlook for ways to make their theoretical positions useful in the treatment of practical everyday problems. Above all, these discussions prevented the participants from seriously dealing with the structural dynamic between their private reservations and their socio-political pretensions. As long as all that was discussed was the legitimacy of the group-dynamics methods used by trainers and consultants, the skeptics remained outside of every practical dispute. Even when they actively interfered with social processes, they could still retain undisturbed their familiar way of behaving, their attitudes, their evaluations of the situation, and their tactics.

For some years numerous politically active participants with social-scientific or educational backgrounds took part in group-dynamics seminars. They described their motives for participation as a desire to learn more about interactional connections and about how to translate their theoretical ideas into practical effects. None of these seminars was complete without the obligatory discussion of ideology. This usually took the form of a pretentious and highly academic debate about the interests behind the "rise of group dynamics" as well as about the relative validity or irrelevance of group-dynamics insights in relation to the understanding gained from, for instance, a Marxist analysis of sociopolitical developments. Although these discussions were usually very penetrating and exciting, their main effect was the creation of an unwillingness even to pay attention to the given interaction processes and their particular dynamics, let alone to think of using this material to understand actual strivings and activities. Everyone remained convinced of the superiority of the old ways of thinking. The contradiction inherent in group dynamics—that the practitioner should not be interested in this kind of demanding one-man show, confining himself to a relatively narrow sector of social reality, but instead should be open to cooperation rather than competition with other disciplines—made the discipline even more questionable to those who criticized this ideology. It sounded like eclecticism and scientific pluralism, and from there it is only a short distance to positivism and its relative notion of the truth.

The disparaging way in which German intellectuals received group-dynamics methods goes back to the introductory seminars given by American colleagues from NTL. It also accounts for the fact that potentially interested politicians, union leaders, and administrators later characterized group dynamics as "controversial" or "dubious." Practitioners of group-dynamics methods did not come from established institutions such as prestigious universities, but instead were invited by interested and well-informed people from less well-known institutions such as adult-education (colleges which became important some years later and are still growing in significance), and arrangements within political and public education, which at that time were still downgraded by Cold War propaganda. These arrangements were distrusted by politically engaged university graduates. Germany had succeeded only too well in changing from nationalistic to anticommunist propaganda, and even politically well-informed employees were not quite trusted in this atmosphere of pseudo-intellectual "boy scout" attitudes. The beginning of group dynamics within these institutional settings gave rise to many additional prejudices (against this "pseudocritical welfare technique"), and the situation was certainly not improved by the occurrence of some overplayed and overdramatized psychotic episodes among the participants in the first laboratories—episodes that gave even the sponsors pause. Since these events ruined the relationship of group dynamics to the critical intellectuals and the like-minded experts in departments, administrations, and unions, even less support could be expected from the official university psychology departments in these first years.

In the 1960s academic psychology considered Lewin and his field theory a small, obsolete appendix to the old Berlin School of the 1920s. Eager to make up for the absence of scientific development under the Nazis, academics welcomed every new fashion, together with the belief that yesterday's theories could be sacrificed. Behaviorism and at best functionalism were in vogue in psychology, whereas in its neighbor discipline, sociology, only positivistic abstractions and platitudes were considered interesting.

This is why the first NTL people when they arranged group-dynamics training in Germany, appeared as quacks and followers of an obsolete theory in the eyes of both university psychologists and critical social scientists and their students within the Frankfurt School. The first group considered group dynamics old-fashioned stuff, dredged up again for use in "national education"; the second group saw it as yet another variety of American positivism with its curtailed perspectives whereby social problems are seen and analyzed in a disintegrated way, with the fundamental contradiction in the capitalist economic and social system not coming into the picture at all. These social scientists feared that the method would offer a way of curing the symptoms of these contradictions while retaining the impression that the total social system was healthy, apart from some minor problems.

It is no contradiction that Tobias Brocher was connected with the organization of the first laboratories and group-dynamics ways of working. At that time he worked for the Sigmund Freud Institute in Frankfurt, and psychoanalysis and the independent Freud Institute were not approved by the university psychologists but were at best tolerated under the appellation of "medicine." Brocher's coworkers were primarily interested in their own recognition, with little interest to spare for something new that seemed to be as poorly established as they were and that might also be a partial competitor in the psychological field. In fact, feuds went on for years between psychoanalysts and people representing group dynamics about the latter's competence and right to practice professionally in psychosocial cases.

The third possibly interested group, the members of the extraparliamentary opposition, did not want to devote themselves to considerations of interaction analysis. They were just getting started at that time, and they certainly had numerous unexplained dynamics, not only internally, but also in the relationship between the active revolutionaries and those they sought to mobilize in opposition against the existing social system. But their eagerness for action left no room for a serious analysis of the situation, and they rapidly developed into a blindly unreflective activist movement. Group-dynamics perspectives emphasize the understanding of "connections," but the opposition movement believed that these connections had been understood long ago and found to be negative in their impact. Thus the only thing left to do, in their view, was to fight the establishment. Tactical reflections, which should have paid some attention to structural considerations, were often abbreviated and restrained in the service of short-term alliances.

THE PRESENT FIELDS OF WORK

Thus the introduction of group dynamics in Germany was both disadvantageously staged and also influenced by a too strong field of forces that made it impossible to use group dynamics as a working model to analyze the interaction processes in the resistance movement. The predominant sociocritical way of thinking was definitely more radical and negated the existing conditions in a much more satisfactory way; the "teach-in democracy" of the extraparliamentary opposition was much more action oriented and did not ask anyone to reflect about his impulses. Thus group dynamics ended up, on the one hand, as a social-scientific sideline, and on the other as a source of therapeutic and technical help.

Later a new field developed from both these positions. The failure of the political and social revolt led to a retreat from the fight for social reconstruction into introspection and examination of individual problems. In this connection there was a massive increase in psychic symptoms such as chronic depressions that revealed extensive defects of the ego structure. Thus a need arose for therapeutic techniques to deal better with these damages than could conventional psychiatry. At the same time a demand for explanatory models developed, models that were less rigorously linked to "postrevolutionary" ideas, but rather would provide both connections to work on and new perspectives about togetherness, mutual protection and

and help, motherly care. Both these expectations can be fulfilled by concentrating on the details in interaction sequences and relation structures.

With the strong demand for therapy, a group movement developed. Even when its activities were summarized by the catch phrase "group dynamics," this movement had little to do with the old notion of applied social science. The notion of "new therapies" would have been more accurate since—beside established forms such as psychodrama, gestalt therapy, and behavior-therapeutic techniques—a multitude of new forms were employed: variations on encounter groups, massage techniques, sensory-awareness training, and Eastern meditation techniques, along with the products of the epigones of all of these. The here focus is not on collective processes and the reciprocity between a person's aspirations and behavior and their social impact and consequences. The focus is rather on the single individual, with the group as medium.

In addition to the comforting and therapeutic importance of the present-day group movement which sprouted with such exuberance that in addition to its serious exponents the door was opened for any charlatan, there is also a new interest in the methodological help to be used in analysis, control, and organization of social processes. This is predominantly limited to pedagogical and social welfare areas. In these areas the massive management problems are evaded, and there is no way to deal with the present tendency toward professionalizing. One example is the growing interest in group-dynamics counseling for university teachers, who hope to get help in handling teaching problems as well as support for the management of the constantly increasing mass production of education. Moreover, university teaching methods is an area that some years ago was considered scarcely worth mentioning by "serious" scientists, since it relied on the notion that "correctly" presented content would speak for itself and be understood by the students. Today there is a growing tendency to require additional pedagogic training as a qualification for a university teaching position.

The strongest interest in getting methodological help from group dynamics is seen in the area of social postgraduate training by physicians, social workers, prison staff members, and teachers. This is definitely related to an interest in raising the individual qualifications required for these positions. The fact that all these professional groups have undergone relatively sudden changes in their social roles as well as in the structure of their institutions, and that they therefore have to learn a lot about things never mentioned in their previous education, has not led to any seeking for advice on the part of those who are responsible for the training and practice of these workers. It is still up to the individual worker to manage his or her job—or not. Corresponding to this tendency is a declining interest among politicians, administrators, and organizers of municipal and regional reformatory efforts to ask questions or seek advice.

The emphasis on individual needs for help and the widespread blurring of sociostructural and institutional consultation assignments has an effect on group dynamics itself. There are opportunities for work in hidden positions within specialized postgraduate programs or in academic collaboration, or else in presenting a variety of fashionable encounter techniques to training organizations or social institutions that want to be "modern." Some practitioners undertake their own marketing and have had some success in establishing training and consulting activities.

Group dynamics, meanwhile, has attained a certain academic reputation owing to the work of some colleagues who never left the academic field, but persevered, going on unperturbed with group-dynamics ways of working as they climbed the ladder to professorship. Afterwards they could advocate their ways of working ex cathedra, letting the convinced pluralists of the academic world get accustomed to the fact that a new school had come into existence. They have followed a traditional path to a position of power, and this now permits them to disseminate methods for analyzing the impact of this power and of those dependent on it. This is successful when they are meeting an already concrete demand for advisory help; in this situation, professorial prestige facilitates the task. But when there is a question of conflicts within the university, it may be difficult for these professors to speak, since the traditional position of power, in this case, is generating the conflict and thus is not able to be freely discussed—least of all by the adviser himself, who might thereby eliminate his own position.

It is extremely difficult to open up new fields of work in which we as professionals could take part in political decisions and organizational processes. It is difficult to penetrate the resistance against our central ideas, which actually amount to the social relevance of group dynamics, because of the preexisting self-images and perceptions of roles, not only among politicians and administrators but also among traditional as well as critical and politically engaged academicians. When we add the notion "applied" to our work, we mean applied social science. But we are not considered true scientists as long as we are neither satisfied with describing what we see, in the tradition of the sociophenomenologists; nor remain stuck in declaiming an unredeemed pretension as the "activist researchers" do. Instead, we say that there are no general recipes for managing social problems and organizational tasks, only more or less useful methods of exploration. Therefore, we must constantly make our "labs" in places where social tasks or conflicts exist. In the eyes of the scientists we pollute our practice with naive discussions about interests and with inaccurate thinking. This is why, until now, group dynamics had no chance to be taken seriously as a theory of cognition in Germany. The existence of an "intellectual trade" that makes it possible to diagnose the respective social structures and to produce a basis for balancing and managing divergent interests, appears to the traditional scientist to reduce his status. And for critical scientists interested in changing society this intellectual trade is not sufficiently affixed to a program and can too easily be claimed by some opponent for the promotion of his or her interests. Representatives of group dynamics may now and then be used as gurus, but with their dubious reputation they estrange themselves from the responsible administrations asking for methodical help in resolving social conflicts. Politicians and administrators generally think they know the answers, and need scientists to confirm this, give them publicity, and bolster their images. Therefore, those who work with group dynamics and who offer methodological help in understanding tasks and decisions must compete with the official experts. Lawyers are always preferred for these positions since they are most likely to follow the rules.

Nevertheless, our attempt to do our job at the level where important problems are solved and the structures of social development are laid down, leads regularly to situations that support in various forms my thesis about the relationship between democratic conceptions and dependent thinking.

EXAMPLES OF THE DIFFICULTY IN WORKING WITH SOCIAL STRUCTURES

Two examples will show, on the one hand, what my main theme looks like in daily life and, on the other hand, the kind of difficulties one must face in trying to deal with false stereotypes. I hope in this way to stimulate the important discussion of how to open up relevant fields of work for us.

1. In 1977 the German parliament passed 514 laws. In the same year there were vehement discussions of planned nuclear power plants and of administratively enforced regional reforms. In addition, results of opinion polls showed a clearly increasing distrust in the established parties. There was also a considerable increase in the number and strength of actions initiated by the citizens.

In this connection I remember a particularly difficult and frustrating assignment with a group of ministerial functionaries. Their task was to develop proposals for reform of government and administrative work. As they did so, certain work problems arose among them that represented boundary difficulties between departments, competence problems, and questions about status. They therefore expected the group-dynamics consulting to provide help in systematizing and improving their way of working. The content and goal of the tasks were not to be touched.

The difficulty was that although they were expected to prepare recommendations for change, they were not prepared to discuss the sense and nonsense in the previously existing regulations—in what ways these were still applicable and in what ways unnecessary and outdated.

They needed to come up with proposals for dealing with their mutual boundary problems, but they already had their demarcations so carefully defined that, in order for them to be able to see their task, they first had to realize this fact. This was informally but thoroughly discussed with some of the participants, who appeared open-minded and somewhat politically engaged. In the group as a whole, however, the behavioral norms were so powerfully conditioned by status and professional role that privately presented interests and viewpoints could not even be mentioned seriously, let alone be used in negotiations or as a basis for decisions.

Their wish to limit the consultation to formal work procedures and their flat rejection of any discussion of the content and goal of their tasks appeared to mirror what had happened within themselves: their dread of being rejected by those they addressed if they presented any viewpoints not officially authorized by their superiors.

This experience was significant and disturbing because the strict division between personal opinion and ordered thinking and acting in the official role was impossible to deal with as a discrepancy. Instead, it appeared self-evident and legitimate within the administrative machinery. This behavior had a separate reality, wherein problems from everyday life and common sense solutions were seen as unnecessary or disturbing. Thus it would be possible to pass a flood of laws, yet hardly touch the highly explosive problems existing in everyday life.

2. The measures related to the educational reform taken during the last ten or fifteen years were connected with a thorough discussion of didactic and methodological questions within pedagogics. One of the important questions in the debate concerning the deschooling in the school system was the institutionalization of learning (a parallel to the antipsychiatry debate about the stigmatizing effect of the institutions). In the relevant literature dynamic viewpoints were productively discussed more and more often. Notions of "situation," "structure," and "process" replaced isolated examples. It was no longer only specialized aspects or individual distribution of guilt that had to be considered when mistakes were investigated. The teachers who became interested in group-dynamics seminars were more and more considered typical rather than distinctly politically conscious and active people who wanted to improve their understanding of the pedagogical interaction in order to turn to their own pedagogic goals with more efficiency. It soon became clear that the external seminars alone could not meet the demand for continued studies, because the problem only manifested itself again when anyone tried to transfer their experiences to

the daily life in their schools. This realization led to the development of numerous groups of teachers that mutually helped one another in a common effort to improve their teaching. They soon noticed that the schools were uncooperative, and they applied to group-dynamics advisers for help. This gave rise to two significant effects. The first was a pointless squabbling with the school boards over the desire to seek advice from external specialists. The incredible degree of irritation shown by school administrators ranged from complaints of the lack of money to finance such services, to legal scrutiny of the right for such persons to set foot on school ground at all, to sarcastic instruction from supervisors who told teachers with disciplinary difficulties in their classes not to burden themselves with psychological questions. These are not just isolated cases but are typical of six years' experience with continued education for teachers in a country with 42,000 teachers.

The second effect was gratifying: More and more teachers used the customary one-week class tours, carried out in every school year, to attend conference centers, and asked for help from group advisers whenever possible.

One of these school classes had worked with the problem of industrial conflict for some weeks before the week of its seminar. During the students' stay at a municipal conference center they unexpectedly experienced a public employees' strike. The conference center stopped its services, and the guests were asked to leave in solidarity with the strikers. This made it clear that they had not succeeded in applying the material studied to the concrete situation. No diagnosis and no understanding of motives or actions emerged. The teacher was very disappointed, as he saw himself deprived of his teaching efforts. But he saw no opportunity to use the situation pedagogically or to close the gap between theory and practice by helping to interpret and by guiding a collective analysis of the situation. He lacked the experience to deal pedagogically with situations other than those prescribed in the instructional scripts. He was too preoccupied with his theoretical insight to be able to help his students explore an example of social realities.

In this case it was possible to attain the mediation with the aid of the group adviser. But this made it clear that both the training of the teachers and the ordinary organization of daily school life represent unsuitable and hindering conditions for a realization of the social learning required in the planned educational reform. That realization in itself is not bad; it can be seen as providing an occasion for considering remedies. What makes the situation bad is the administrative hampering rather than support of a training set-up for the understanding of pedagogical processes as something more than a private hobby for the individual teacher. At the same time, there are complaints about dislike of learning, pressure for performance, and fear of examination, along with demands for more realistic preparation of the students for the increasing changes in the requirements and conditions of their subsequent vocational world. The politicians (and the parents) require from the teachers something they cannot give. Those who suffer are the students who find themselves helpless when they leave school—in a situation for which the school should have prepared them.

UNDEVELOPED ASSIGNMENTS: TO BREAK THROUGH THE COMPULSION FOR HISTORIC RECAPITULATION IN SOCIETY

These examples do not give us an optimistic picture, they may appear as exaggerated complaints or as expressions of personal dissatisfaction. There is some truth in this impression: working for some years with group dynamics in Germany has led me to the conclusion that we often fritter away our possibilities in privatism. What is flourishing is the multifarious application of interactionistic ways of working for individual-therapeutic purposes. This is important and should not be criticized or disparaged whenever it is handled in a responsible and reliable way. But at one extreme it has developed into a playground for charlatans, and we have done nothing to denounce or hinder their activities. At the other extreme a sociodynamic perspective makes it possible to work with something other than individual therapy in group settings. It gives us a perception and a methodological analysis that permit us to work with psychosocial factors and with those structures in which individual suffering originates and in which social conflicts and problematic developments are based.

But this task must be undertaken cooperatively. It is no work for "centers" who want to skim off the market. Germans who work with group dynamics have as their motto that the point is not to change someone else but together with him to find common possibilities and ways of life in which both can come into their own.

This comforting statement has always softened widespread anxieties about "psychological striptease," but at the same time has overshadowed the other side of the story, namely that the consequence of this motto is a constant review and change of the institutions in order to avoid their developing a separate life and thereby restricting individuals' free play to such a degree that individuals are no longer capable of forming their own life, let alone of coming into their own in this way. The common reproach that group dynamics individualizes and psychologizes social problems therefore holds true, although the critics, with their strictly theoretical position, have nothing better to offer.

In Germany we are still highly preoccupied with individuals and their awareness of themselves and their interests. We have scarcely begun to let these individuals work with, examine, criticize, and jointly remodel the structures in which they live—with the exception of special fields.

So far there has been no demand for expert help in areas where group-dynamics knowledge and ability could first be applied, such as the development and change of social organizations and the translation of individual demands and interests into common structures for action and satisfactory institutions. Those who are "responsible" at any time imagine, furthermore, that their special criteria for judging and parameters for action are the proper ones, and that any opposition is a sign of ignorance. As a reason for this belief in "practical necessities" and faith in technology, I have attempted to describe a recapitulation model in modern German history.

The constant prevention of the elaboration and constitution of a social order, the retreat of those with developmental and innovative impulses, and the displacement of their energy to the fulfillment of prescribed goals and a life within prescribed structures, have all prevented the development of social responsibility and social cohesion to a noticeable degree. Instead, a subordinate bartering mentality has developed, with clear signs of dependence and craving attitudes. There is a broad readiness for the idea that everyone must do his part. But "his part" does not originate from his abilities and interests but rather from the job description for his occupation or function, that is, from an anonymous authority. The responsibility is not so much of a moral nature but is rather the result of an idea about normality that allows only those who have accomplished the prescribed performance to make any demands or claims on the system.

Once the accomplishment is finished, the individual is usually happily indifferent to the question of whether the actual social situation permits the expected reward. He is primarily interested in the "right" that has been promised him, again by an anonymous authority. (These descriptions are not meant to characterize the workers who demand wage increases. They are, rather, an outgrowth of official status, whose occupiers claim the most obscure customs to be "protection of social ownership." An example is the behavior of the medical association, who recently were criticized by the health authorities for excessive increases in their fees and cost calculations.)

Even if the reward does not follow as expected, there will be no inquiry into the social scenario in which the barter takes place. There will, instead, be complaints about injustice and the lawyers will be called on to protect the "rights" of the individual.

This rather defiant belief in authority corresponds with the difficulty so many people have in Germany in taking over positions of authority and filling them in an appropriate and selfcritical way. We have instead an accumulation of bad examples of authorities who overemphasize the administrative function of the role in a self-satisfied, inaccessible, and often cynical way, without being able to see the protecting and assisting side of their role at all. There is a tendency connected with this to be unable to take personal responsibility or to attempt to come to terms with critics by talking things over. Instead, responsibility is seen as a prerogative that is lost when something goes wrong or one has bad luck. This corresponds to the authoritarian trait in the irresponsible elitist politician who in any conflict will recommend cutting the matter short ("If I had anything to say in Bonn, all the terrorists would sure enough be a head shorter.")

After World War II there was the famous attempt to "reeducate" the Germans democratically. In that connection a pedagogically understood type of political learning went on for a long period. Many members of the first generation of people who worked with group dynamics played an active and committed role in this reeducation. But with what we know today, we should try something else. We should intervene in the numerous everyday conflicts that occur, offer our services, and set examples to show that our way of working and our viewpoint is a serious alternative to the authoritarian "ownership of the right" and its related social order. We should collaborate on the "deschooling" of the school, on a sensible development of the debate around nuclear power and its consequences and alternatives, on new ways of dealing with the "north-south conflict," and on the innumerable other tasks in our society. In this connection, EIT's Norwegian-trawler-fleet case (chapter 17), where what was originally a consulting job developed into an extensive social intervention, is a good example of a constructive way of using our potential—and not only in Germany.

Chapter 12

Certain Aspects of Group Dynamics of a Specific Country

Ramon Meseguer

In this paper is presented a synthesis of extensive research into the group dynamics of Spain.

The history of this nation has been analyzed by way of a conjunction of diverse methods from the social sciences: history, economics, sociology, linguistics, psychosociology, and group dynamics.

THE DYNAMICS OF SOCIAL GROUPS

Galaxy of Contradictions

When analyzing the Spanish population as a whole, the first impression one receives is bewilderment. And after making a more thorough study, trying to recover from the discouragement that bewilderment causes, one begins to see clearly that Spanish people are characterized by paradox.

I shall attempt to explain the following series of contradictory features of the Spanish people. These features, drawn in outline, prove all Spanish people to have very complicated, paradoxical personalities.

The following are the contradictory features:

Seriousness: Ranges from tragedy in many situations to verbosity in a series of official statements.

Frivolity (Chachondeo):   If you will forgive the vulgarism—the word is more precisely translated as "screwing off"—but modern Spanish has acquired this word and it expresses exactly what I want to say. This is very frequently the foundation on which some of the most important Spanish statements or declarations are based. In other words, at the base of the most important Spanish activities, one cannot deny the existence of a deep layer of frivolity.

Obedience: Ranges from the obedience that yields to each innate symbol of the Jesuits to the sheeplike obedience of thousands who, throughout history, have suffered on countless occasions without the slightest protest.

Anarchy: Ranges from people who are very sheeplike in thought, people who withstand countless abuses, yet because of some reason no one really understands, still preserve their own personality, to individuals and groups that, in the most important situations, jobs, and official functions of the country, act "just as they please" without paying any attention to hierarchy or established law.

Fear: Ranges from the inability to defend the least of rights against any authority to the inability to think for oneself (this includes the best educated intellectuals of the country).

Courage: Ranges from the ability each individual possesses in the case of a declared war to perform the most heroic deeds, to taking in his stride daily-life situations that would tax all the energies of individuals or groups in other countries.

Religiosity: Ranges from the most rudimentary functions that are included in any kind of activity or simple official ceremony, be it politics or football, to the adornment of the most important state functions.

Paganism: Ranges from the most primitive and simple eagerness to enjoy oneself, using a religious holiday as an excuse (like the Greek drunken orgy), to the scoundrel and close friend who, every once in a while, discovers himself through the mystic texts when the mystic throws his arms around the shoulders of "his God."

Perfectionism: Ranges from the officials in the most rudimentary institutions of any Spanish municipality who never find any good in anything nor permit anything to be attempted because they know it will not be done perfectly, to the intellectuals who never succeed in completing their works because they can never get close to the pure, all-powerful ideal that they want their writing to achieve.

OKism: Ranges from the OK of any slipshod mechanic to the OK of any full professor who deals with the most rigorous of the sciences yet teaches his class as if he were a bull rushing out of his bull pen just to see what might happen.

Revenge: Ranges from the most cruel vengeance taken in the darkest corners of the office to the continual persecution of some VIP or group that is considered to be "evil." Even homicide is permitted!

Forgiveness: Ranges from the capacity an individual has at one time to prove himself tremendously cruel and to forgive in secret some insult inflicted by his best friend, or his wife, or his brother, to those unreconcilable blood enemies who at some weak sentimental moment forgive one another as fast as lightning for everything that has previously occurred between them.

The Joke: Ranges from the one that arises from some esoteric situation in any small town on the peninsula, to the superb joke that depicts a momentous sociological event with the same perfection as the masterful hand of an inspired painter.

Lack of Humor: Ranges from the inability of any given person in any Spanish town to tolerate joking or ridicule, to the inability of the national leaders, during the most important functions of the Spanish community, to accept and participate in the irony, joking, and sarcasm they receive either personally or in their public role.

Inability to Form Teams: Ranges from the demonstrations held in the national schools when the moment comes to make up an athletic team, to incapacity at the international level to form a group of investigators.

The Tremendous Ability to Form Fanatical Groups: Ranges from the fanaticisms that have set town against town in the smallest district on the peninsula; to the ability to form groups that have repercussions on a worldwide scale.

Thus, scanning these traits that illustrate the characteristics of the Spanish people, one could construct an interminable chain of contradictions which, considering this extremely tense atmosphere of assault and onslaught (setting one against the other) would eventually portray the paradoxical national situation that has existed throughout history, continues today, and moves on toward the future.

THE NEED FOR HAND-TO-HAND COMBAT

One of the issues that most profoundly affects the observer of the Spanish people is the foolish, enthusiastic violence ("hand-to-hand combat") into which the most distinguished Spaniards are ready to plunge over some disagreement. Spaniard is almost always against Spaniard, both men and women.

If one wanted to know who has most afflicted the life of the Spaniard since the nation was founded, the one who has made him suffer the most, destroyed and hurt him the most would almost invariably prove to be another Spaniard.

This enormous bow of unrest tightens. On the one hand, we find two journalists, two artists, two scientists, or two professors quarrelling in newspaper articles for weeks on end. As the battle progresses, they forget the central scientific or artistic subject their articles dealt with in the beginning. Each successive article introduces some new bitterness, until finally ridicule, mockery, and insult become the central theme. The initial concept is lost. On the other hand, we see (throughout history) the recurrent phenomenon of Spaniards fighting and murdering each other in the bloodiest ways imaginable.

There seems to be a more passionate, profound pleasure in destroying something belonging to another than in creating something of one's own. There is much more intense delight in personal attack than in an objective discussion about the topic; or the destruction of a playwright through criticism rather than making a thorough analysis of the content of his work (be it a book, play, or whatever). And so, we see a huge, mystic collection of ill-assorted people, who are not aroused by the fury of passion to create new things or to revise and improve the old, but who are readily disposed physically to attack the man or woman who has had an artistic idea or a creative thought.

In response to a book written by an unknown author, a movie made by an unknown director, the unknown poet's verse, a professorship awarded, or any outstanding achievement by an unknown person, there is an expression used to refer to such people (here I will intentionally use a vulgar expression again—yet not all that vulgar, as it is on the lips of those who hold the most prominent positions in the country). They say "Who's this bastard?"

I am not saying that our people do not admire the traits or qualities of others. On the contrary, they frequently idolize them and even exaggerate by boasting. A doctor's friend, even though he hasn't any understanding of medicine, will introduce him warmly at a meeting as "the best doctor in Europe." One of the first stipulations for the admiration of another's character is emotional glorification.

In this chapter, I have examined three exploratory themes that are closely allied in our cities. They are: the violent need for hand-to-hand combat, glorification, and the formation of fanatical groups.

In the unconscious world of each person in the country and in the collective unconscious of the different cities, the concept or image of the other is so disarming, so disturbing that the love and hate felt for the other becomes exaggerated. This exaggeration reaches such a point that this love/hate is transmitted through a form of social inheritance. The hate felt toward the image of the other reaches a point at which, when people are about to encounter one another, they are already conditioned and predisposed instantly to attack, to idolize or to gather a few people together (almost at random) to make up opposing families. What could have been a mature, healthy family becomes an illusion, burdened with fears and terrors that convert our groups into reservoirs of mutual restraint and repression.

THE IMPOSSIBLE GROUP AND THE FANATICAL COLLECTIVITY

If something is to be done as a group, the spontaneous reaction is to sneak out of it or to escape. The feeling is that the problem should be solved alone, never by a group.

This view of the question of group formation can be proved by direct observation in the streets or by experimental investigation of group dynamics.

Initially one would say that without motives of glorification or destruction (the annihilating factor), the Spanish do not spontaneously form groups. In other words, throughout our history, we find groups that were formed through some common objective of a few mature, clear-headed people. These people came together harmoniously to achieve some creative goals that they should share with the districts, states, regions and the nation. They brought us riches, inviting us to enjoy life while we can.

Their aim was to form groups motivated principally toward the growth of creative ideas; individual movements based on devotion and love for the truths that bring them together; the serenity of determined objectives; joint action based on rational flexibility, criticism, and mutual demanding of one another; mutual respect while discussing and integrating the opinions of each and accepting the opinions of others; peer-group pressures to respect the individual rather than subjugating him, to direct the energy of these groups more toward creative richness than emotional violence. Because one is part of the same community, there should be the flowing communication one enjoys when reinforcing in another the good qualities he has so that he realizes them. There is no need to indoctrinate the other, to change him or make him fanatical. It is constructive to plan objectives within the limits of reality so that human beings can experience the satisfaction of achieving their goals. In marked contrast, however, as a result of the inability spontaneously to form mature, serene, constructive, flexible, coexisting groups, there appears a predisposition to form glorified groups.

We see throughout our history that every time an attempt is made to achieve something ethically, save something gloriously, change something through reform, attack something belligerently, impose something fanatically, associations are established with an almost inexplicable emotional stimulation that, for a few years, hold men tightly in groups like a busy bee colony. This makes them capable of implicating themselves, capable of setting the most absurd objectives, of believing in the most incredible things, and of maintaining a euphoria, the description of which has almost (I say "almost" to be prudent) been copied line by line from a number of different psychology books. These books describe both this state of glorification and the features of these associations.

A common feature of these diverse groups that have been forming throughout history in different spheres of national life is belief in "the grandeur of the mission." Therefore, those individuals who enthusiastically join and become part of these glorified groups do so almost always because of some unconscious motive of omnipotence. They want to be part of the omnipotence of some glorious mission, even in those cases where the group might have as its objective that its members should not be important or when they might consider themselves insignificant or worthless. Here a comment made by a European psychologist to a man who was belittling himself comes to mind: "Don't belittle yourself so much because in reality you are not so big."

Many members of the glorified groups in our country have become part of history, in their glorified position, by great heroic deeds, great impudence, impertinence, incongruence, lack of respect for the law, lack of affection for their fellow man, lack of respect for others' opinions, and so on. In the glorified groups our individuals, when they are right, are absolutely right, and their achievement is exclusively theirs. From here arise all of the intricate procedures of justification of the unjustifiable. These procedures are obviously absurd, but glorification justifies everything.

Many of their deeds, treated separately, arouse great admiration because, as a result of the situation and the kind of human phenomenon involved, they became heroes.

Unavoidably, the identification with this strange uncouthness (the capacity for heroic deeds) attracts a great deal of attention, because it happens very frequently in extraordinary circumstances—so much so that one would say the individuals in our cities, who spontaneously carry out these unusual deeds, do so because they find themselves in extraordinary circumstances.

If it did not happen this way or if they were not in this atmosphere, they would not be in the least inclined to do these deeds, because they would only be normal everyday occurrences.

If we made a unilateral conclusion and stopped talking so impulsively we would say that throughout history the life of this type of individual moves through a kind of depression or void where nothing is worthwhile or meaningful; since everything works poorly, this country is worthless, and so on. Then suddenly there is a change, a new leaf is turned over, and the task is accomplished.

The next question is: Can one conclude that life for these particular individuals is worth living, or do they only come alive when there is a change of fame through doing something extraordinary?

THE JOKE

The people of our different cities have an inspired capacity for witticism and ridicule (they ridicule one another, national events, and others). Yet except for some rare exceptions, they do not have a sense of humor, if we consider that to be the ability also to accept ridicule, on the expectation that the other will spontaneously come back with some witticism and thus establish some kind of authentic cordial dialogue.

The Aragonese joke touches a sore spot in the flesh, and the blade of this sword cuts in both directions, toward the person who ridicules himself and toward the person who ridicules others. The following is one of the archetypal jokes that exemplify this phenomenon.

An elementary-school inspector made his annual visit. He was one of those who usually visit the towns when the town hall, the priest, local industry, commerce and banking, teachers, and students are celebrating the end of the school year. The inspector, a reserved man with skinned elbows and feet caused by his running around a lot of schools and towns, rapidly sized up the intellectual and cultural level in that school.

Inspector: Teacher, I don't need to ask these children questions. I can see that they are excellently prepared; so we can go on to the last part of the program without testing them.

Teacher: No, Inspector, you must question them. I've got them as sharp as a razor that cuts at both ends. Ask, ask, ask them anything you like and you'll see how they respond.

At this point the inspector was trying to change the teacher's mind through a few long digressions, but finally the tenacious teacher won out and compelled him to pose questions. The inspector, after a long, profound, and inquisitive look, attempted to choose from the students in front of him one he felt was the most sensible, intelligent, and prudent and the least resentful of the group. Finally, since there was nothing else left to do, he decided on one:

—Well, son, let's see, who were the four evangelists?

—Samson and Elias!

At this point the teacher, looking magnanimous, radiant, and clever, winks and then elbows the inspector in the ribs and murmurs to him: He's only eight.

I have just left resounding in the listener's ears this marvellous story from our old Aragon. Now, I invite him to take a look at Castilla. I have said that their exemplary joke is one of transcendental or metaphysical irony.

Let us conjure up and allow to chill our bones the picture of a couple of gendarmes taking an assassin, condemned to die by all the known and unknown death penalties, to the adobe wall of the cemetery of Guadalajara. The convict, with his wrists handcuffed behind his back, walks silently. There is a monk beside him murmuring deep, simple, cordial, comforting words. Following behind, with an uncertain look, are two gendarmes. They get to the cemetery. They take the prisoner to the wall. The gendarmes remove the ramrods from their rifles and begin to clean the barrels. The priest opens his gospel and begins to read aloud to the prisoner passages concerning eternal life. Meanwhile the accused, courageous even in the last moments, feels a special tenderness toward his fellow man and a need to be courteous even to death. He turns to one of the guards (who is indifferently concentrating on cleaning the bore of his rifle) and says:

Accused: It's cold this morning, isn't it?

Guard: What are you complaining about? We have to go all the way back to town on foot!

I will now attempt to tell an archetypal Andalusian joke. There is a father and a son. Both are leaning against a wall side by side. They are engaged in the eternal task of killing time. Time goes by and the sun rises to a point where it shines directly into the father's eyes. He slowly turns his head upward to where his hat hangs on a wall board. He then looks at his son and says softly to him:

Father: Son, give me my hat.

Son: Father, I've got my hands in my pockets.

Father: Like father, like son.

ANARCHISM

The Jacob's ladder of the anarchists, which they had to climb to reach the heaven of universal justice, was constructed of the following steps:

1. the idea
2. possession of the earth
3. the apolitical
4. the coming of the great day
5. lyricism
6. mysticism
7. the definitive revolution
8. the disappearance of power
9. the ruination of the capitalists
10. exalted rhetoric
11. human dignity above all else
12. value
13. individualism

There could be other steps to add, but I think with these the skeletal outline of Spanish anarchism is sufficiently clear.

Alongside this ladder there existed another, rising to the heights of the utopian, one of intrinsic contradictions:

1. The idea of a common possession of resources contrasted with the burning desire to redistribute land. Especially among the agricultural anarchists the great day, when all bad things would come to an end and the good would begin, was to occur quite simply when each anarchist should become a small landowner. This ancestral desire to "acquire," to be an owner, is one of the principal unconscious driving forces of the present consumer society in Spain.
2. The apolitical: the belief that politics are destructive in contrast to the formation of anarchist federations, which automatically become political pressure groups, against their original intent.

3. Pacifism contrasted with fierce struggles and dreadful violence, which were almost apocalyptically acute in the first months of 1936.
4. A human phenomenon that is alarming to consider and review is the religious wars. For the love of God and the salvation of the human race, millions of brothers have been killed.
5. The arduous preparation for the great day in contrast to the total lack of planning to guarantee that it survives in the long term.

Spanish anarchism pulls the hearts of the passionate along with it and fascinates the sensitive because it carries in its train a host of Quixotes, Christs, John the Baptists, rebels, Prometheuses, and valiant, visionary, generous bandits who preach the beautiful utopia of anarchy: Nobody will be the slave of another; all are capable of giving their lives to save the oppressed; and, finally, all can fight against the capitalist tyrant.

In the conduct of the great caudillos of Spanish anarchism, especially outstanding is an extraordinary bravery, at times combined with a stoic spirit that the anchorites would have envied, and at other times linked to a profound exaltation of human values. The second of these characteristics astonished both insiders and outsiders during some of the anarchist congresses; when everyone else was discussing money, the Spanish anarchists spoke of the dignity of man.

ENVY

At times the envy reigning among the Spanish peoples has been explained as based on hunger. It was argued that from the first moments of infancy for each one of this multitudinous population, the fact that a brother was at the mother's breast meant hunger for the other. It is possible that this unilateral attempt at explanation has certain components, certain arguments that may be convincing. However, it is unsatisfactory because no reality, especially social reality, can be explained by one single historical cause. The characteristic of complex phenomena is the combination of different realities. Therefore, envy cannot be explained solely by hunger, even though this hunger may have existed through long periods of history, as has happened in our country.

In answer to the simple explanation of hunger, one may argue that envy also fills the life of people who have not known physical hunger and who have been very successful. Despite this, they are constantly envious of other people, sometimes of competitors in their own field. Perhaps envy toward a man who "is also successful" explains many things that hunger cannot.

Not even people who have achieved considerable success have managed to escape the gnawing feeling of envy toward others. Therefore, as envy constitutes a basic characteristic of our people, its origin is to be sought in something much more complex than deprivation.

This picturesque panorama of national envy results in an intense state of disquiet.

.   In the Golden Age, the century in which this nation reached its highest achievement in every field of action, of contemplation, and of aesthetic creation, many thousands of people made us acutely aware of envy as a dominant theme of the time. They portrayed the mutual envy of the literary giants, of the great conquistadores, of religious orders, the envy of one *picaro* (rogue) for another, the envy of the avaricious for the avaricious.

Envy as a collective phenomenon is truly unnerving.

1. When a comment is made about the worth of another, the disagreeable voice of one who delights in pointing out a number of deficiencies in the character of that person is always heard. Thus we are frequently left with the impression that in our country nobody is worth anything, nobody is satisfactory. A serious consequence of this habit of devaluing others is the unconscious self-devaluation, resulting in a general discontent.

2. Linked to this is the demand through passionate, violent coercion that others recognize one's omnipotence and perfection.

3. This aggressive behavior may take different forms: constant attack, stabs, and criticism; life-long persecution (from Fray Luis to Ortega, one is defined as: "I am me and those who envy me") continual harassment of friends, leading the nation into a destructive civil war and massacre.

4. There is a tendency toward boasting of rich mental endowment or great success. Not only in bull fighting but also in every profession and position, there is self-advertisement and the claim to be supreme. This is so widespread it has become a national custom. As a result, journalists, when they meet various figures in the arts and sciences, attempt to compromise the interviewee by first flattering him and then inquiring whether he believes himself to be the leader in his field. Thus, they convert our society into a motorcycle race, giving everyone a number on his back.

5. Another form of envy is what I call "intolerance of the fault." This means that if an imperfection is discovered in any person previously praised, however insignificant it may be, he is knocked off his pedestal with explosive fury. Let us summarize the process: a god is raised, an idol placed upon a pedestal, it is scrutinized until a chisel mark is found in the marble, and then, with the speed of lightning, it is demolished.

Perhaps this means that the destroyer unconsciously attacks himself because he cannot tolerate the limitations that, as with any being, nature has imposed upon him.

I will now sketch a diagram to show how the archetypal envious person fits into our national scheme:

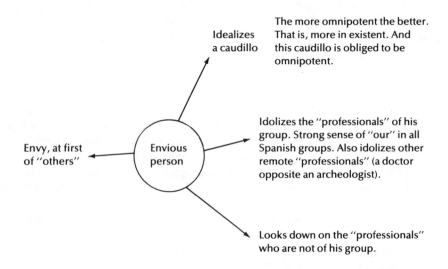

Idealizes a caudillo — The more omnipotent the better. That is, more in existent. And this caudillo is obliged to be omnipotent.

Envious person

Envy, at first of "others"

Idolizes the "professionals" of his group. Strong sense of "our" in all Spanish groups. Also idolizes other remote "professionals" (a doctor opposite an archeologist).

Looks down on the "professionals" who are not of his group.

A truly noteworthy aspect of the repertoire of the envious is that envy recognizes both those who fail *and* those who succeed.

The matter is potentially more complicated: It is probable that the highly endowed person, enslaved by treating himself as an object and others as a narcissistic mirror, is always doubting himself. If that is so, when he sees another "who *is*" he feels an inner disintegration "because I am *not*." As this ruinous collapse becomes unbearable, he destroys that which can reveal he is "not a man."

But up to now we have only described and not explained. What gives rise to our typical forms of envy? We can imagine running a film: Diverse forms of behavior move across the screen, and the mania for greatness is continually being portrayed—the ideal of the "deed," to be a great warrior, to be a great saint (it is not enough to be a warrior or to be a saint; one must also be great); geniuses continually appear on the screen, as well as, the necessity of being a genius (what an intimate delight the word "genius" produces in us! and genius and support carved in our tombstone), and then nobility, the degrading nature of work, the supreme purity of caste.

Every Spaniard carries a king withim him. I have frequently heard German businessmen commenting that Spanish workers are very productive but must be treated with great tact as each one feels himself to be a king. Such is the force of the archetype that Schiller puts into the mouth of the king of Spain these words: "I want the Spaniard proud!" In central Europe the admired Spanish archetype is of pride and worth.

But at once one sees that among so many kings nobody wishes to be treated as a vassal.

It is possible that over the centuries in our country, a number of concepts of the "I" have overlapped in the structure of personal identity and have thus precipitated a social trait of envy.

The "I" concept of the envious leads to the scale of consequences that I now present:

Concept of the "I"

Perfectionism

Competitiveness

Incapacity to recognize destructiveness

And this derivation fits into the following chart of attitudes:

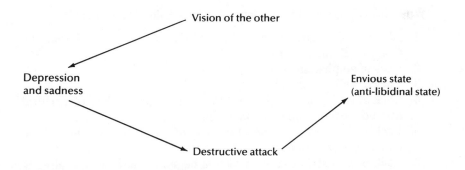

An envious person is tired, depressed, wishes to destroy the other for the good he has or could have, or even for the "perfectly good" he should be.

I have tried to explain a little the dialectics of envy, which causes so much death in our country. I hope to be able to devote more space to it and explore it in more depth, because I fear that in the dynamics of the family there are bitter roots that have not yet been explained, roots that are later nourished at school and at work.

THE LACK OF GROUP EVOLUTION

The countries of Western Europe, from the fifteenth century to the present day, have moved through the following phases:

1. The Renaissance
2. The Reformation
3. Empiricism
4. The Enlightenment
5. Rationalism
6. German ideation
7. Socialism
8. Anarchism
9. Industrialization
10. Marxism
11. The set of "subevolutions" that range from phenomenology, social-ism, structuralism, and the latest philosophical scientism, to tech-nology, the consumer society, and the postindustrial society. All this is leading to chaos as Western humanity is currently experiencing an intense motivational protest.

What does Spain present in contrast to this scale of evolution?

1. Absence of Reformation (and in addition, a specific involution: the Counter-Reformation)
2. Lack of empiricism
3. Lack of enlightenment
4. Lack of rationalism and therefore a corresponding lack of a critical attitude toward superstition and magic
5. Lack of idealism and therefore also of a philosophical base for a dialectical evolution
6. Lack of industrialization, which is beginning now, as the already industrialized societies are entering the era of postindustrialism
7. Existence of an anarchism exalted as an archetypal phenomenon of what might be called "style of national life."
8. Brief existence of an organized Marxism which resulted in a blood-bath
9. A period of thirty-eight years of unflinching authoritarianism.

The two most serious consequences for Spain resulting from not participating in the vital evolution taking place in other Western countries are,
first, the separation of Spain from the rest of Europe, thus making it
develop in a way quite foreign to the rest of the European organism. As a
secondary consequence I will note here that when we speak of European
philosophy, European sciences, new European aesthetics, something is
being spoken of that is not lived deeply, which is not an authentic existential
experience of the Spanish people, which does not correspond to our deepest
personal identity, all of which creates a certain schizophrenia of dialogue
between Spain and the rest of Europe. This point is so serious that it alone
demands extensive research.

The second consequence is that since Spain has not followed multiple and
periodic evolution like the other European countries, each time a revolution has been needed, the country has been obliged to undertake a titanic
effort in the attempt simultaneously to bring off five revolutions, to re-
cuperate lost time, and thus to be brought up to date.

UNCONSCIOUS FANTASIES IN THE FIGHT FOR POWER

Whenever individuals began to wonder, "What will happen to the
organization of the nation if the populace is allowed to regroup freely to
discuss the forms of power, the ways of participating in government, and
the ground rules of negotiations and discussions they desire," in the
conscious fantasy of millions and in the collective fantasy of the nation
there was written in vivid colors the following sentence: "They will murder
each other." This was the key fantasy affecting the future of power, peace,
and violence in the country.

If this imaginary process just described were to exist in the majority of
nations' consciousness today, the future of any country would not have a
mature solution until the day when the question is spontaneously asked by
the majority: "What would happen if individuals were allowed to regroup
in a different way?" and is answered naturally: "They will understand each
other even if they have to make sacrifices."

The fantasy of mutual homicide was ignited in the imaginations of the
illiterate just as it did in the minds of the most acknowledged intellectuals.
It was not a simple fantasy of imagination but a radical, visceral, emotional
jolt visualizing the spilling of blood and death.

The simple desire of some individuals to come together freely to choose
the form of power they prefer, to negotiate the different forms of participation in government, inflamed like a forest fire the sleeping forces of
destruction in the unconscious of many others.

What fantasies burned underneath all this? A Dantesque vision in which were combined the circles of heaven and hell: the celestial circle of powerful sons preferred by the father and the sons hated by the father in burning collision with each other, while an unbearable vision passes of angelic sons, elevated to sanctity by the mother, flying over the filthy multitude of sons castrated by the mother; against a background of condemned demoniacal sons pursuing in vain a tyrant at the pinnacle of hell, who is laughing loudly over the mountains of castrated sons, bewailing their fate of being condemned never to overthrow the tyrant.

From one side comes the idea, "They will lose the truth," from the other the idea, "Liberty will be lost." Both of these ideas are opposed to the notion, "We will impose liberty and peace." This Dantesque vision invaded the root of the instincts of various groups when they imagined a hypothetically free populace confronted with the possibility of choosing a form of political participation.

For this reason the historical problems of our country had to be resolved at the source of the instincts and in their battle dress. It is possible that remains of these fantasies still exist in the majority of our population, with more or less potential for action. But it is also feasible they are hidden only in the following groups: (1) extremist minorities, especially university students and workers; and (2) minorities with unreconciled historical conflicts.

It is quite possible that these fantasies are not in the mind of the masses who are restricted by conservatism and the habit of being governed, by economic security, and by unawareness of the personal energy required for full participation in the confirmation of power and its distribution.

Furthermore, it seems to be true that there is a minority of groups who faithfully embrace the illusion that power can be decentralized into subgroups with discrepancies, but with harmonized influences in the overall national organization.

If I were to let myself be guided by my intuition and instincts, I would say that the number of groups and individuals willing to settle their differences is greater than it seems.

Have civil conflicts served to eliminate destructive fantasies? Would new conflicts serve to spread unconscious destructive fantasies? And from this point of view, if we look at those with a program for a change of power who say, "This time there will be no mistakes," the reaction of millions of spectators is a fatalism encapsulated in the sentence repeated thousands of times in our history: "Nobody will be able to fix this." Why does this belief that "nobody can fix this" surge up at the prospect of change? On everyone's conscience weighs the memory that each attempt in our history to solve the root of the problem of national organization has only succeeded in making it worse.

Different generations have found in the fight against archetypal abusers of power (an individual supported by and supporting abusive structures) that they have only gained one thing: another archetypal abuse. And because tyranny always won out, the nation was fundamentally divided into two strata, the upper occupied by those who were sustained by the sufferings of the others beneath them. The history of Spain, with little exception, has always been a horseman's history: certain groups of Spaniards bestriding other groups.

Underlying these conscious fantasies are other chilling unconscious ones—that as individuals or in groups the Spanish are fatally condemned to be slaves of the omnipotent patriarchs and never free sons; that the patriarchs will only allow castrated sons to survive, either as functionaries of the patriarchs or as slaves of the functionaries.

And even deeper, like a geological layer of rigid rock, extends a region of fantasy firmly anchored in the unconscious of fatalists: "The people of this nation will never become complete human beings; they are men who have never been able to reach autonomous virility, sexuality, love, and the freedom to participate in government because biologically they are beings of an inferior race historically trapped in immaturity." (They marry because their mother gives them permission, their father says nothing, and the priest finally authorizes it; in the last fifteen years it is not the priests who give permission but the Catholic Kamasutrists, creators of the equally ineffable Catholic geisha girls!)

We will move from this class of fantasies to one that merges into the religious. (1) Historically, on our peninsula everything ended up sanctified; thus (2) political beleifs were true and holy, scientific beliefs were true and holy, and so on.

From the time in our history when everything became sanctified, the natural consequence was extreme: The religious hierarchies could never be free from having to exercise political, financial, or military power. In those epochs ecclesiastical hierarchies were everything except what the Catholic mystics asked them to be: ascetic, essentially based on a distancing of the spirit from possession and power. In sanctifying everything it was not only religion that became deformed. Thinking, loving, commerce were also sanctified; and this is the reason why every affair, every theme, every situation that becomes an issue among our citizens is necessarily and radically dogmatic.

This phenomenon has deep historical roots. Our country, unlike any other European country, has been the center of invasions by others who, one after another, have imposed their religion, be it by war or by a combination of seduction and intolerance. These two have been fundamentally a form of violence, ramified like the capillary roots of a tree, enmeshing a continuous historical attitude adopted by Spaniards toward other Spaniards, the attitude of inquisition.

In the last stage of the conflict to decide which religion would prevail, Christians fought for centuries to impose their culture on the Mohammedans. The first national organization was, among other things, a religious coercion, a process of religious imposition. The historical theme of religious fighting among Spanish peoples has been well documented. Here it is cited for the value it has to explain the dynamic of conflicts in a group whose subgroups confront one another over hundreds of different issues consciously or unconsciously dominated by religious dogmatism. The result is that the forces in competition always have something of an "antigentile" component in their makeup.

THE EVOLUTION OF NATIONAL GROUP DYNAMICS

The country is, in a very specific way, emotionally a nation, and a profoundly irrational nation. I do not use the word irrational in a negative or pejorative manner, but rather, on the contrary, with a very positive meaning.

But this irrational base makes the following two tasks difficult: (1) the nation's attempts to acquire societal characteristics in the strictest sense; and (2) the combination of the discovery of methods by which the great potential wealth of our irrationalism can be respected and stimulated, with other features of a society, such as a strict empirical sociology would define it.

From here on I will expound the positive features currently possessed by the nation that enable it to become a society. At the same time I shall take advantage of the great possibilities of irrationalism.

The list of evolutionary factors is as follows:

1. The disappearance of the tragic repression of sexuality.
2. The disappearance of hunger.
3. The general ability to earn money.
4. The widespread disgust felt toward the civil war.
5. Social security in its two aspects.
6. The general possibility of acquiring property.
7. The disappearance of fratricidal hate.
8. The absence of hostility between Spaniards (or irritating and repetitive hostility between organized bands in confrontation).
9. The long history of labor security.
10. Easy emigration.
11. The feeling of well-being.

To emigrate while having almost complete security of return within a few hours to the place left; the possibility of being able to show off on holiday the success had while abroad ("one is not just legs, but is a conquistador"); and the maintenance of the illusion, more or less remote, of being able to live in a better economic situation and at the same time in a more advanced society, make a great number of emigrants, consciously or unconsciously, suffer less during their absence. The journey away is not a blind and obscure adventure to America with no knowledge of how it might end and offering little possibility of a return to one's own country.

Nevertheless, it is evident that when a large-scale emigration from in the country occurs, it is because it has serious problems to resolve.

Large numbers of Spaniards confronted with mutual annihilation have disappeared. Among certain intellectuals, among certain poets, among diverse people who are "in opposition," the tragic subject of the "two Spains" is continually brought up. The archetypal features of these two Spains mortally in combat with each other would be:

1. One Spain is characterized by fanatic, intransigent, inquisitional, excommunicative, and warlike religiosity. It is intimately linked to the fiercely capitalist structures that are exerters of a suffocating financial pressure on the poor classes. Moreover, the two previous structures are allied to armed forces willing and ready to fight against the people if they declare themselves against the religious or financial dictatorship. These three structures are also intimately linked to a prohibition of thought and to an obligation that all believe the same, in philosophy, in religion, and science, such that freedom of thought becomes a "national crime."

2. The other Spain would be the nonreligious, atheistic, tolerant Spain with all kinds of religions and unbelievers, or even with a clear tendency for all churches to disappear. There would be a basic tendency to socialize capital. The two mentioned tendencies are linked to a wish only to commit the armed forces to the defense of domestic order in an extreme case of total chaos within the national boundary, or to the defense of the nation if it were attacked from abroad. But it would always keep itself apart from political interference. (In certain cases, the disappearance of the army is advocated.) Intimately linked to the previous structures is the acceptance of freedom of thought, creative spontaneity, open house for the most diverse ways of thinking without anyone having the right to interfere in the ways of thinking of others.

If this description corresponds more or less to the real characteristics of the two Spains, and if these two Spains have been this way historically, it should not be surprising that they have confronted each other aggressively even to the point of shedding blood.

We are at a stage in which the two Spains are no longer effective as they once were. They are beginning to lack meaning and possibly within a certain time it will merely be amusing to speak of them.

But at the present moment we find that, in the religious field, the Spanish ecclesiastical structure, its influence on society, its monolithic faith, its authoritarian functions, and perhaps its continuity are in profound crisis. Let us not forget that the average Spaniard is no longer accustomed to fulfilling religious duties. Youth does not feel itself attracted in general to the church, and within the hierarchical structure there are deep divisions. The hierarchical structure, from the cardinal primate to the last Marxist priest, is undergoing a crisis so profound that it currently presents the archetypal features of a group crisis.

On the other hand, there have arisen a series of tendencies against dogmatism and in favor of tolerance, flexibility, and adaptability. And, what is more important, the whole attitude of the church is being rethought in a country where in the past the church has acted as a pressure group.

As for dictatorial capitalism and financial pressure groups, the tension that has existed through many phases of history has decreased considerably with the development of the Spanish consumer society in which millions of Spaniards have been able to acquire money and a higher socioeconomic standard. Nevertheless, there is still a group of excessively capitalistic and intolerant institutions, although in some of the leaders of these institutions there is being engendered a healthy crisis tending toward better socialization.

In conjunction with these groups, the army's attitude has been to opt for maintenance of order within the nation. Besides, it is tending to maintain detachment and neutrality toward the laws that Spaniards are formulating and voting for in their attempt to organize themselves socially and develop their own particular form of government.

At present, there is an attempt in the universities to do away with dogmatism and the compulsory curriculum and to introduce a study plan founded on elective courses.

We have labeled the first feature of the present evolution "the disappearance of sexual repression."

The history of Spain has in many respects been the history of a national sexual conflict. This conflict cannot merely be reduced to a rough scheme that pretends to synthesize the whole problem by stating: For socioreligious reasons, it has been hard for the Spanish couple to make love.

Millions of Spaniards over the centuries have been aware that the country clearly suffered from sexual repression. It does not interest us that other cultures have also experienced this. Our men and women throughout the years have suffered unspeakably.

This was a tragedy that closed off and thwarted the sources of creativity, of love, of curiosity for discovery, and that made many vital manifestations impossible because repression of sexuality leads to a repression of vitality. It began to change and disappear in the 1950s. This has reached such a degree that at present exactly the opposite is taking place. Some minorities in the large capitals have reached levels as destructively out of control, as inhuman and abject as one can find in New York, in London, in Hamburg, or in any other city in thrall to the monster of technology or the consumer society.

The progressive disappearance of this conflict makes one foresee an optimistic future for the nation with regard to the possibility of civil wars. This sentence is naturally a simplification, but it is posssible that it embraces broad reality—the sexual activity of thousands of Spaniards in whom the following phenomena coincide:

1. Sexual satisfaction.
2. Earning of money.
3. Continuing recreation for months on end, not only in the specific sense but also in the broader expansion of the entire personality.

We must note that in Spain, apart from a great love of diversion, the fact is that it is cheap to have fun: wine, "tapas," tobacco, dancing, and certain kinds of food, with the added advantage of the Spanish sun.

To this one must add something much more profound which forms part of the repeated crisscross of contradictory constellations that are typically Spanish: Spain is a fun-loving country. This cannot be said of any other European country except perhaps Italy. But even Italy, caught between technology and Marxism, is becoming tedious. Luckily for many Europeans, Italy is the hope that Marxism may yet have color, life, and poetry. In the same way, in Spain the hope is held that, if some day Marxist fanaticism enters the country, it will eventually create a sublime, almost ineffable, Marxism: the Marxism of Andalusian song and dance.

Fortunately these hundreds of thousands, satisfied vitally, economically, at work and at recreation, feel a deep disgust for war, not only because it means death but also something worse: It would take the good life from them, and that is the only truly serious thing.

The second positive feature that can give rise to the formation of a large national structure divided into subgroups is found in what we have described as "the ability to earn money."

The positive resonance of this ability is immense. The Spanish have always wanted to be lord and gentleman, owner and possessor, traveler and free, dominating and expansive, artist and comedian. None of this have they been able to realize because, among other factors, they have been unable to earn money.

The possibility of acquiring money is renewing and transforming the Spanish people with the potential, for the first time, of becoming owners and with the promise of the good life.

The third positive factor after those of sex and money is the *disappearing specter of hunger*.

Hunger has contributed to the development of literary genres. Among these is the picaresque novel, which occupies a special place in world literature, representing a peculiar vision not achieved in other countries. The picaresque novel is perhaps the most inspired genre of humor known to world literature.

Hunger has been the cause of massive sublimations, which have echoed in the ears of Spaniards, making them split their sides with laughter and covering the whole country with the image of the underfed and skeletal cachinnator. A sign that hunger is vanishing from Spain is to be found in the disappearance of jokes about it.

The fourth positive factor is the development of *social security*.

Until 1936, the worker and peasant knew that if they fell seriously ill, the likelihood of death was high. Since the 1940s, this anxiety has been greatly lessened and the indexes of social security achieved are among the highest in the world.

When we analyze this further, not only has conscious security increased, the disappearance of the specter of sickness and irrevocable death, but also unconscious liberation, the disappearance of tension and anxiety, depression and pessimism as a result of the annihilation of the prospect of death. Thus we will perhaps discover that a very profound turn of events has taken place in our society in these last thirty-five years.

Next we will discuss the following factor: *the desire to work*.

Since the end of 1939, the enormous belligerent dynamism of the Spanish has been transformed, for differing reasons, into a dynamic of work that has been increasing steadily and has reached an extraordinary intensity at the present time. Most remarkably, this movement still has not reached its saturation point: It is capable of further output, greater diversification, more jobs, and more creativity. The Spanish people, in general, are taking a great delight in the regulating, tranquilizing, creative, and structuring work of their new society.

The most important positive factor for the building of a Spanish nation is *the disappearance of murderous confrontations between different groups of people*.

Endemic in the history of Spain has been the bloody encounter of two enemy alliances. This confrontation has been repeated throughout the centuries. Finally the moment arrived when, in the most recent phase of Spanish history, the two Spains took shape and were personified as two devils in combat with each other, who were going to establish a hell on earth in the form of the Spanish nation. These two Spains had a typical configuration, and after a century and half of mutual provocation and cruel inflammation, they attacked each other in a fury of destruction.

If we examine the *general disgust toward war*, we can say that it is quite clear without needing philosophers, sociologists, statistics, or profound psychosociological analyses to tell us so. The Spanish population is being transformed, for the first time in history, into a happy people; and happy people turn immediately away from war, especially war within their own national boundaries.

In thousands of towns and villages throughout the nation, people dress well; the young are growing in such a way that the average stature, in a number of provinces, is demonstrating the potential for healthy development. Spaniards are increasingly taller, more athletic, and more attractive. In the past few years the archetype of the physically strong and attractive Spaniard is again reviving.

Finally, there is the absence of a *continual hostility among the Spaniards*. For years I have devoted myself to the historical study of civil wars in different countries: regional wars, religious wars, in short, the wars that have set citizen against citizen. I have found the following common features:

1. The more or less sudden appearance of irreconcilable differences.
2. A mutually hostile view of each other and a projection of conscious and unconscious fantasies of destruction of the other.
3. Isolated hostile outbreaks that little by little involve everyone.
4. Intensification and extension of those hostile manifestations until total conflict has broken out.
5. Outbreak of the mutual confrontation that has provoked the war.

All of this I call *periodic hostility*, which leads to the final catastrophe. Fortunately for us, many years have passed since such hostility has been experienced in Spain. Spain now, for the first time since it became a nation, is about to escape the necessity for fanaticism.

CAN SPAIN BE FANATICIZED AGAIN

The active members of Western culture lost their faith in both science and religion years ago. The more passive members of this culture, those who follow in the path of the minorities, have also lost these two faiths.

But suddenly, like a depressive mental patient, sad, ruined, guilty, desiring to die, who is excited into manic alertness by a chemical stimulant, Western man has been lifted out of his depression by the new technology. It has shown him the flight of astronauts, the transplants of pulsating hearts, the bombardment by radium of cancerous cells; and it has intoxicated him with a new euphoria that goes to his head. At a deeper level, however, he cries out at the growth of pain, the suffocation of technology, and the immense question of the atomic bomb.

We Spaniards are, more or less profoundly, passing through a similar phase. Nobody knows what will be the outcome. Apocalyptic fear has always existed, and confronted with the immediate reality we wonder: "Would it be possible to fanaticize Spain again?"

The instinctive answer is no. Who or what circumstances could fanaticize the Spanish masses? An ideology, a "caudillo," or a war? But for this it would be necessary for Spaniards to be hungry for a caudillo, a religion, an ideology, or a war. And it seems the country is not really hungry for anything.

By hunger I refer to that peculiar state in which individuals and groups sustain boiling fantasies swollen with motivational forces that move toward a great storm. And if these fantasies are perceived by a caudillo, who with his gestures and words can translate them to the language of the bullet, the masses will fire.

Let us review the various forms of historical identity of the majority of Spaniards: They are incapable of teamwork yet capable of forming any sort of exalted group, serious as the grave yet permeated by a rare sense of humor, born protestors yet bearers of the unbearable, supreme individualists yet tamed for centuries, a hostile people yet compassionate to others' misfortune, timid in daily life yet heroic in any emergency.

Alongside this system of contradictions exist the solitary Spaniards, ostracized and even laughed at by all, but still gentlemen, unshakable in their honor, their love for study, conscientious workers among legions of loafers, honest men among thieves, well-ordered men among the chaotic. Perhaps this country has survived historically because of these men.

Do the Spanish still exhibit the behavior we have described as typical of other periods? It seems that they do, but there is a diminishing of the exalted extremes and the addition of notions of organized conduct, a more or less constant attempt to work toward social well-being. Most important is a decline in the level of delusions of grandeur and even their disappearance.

To ask a deeper question: Is this country in the mood for religious crusades? It seems not. In the large cities religious activity has diminished to an extraordinary degree, and the majority of Spaniards live in cities. Migration from rural areas to the cities has grown. In general the attitude of most young men toward the church has greatly changed, even radically in some cases.

In the villages, especially those with over 2,000 inhabitants, religious attitudes have also changed. For example, not long ago people were more afraid of the priest than of the policeman. Now the priest is not a source of fear but, in some cases, of laughter, which apart from indicating a lack of feeling is socially impoverishing.

Summarizing what has been covered in previous chapters: The church is in the midst of a fierce internal crisis; religious vocations have fallen off heavily; in the younger priesthood unnatural tendencies occur for political activism, strange obsessions with sexology, and enthusiasm for social economics. It is possible that these phenomena are caused by the inherent failure of the vocational calling. What would be thought of a doctor who trained guerrilla fighters or a chemist who devoted himself to political oratory?

But the more profound problem is the more serious: The archetypal figures of religion who so attracted men and served their models have today lost that capacity. The causes of this phenomenon are universal and should be analyzed by research into the profound symbols of religiosity. We can say, however, that in Spain there are particular national reasons in addition to universal causes. Among these are the lack of extensive and responsible experience in the face of religious practice combined with government officialdom.

The second question is: Are the Spanish people inclined to be fanaticized by a political ideology? It seems not. The only ideology that could achieve this today would be Marxism. And the country is not ripe for Marxism for many of the same reasons that it is not open to religious fanaticizing.

If the quantum loss of religion were to correspond in time with a state of depression in the Spanish people, it could lead to the possibility that a new religion, communism, would set fire to Spain. But the country is not suffering from delusions of grandeur. The nation in general wants well-being, wealth earned by work, leisure time, and to be allowed to live in peace.

The Spaniards destroyed mystical communism in the period 1936–1939, and mysticism like all vital cycles goes in and out of season; the communists know that if current trends in Spain continue for fifteen more years, Spain will say good-bye forever to the communist mystique. A minority remains, but only within the context of other political groups. It is estimated that only 10 percent of the Spaniards struggling for political power are communists.

Another question that goes to the core of the problem: What do the Spanish people want? If at this moment there were a paranoid caudillo in Spain, he would discover our most secret and urgent desires more directly and immediately than any public opinion poll. But I believe that Spain does not have paranoid caudillos now because the country is not as paranoid as it has been in previous times. Such a caudillo emerges as a specific response to the collective paranoia. And I repeat: Spain, fortunately is *not* paranoid today. But to return to the question:

Does the nation want a political or religious holy war? No.
Does the nation want a civil war? No.

Does the nation want a fanatical ideology? No.
Does the nation want a paranoid "caudillo"? No.
Does it want to enjoy life? Yes.

I believe that in Spain we will not have a conflict of collective fanaticism. But we would have one for these reasons:

1. If there is no change in the ways of access to power. We must not forget that, statistically, three generations of Spaniards have been born since 1939.

2. If the development of economic well-being is not accompanied by an elective and polivalent (the recognition of different groups) way of creating and distributing power. Experience has shown us that when groups acquire some degree of well-being, they react against fanaticism and toward plurality, dialogue, and mature interdependence. The more mature they are, the more implacable are their demands for these rights.

Chapter 13

Sweden—a Rapidly Changing Society: How Group Dynamics and Other Factors Can Interact in Social Change

Arne Derefeldt

The Swedish Council for Personnel Administration (The PA Council) is a foundation that is sponsored by the Swedish Employers' Confederation (SAF). The Board includes representatives of SAF as well as of the Swedish Confederation of Trade Unions (LO) and the Swedish Central Organization of Salaried Employees (TCO). These representatives are also members of the council proper, whose purpose is to discuss activities and their objectives. The council also includes representatives of industry, government, the Cooperative Union and Wholesale Society, and research institutions. SAF makes an annual contribution as a basic budget for research, which is otherwise financed by grants from research funds. Consultancy is financed by chraging fees for every assignment.

BACKGROUND

"Sweden—The Middle Way" is a phrase from the 1930s for a picture of Sweden which the then Social Democratic Prime Minister, Per Albin Hansson, called "Sweden, the People's Home." In the early 1930s

This chapter, originally titled "Sverige-ett samhıalle i snabb fıorıandring," was translated from the Swedish by the PA Council.

Sweden was a poor country. Like many other countries it was hard hit by economic depression and unemployment, but it also had a labor market characterized by strikes and lockouts, which caused a high percentage of working days to be lost every year. The labor movement, after an uphill struggle waged since the turn of the century, had achieved a high percentage of union membership and a strong position as collective bargainer vis-×a-vis the employers. In the same way the employers had developed a powerful organizational antipole to the manual workers' union groups.

After negotiations, an agreement was reached in 1938 between the labor-market parties that was to safeguard arrangements for settling industrial conflicts. This compact, familiarly known as the "Saltsjiobaden Agreement," was signed by the SAF and the LO. It later became an important cornerstone of the policy of cooperation that also characterized the postwar period. This period and most of the 1960s were in addition marked by a consensus between the labor-market parties and the political parties, which called for the attainment of a high level of productivity in Sweden on which to build material prosperity for its citizens, and paved the way for the system of social security that was built up during this period. As from the 1940s also, the white-collar workers employed within private industry and public administration had been organizing themselves, whereas the university graduates formed their own professional associations.

So by the time we get to the 1960s, a very high percentage of all people employed in the business sector were affiliated with trade unions. Collective agreements were reached directly between the labor-market parties, and very little legislation was to be found in the industrial-relations field.

During the 1960s the material standard of living, as well as the expanded system of security for citizens, came to underpin value judgments that went beyond assigning top priority to the material welfare state with its high standard of social services. Questions of working life—the world of work—began to come to the fore.

Sociotechnology—Self-Governing Groups

The labor-market organizations as well as various research bodies closely followed the experiments being carried out in Norway with sociotechnology and partly self-governing groups. In Sweden the employers, blue-collar unions, and white-collar unions formed a tripartite body, the Development Council for Collaboration Questions, to keep up with the Norwegian activity, initiate experiments within Swedish firms or companies, and later evaluate the application of these experiments on a larger scale.

Political Radicalization

The radicalization of political life, notably as manifested by the Paris riots in 1968, also very much colored the Swedish scene. It was a radicalization that came to affect all parties dialectically because it enhanced interest in the political debate. Political debates and action centering on the Vietnam War permeated the whole society. Wildcat strikes injected a new element in the once peaceful labor market. Moreover, the most conspicuous wildcat strike—the one that hit the mining company, LKAB, in 1969–1970—set off an alarm clock within the trade unions, urging them to intensify their activity in the working-environment and labor-law fields. So by the time general elections were held in 1970, every political party had built a plank into its platform to reflect this debate about democracy. The consequence of this parliamentary pressure was to lay the groundwork for a great many statutes, which during the 1970s have been passed and will drastically change labor law and the working environment both within private and government enterprise and public administration.

The Working Environment: Mental and Physical Health

Conditions at the places of work, considered to have been one of the factors that triggered off the wildcat strikes, have in their turn formed the basis for comprehensive new statutes that confer greater power on official safety stewards. For example, it authorized them to halt hazardous work; it let companies set aside reserves to finance improvements to the working environment; it gave employees a say in the use of these funds, and so on.

The Total Environment: Ecology

The worldwide debate concerned with pollution, toxic substances, and other ecological aspects has also impinged heavily on the Swedish world of work, with discussions about *what is* to be manufactured, *how* it is to be manufactured, *how* the environment is contaminated, and so on. As a result of laws enacted on these matters, far-reaching interventions are being made in the production and marketing decisions taken by companies.

Foreign Manpower

In the overheated labor market that prevailed in Sweden during the 1960s, we maintained an open-door policy toward the entry of workers from other countries, chiefly Yugoslavia, Greece, and Turkey; as well as a free labor market within the Nordic area (consisting of Norway, Denmark, Finland, Iceland, and Sweden). Starting in the 1970s a more restrictive policy has been pursued with regard to eligibility for work permits. Among other things, companies are now required to mount major training programs in the Swedish language and other subjects for their foreign-born employees; also, other linguistic groups are to be given greater opportunities to live within their own culture in Sweden —all to reduce the social problems for groups of people who would otherwise be left outside Swedish society.

Equality—Quality of Life

In like manner during the 1970s, equality has become a politically vital issue to level out differences between social classes. Toward this end tax scales have been made progressive, welfare allowances graduated, greater attention paid to complex problems bound up with sex roles; and, as an underlying trend, ideas concerned with the total quality of human life are being fostered. Moreover, discussions and official inquiries aimed at creating another world of work and another society for the 1980s and 1990s are in progress more or less intensively.

Social Changes

The school system has been continuously changing and expanding since the early 1950s. Today, education is free in principle to everyone, and students qualify for financial assistance up to tertiary level. In the new school system that comes into force in successive phases beginning next year, added provision for day-care and after-school centers will build leisure activities for schoolchildren into a more complete workday for this age group, which can give greater opportunities, richer variation, and more stimulus to school-age children than that provided by merely plugging away at lessons as at present. It also signifies a more group-oriented education and a reduction of existing classroom schools.

Economic Democracy

The Swedish Confederation of Trade Unions has put forward a proposal on "wage-earner funds," the intention of which is to transfer the ownership of companies to the employees in stages, as profits are allocated to these funds. Parliament is expected to act on this proposal, either in its present or in a modified form, before the 1970s have run their course.

Changed Attitudes—Values Held by the Individual

Thanks to the mass media—press, television, and radio—all these changes unfolding on the labor market, in the community at large, in schools, and in social services are exposed to sustained publicity. In a country like Sweden with its homogeneous population, the result has been to produce relatively striking and rapid changes in attitudes and values on these matters. So even if one lives in Sweden, there is no mistaking the signs that Sweden as of 1976 is a recognizably different place from the Sweden of 1966. Interpersonal attitudes are more open; there is much less formality, fewer rules and restrictions between people. The Swedes, once known abroad largely for their stiffness and formality, have wrought a remarkable change on these counts during this ten-year period. In the course of a decade this change in attitudes and increased openness between people can be recorded with every bit as much salience as the changeover from left-hand to right-hand traffic in 1967.

The heavy commitment in Sweden to change the working environment, to codetermined or participatory management, and so on, which in its main features can be said to enjoy the support both of the employer and employee organizations, as well as that of all political parties, is unique if we compare it with the rest of the Western world.

However, every country, every culture is unique—which of course explains why the Swedish experiences cannot be directly translated into other countries and cultures. Some features distinctive to Swedish society that have affected this development and the world of work are particularly deserving of mention:

A homogeneous population structure (even though a growing number of people in Swedish society were not born or brought up in Sweden).

A relatively uniform system of values, not least those derived from the Protestant work ethic, that it is immoral not to work.

A full-fledged school system.

Traditions of cooperation in the labor market.

Strong organizations in the labor market.

A high percentage of union membership among employees (both manual and nonmanual workers).

In my opinion, therefore, Sweden is better placed than other Western countries to implement industrial democracy in the world of work, throughout all the phases of its development, consistent with keeping productivity intact.

Group Dynamics—Group Development

The first group-dynamics laboratory in Sweden was run by the PA Council in January 1957, notably in partnership with the Swedish-American behavioral scientist, Don Nylen of the National Training Laboratories, U.S.A. More than ten years were to elapse before group dynamics returned and slowly began to enter the world of work. Somehow group-dynamic learning methods did not harmonize with the Swedish labor-market picture or with Swedish society as it was in 1957. Even at the end of the 1960s, when the PA Council and several other institutions began group-dynamics laboratories, team training, and similar programs, there was great opposition to these educational forms. But in the same way that big changes have taken place in working life and society, the period since the late 1960s has witnessed an enormous growth in the use of group-dynamic learning methods in virtually all sectors of Swedish society. Just about every training program is now being advertised or compared with some form of group-dynamic actiity in fields like social welfare, primary and secondary education, penology, military service, working life, and language training. Parallel with this development, gestalt therapy, creative drama, family therapy, encounter groups, transactional analysis, and so forth have made rapid headway and expressions like "I feel for this" or "I don't feel for this" have become so-called buzz words.

Institutions That Employ Group-Dynamics Methods

One of the ice-breaking institutions in this subject field is the PA Council, which was formed in 1952 by the SAF and whose board includes directors representing the LO and TCO. The PA Council has performed this function in various ways: with individual and group development and with leadership and organizational development.

ALI-RATI, which is SAF's training body, is responsible for the broad and considerable quantitative input of group-dynamic learning, as represented by its programs for training executives and managers.

Similarly, civil service departments and other government agencies run a number of educational institutions, all of which employ group-dynamic methods in their executive development and other leadership-training programs.

Another characteristic feature of Swedish working life, both in the private and public sectors, has been the operation of coordinating bodies. Since the late 1960s these have dedicated themselves to initiate and follow up experiments with "industrial democracy," a field that goes by many other names, among them "corporate democracy," "plant democracy," "multiple management," and "worker participation in management." A number of these projects also have introduced group-dynamic learning methods into these experiments.

WHY THE PRESENT SITUATION?

Against this background, I propose in the following sections to expound my personal views of organization development with group-dynamic learning in Sweden. On the one hand, I will add a few words about those issues that have affected current trends in the Swedish world of work; on the other hand, I shall comment on how Swedish society (meaning the public sector) has reacted during the early 1970s. In addition, I shall digress on some of my own experiences gained during the years in which I have been actively working with organization development and group-dynamic learning. In short, I present some reflections that have arisen in connection with all these things, plus my highly personal opinion of some future scenarios that tie into social change and group-dynamics development.

Generally speaking, up to the late 1960s the unions took no more than minimal interest in questions to do with training executives and other personnel, other aspects of personnel policy, organizational structures, and so on. This relative absence of motivation appears to have existed at both central and local levels. Productivity was an unchallenged goal for private enterprise, a goal that was endorsed by the trade unions.

Up to the end of the 1960s, all private enterprise was dedicated in principle to one overriding goal: "optimal profitability." All other goals were subordinate. From this point of reference, the conditions under which companies have been managed have changed these past five years in a way that was scarcely predictable during the "productivity" decades of the 1950s and 1960s.

Today, this "optimal" goal has to make room for many other goals that the companies must take into account, as we shall see in what follows:

Union pressure in the late 1960s for increased employee participation, and so on.

Concerted political pressure relating to issues of industrial democracy in the 1970 general elections.

Productivity demands in the 1960s led to:
—executive development/management by objectives (MBO)
—organization development
—sociotechnical systems
—partly self-governing groups

Which set the legislative mill churning with various results for the world of work, among them
—security of employment
—greater decision-making power for employees and their organizations
—the right to take time off from work to pursue studies
—protection for union officials
—older laws/adjustment groups; that is, security laws for the employees
—the change in "Paragraph 32," that is, the employer's unilateral right to "direct and apportion the work," was be abolished on January 1, 1977.

Demands for an improved physical and mental working environment:
—legislation dealing with the physical and mental working environment
—discussions commenced to lengthen paid vacations (five weeks beginning in 1977), to lower the retirement age, to shorten the hours of work (a six-hour workday), and confer eligibility for half-pension from 60 years of age together with half-time work.

A PHILOSOPHY OF CORPORATE GROWTH

In the late 1950s and early 1960s, Sweden could have been described as an administratively underdeveloped country as far as the private business sector was concerned, that is, if today's administrative development is used as a yardstick. For example, very few companies trained their executives in personnel management, supervisory psychology, and so on. Of the courses offered by ALI, the Institute for the Training of Foremen, 99 percent focused on the training of supervisors and very few courses were addressed to other executives. If anything, the latter courses were orientation courses, which gave these other executives some idea of what the supervisors had to go through. However, there was one shining exception: the management-training programs run at SAF's residential school, Yxtaholm.

Insofar as companies had any kind of personnel and training departments at all, they were more or less rudimentary, and the programs they offered were chiefly concerned with meeting the needs of supervisors and apprentices.

Financial controllers began to take up executive positions, and financial departments were built up from the old accounting departments. Sales departments were extended with marketing departments. Psychological aptitude tests were widely used to help select supervisors and apprentices, but their use in order to fill high-ranking positions was extremely limited. Written corporate policy, corporate goals, job descriptions, and so on were unknown at most companies. By contrast, merit rating was very much in fashion.

Although many business firms and government agencies got programs of executive training and development underway as the 1960s proceeded, these programs were not integrated with organizational goals to any greater extent. Executive training adhered to the model that American experiences had already warned against in the late 1950s: "dollars down the drain." In other words, unless training is integrated with the company's goals and other development, as well as with the individuals' own goals, training will have little effect on learning and change.

After a ten-year period of personnel and executive training, that is, by the beginning of the 1970s, we could nevertheless observe that job descriptions, leadership development, and other MBO (Management by Objectives) activities had come to be installed in many companies and agencies; not only that, but these programs had also begun to function pretty well in some phases. So a degree of integration had begun to operate between corporate and individual goals at the executive level, as a link in the managerial control systems.

The term, "organization development," regarded as a collective concept for a company's change functions, was introduced in Sweden in the late 1960s. Perhaps the organization-development projects so far carried out have not been particularly numerous or far-reaching, but companies and government agencies have generally accepted the philosophy on which the concept is based. In the same way that group-dynamic learning methods can now be said to be an established and accepted learning form, organization development is now a relatively accepted term to describe the methods used to bring about change that are used inside companies, civil service departments, and government agencies.

One way to see these changes in the Swedish world of work may be to describe them as delimitable factors or phases over time. Obviously, this is only a theoretical descriptive model, but as such it can still be used to describe and illustrate schematically various "states" that have affected companies as well as their management philosophy, training policy, and so on. In the tabulation shown below, I have also marked some of the "buzz words" that I feel describe the shift of power from owners/employers to employees that has occurred in the Swedish world of work during the past twenty-five years.

Phase IV has a concept which I have chosen to call "quasidemocracy." I have used this to designate a fairly common attitude among company managers and executives who tend to regard "partly self-governing groups," "sociotechnical experiments," "group consultation," and the like as methods that one has to learn in order to be able to "manipulate" and "control," in the manner of bosses, the elements of change in companies. I can see this as a natural way for many top executives to react, trained as they have been to be entrepreneurs, to be responsible for efficiency and productivity in their roles as bosses. In many cases it may be assumed that discussions of values centered on changed human attitudes toward shifts of power in the private and public sectors came later to these executives than appreciation of their own needs to see quickly, as new opportunities for "chief engineers," the new techniques for working together in companies.

With the passage of time, presumably, they have been dialectically influenced to adopt another attitude than the one that can be said to have

Table 13.1

Phase I to 1950	Phase II 1950–1960	Phase III 1960–1970	Phase IV 1970–1975	Phase V 1975–1980	Phase VI 1980
View of firm and management:					
Patriarchal/ authoritarian corporate system	Personnel administration/ welfare Budget Data	Executive development Managerial system MBO/adminis- trative system MTM/UMS	Organization development Resource coordination Quasidemocracy Holistic view of firm	Open system Conflict/ confrontation Holistic view of firm, industry, society	Total life environment Quality of life Holistic view of work, leisure, school, society
Significant concepts:					
Cooperation	Consultation	Interaction	Participation	Codetermination	Shared deci- sion-making power
	Representative systems			Changed right of first interpreta- tion and bases of labor law	

been the "boss philosophy" that prevailed in Sweden in the transition from the 1960s to the 1970s. No doubt everyone who has taken part in the development of his society has been influenced. This is by way of saying that an authoritarian boss in Sweden functioned in one style back in 1950 and an authoritarian boss functioned in another style in 1975. Obviously, one part of a different style of functioning lies in the insight into what one "can do in today's companies," but I should also like to argue on behalf of a dialectical insight change that has to do with changed values. I can notice the difference when I get together with Swedes who have been living abroad for many years. They often have a subjective picture of Swedish working life from the time they left Sweden, subsequently colored by what they have read and heard about Swedish developments through their "appraising spectacles," which they "acquired" prior to the outward journey. In a sense these expatriate Swedes take perhaps a more conservative view of Swedish developments than the executives working in Sweden, or perhaps it would be truer to speak of a "different philosophy."

With phase V, "open system," I refer to a corporate system that interacts more and more with the external environment, including the surrounding society. More and more decisions have to be taken which defer to other decision makers/actors than those within the individual company. I also see conflict/confrontation as one part of this openness, and as such it should be recognized with approval.

Phase VI, "Total life environment/quality of life," is meant to describe an altered attitude to such things as work, leisure, environmental protection, and demands for solidarity. I am well aware that neither the economic resources nor the value-based parameters exist in Swedish society and working life for a turn of the tide so swift that it could be covered by these headings. But the tendencies toward change in that direction will become more sharply noticeable beginning in the 1980s.

Questions of assigning priority to a shorter working week/day versus solidarity with developing countries if we lower our productivity by opting for a better quality of life may become areas of conflict/confrontation during this period, as may other questions that totally change the parameters compared with what now looks likely to happen.

INDUSTRIAL DEMOCRACY/PARTICIPATION

For most companies and government agencies in Sweden, industrial democracy up to the end of the 1960s was identical with the proceedings of works councils, departmental committees, or equivalent bodies. However, two pamphlets put out by the Swedish Employers' Confederation, the one called "Företagsdemokrati och företagsorganisation" (1964) and the other "Samarbete i framtidens företag" (1965), exerted great influence over the debate on "executive and specialist fields" in the Swedish world of work and were consequently very useful in making these groups more knowledgeable about industrial democracy. But in actual substance not very much work toward change got started on industrial democracy beyond this debate until the late 1960s, when renewed interest was triggered by the Norwegian experiments with "self-governing groups." Thorsrud-Emery's book, *Mot en ny Bedriftsorganisasjon*, was published in 1969. The questioning period in Swedish society from 1968 to 1970 also had a highly seminal effect on the development of industrial democracy. Experiments with change and growth were mounted at a great many workplaces. The development council, together with counterpart bodies in public administration, became an important vehicle for initiating and evaluating experiments with industrial democracy. As a result very substantial portions of the Swedish world of work acquired their own—and new—experiences of industrial democracy/participation over a period of about five years.

Companies have chiefly focused on something called direct workplace democracy. The interest shown in self-governing groups, for example, may be seen to reflect, first, the desire to make better use of human

Table 13.2

1950	1960	1970	1980
Representative democracy	Union representation on boards of directors, etc.	Direct democracy (workplace democracy)	Economic democracy (shared ownership collectively-locally or wage-earner and/or community funds)

resources at a workplace so as to increase productivity; and second, a desire to achieve greater motivation among the employees as an indirect means of increasing productivity. A fear that companies will become more bureaucratic when enlarging the representative system, combined with shifting power to elected representatives, can also be noted among companies.

As yet economic democracy in companies has not progressed beyond the discussion stage, but some form of it may be expected to become a reality for companies to work with, beginning in the 1980s (Table 13.2).

Industrial Democracy—Organization Development

Industrial democracy as a working method or idea, need not be an engine of change in a company. By *idea* I refer to that form of industrial democracy/ job participation that has been introduced in the United States and to some extent in England and Ireland as well. Here the usual aim is to get the employees to become more work-motivated: Increased power to bring influence to bear is possible for the individual, but not primarily for groups of employees. In principle, therefore, the status quo persists as far as shifts of power are concerned.

Given this *ideological* background, industrial democrcy that seeks to change the power relationships between, say, owners and employees, management and manual workers and nonmanual workers, companies and unions, will be more conflict-oriented than the aforementioned "participation model," if it is implemented with a high change tempo.

The programs for deepening industrial democracy that "steer" the job-participation changes in Sweden are thoroughgoing and fast-working in their power-shifting effects. How the practical reality looks in a particular firm is bound to rub off on the form and the speed at which power shifts occur. One company may put the pivotal weight of its industrial-democracy development on the representative plane, whereas another company will put it closer to the task or the "shop floor." A company may represent a wide variety of industrial democracy changes. Industrial democracy may live its own life in the company or it can coexist with the company's total development. It can become a program for changing things together, where the engine of change is a steering committee jointly appointed by employees and management. Industrial democracy and organization development then become concepts for a process of growth shared in common.

Organization Development with Group-Dynamic Learning Methods

The group-dynamic working method has several different interacting objectives. Among other things, it seeks to equip individuals, groups, and organizations with a higher degree of readiness for change, and to enable business and other organizations to intensify the pace of change. In that way companies and their employees are enabled to learn a better technique for dealing with changes through their own group-dynamic experiences. The individual can learn more about how he reacts and how other people react. That is to say, change will not only be a matter of practical and theoretical craftsmanship but also something that takes human feelings and relationships into account. At the same time the group-dynamic method of working makes it possible to instill greater awareness in the participants. It gives them insight into the fact that they themselves can be brought in to exercise influence, and it also raises their resistance to manipulation. Sensitivity training was banned in a number of American companies not because it was useless but because people began to question and be demanding. So the group-dynamic working method can be one way to set a company off on the path to industrial democracy. This also explains why the unions must not only be informed but perhaps also be persuaded to familiarize themselves, at least more actively than has so far been true of the Swedish scene, with what group-dynamic learning methods mean for them and what their significance is for fostering change in companies.

Industrial democracy can cope with its own development and does not need organization development as a change method. For its part, organization development cannot function unless allowance is made for the particular path that it takes in each company and government agency. Industrial democracy can also step up its own change pace in each company/agency by taking the total organization's developing activities into its respective corporate program.

I should like to contend that group-dynamic learning methods as well as organization development can accelerate the implementation of an industrial democracy program in a company.

EDUCATIONAL NEEDS FOR TRAINING IN THE ART OF CHANGE

For a human being to learn he must be enabled to draw upon his own experiences. The cardinal changes that have taken place in the Swedish world of work over the past five to ten years have certainly given individuals and organizations experiences of different kinds, for instance insight into the need for the individual to build up his corpus of knowledge, the better to enable him to tap his influence-wielding potential; increased training in the art of working together in groups; and human relations and confrontation training.

To a great extent changes have "hit" people, companies, and government agencies as phenomena that have been susceptible to little, if any, control. Many people have therefore perceived these changes to be threats; indeed, not a few of these threats have become real due to shifts in power relationships, value judgments, established positions, and so on. Group-dynamic learning methods have been used in many companies and government agencies to help smooth this readjustment for individuals and groups. Then, too, no doubt many individuals have felt that these learning methods threaten their personal privacy.

If I could turn the clock back, I would have liked executive development programs to have used group-dynamic learning methods back in the 1960s. The result would have been a higher level of contingency planning to cope with the rapid readjustment in Swedish working life during the first half of the 1970s.

If industrial democracy is going to succeed, it is also necessary to change patterns of communication for both the executives and their associates. An additional step required to change the working environment is to change the hierarchical philosophy and to reduce the dependence on authority. For the executive/specialist this means cutting down on his formal power, for the associate it means training him to exercise greater influence over decision making. Perhaps we can call this changing the power distribution or the division of power in an organization. If we want to change the low utilization of "human capital" in private and public employment, we must also clarify people's experience of power/impotence at their place of work.

It follows that I see yet another commitment to individual and group development with reference to these questions, as well as the questions taken up below, which deserves top-ranking priority in the Swedish world of work.

If we want to achieve a formation of values, opinions, and norms in the world of work (and naturally extending across the total life situation) that can enhance the individual's ability to enjoy work and a whole quality of life, we must deploy time and educational resources to this end within business and government. If we want to counteract emptiness, indifference, competition, and discord between people at a workplace, we must give them the opportunity to realize their potential both as individuals and social beings.

The ongoing and rapid process of change in Swedish working life and society results in something that many call "anomie" or "normlessness" for individuals and groups. Since the word "normless" has ethical overtones, I should like instead to use a term like "norm uncertainty," which often goes with individual/personal uncertainty. The concept of solidarity has also become unclear to many. Solidarity solely toward oneself, one's group, one's buddies—or what? The values of the competitive society penetrate the individual's values.

I should also like to emphasize that it is not the philosophy held by any one or more persons which should suffuse any training in value judgments. If anything, the educational situation must be such that it lets people join forces to prepare a "rating platform" for their work together in the company.

If one wants to achieve positive results of change in an organization over and above those of the more facile type ("Well, we're doing something about it"), resources will have to be invested in training for change. By that I mean knowledge, learning experiences, and attitudes that let the employees themselves get in on the act of deciding whether they want future changes, and not only be trained to accept changes after they have occurred.

My sole purpose in presenting these brief ideas on change, power, values, and norms has been to highlight areas that have been far too much neglected in corporate and administrative training during the past ten years—not least in Sweden.

Group-Dynamic Learning in the Development of Industrial Democracy

By group-dynamic learning methods I mean, in the following, the collective term for experience-oriented learning that is chiefly based on theories taken from social psychology. Put concisely, the methods build, first, on learning to see *what* happens between individuals in the course of (say) problem-solving, discussion, and so on; and second, on letting the individual learn more about *how* he reacts and how others react: that is to say, in the latter case they increase the chances for self-awareness and awareness of one's own and other's resources. With the expression, "learning to see what happens," I allude to the underlying message that is nearly always to be found in contacts between human beings. In the political, technological, and behavioral-science experimentation that has been conducted in Swedish working life since the late 1960s around changed work structuring, social engineering, changed working environment, and applied creativity, the group-dynamic learning methods have come to be used not least in the experiments that changed work-structuring and social engineering as well as in the field of executive development.

My experiences of participation problems and group-dynamic learning, plus first-hand experiences of how hard it is for people to establish true rapport with one another, have reinforced my faith in group-dynamic learning methods as an integral part of the development of industrial democracy. The prospects for a real breakthrough of direct workplace democracy must allow for interpersonal relations at the workplace by breaking off, root and branch, from past practice. This observation applies not least to Swedish workplaces.

Group-dynamic Methods in Companies

Now, how are group-dynamic learning methods used to promote organization development in Swedish companies? I shall give some examples of such methods in action.

When it comes to training located outside the company, the individual employee encounters it as follows: If he is climbing up the career ladder and taking a course in management at the IFL College in Sweden or its equivalent in one of the other Nordic countries, he will be engaging in different training sessions of a group-dynamic character. First, in order to learn the methods as such; second, in order to gain added insight into himself; and third, so that the training group as such will, by virtue of group training, be better able to assimilate the remaining course content.

This will also happen if the employee chooses instead to attend one of the international top executive courses, as in Switzerland, France, or the United States. Other executives, including members of the supervisory group, will encounter group-dynamic learning methods when they enroll in, for example, manager-training courses mounted by the Swedish Employers' Confederation. Other people may have made known to the training department that they would like to attend a sensitivity training laboratory or a creativity course where they can obtain their own experiences of group dynamics.

Internally, in the company, he or she may take courses in subjects like teamwork training, group training, creativity training, or encounter groups. Many companies and government agencies run their own courses in leadership and cooperation, which vary from one to four weeks in duration.

Perhaps the company also has a professional group-dynamics trainer or external consultant who takes a direct part in committee meetings, departmental get-togethers, or project meetings. Here his task will often be to contribute to analysis of problem-solving conflicts, and so on; in addition, he may conduct training in interpersonal relations.

What Can These Methods Give the Individual and the Company?

Group-dynamic learning methods can give increased insights to the participants about their own resources, and about obstacles to the use of those resources, as well as knowledge of how other people react and of how groups and organizations arise, develop, and interact.

These learning methods play a major role in the large-scale process of change and employee participation that is going on in the Swedish world of work. By the same token they can contribute to improved self-awareness and thus indirectly to a better quality of life for many employees.

Group-dynamic learning experience can help people learn to become more genuine and sincere, traits that in their turn promote a real development of industrial democracy. Insight into one's own way of functioning can bring heightened awareness of the innate potential and resources that can be brought to bear to change the personal situation. Group-dynamics training can broaden the participants' perspectives on life, existential problems, and so on. It can also effect changes in values that are conducive to increased group solidarity.

Bokslut från LM, a book by Göran Palm, which describes his experiences of working on the shop floor at LM Ericsson, the well-known telecommunications enterprise, takes up the significance of language for contact or lack of contact between groups. Not only on the shop floor but also in offices, verbal communication and togetherness at work suffer because people are unaccustomed to expressing their feelings and sentiments. Changed/improved relations between individuals can alter a group's mode of functioning: That is to say, pressure may be brought to bear on the climate within the work group, in the workshop, or in the office. I should like to emphasize that it is important and imperative to have the tasks at work themselves take on a higher degree of meaningfulness for as many employees as possible. But unless this greater meaningfulness is accompanied by training in how to increase the meaningfulness of interpersonal relations at the workplace, we shall each of us stand there with our meaningful jobs but will not have learned to establish meaningful rapport with one another. Moreover, it is not least essential to afford opportunities for increased contact between employees from different language groups or hierarchies. The work team that is given more and more discretion to plan its own work, or affect wage payment systems, product quality, and so on, may tend to become ethnocentric vis-à-vis other groups. Here again, group-dynamic learning can be an instrument for bringing about greater insight into the brotherhood of man and into the need for solidarity between groups at the workplace. The loner at the workplace who from his childhood years has learned never to rely on anybody else feels lost in group situations. If he or she so desires, enrolling in some form of group-dynamic insight training may provide the key to that knowledge of self that can only come from being allowed to share in the experience of group fellowship.

The Development Council's experiments with changed work structuring and the reports that emanate from the experiments going on inside state-owned companies, as well as my own work with in-plant groups, have strengthened my conviction that some form of group training is needed to get both partly self-governing groups and other group activity relating to employee participation to function. Group-dynamic learning methods can be one way.

To care for one another, to care for those who cannot take the work pace, to care for those who are older, who are somehow deviant or erratic, to care about what happens outside the workplace—all these things are also part of the quality of life and at the very least should be a demand that we can impose on the climate at a workplace.

Risks in Organization Development

In the following I should simply like to call attention to some problems connected with organization-development programs in companies and government agencies, without dwelling at great length on other forms of effects or positive results.

Organization development (hereinafter referred to by its Swedish initials, OU) brings with it the risk that large groups of executives will learn methods of cooperation that can be used quasidemocratically, especially if the training is exclusively concerned with cooperation and used as special technique for exercising leadership. Moreover, the confrontation must actually take place and be thrashed out and become a meaningful part of a work group's way of functioning together. It is also important to give a present reality to the values held by the participants, values that are bound up with quality-of-life questions, working environment questions, and so on. I very much doubt whether many OU programs have been doing this sort of thing, either in Sweden or elsewhere. Here I feel particularly dubious about the structuring practice training, where people use some form of training kit to go through a series of group-dynamic learning exercises. This is not to suggest that the structured exercises are useless

—far from it—but my experience is that one does not actually get beyond the objective for the training program or change activity in which they are included. Organization development and group dynamics have penetrated more rapidly than the ethical guidelines and the interest in value-judgment problems.

An additional risk with OU lies on another plane. Increased work commitment and increased work motivation encourages many employees to start using resources that were not demanded earlier. Special group training helps with this to a great extent, and obviously so do the intensified efforts on behalf of employee participation, which will create, in some instances, more stress and psychosomatic problems. Even so, results from a number of OU projects indicate the risk that another form of elitism may be developing: those who became committed, and those who were not—or tried to be but lagged behind in their "development." Competition—instead of cooperation—may also enter into group-development and participation problems. Distances lengthen between the committed and the noncommitted, who may become more alienated than before. Besides, OU can become a new instrument for committing/exploiting people who unsuspectingly give "more" of themselves to the companies without being clear about the consequences. So unless OU is rooted in industrial democracy, it may turn into a manipulative modus operandi that in the longer run reduces people's commitment to work and working life.

In the following we shall look at the experiences gained from a group-dynamic method used in OU to change working life.

Sensitivity Training and Changing the World of Work

Sensitivity training undertaken in a greatly changing society can be expected to produce more positive long-term effects than in a more "change-static" society. Although I am in no position to make comparisons for this purpose, I should like to present quite briefly some results from a Swedish follow-up survey of sensitivity training laboratories (ST).

This survey relates to 406 people who took part in ST's organized by the PA Council in the period from the spring of 1972 to the spring of 1975. Altogether, 374 completed questionnaires were analyzed and tabulated. Control tests gave no reason to assume that the nonresponse group deviated in any material respect from the analyzed group.

The survey participants spread rather evenly across different gainfully employed ages, 23 percent were women, and nearly 60 percent had a university education. Slightly more than one-third had personal problems with which they hoped ST would help them. Nearly 90 percent of the survey participants felt that what they learned had been rather or very useful for their work. About 90 percent said that through taking part in ST they had learned something rather or very useful about themselves, about others, and about groups. More than 80 percent felt that ST can generally give working people something worthwhile.

Over 60 percent had taken initiatives to change conditions at work after taking part in ST. Somewhat more than 50 percent had taken corresponding initiatives to change a situation away from work. The direction taken by stated wishes to change the world of work was toward more open and democratic forms of working together. Among the change-oriented initiatives were increased group activities, greater delegation, and a more active commitment to prevail on the "powers-that-be" to rectify anomalies.

Most participants felt that the openness that developed during the courses was constructive, liberating, beneficial, and reciprocal.

SUMMARY—AND SOME THOUGHTS FOR THE FUTURE

Summary

In this chapter I have primarily accounted for:

Why the Present Situation in Sweden?

1. Union pressure in the late 1960s for increased employee participation, and so on.
   Concerted political pressure relating to democracy issues in the 1970 election
   Productivity demands in the 1960s led to:
   a. executive development/MBO (Management by Objectives)
   b. organization development
   c. sociotechnical systems
   d. partly self-governing groups
   e. group-dynamic learning methods
2. Led to legislation relating to:
   a. security of employment
   b. increased decision-making power for safety stewards
   c. time off for training
   d. protection for union officials
   e. the working environment
   f. paragraph 32.

Attitude and power changes, 1968–1976, plus laws/agreements relating to:

1. Older-man power
2. Power to safety stewards
3. Employment security (1/7/74)
4. Instruction in Swedish for immigrants (1/7/73)
5. Fifth vacation week
6. Right to time off for training (1/1/75)
7. Protection for union official (1/7/74)
8. Law promoting adjustment (1/7/74)
9. Section 32 (right of first interpretation)
   Section 32 Bargaining/right of contract labor (law 32, 1/1/77)
10. Expanded day-care facilities
11. Methods:
    a. group dynamics
    b. OU
    c. self-governing groups
    d. experiments
12. "Worker-directors" (1/4/73)
13. Discussion re:
    a. Economic democracy
    b. Six-hour workday?
14. Changed school system
15. Three-shift
    Five-shift
    Six-shift
16. Equality issues, women's issues, quality of life.

Group-dynamic learning in Sweden has been based on:

1. Group development within
   a. the private sector
   b. public administration
   c. schools
   d. the care sector
   e. the armed forces
2. Group development through
   a. process consultation
   b. group training
   c. laboratory training.

Naturally, the enormous commitment to group-dynamic methods within Swedish society and working life made during the past five years will exert great influence over coming events with respect to employee participation and organization development within companies and government agencies. If we take a parallel to MBO (Management by Objectives), job descriptions, and so on, the discussion began to be taken up in the early 1960s, and quite a few programs were being installed by the mid-1960s, followed by general acceptance around 1970 when it was just about time to install other organization systems. So by 1980 OU should be pretty well moored in companies/agencies, and integrated with the development of industrial democracy.

As to changes of corporate power in Sweden seen over a longer perspective, we can describe them like this:

1850	Owner/managers
1900	Owner/managers
	state
	unions
1950	Owner/managers
	Employed management
	state
	unions
1970	Owner/employed management
	state
	unions
1975	Different ownership patterns, changed management patterns
	Other interests
	state
	unions
1990	Quality of Life
	state
	unions
	employees
	owners
	other interests

The Wind Has Subsided

It was when Swedish society and the world of work dipped down into "cold water" in 1973 that the experiments with "partly self-governing groups" in the world of work had largely spent their course. Legislation had come into force or was on its way in many sectors of working life. A government commission had been appointed to inquire into "Paragraph 32"—that section of the Swedish Employers' Confederation's document concerned with the right to manage; and a pretty good idea could be formed of what the commission was going to say about employee participation.

Up to 1971–1972 most initiatives concerned with such matters as organization and the training and development of personnel had come from managements or from associations of manufacturers and employers. Today, it appears to me that the wind has gone out of management's sails in these matters. The managers feel squeezed and unsure about the strength and scope of power changes in the world of work.

Personally, I think it a strength of society and working life that the unions have pounced so quickly and conclusively on areas of work that used to be exclusively reserved to management and its specialists. If we compare this with the course of events in, say, the English-speaking countries, this assumption of responsibility is unique as well as a positive challenge and opportunity, not least for our companies.

However, there is one drawback in this: It might cause top managements to lose interest in also taking initiatives and urging development in these areas.

On January 1, 1977, a new law entered the statue book: enlarged "codetermination in working life" for the employees. Briefly, the new law abolishes the employer's "right to direct and apportion work," as spelled out in paragraph 32 of the Swedish Employers' Confederation's earlier agreement with the Swedish Confederation of Trade Unions and the Swedish Central Organization of Salaried Employees. In principle, moreover, the workers (manual and nonmanual) will enjoy an unlimited right to negotiate and reach agreements. On top of this, in most disagreements about the rules, the *right of first interpretation* moves from the employer to the trade unions, which are specifically designated to represent the employees. Hence, January 1, 1977 can be seen as a date that will usher in a period that will be marked by large shifts in the distribution of power, the assumption of responsibility, and the utilization of human resources.

Toward 1985–1990

One transitional problem that will be accentuated up to 1980 is that top executives will find it difficult to change over from hierarchic authority decisions to a greatly expanded system of joint consultation and participatory management. The employees are unaccustomed to bringing influence to bear on decisions that fall outside their immediate work situation—and their educational backgrounds are deficient, too. Middle-aged and older employees will find it hard to change their attitudes on questions of the who-is-going-to-decide type toward a more informed and less authority-dependent right to function. These are all habits and attitudes that are the result of earlier systems of childrearing and social development.

As every year passes, new cohorts will be entering the job world with a better education behind them, and values and attitudes other than those of the age group that is due for retirement. Add to this the "experience learning" that will take place in Swedish working life and society in the years just ahead, combined with massive training of group-dynamic and other group-developing character. Accordingly, the following assumptions can be made about "working life in Sweden as it will be in 1985":

The concepts "superior-subordinate" will be "historical" and superseded by "employees with different tasks."

A more open—more authentic—climate between people on and off the job.

Greater awareness and assumption of responsibility, that is, more and more people centering on themselves, on relations with others, on business and civic activities.

New problems and terms of reference that spring organically from the development, and that cannot be foreseen at present.

CONCLUDING WORDS

My personal philosophy is optimistic, and my view of man is imbued with confidence in people and their resources. I feel convinced that the more individuals and groups obtain knowledge, insights, and experiences, the more they will also make use of these.

Values and norms in the school, family, working life, and society, which may move in stages from competition to cooperation, from egoism to solidarity and consideration of the less well-to-do and other buffeted member of society, can contribute to shaping that value reference frame that enables us to approach concepts like positive human coexistence and increased quality of life.

I am realistic in my optimistic philosophy and quite clear about everything's innate dialectic antithesis; but through this I also see the dialectic potential for continuous development—with people who are aware. Abuse of power, excessive bureaucracy, conflicts betwen trade unions and their members may be some of the risks that lie ahead. As I see it, a too slow pace of change in the school system, which serves to retain competitive attitudes and dependence on authority, is one of the biggest obstacles to shaping a more human society in which to live. What about group-dynamic learning methods? Well, they have come to stay, but in my opinion they will have to be raised to higher levels of sophistication.

Chapter 14

Cross-Cultural Aspects of Organization as Experienced in Expatriate Family Moves

Harold Bridger

"Le poisson ne sait qu'il vit dans l'eau que quand il est sur la rive."

Old French Saying

"He only says, 'Good fences make good neighbors' . . .
Before I built a wall I'd ask to know
What I was walling in or walling out,
And to whom I was likely to give offense.
Something there is that doesn't love a wall,
That wants it down, . . .
He says again, 'Good fences make good neighbors.'

Robert Frost
(Extract from "Mending Wall.")

INTRODUCTION

The unknown French wit and Robert Frost are at one in recognizing that cross-cultural perception and experience may all too frequently be gained at considerable risk; on the one hand, dying for want of one's own medium of values and standards, and losing the water one knows; on the other the danger of being aware of other territory only when giving or receiving offense. The history of intergroup and international growth and tension in a world of increasingly interdependent countries, organizations and institutions of many kinds has pointed up the necessity for greater

This contribution is derived from a paper read to the International Occupational Health Conference at Le Vesinet, Paris, September 1973.

awareness and understanding of the comparative and contrasting aspects of different cultures. Language teaching has become a growth industry in itself but it has also been discovered that professionals and members of a common business function or discipline may get along more readily across natural boundaries than within their interdisciplinary project teams.

Learning the other language can be of great assistance, especially when combined with discovering and deepening one's knowledge of customs, conventions, and norms. At the same time, as those who remain in another country for any length of time are aware, there is always the quandary that Robert Frost expresses so beautifully and crisply in more than one poem, of becoming part of the culture at the expense of losing one's own. Increasingly there are expatriates who are experienced as "half-members" of other countries; there is also the new acultural "jet-set."

While much has begun to be compiled about different national cultures and preparatory setting established to allay culture-shock in some measure, few multinationals and other institutions have fully recognized the critical relevance of these issues to the effectiveness of the enterprise in operational, planning, or decision-making terms.

Over a period of about five years, however, a deliberate attempt was made by a few multinationals, banks, and government bodies in the late 1960s to study the issues, concerns, and problems experienced by international managers and their families. In periodic courses ranging from four to six weeks the selected fourteen or fifteen members explored a series of organizational, economic, and cultural dimensions. Wherever possible these were not only concerned with the general international environment and the personal or organizational interests of those taking part, but more especially directed towards the multidisciplinary, crosscultural institution that the members themselves formed—and that also had its own organizational aims and developing culture. These components of program studies and institutional self-study were further developed with respect to those wives—and their families when available—who could spend the last half of the course with their husbands. Wives had their own program, shared part of their husbands' when appropriate for all, and also conducted their own self-review.

Although it is impossible in one article to communicate the rich and varied experience gained in working with the wives' groups over a significant proportion of these courses, an attempt will be made to report in detail one such group while including the experience and derived concepts from others.[a]

[a] The classic approach developed by Laurence Wiley in *Village in the Vaucluse* (Cambridge, Mass: Harvard University Press, 1961) has not been surpassed. An equivalent in the cinematic medium was *Kermesse Heroique* 1926.

INTERNATIONAL AND CROSS-CULTURAL ASPECTS IN THE GROUP OF WIVES

The group consisted of two German, four French, one Canadian, and three American wives; and the group consultant was British.

There were many other cultural divisions in the group. There were those who were experienced in moving around in different countries; some still resident abroad; and some now back in their home countries. Some had grown-up families and others had young children. Then there were the different kinds of management and organizations that their husbands were in—some more like each other and some more different from each other. Similarly, there were different kinds of interests; whether they were allied to his, or whether these were independent of one's husband's interests; doing things together or complementing what he did in the free time together. All these dimensions, as well as others, brought different subgroups of the whole group into being. Thus while we did speak a good deal about national and cross-cultural matters, these other subgroup cultures were always bringing new patterns into the life of the group.

While there was always some difficulty—depending on circumstances—about settling into the culture of a different country, there were other situations that indicated that the difficulties were not always international. We were given examples where the problem of being accepted into a community in one's own country could be more difficult than being received into one of another country where the subculture happened to be more open to strangers. From another example of a large number of families moving from one part of a country to another, there was great reluctance on the part of many wives to do this, although their husbands were ready to go for their career and work in the organization. No one was really happy about leaving a settled community for an unknown one, and it was understandable that some wives were not fitted for moves and could not meet the demands and problems that occurred in these circumstances. A man might be personally suitable for a new job or promotion abroad, but his domestic circumstances might not stand up to the pressures on it. Whether wives welcomed such moves and experience and whether they found satisfactions and a deepening relationship with their husbands and family, it was far from easy when the settling in depended on so many more factors than the cultural environment: on the capacity, and attitudes of the wife to such experience, on the receiving community, on the degree of support and help one received from one's coexpatriates, and on understanding and help from the husband's organization.

For the wife, with her anchor in the family and home, it was harder because with the husband's absence she missed the neighborhood she had grown up in or in which she had built her connections and basic friend-ships—often including her own family ones. The husband moved with his organizational networks around him, although he too shared most of these feelings of separation with his wife and family. Keeping together, how-ever, was the main thing; and it was always something of a problem when, because the length of stay of a husband away did not happen to reach the time allowed, the wife or wife and family could not go too.

When one did move away to another setting, whether to another country or even to another part of one's own country (as in the previous example) there was always the need to consider how far one could find one's feet and settle into the new environment and community—and how far to spend time and relationships with families and friends of one's own culture or subculture. There were many national families who seldom moved outside the relationships they built with each other—a foreign community in another country—built inside national and language barriers or inside the husband's organizational one. Getting the right balance was difficult for those who wanted to grow some roots and friendly relations (and find real friends) in the receiving community, while maintaining their own culture with families of similar background. Much depended on the openness of that receiving community and indeed of the fellow-culture families. Any tightness and rigidity on the part of either could make life very difficult for the wife in particular and for helping her children develop flexible attitudes for themselves. To earn the right to settle in required much mutual understanding between husband and wife but, not least, they would be helped or hindered by the climate of opinion between the two cultures, the one of which they were part and the receiving one.

It was a French member of the group who drew our attention to the need for reflecting on the international and cross-cultural aspects of the group itself, which was, naturally, not found to be easy. It was always easier to discuss a topic or some material provided from outside the group—either by a speaker or by "authority." This was something that, as the saying goes, one can "get one's teeth into." We found that to express personal experience and views meant taking something of a risk because it opened ourselves to let others see a bit more of us—and how could we be sure that we would not be seen as an exception in some way or be ridiculed? How could we be sure that people, and especially those from another country, would understand our values and standards? Would they think us strange—and if we asked *them* questions, would they think that we were criticizing or attacking them? So one of the main difficulties in the group was recognizing national differences even in this respect, and trying to understand how they arose. We found, for example, that for French people to discuss personal experiences was far from easy because it went against their culture. There could be plenty of cut and thrust on the given subject from outside or on intellectual affairs not immediately about people in the group. If discussion was used to "get one's teeth into" (like food), one could hardly be so aggressive perhaps as to do this with each other's experience. (The expression used was "couper les cheveux en quatre"—the nearest equivalent of which was "splitting hairs" in English.)

Of course, it was recognized that we all tried to sense what other people thought or implied without openly asking in words. So we tried to get it through the "music behind the words." But often we took what was said in the way *we* thought or understood it—which may not have been what was intended at all. How was one to get feed-back, confirmation or otherwise? Then there was the problem of saying something in a certain way *in case* they took it the "wrong way"—which often led to even more confusion. Could we establish our *own culture* for *this* wives' group which would mean establishing conventions and customs for our group without infringing on the way we behaved in our other groups and communities elsewhere? Could we give ourselves permission in *this* group to speak of our experiences and find out what the others thought? And this of course meant that it was not just the people of the *other* countries and cultures about whom we were concerned, but more particularly the *people of one's own culture* —with whom we would be transgressing the cultural pattern and mores. As was said on different occasions by a number of the group, "When I go to another country, X, it is not difficult to take part in their kind of life and even act in their way." But in doing so, one is not giving up one's own culture or taking part with one's own people. In an international setting, therefore, it can be harder to settle in with one's own people around than because of the others.

Many of these issues and others were discovered, particularly when we tried to establish how we should address each other. The consultant described how he had run into trouble in the men's group when he took certain things for granted. We soon discovered that although the American and Canadian approach would easily allow first names to be used, the German members also liked the idea but needed to have the agreement or approval of the acknowledged older (representing experience, wisdom, authority in *their* culture) members of the group before being able to adopt it comfortably. There was no question but that French members in their own culture would use surnames with Madame or Mlle. even though they might know one another well for years. Much depended on the degree of intimacy in other contexts and there were quite clear guidelines in this respect. The differences in the French members of the group about the readiness to use first names could be simply one of how accustomed one was to being in other groups, for example with Americans. It was becoming more the custom in Britain, but even there it was far from common to use first names early on in an acquaintance. The European, even when first names were used, had a different approach to early relationships and modes of address. But between Europeans there were also differences in custom and convention, as we have seen. As discussion progressed, we came upon an important understanding of some of the issues that perhaps lay behind these apparent reservations. At one point when a French member said that she was prepared to go along with what was agreed by others, there was a strong wish by the German members that this would not let them comfortably use first names because the particular person was one of the "permission-givers" in the group as far as they were concerned. It also transpired that for the Americans, using first names meant that in this way they were being given an *identity* as *individuals*. It then became clear that using first names in France did not have that particular connotation or inference. In fact, to do that one would use the proper title and surname. Thus all the modes and conditions attached to addressing people would seem to suggest that *all* were trying to give people a *full identity in their own culture*, but that this was done in different ways in different countries. An American suggested at one point that we should perhaps use the French mode of address since we were in France. But it was agreed that although we were in France, we were here to consider ourselves in an international setting.

Thus in the United States and Canada, the first name gives a personal identity and a sense of being individually recognized. In France it could be said that first names could only readily be used, with regard for the individual's personal identity, when ça va sans dire that his identity will be fully recognized—and this required special conditions and perhaps time. *Time* and *friendship* were certainly factors in Britain in this respect; and until these conditions were satisfied the use of first names might be frequent but was more of a formality. For German members personal identity was, in the culture, accorded by those in special positions in the community and in the culture itself—but this aspect too might be changing and becoming less rigorous, as it was elsewhere.

THE WIFE'S POSITION

"Shared troubles are halved troubles,
Shared joys are double joys."

(German saying quoted in discussion.)

The wife can be more exposed than her husband; his work and organization give him special roles from within which to establish his relationship with others. A woman needs to be more "natural" with her children and domestic responsibilities around her. Her way of doing things, the conventions and customs of her culture, are therefore more open to the community in which the family is living. This can be advantageous or the reverse, depending on the community around and the circumstances, whether business or social, with which the wife and mother has to cope. The wife's experience is therefore open to more understanding and to more misunderstanding.

There was some discussion of whether any destructive criticism of one's own country reflected on oneself. There was the recognition that one was representing one's country abroad and also how far the criticism of an individual could reflect on, or be an affront to, one's country—and similarly for matters of merit.

Various aspects of responsibilities and circumstances were mentioned, such as the feeling that one should keep many troubles and anxieties away from husbands so that they could concentrate and do their best in their work; on the other hand, recognizing the need to share things in marriage. The husband on his side had corresponding feelings about his concerns, whether career or work, at various times. It was in the marriage that the two individuals grew a *joint* set of values and agreement on such matters, and this formed the basis of interdependence. On the other hand, day-to-day happenings did not by any means fit neatly into a set of rules and there were bound to be times when one found (or felt) that one bothered the other too much, or that one had kept away too much. Certainly this was likely to be more true for the international family and the less-settled existence. Yet coming through such experiences could make opportunity for having a unity and joint individuality stronger. There was also greater opportunity for the marriage to be more mature and deepened with the experiences gained in building the family with the children, and with the various associations and friendships developed with other families, groups, and organizations.

While each marriage worked out its own *unique* set of ways of relating to the family itself, to the community around, to the husband's organization, and, not least, to the individual development of each partner of the marriage, were there any common patterns for families of one culture? And was there any kind of common pattern for families of the international manager? For example, might not wives of international managers have some *common* values and mutual understanding that could not easily be shared with other wives who had lived their main family lives in their own country? On the other hand, there would, for example, be attitudes and behavior toward ways of bringing up children and toward running one's home that might bring a different alignment. Even within one country, there were differences that related to religion, class, education, part of the country, ages of couple, duration of the marriage, and so on.

FIRST THOUGHTS ON THE COMMON GROUP EXPERIENCE OF HAVING HUSBANDS AWAY

While the strength, strangeness, reactions, and feelings of the experience depended on so many factors (especially on how often it had occurred and with what intensity), everyone in the group recognized that they shared different degrees of *similar concerns and expressions*. In fact, one of the most significant aspects of the discussions was this finding of being "sisters under the skin." Naturally, at the same time there was some need to explore further why these differences of degree occurred; for example, those with younger children had much more to contend with in acting for, and "being" father as well as mother during a husband's absence. But while the *signs* and extent of missing one's husband would vary in type of *expression* (for example, accidents and incidents of different kinds) there was relief and understanding in finding that the *common* emotional missing of one's husband needed to find outlets in so many ways. These ways might seem strange and even sound foolish to express were it not that they showed the human reality of wanting to keep a loved person close or even of wanting an unloved one far away. In either case his actions and part in family and social life had become part of life itself. Thus for a loved person to be absent meant finding how much one missed and needed him and also how much *he* ought not to go away—however much reason could point out that it was for so good a cause in the future of the family and for the value and development of the man himself. The incidents or situations themselves could be important or trivial, but we saw that they could all be "justified" to show some safe way of blowing up against the husband not being home when he was needed—to indicate how much he was missed and loved, by saying, "See what happens when you are away."

The sense of absence seemed to be strongest immediately after one's husband left and then continued in those experiences of usual joint or complementary activity, when normally the parents or family would do things together or in those many accustomed circumstances: "I do this" while "you do that."

It was understandable, therefore, that the accidents or incidents would tend to take place at times when one was trying in all kinds of ways to do two things at the same time that had a degree of contradiction in them. For example, wanting to ensure that one's husband could stay away and fulfill his own career development and capacities for being the father and husband —and thus one keeps oneself busy and resourceful; on the other hand, wanting him back not only to help, but also to be with one at home—and thus finding oneself unable to do something or letting something slip. There was a recognition that the absence also meant having to find again those personal resources that one had had to develop for oneself before being married. In some instances, one wondered whether one could still use that capacity, and it was good to find out that one could. The absence also meant that one had to invent and develop activities, particularly where the children were concerned, to ensure that husband and father could still be present and alive at home even though he was away.

Many of the examples of all these kinds of situations and incidents showed how all shared this general experience and yet each wife and family found its own *unique* way of expressing it. A few will be recalled here, but only members of the group would be able to fill in the gaps in the references, and the many other examples that have not been given. Many were often accompanied by involuntary tears and a strong sense of missing at significant breakthrough points.

What to do on one's son's birthday?

Choosing and opening a bottle of wine.

Attending to the freezer or to the furnace.

Arranging a program of the children sleeping with one and in the guest-room.

Working in the garden.

Making dresses.

Spring cleaning activities and keeping busy longer.

Not sleeping.

A hand "going out of action."

Child becoming ill.

Reading a lot more.

Using the telephone to friends; talking to the dog.

How far one will be able to stand, for example with driving the car and other activities.

"It's all right to talk to yourself so long as you don't answer" (that is, don't close the circuit yourself—keep the missing one).

Generally speaking, the greatest difficulty was being out of contact, and this was felt despite letters. It was also recognized that with young families—and the younger the family, the more difficult—the problem of maintaining contact and all the aspects mentioned above, as well as others, were raised again with the wife coming to the course. As one person put it:

"When our husbands went we were at home with the children. When we come here, everything depends on the people who are caring for them and the contact we keep up." At the same time, it was good to come to be with one's husband.

When one gets married and builds a family together, one grows into a different life, particularly for the woman who may have had an independent work and career experience beforehand. (And this earlier independent career experience was felt to be certain to increase in the future with the equal likelihood that wives would go back to that career or another one as and when the children became old enough.) The fulfillment of the wifely and maternal roles is accompanied by relinquishing those roles that are mutually arranged, explicitly or implicitly, by husband and wife to make their own unique combination. At times a wife wonders whether she can, or will later be able to, recapture the resources she had in her independent days. In absenses such as these there was an element of rediscovering some of these resources—not just in the particular incident, but in finding whether one could be resourceful or self-reliant in other ways outside the family circle itself. This gives a clue to reentering work life or other interests later on.

SOME CULTURAL AND CROSS-CULTURAL ISSUES

Among other aspects that were raised, it was suggested that Anglo-Saxon and German members could take part more readily in general discussion, for the reasons given previously, in ways that were nearer to the experience and closer to life, whereas French people would expect to be more theoretical and logical. It was pointed out that the French person would ask "what is the *aim* or *purpose?*" Even though this could be expressed in the present situation as "sharing experiences to learn about cross-cultural and other aspects of international living," the method itself could appear to be "inconsequential chatter to while away the time," "doing nothing," and so on. On the other hand, bringing out and raising these differences of attitude, culture, or behavior in the group could lead to new awareness and understanding of each other, whether individually or nationally. It could also produce the rules and customs needed to build a group identity. Certainly it would avoid making the *assumptions* we were all making when we only had limited experience of others on which to base our impressions and find some rationale—or to identify the *other* people on our own *personal maps* of the world. In sharing these personal maps we were testing and risking some of our treasured beliefs and expressing our half-baked or partially formed ideas to the views of others.[b]

[b] In some way we all shared anxieties with the artist—the painter, musician, essayist, sculptor, and so on—because we exposed an 'unexplained' (and even unfinished) product to the world and risked hearing what others thought about it—and its author or creator (oneself). Of cousre, while this was true of all of us in the group meetings, it is also true of this communication—and me!

What is true for expressing personal experience and views is also true for other aspects of communication, such as language. Learning to speak in another person's language can also indicate that one wants to get across to the other person and to receive him. But sometimes not speaking or not bothering to learn can be felt as not caring or bothering to get to know— although there may of course be many other reasons. As before, it was all too easy to attribute the wrong assumption, for example, they are "reserved" or "volatile." We tend to look for some *common* attribute in the other country or culture that will seem to be *common* or *general* to more than one. Naturally members looked for such confirmation unconsciously on meeting each other in the wives' group and in the rest of the staff and members of the course experience.

We are more or less conscious of being ambassadors at different times, but we want to and can be ourselves as we begin to feel free with each other while retaining our own culture and identity.

There was some discussion on *prejudice and stereotypes*. It was recognized that they had little or nothing to do with intelligence or intellectual knowledge, and hence they could be described as unreasoning attitudes, without reality foundation but arising from early experiences, built-in attitudes, and anxieties developing through life. Besides prejudices and stereotypes concerning people of other countries and cultures, there were those one could easily recognize in one's own country. Each of us also knew that we *all* had prejudices and formed stereotypes of different kinds depending on our upbringing, experiences, and relationships we had met with both as individuals and in the groups to which we had belonged.

In the course of various discussions, members often referred to people or other groups that we tended to use as "marks" or "bearings" from which we could judge where we stood in our views or experience. Such *reference groups* gave a clue to our standards and aspirations.

These reference groups were ones to which we tended to attribute certain virtues, values, or standards, and which occupied certain positions in the community or society at large. Having identified some of these groups, we could see that they could be regarded positively or negatively depending on the purpose we used them for. The consultant used the police in Britain as having generally a positive reference value for most people in and outside the United Kingdom. On the other hand, very many years ago when a policeman (bogeyman) might be used by a mother to threaten her children when they were naughty, they could be a negative one for those who experienced police in that form—as punishing. Another negative example was Governor Wallace. Further interesting origins of reference figures, particularly in Germany, were mentioned.

The reference groups could be used from one's own or from different countries, and this is increasingly so today as we know so much more of what is going on elsewhere. Besides special companies, governmental bodies and figures (for example, the Ambassador), and banks, which stood for certain attributes in one's own country or abroad, we could compare the status and values associated with different groups within any one country with that of similar groups in other countries—for example, doctors, lawyers, aristocracy, network groups like Les Grandes 'Ecoles, teachers, nurses, and so on.

In Germany, it appeared that the professional groups were highly regarded: "Herr Professor, Herr Doktor," and so on.

In France, it was the intellectuals and bodies associated with that term, such as L'Academie Française.

In the United States, it was the successful individualist, the merchant prince, and the self-made man. Gradually, however, this was already changing, because the scientist was so highly regarded.

Generally this was an era of change in this respect because the positions and values associated with groups such as diplomats, technocrats, and so on were changing within countries—and managers were becoming professional.

The teachers were used as a special example. They tended to enjoy their work and to be dedicated, deeply interested in it. As such they were underpaid according to a past and even present culture. However, as other groups, like managers, began to enjoy their work and yet earn good money, teachers were striking. It was pointed out that in the American culture it would be necessary for teachers to organize and strike if the United States was going to respect them and to feel that they should have more money. In view of what had already been said about success and power, the teachers could not be seriously regarded unless they demonstrated that they merited it by American standards.

In referring again to representing one's country abroad, it was felt that foreign figures could be regarded differently and felt differently themselves depending on whether one was:

1. a working representative of an organization traveling abroad or stationed in the country—feels very responsible;
2. on holiday, in a private capacity—does not feel so very responsible.

CUSTOMS CONCERNING ENTERTAINMENT OF FRIENDS, BUSINESS ACQUAINTANCES, AND DEVELOPING FAMILY FRIENDSHIP

There was a liking to receive people at home, but a general dislike of cocktail parties. There was some connection between inviting people to one's home and being able to speak the language. Everyone preferred to prepare the food herself.

In Germany, most people want to sit down to a meal and talk. One also took unwrapped flowers when invited (a double symbol of a formal gift, but given informally).

With a cocktail party, it is easy to get rid of one's social obligations at once—but perhaps that is part of the reason why one does not like to attend them! It was, however, also useful to have a cocktail party for fund raising in social affairs.

There was general agreement that it was part of one's job as a wife to entertain, especially abroad where the social life can be more varied.

Generally, it was agreed that the smaller, more intimate few guests at home was best: There was the cold buffet for eighteen to twenty and the dinner at home for six to eight guests, husbands and wives. It was increasingly difficult to obtain help for the meals although all preferred to prepare their own meals.

In France, differences were drawn between customs in Paris and the provinces. In Paris, wives described how husbands were mostly invited on their own, and then to a restaurant, seldom if ever to the home. There was a suggestion that one needed to speak French to be invited home. The provinces were different in certain respects from Paris. Home was more naturally used, but those invited had to be accepted.

In certain respects, having too many friends or acquaintances from one's home country (or home town in one example, even though only a few hundred miles away) in a foreign location can be a disadvantage and prevent one from settling down and getting to know people better in the country where one is living.

It was becoming clear during this discussion that many of the trends described for inviting and visiting could be used as a metaphor or comparison for the way people related to each other in a group. It could apply to any multinational group where one either invited or visited another person by the way one addressed them and what one said.

For example, "taking people home" in the group discussion meant communicating one's own impressions, describing parts of one's own experience and that with family and community. Alternatively we could "take people out" by discussing subjects and topics that did not affect the group itself and the relations between the members of it. In fact, one could say that there were many ways of extending one's hand and different ways of receiving it. There were also many ways of indicating whether one wanted to continue the relationship or not.

Latin America appeared to raise special difficulties with regard to newcomers. There were much sharper lines of class distinction, and family structure was still traditional and often rigid, with arranged marriages. There was no middle class of any real size and the upper-class man often had his "querida" as well as his wife, so that the entertainment of guests meant making a problematic choice for the South American with respect to how, where, and with whom. This became intensified when it was a question of developing an acquaintanceship between families.

Social responsibility as Europeans and North Americans understood it—despite the variations between the different cultures and countries within that very large group—was lacking in South America. For example, at the simplest level, South Americans will accept invitations and not come and, alternatively, will not accept and still come.

We seemed here to be exploring *different combinations* of underlying philosophies and sense of values that the South American (or anyone else) experienced in his life through the different groupings to which he belonged. The South American, for example, seemed to be *constrained* in a rigid family structure, both in his family of upbringing and in his later-life family, with regard to choices in *that* part of his existence. Where, therefore, would he learn to *develop* group or social responsibility as a personal relinquishment of freedom for the good of his working colleagues, friends, and hosts? Even his querida might not represent much freedom.

Even though there might be an element of personal choice with the querida, she was also a further restriction on his time—however pleasant! Even license and rebellion would seem to be brought into the general social environment, so that even irresponsibility is socialized!

LINK BETWEEN FAMILY, HOME, MOVING AROUND, AND HOUSE

There were different attitudes expressed about house and home and the different ways in which members of the group related to having a base or not—and if so, at what point in their lives. Although there appeared to be some national characteristics in this respect, there would appear to be greater variation in the American culture. For all there was the base of one's own country and culture and then the base one had built together with one's husband in the family. While the *home* was the family, it could also be closely identified with the *house*. For some it was important to have a *house* somewhere back home, which could have a special place in the family life even though the family itself might be living abroad or traveling around. (This was also quite common in the United Kingdom where, with the fences and front gardens, one's house is one's castle.) It was indicated that Germans love their houses and take a deep pride in them. We did not perhaps spend long enough on this question of putting down roots, having a home to go to, and when was it best to have a base—if at all, depending on the particular circumstances of the family itself and the conditions of the husband's career.

Another common experience in all countries and cultures was the effect on families of the continuous rise in the cost of living. It had had an important effect on the husband/wife/family/house relationship. This rise was accompanied by evidence of bad workmanship and the difficulty of getting appropriate help (and the price) for the home or family. Where the husband can transform such need into a *constructive hobby* it was most valuable and rewarding in many ways. This applied to gardens and other aspects of the home. The important issue was generally agreed on—that this was fine as long as he got pleasure out of it and did not feel that he was a slave. He might actually get pleasure out of doing certain things in the garden or the house, and he might get pleasure out of doing something he did not necessarily like so much but because it was giving a special satisfaction to his wife or children. All felt, however, that for something to be continuously an unrelieved bore or chore would be damaging.

SETTLING-IN AND RE-ENTERING PHASES

This type of course experience had been an opportunity to try out different ways of looking at relationships between different families, and between wives whose husbands had different kinds of work but who shared a common interest in senior *management responsibilities* and *international* fields of operation and movement. Trying out relationships with each other both separately and together in such a way would be impossible back home where the customs and rules associated with one's own culture could act as a barrier to such exploration. This was apart from the difficulty that would be experienced in trying to set up such an opportunity. Of course, it was occasionally possible to exchange such direct testing out with one's closest personal friends, with whom one could express these viewpoints. It was recognized, however, that some difficulties arise in the early interchanges here during these discussions because in a way they may appear as an invasion of privacy. It seems to suggest that meeting as strangers, we are adopting an approach and treating each other in ways that are usually reserved for personal friends with whom we can afford not always to be polite, whom we can interrupt, and to whom we need not always listen. We momentarily looked ahead to the need to consider thinking about the return home. Of course there would be the welcome home, and of course one would have been missed. But would it also be all right to have had some enjoyable moments away from parents or away from children without feeling a bit guilty? Adults can cope better with these experiences because they have been through many separations and rejoinings. Children do not find it easy even when they are too good about it. Do you remember the game of peek-a-boo, which we play with very young children? It takes quite a while before children discover that the parent or adult has not actually disappeared and that he is behind the handkerchief or hand or around the corner.

We have to learn that our loved ones will come back—and when they do, we have to test them out a bit to be sure that they will not disappear again. This often means looking for trouble, provoking aggression, or being aggressive oneself.

A LEARNING EXPERIENCE FOR DEVELOPING EXPATRIATE HEALTH

It was also realized after a time that the different individual circumstances made for different concerns. Some had had the international (cross-cultural) experiences in the past rather than the present, for others it was new; some were coping with young children, while the children of others were grown up; some were living in their own country while others were living in another; some husbands were based at home, others traveled a lot; and there were many variations of the husband's managerial life and circumstances.

It would be impossible, therefore, to pretend that these few notes could reproduce all the nuances or music of the words and talk that were exchanged. But perhaps they will serve to reflect that even in pleasant surroundings and favorable circumstances, it was quite a big step from being a social meeting of wives whose husbands happened to be on an international course together, to earning the right to cross boundaries with each other.

The learning institution of the group was one that all members wish they had experienced many years before. There was much for organizations— and expatriates themselves—to realize that the main resources lay within themselves to achieve health in transitions.

THE EFFECTS ON CHILDREN

Although much shorter space will be given to this specific aspect of the total problem, it will not be because it is of lesser importance. On the contrary, the cumulative and reinforcing effects of moves on children— and of children on the moves—can be a determining factor in the individual's, the family's, and the organization's effectiveness in their different ways.

It will be seen, however, that whereas the basic stability of the child and the relationships within the family may be sound in themselves, a cross-cultural move may upset the parents if they do not or cannot adapt to the new community—and in turn the children suffer.

It is not unknown for moves to occasion child and parental stress on such questions as whether to leave them or to take them on the new assignments or whether to split parents for a time or to find another type of compromise solution. Each case is different, and the ages of children and their maturity are always vital. We must also bear in mind that today children may adjust better to moves than their parents, but, with all the variable factors to take into account, general rules are few—except that of taking note of the way the children are dealing with the different situations. Some will be coped with better than others, and taking it all in his stride may infer a good adjustment or a defense against anxiety; it depends on the child and the circumstances. If I select one particular example of stress that often passes without notice, it is because of the impairment for later life that is not infrequently seen in those who have moved frequently in early years—the capacity for making and keeping real friends. If, on establishing a friendship, some powers that be take the child and/or his family away so that he has to start again, there can be a weakening of the making of friends on succeeding occasions, to avoid the pain of losing them.

THE EFFECTS ON THE ORGANIZATION AND THE ACTIONS IT CAN TAKE

Least will be said on this score because this should be considered when all dimensions of the problem have been explored and interrelated. Certainly institutions employing international workers must consider the total life space of the people as individuals and families, but they also have a responsibility for ensuring that the possible implications of moves and returns to base are fully considered. No one expects organizations to be guarantors of the future or owners of family lives. But the opportunity to explore implications and prepare for moves could reduce the many tragic and disabling effects on the family *and* the organization's effectiveness. While privacy and choice must be respected in the organization's dealings with its international managers and their families, it is all too frequent that the avoidance of issues that could appear as invasion of privacy is overdone. The collusive aspects of individual and organization can only be affected by giving sanction to various types of exploration before and during a move. Providing opportunities and making them available for use without insisting on their use could obviate many a casualty situation at a later date. Experience with one particular multinational organization where such opportunities are provided has demonstrated this in manifold ways. And while managers, civil servants, and more senior people have been the focus of attention in the past, we must recognize that large populations are now on the move as well as individuals with skills—at all levels and in all kinds of organizations.

Chapter 15

The Third Road

Hanne Sjelle Ernst and Peter Holbøll

DILEMMAS OF TRAINING PROGRAMS

Management training frequently takes place in the form of training programs for which participants sign up individually and from which they, as individuals, each return to their own organizations. This is also the case when the objectives of the training program are to change attitudes and behavior; for instance in training in cooperation, group dynamics, and sensitivity training.

In organization development, where the objective is to examine and change the existing working conditions in a specific organizational context, the process interventions are frequently within the physical framework of the organization itself. It may be implemented by assistance from outside consultants, for example process consultants. This method implies that the participants will not be in contact with any people other than those with whom they work, or than those who are at least employed by the same organization.

Both situations are characterized by relative isolation: In the training programs the individual is like a guest at the conference house. In the learning situation within the organization the participant is prevented from contact with, and influence by, outside groups or organizations, apart from the presence of the consultants.

Our conclusion is that both procedures limit the possibilities of influencing as well as of being influenced. We wanted to try a third road, where these limitations could be minimized, and where the following conditions would be attainable:

1. Confrontation and comparison with other organizations and their cultures.
2. Analysis and development of own roles and functions compared with corresponding role and functions in other organizations.
3. Analysis of own organization and planning for change.

Our hypothesis is: if these conditions were fulfilled, the "third road" would provide an opportunity for development and/or change in the organization as well as development of individual resources.

THE OPPORTUNITY FOR PRACTICAL TESTING

One day we received an inquiry from one of our client organizations. A group of managers—executives—from an autonomous unit within the organization wanted to get more experience and training in social psychology and human relations. Furthermore, they wanted new inspiration from outside to apply to their "back-home" situation in order to function better as a policy and management group within their unit. One week away from the working situation together with an outside consultant was what they wanted. We felt this would give us an opportunity to take our third road: The organization in question and we—as outside consultants—made contact with other organizations to explore if there were similar groups interested in joining us in a four-and-one-half-day conference. We ended up with three groups coming from three different organizations.

A. The original group of six from A form a steering group within a private company dealing with building and contractor activities. The group is a project management group in a matrix and project organization. At the same time each of the group members is head of a special department in the parent organization.

B. The members of the group from organization B do not work together as a permanent group, but know each other from various project groups. All five are in top-middle management. The organization is a private company for building and project activities.

C. The seven members from C do not work together as individuals in their organization. C is a concessionary telecommunication company. The members are placed at the same top-middle-management level in the organization and work in different functions at the same geographical location, or in similar functions at different locations.

Common to all participants is that they have an academic degree: engineer, economist, architect, or the like.

Everybody from C, many from A, and none from B have previously attended training programs in which the objectives were similar to those of this conference.

OUR THEORETICAL BACKGROUND

As a beginning we will describe the most significant theoretical references for our formulation of the conference objectives, and consequently for the planning of the design. Also, these references have guided us in our roles as consultants in the various situations during the conference. It is not possible to classify our references according to importance; all of them were in our minds before, during, and after the conference. As a consequence all six will be described in the following:

Kurt Lewin [1]

Lewin was one of the founders of laboratory training and organizational development. His concept of change, development, and learning is still fundamental and relevant: In order that man can change, develop, and learn, any situation that aims at these objectives must be based on:

1. The whole person is part of the learning process. This process involves at least three areas:
   a. The person's ways of conceptualizing.
   b. The person's motivation
   c. The person's modes of behavior.
2. Only by change in the ways a person perceives himself and others is it possible to create change in that person's behavior toward other people.
3. Transfer of knowledge is not sufficient to create change in the ways a person perceives and behaves.
4. Even personal experiences do not necessarily create change in perception and behavior. Personal experimentation as well as personal experiences is necessary.
5. An active and emotional involvement in the learning/changing situation is necessary to secure that information and knowledge obtained will influence the perception and behavior of a person.
6. A person accepts new values and attitudes by accepting his relationship to the group in which the new values and attitudes are norms.

These six basic thoughts are fundamental for Kurt Lewin's well-known description of change, both on individual, group, and organization level:

1. *Unfreezing:* creation of a climate that makes it possible to overcome resistance by reduction of forces against change rather than supporting forces for change.
2. *Moving:* change of the forcefield so that a new balance of restraining and supporting forces is obtained. This can be made by experiments and tryouts at a conference.
3. *Refreezing:* here the intention is to stabilize the new balance of restraining and supporting forces, and to keep the balance.

The ideas and theories of Kurt Lewin are to a great extent a product of conferences and learning situations, where participants and consultants have been away from their daily work situation for a shorter or longer time. Being away from the work situation for a limited time in order to concentrate on change and development, has particularly been described by Matthew B. Miles.

Matthew B. Miles[2]

Most of our organizations and social structures are created for an unlimited time: schools, universities, state departments, private enterprises, and so on.

Other social structures and organizations are temporary, which means that they have been established for specific objectives/tasks with clearly defined membership and time or criteria for resolution: conferences, workshops, research projects, consulting tasks.

In a temporary system certain characteristics that enable change to occur can be seen:

1. *Time utilization:* better use of available time.
2. *Goal redefinition:* goal differentiation and clarification.
3. *Procedures:* critical development and change in procedures.
4. *Role definition and socialization:* experimentation with new roles and different role performance.
5. *Communication and power structures:* increased communication, development of shared concepts, openness, and trust. Development of more equal distribution of power.
6. *Sentiments:* a change from formal and defensive behavior through experimentation to acceptance of closeness and group identity.
7. *Norms:*
   a. *Equality:* an increased belief in the appropriateness of equal status/relationships.
   b. *Authenticity:* importance of openness and trust.

    c. *Inquiry:* problem solving with use of all available data.
    d. *Hypothesis:* experimental and tentative tryouts.
    e. *Renewal* is supported.
    f. *Change for its own sake:* value of experimentation.
    g. *Effectiveness:* hard work and energy investment.

The processes described here create better opportunities for

1. Personal, group and organizational change in attitudes, insight and behavior.
2. Changes in relationships.
3. Decisions for action.

Gunnar Hjelholt[3]

Regarding the experiences from Gunnar Hjelholt's "minisociety" laboratories, the following has been of particular importance to us:

Through the laboratory it was possible to obtain greater insight into the relationships between different groups of our society.

The minisocieties consisted of homogeneous groups that in one or several ways had relationships with each other: economically wealthy/poor, workers/managers, children/grown-ups, professional helpers/clients, and so on.

By exploring, testing, and confronting the homogeneous groups with each other, differences in culture, values, norms, became visible. This visibility gave the individual and his social group an opportunity for greater insight, understanding and basis for action, both in the minisociety and in real life.

Gurth Higgin and Harold Bridger[4]

It was stimulating for us to read about a Tavistock conference where the interaction between just three groups was described and analyzed within a psychoanalytical frame of reference. A clear configuration of the inner life of the groups and their relation to each other was seen.

Two of the groups matured on a work level by projecting their emotional problems on the third group, which integrated the problems as its own (introjection)—and to such an extent that it was impossible for the group to solve them, and it was thereby blocked from further development. We think that the description of this development is valid also as a description of general relationships between groups inside organizations, for example, the so-called "normal" conflict between production, sales, and finance. The scapegoat theory might be seen in this context.

Richard Beckhard[5]

Facing a conference with three different organizations represented, we also felt inspired by the *confrontation meeting* designed by Beckhard.

The confrontation meeting is a strongly structured design where the objective is to diagnose problems, create procedures for solutions, and allocate responsibility for the implementation and evaluation of these solutions. Focus will often be on interdepartmental and intergroup conflicts. The key point is to reach common concepts and acceptance of the nature of the problem(s). A prerequisite for this is an open climate where all relevant data can be produced.

If the interdependency between departments and groups is made visible, unsolved problems may often be spotlighted and thus clarify the actual mode of operation and the need for changes in structures and functions.

Trygve Johnstad[6]

Thinking about the confrontations between the cultures of the three organizations we were inspired by Trygve Johnstad's reflections on the themes of life and death in organizations. Johnstad suggests that these two fundamental themes exist in any organism: individual, group, organization, or society. The theme of life is anything connected with differences, new inventions, uniqueness, incomparability and *growth*.

The theme of death is anything connected with similarities, "do as we always do," generality, consistency, and *security*.

In any organization there must be a reasonable balance between themes of life and death. This implies that any organization can be described in terms of an equilibrium of these two themes. Having this in mind, we could make profiles of each of the three organizations as a foundation from which to explore what was common to and what was specific in their cultures.

Planning and Design

In a letter to the participants before the conference, we stated the following objectives:

1. To deal with conditions that *support* and *restrain* development of groups.
2. To work with relationships with other (organizational cultures) groups and mutual influence.
3. To explore communication, leadership, decisionmaking, forms of cooperation, and so on.

The overall objective was to give each individual experience in—and thereby a better understanding of—these areas and to make sure that the application to the back-home situation would be the strongest possible.

Our main ideas for the conference were:

1. To provide time and opportunity for each of the three organization groups to work separately with the essential problems in their daily work situation.
2. To have confrontations between the groups to ensure feedback about their specific organizational cultures.
3. To work with new groupings by mixing members from A, B, and C in order to release the individuals from restrictions in their daily work situation to experiment with personal behavior.

The conference lasted four and one-half days. The first day was planned for work in organizational home groups and to have these groups preparing presentations of themselves in various ways on individual, group, and organizational level. The presentations were partly the perception of their own organization, partly how each participant looked upon himself as an individual in his daily work situation, and partly his expectations and objectives for the conference. The presentations also outlined the benefit each group expected from the presence of the two other groups.

On the second day the morning was devoted to confrontation activities between the three organization groups.

The focus was on the following:

1. How do we see ourselves in this situation?
2. How do we think the other two groups see us?
3. How do we see each of the two other groups?
4. How close/distant do we see ourselves in relation to the other two groups?

In the afternoon the groups were reformed, and through a long series of very fast and varied activities each individual got into closer personal acquaintance with the others.

By the end of the afternoon three new groups were formed by mixing the three organization groups. The new groups were only meant to exist during the third day.

The first task for the new groups was to decide with what they felt it would be most important to work. Two of the groups very quickly chose to work with sensitivity-oriented activities to obtain greater knowledge of themselves—how they were seen as individuals, how they influenced and were influenced by others. The third group spent a lot of time deciding what they wanted to do, and then never really got started.

In the last one and one-half days the participants were back in their organizational groups to review and sum up what they had experienced during the previous days, what they had learned and how to apply experiences and learning to their daily work situation.

It was extremely exciting to work with the differences and similarities as these became visible between the three organization cultures. The two contractor groups (A and B) were clearly different from the concessionary company group (C), for instance with regard to punctuality: A and B were always present in the room for plenary meetings almost earlier than the planned time, whereas the C group always were 3–5 minutes late. The groups' different attitudes to time were also evident in the way they worked: the group from the concessionary company took their time in the beginning when they worked on solving common problems, and were rather slow in their decision making: "We cannot press things through. Development and change take time." The contractor-groups were very quick and tried to press their decisions through: "Efficiency in decisions and speed are closely connected."

Another topic for discussion was: Which level of personal security gave the most benefit and efficiency in the work situation? To live in the tough business world, as did the two contractor groups, or in the safe, protected world without any competitors, as did the concessionary group?

We consider this design as an opportunity for the same amount of learning on individual and group level as traditional designs, and in addition as providing explicit insight into the specific culture of one's own organization.

The immediate results of the conference were a reasonable level of achievement of the objectives set for the conference:

1. To deal with conditions that *support* and *restrain* development of groups.
2. To work with relationships with other organizational cultures and groups, and to study mutual influence.
3. To explore communication, leadership, decision making, forms of cooperation, and so on.

Concerning long-lasting results we have especially followed up organization A. The involved group has been able to implement drastic structural changes in the organization as a whole, and in individual function to such a degree that both personal and organizational resources have been maximized.

Our subsequent experiences indicate that the same design is helpful when used inside multinational organizations where cultural differences exist among departments.

REFERENCES

1. Lewin, K. "Frontiers in Group Dynamics," I, II. *Human Relations* 1 (1947); Lewin, K. *Resolving Social Conflicts.* New York: Harper, 1948.
2. Miles, M. B. "On Temporary Systems." In *Innovation in Education*, edited by M. B. Miles. New York: Teacher's College Press, 1964.

3. Hjelholt, G. "Group Training in Understanding Society: The Mini-Society." *Interpersonal Development* 3, 1972; Hjelholt, G.: "Europe is Different." In *European Contributions to Organizational Theory*, edited by Hofstede and Kassem. Van Gorcum, 1976.
4. Higgin, G. W. and Bridger, H. "The Psychodynamics of an Intergroup Experience." *Human Relations* 17 (1964).
5. Beckhard, R. "The Confrontation Meeting." In *The Planning of Change*, edited by W. G. Bennis, K. D. Benne, and C. Chin. New York, 1969.
6. Johnstad, T.: "Livs- og dödstemaer i organisationer" ("Themes of Life and Death within Organizations"). In *Magt og Påvirkning i Systemer, (Power and Influence within Systems)* edited by G. Haslebo and P. Holbøll. Copenhagen, 1973.

Chapter 16

Group-Process Studies as Part of an Organization-Development Program in a Norwegian Oil Company, 1969–1975

Svein M. Kile

THE BACKGROUND

This is an attempt to describe the general frame of an organization development program in a Norwegian Oil Company and, in particular, the group-process-studies seminar (GPS) that played a part in this program.

During the middle and late 1960s some people within the company had grown increasingly dissatisfied with the ways of organizing their work and collaboration to achieve efficiency and satisfaction. At that time the Norwegian scene presented an abundance of ideas and plans concerned with industrial democracy. Experiments with partly autonomous groups were well under way; the search for humane and satisfying work and life conditions for everybody was expressed in political debate, legislative efforts, collective bargaining and agreements, and in research and educational efforts. One company decided to make its own experimental effort to reshape and reform its own organization and climate in the light of these ideas and those of sound business practice.

According to the personnel director of the company, management felt that in order to use an OD approach they had to clarify and make public to all members of the organization their values and goals. As a group, they developed a set of guidelines intended to mark out the general policy and aims of the OD effort.

These points were:

1. *The environment and the company.* The objectives, structure, and ways of operating must be in accordance with the present and future demands of society and the market, and the organization must be able to change in accordance with these demands.
2. *Objectives and results.* All activities shall be objective- and result-oriented, both qualitatively and quantitatively.
3. *Management.* The management style and the work methods will be group-oriented, with a high degree of autonomy for the individual as well as for working teams.
4. *Decision making.* Decisions shall be made as close to the source of information as possible, with a high degree of delegation as a means of training and motivation.
5. *Controls.* Control functions will be based more on self-control.
6. *The needs of individuals.* The tasks, that is, the jobs, should insofar as possible be structured in order to satisfy human needs, that is, needs for: variation in the job; learning on the job; decision making; support and respect; seeing the relationship between the job and the environment; seeing the job as part of a desirable future. (This was based on the concepts of Thorsrud and Emery, 1969.)

Management quite clearly realized that there were indeed no safe and easy methods by which to attain such goals. Thus they were prepared to be elective insofar as theories and methods were concerned and to proceed by trial and error. They also chose (to my mind, very wisely) to keep the responsibility for and control of the OD program firmly within the company, in practical terms delegating this to the personnel department. They were also well aware of the fact that to work at the intended changes would require time and patience as well as insight and money.

I became involved with the planning of the OD program through my research interest in the evaluation of training and development efforts and through my long experience with sensitivity training. The unit of development was to be the departmental heads and their subordinates—later to extend to the higher and/or lower echelons according to their openness and motivation to participate.

At the outset we made a simple model of expected progress through phases (Figure 16–1). The input phase consisted of the groups reading, discussing, and learning about basic and relevant research results and ideas from the applied behavioral sciences. Thus we hoped to lay a foundation of common knowledge and a set of working concepts for the learning ahead. The diagnosis involved asking the group to take a really hard look at their own work and organization and to give priority to problems that the group itself could solve. In order that the autonomy of the group might

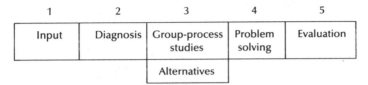

Figure 16–1. Expected phases of OD.

perhaps increase, no diagnoses were made by outside experts; but some small assistance in the formulation of questions and problems was given when it was requested.

The third phase was planned to be some sort of experience with and learning about the internal dynamics of the group. From the very start it was made as clear as possible to the groups that nobody should feel forced or obliged to participate in these rather personal activities. The individuals and groups that might choose to refrain from the group-process-studies seminar had options of, for instance, a one-week introductory course to the managerial-grid program or simply a reading and discussion program about group dynamics.

It is this third phase (GPS) that will be the main theme of this chapter.

The group-process studies generally led to a reevaluation of the initial diagnosis and then to a phase of problem solving which, after a certain period, developed into a broader evaluation process. It was our hope that these phases would to some extent become part of a cyclic effort and of continuous development perpetuated by the group itself—in short, part of their usual ways of operating.

The enterprise, a fully integrated oil company of some 1,000 employees, started the OD work in 1969–1970 with this phase plan accepted by management and with the following basic assumptions:

1. The satisfaction of company needs as well as those of the employees could be improved by a long term systematic program covering the entire organization.
2. Such a program must be based on diagnoses developed by each individual unit.
3. No ready-made package or outside-consultant blueprint approach would suit the situation, that is, it must become an OD effort from within.
4. No one unit should be forced to start OD, but those who were interested should be given assistance—initially from the personnel department. Diffusion of the ideas was expected when results could be demonstrated in practice.

The company enjoyed a good reputation for hard and challenging work and thus had a good many "workaholics" in its employ. The leadership style was generally of an authoritarian character, most of the time mellowed by good fellowship as long as people kept reasonably in line and up to tough standards of work. The power to make decisions had come to rest rather firmly at headquarters, thus making sometimes for extreme dependency on the part of the district managers. Despite this and some interdepartmental strife and conflicts, as well as personality clashes here and there, the company compared well to the general run of larger Norwegian companies as far as satisfaction, efficiency, and morale were concerned. But many people felt that the management, the work, and the organization, as well as the human-relations aspects of their situation, not only could but should be improved. Fairly soon after the program was launched, expectations were raised. Many employees hoped for a better climate, more participation and autonomy, more openness and trust. Many managers expected better understanding of their managerial tools, that would enable them to make better decisions and better use of human resources.

However, underneath this mainstream of bright expectations, we soon sensed quite a bit of suspicion. This suspicion consisted mainly in two ideas; one, that top management had something up its sleeve and would really press for more efficiency; the other, that opening up and voicing in public their real opinions and feelings might cause consequences harmful to their careers or to the esteem of some particular honest person. In some cases this suspicion was not overcome until the second or third year of the program.

The only way to achieve a realistic assessment of the possibilities of the program and to alleviate suspicions was to build on openness and assist growth toward openness and trust. Any foxy and devious attempts at manipulation would have been disastrous.

SOME IDEAS GOVERNING THE GPS

Ever since my first contact with sensitivity training, twenty years ago, I have adhered to the love-trust aspects of this wide and heterogenous methodological field. Over the years one of my main research interests has been to study how such training really might aid personal, group, and organizational development efforts. Early on, research showed that the impact on the organization was rather negligible when managers from different enterprises were gathered for training without a firm backing and planned effort within their organizations (although a great many testified to an important personal experience during training).

As far as I can see the aims of the GPS do not differ in any significant way from the bulk of aims stated by trainer colleagues in the field. The aims to be stated here were frankly discussed with the personnel department and, later on, with the groups who were about to choose their course at the phase of diagnosis. Throughout this work, no promise of actually reaching these goals was made, although a certain challenge was presented by describing the possibilities of the method.

The intention was to attempt to develop for each group and each member:

1. Increased trust and openness in the work and organizational setting.
2. Increased mutual understanding and more genuine, clearer communication.
3. Increased understanding of the needs and feelings of oneself and others.
4. Increased motivation and skill in the understanding and practical handling of interpersonal conflicts within the group, the organization and, if possible, intrapersonal conflicts.
5. Increased perceived freedom for each person to work in his own way on his own development.

To these ends we planned to make the group work for three full days. It was deemed important to get away from the office to be able to concentrate fully; hence we worked at different hotels and residential sites for organizational training. If for any reason the groups decided to break off the work, we stopped after the second day. Only three groups did so. We wanted to behave in such a way that the following rules and aims were fulfilled.

1. Great care should always be taken not to create situations where the mental health of the participants might be endangered. Hence, only mild pressure to open up, to discuss emotions, guilt, anxiety, and so on, should be applied.
2. An atmosphere of personal freedom, warmth, trust, tolerance, and acceptance should be established. The trainer should in all his behavior attempt to act accordingly. (The closest to this model in the literature is the therapeutic ideas of Carl Rogers.)
3. The process of reflection on and feedback to each person on things that really mattered to him in his work should be worked on carefully and one step at a time.
4. The studies should, insofar as possible, be relevant to and centered on the work of the group and the individual. Reflections and recommendations should be given within the frame of applicability and practical usefulness.
5. A rather loose general structure should govern the seminars.

The great need for structure and for meeting expectations—drawn from school—of being taught should in the beginning be partially met. Their

Day 1 Familiar topics of work and organization. Ordinary discussion of group work and problems. Tasks set by trainer.

Questions, interventions, some small feedback, and interpretations offered by trainer.

List of adjectives describing each person distributed for filling in; preparing for the feedback sessions. Turning to the person.

Day 2 Each person receiving in turn feedback from the others, leading to expressed increasing needs for depth and understanding. Testing out of reflections and true feelings. Diagnosis of personal behavior—strong and weak points—attempted.

Day 3 Reflections on and deepening of feedback. Wish for honesty, genuineness, openness. Considerable trust. Advice and solutions proposed for personal and group growth. Analyses and decisions.

Figure 16–2. Psychological structure of GPS.

freedom of choice and to conduct the seminar should be presented early; but these ideas should also be given time to grow and to be accepted. The aged work horses of pedagogy—that is, from the very familiar to the relatively unknown; from the safe, strong, and intellectual to the unsafe, weak, and emotional—were to be put into harness. We would also proceed from group to person and from person to group (Figure 16–2). A few agreements about the conduct of us all at the seminar and afterwards were obtained before we started to get down to work:

1. Everything that happened at the seminar was to be treated by everyone as strictly confidential material and should not in any way be used against any participant later on. (The suspicion that the trainer, or a superordinate who was present, or competing colleagues, might make use harmfully of indications of personal weakness, anxiety, strong criticisms of the company, and so on, loomed large before and during the initial phases of the seminar.) These problems were taken up from the beginning and a clear, responsible agreement was made. This rule seems fundamental for achieving and deserving the trust and openness sought for.

2. To avoid possible harm by going too near any individual too fast or by discussing too painful or disagreeable matters, the rule that everybody at any time could stop the discussion and change the subject was underlined.

3. The common responsibility of giving positive, helpful, and constructive feedback was underlined and stressed throughout the seminar.

THE GROUPS

Over the last five years, twenty groups, comprising 155 people, have been to GPS seminars. Although the groups were given an opportunity to choose other types of courses and seminars, the GPS became the accepted way of going forward. Almost from the very start, the GPS seemed to be regarded by many participants as an interesting, challenging, and helpful activity. When over time no harmful effects materialized, trust and expectations grew.

The groups differed widely on such variables as size, function, organizational level, and group climate. As they ranged from five to fifteen persons in size and covered most of the functional areas of the firm, and as participants varied from the topmost group to ordinary office personnel, it goes without saying that a multitude of differences could be analyzed. Perhaps the most important variables were those relating to the internal group climate, that is, the degrees of good management, genuine cooperation, openness, freedom, mutual regard, and so on; or the opposite, such as grave conflicts, deep-rooted personality clashes, suspicion, defensiveness, and tension, as well as opinions about bad management and dissatisfaction with quality of work within the group and outside.

A rough assessment suggests that five of the groups were located markedly in the "bad" climate or high-tension bracket; six groups could be classified as having a very open and constructive climate; while the remaining nine were found in varying intermediary positions. This rough assessment could usually be made during the first day of working together.

The main approach to the GPS was, however, to take each group as it was found, starting out with the particular tasks, problems, wishes, and hopes of the group in question. The general run of the group-process studies proceeded, however, in a remarkably similar way, despite what were of course the very wide differences in problems studies; in the levels of anxiety, tension, and aggression; and in the degree to which objectives were achieved.

THE TYPICAL PROCESS

The typical group came to the seminar with a mixture of expectations, some conscious, some subconscious. Previous information from earlier groups, the trainer, and the personnel department seemed to have created a mingled set of feelings. Some were highly motivated, wanting to strip emotionally at once; some were rather anxious about precisely this possibility. In the high-tension groups, the need to get at the underlying conflicts were so great that the seminars were marked by this from the outset.

Among the greatest expectations were usually those directed at the trainer: that he should teach, direct, say something worthwhile, and directly contribute to fast solutions to group and personal problems.

Although actively involved in the opening of the group discussion and in the general explanation of the framework of our efforts, the trainer chose to play a rather passive, questioning, and interpretative role—offering alternative things to do, reflections, interpretations; asking for opinions and feelings. Thus during the first day he achieved a reputation of being a kind but somewhat passive and ineffectual person. The drive to do something efficient, to achieve measurable progress, was in most groups intensely expressed. On the average one and one-half days passed before the group realized the sincerity behind the statements about their freedom of choice, their responsibility for progress, their real autonomy in the situation. (Some people unfortunately never understood this.)

Together with this mild frustration in the early phases of the seminar went the increasing frustration of feeling that the discussion treated only familiar topics. Most groups felt relief when, during the first afternoon or evening, a list of some 50–60 adjectives with which to characterize each participant and for self-description was presented by the trainer as one of a set of possible means by which to proceed further toward more personal areas. All groups except two agreed to use this instrument. Asked to describe each other and themselves and to add to the list any adjective that they found more suitable, the group members were then required to proceed by concentrating in turn on each person. In general this process took 4–6 hours. During this period the discussion increased in quality, measured by the increased openness, frankness, and personal exchanges that took place. Slowly but surely most groups outgrew their apprehensions and hesitations, and many people started to try out their interpretative skills at a more than superficial level.

The need to get at genuine, deep-rooted, important themes grew measurably during this period. A common reaction occurred after this part of the process. Most groups felt let down—a sense of great disappointment. They also in general felt that they had not succeeded in really opening up, that they had not been genuinely honest. Quite general among the very many who received very positive feedback was the tendency to believe that this feedback was not really genuine. Whatever this may reveal about the individual, the group, or the company, it certainly strengthened the need for getting at "the real thing."

After a period of groping for a means to progress, the group usually decided on new rounds of attempted real and honest personal feedback. At this point, no further preplanned structure was needed. The groups grasped the responsibility of building for their own progress. The subjects of discussion and the depth of emotion and openness increased considerably toward the end of the seminar. Somewhere during the second day most groups reached this new level, experienced by many as very important, helpful, moving, and genuine. A feeling of warmth and trust prevailed.

Most of the last day was generally used for attempts at genuine problem solving for the individual and for the group: offering to one another honest advice and help; and attempting to foresee and decide on future ways and means of implementing changes necessary for future growth at work.

The most important finding made through this type of group-process study is perhaps how one may, using a rather soft and careful approach, stimulate the very basic need to reach toward genuine existence and relationships at work as well as in other aspects of life. When this need is expressed and accepted, the job of the trainer becomes one of helper and contributor, but also one of a certain professional safeguard against diving too deeply too early. He may have to hold back the most eager and to protect the weakest. To do this, he remains consciously on the outskirts of the group, taking the role of the outside helper, never going far into discussions about himself. The group on hand has to be the important thing; not the personality, feelings, and vicissitudes of the trainer, or the trainer-group relationships.

EVALUATING THE GPS

Apart from evaluation of goals, people, and processes, the main objective of the seminars was to change for the better the group climate and working relations for the greater satisfaction and efficiency of the participants.

To assess the actual results is of course rather difficult. No achievement can be ascribed exclusively to the GPS alone. The input phase, the work of the personnel department, the slow general change toward greater autonomy in the company as well as in Norwegian society in general, all played a part.

Two somewhat restricted interview programs, with some of the participants conducted by me, seemed to show that the great majority of the groups regarded the GPS seminar as a very fruitful experience on which they had attempted to build further. Most of these groups had also succeeded; though in 4 or 5 groups changes of personnel, workload, and so on had prevented further development. Some groups explicitly wanted a new phase of work at GPS.

The effects most frequently mentioned were those of really increased trust and openness; better, easier, and clearer communication and personal relations; more skill in handling differences of opinion and conflict; and, at the personal level, greater self-reliance and satisfaction.

Some groups maintained that the GPS had been the turning point of their attitude and motivation regarding the OD project as a whole.

Top management, after participating in a GPS seminar, has been fairly convinced that this effort is helpful. One other practical measure of success is that the GPS seminar remains a steady feature of the OD program.

Two cases of unintended and, to the individuals concerned, somewhat harmful consequences have been brought up. In one case, someone reported feeling very stressed and tense for a period of time during and after the GPS seminar; in the other case, the feeling of the individual involved was that participation had been harmful to his career.

The OD program as a whole was evaluated by the company's personnel director. He stated:

Results so far have emerged on three levels:

1. *Objectives, procedural changes, etc.* The majority of the groups started by clarifying their department's objectives and their relationships to company objectives and the objectives of other departments. Most of the groups also effected some changes in day to day procedures, such as changes in the composition of weekly meetings, flow of information, etc.

2. *Inter-personal relationships and minor organizational changes.* The next level of results concerned inter-personal relationships between bosses and subordinates and between subordinates themselves. Several OD groups reported improved effectiveness in decision making, less time spent on meetings and on searching for solutions to outstanding problems.

The Finance section, for instance, reported that OD had led to a less formalistic approach to problems; to the abolition of organization charts, which had been replaced by task/person matrices; to less control for the sake of control and better interfunctional co-operation in financial matters.

At this point also some structural changes took place. Two marketing districts started to operate on a partly autonomous basis, i.e., with no district managers, and to act as a group to discharge the manager's responsibilities. This led to improved sales results, better utilization of the employees' abilities and some sharing of tasks between engineers, salesmen, planners and retailers.

A more participative management style emerged. In the automotive market, for instance, the market manager with his staff of specialists previously ran eight districts as separate entitites. They re-organized, and established a retail management group consisting of the marketing manager and his district managers. Together they became responsible for the planning and policy-making in that market as a whole.

3. *Organizational structure of the company.* The third level of results is concerned with the organizational structure of the whole company. The "class of market" concept had shown some weaknesses, for instance in terms of sub-optimization and lack of co-ordination, which, together with some undesirable effects of the functional split between Supply/Distribution and Selling, made the OD groups search for improvements. Co-ordination groups at district level were established with the objective of making optimum use of all the resources in the area and the whole question of the organization of Head Office was taken up for discussion. Linked with top management's strategic studies on organization this is likely to produce a new organizational structure, with integrated units at district level and with Head Office on a task-oriented matrix organization basis. No pre-set solution is in mind, but amongst the results so far there is the possibility of a further reduction in manpower, based on better utilization of peoples' abilities coupled with a more suitable organizational structure. The new organization will take account of the interdependence of peoples' abilities, the changing tasks of the organization and the organizational structure. It will be the result of a process with direct employee participation from all levels in the company."

These were the personnel director's observations.

The experience and data accumulated so far provide, at least in my view, rather convincing evidence that in this context the love-trust model—the careful and kind way of working with group dynamics— helped by the whole program to transfer into action, really is a workable one.

Three students are at present working throughout the company on an evaluation of the OD program including a detailed examination of the GPS. This study will be reported at a later opportunity.

REFERENCES

1. Kile, Svein, M. *Virker Det? Evaluering av Bedriftsopplæring (Does It Work? Evaluation of Personnel Training)* Bergen: Universitetsforlaget (University Press), 1971.
2. Kile, Svein M. "Evaluating a Course of Management Training and Development in the Norwegian Business." Lecture to the European Congress for Insurance Training, IFAP, NHH. Bergen, 1974.
3. Thorsrud, Einar, and Emery, Fred E. *Mot en ny Bedriftsorganisasjon, Eksperimenter i industrielt demokrati (Toward a New Industrial Organization: Experiments in Industrial Democracy).* Oslo, 1969.

Chapter 17

The Norwegian Trawler Fleet Case

Trygve Johnstad

BACKGROUND FACTORS

The subject of this case is a community located some 600 miles north of the Arctic Circle. The landscape around is bare and can best be described as a rocky wasteland. In contrast to the meagerness on shore, the sea around is a horn of plenty. Some of the richest fishing grounds in the world, which are just off the coast, have, for as long as people have settled there, been the foundation of their economy. With their seagoing tradition expansion came naturally with people setting out for larger expeditions in the Arctic areas and being away for three to four months at a time.

In earlier days these men were the heroes of the community and held a status that was comparable with their economic significance. In recent years this picture had changed.

During World War II the total area of North Norway was demolished by the Germans. After the war the government got heavily engaged in rebuilding the area. A plan for the development of the district was established, and government support was given to a variety of enterprises. So when initiative was taken to establish a freezing factory in this particular community, substantial support was given.

The community itself had about 7,000 inhabitants. Bearing in mind that the company employed in all 1,400 people, it is easy to understand the company's dominant position in the economic life of the community. As someone put it: "If the company stops, the community stops."

Of these 1,400 people, around 1,000 were working in the processing plant, which had a modern, highly automated operation. Because the product was food which needs to be carefully handled, the plant was totally dependent on daily supplies of fresh fish. It was part of the contract for the people employed there, mostly women, that they could be asked to leave without any pay if supplies failed to come in. Luckily this happened only occasionally, and then only for two to four days.

The 400 people obtaining the supplies were working on some twenty ships. This was the trawler fleet that was operated by the company. According to legal regulations, the company was not allowed to own any of the ships. They therefore had to deal with a somewhat variable group of shipowners, who were paid a fixed price in return for the company's right to control the ships over a negotiated period of time.

It was the shipowner's responsibility to keep the vessels in good order; and the company—the user—informed the shipowner as soon as anything needed to be done. A shipowner who did not fulfill his obligations would have difficulty in getting his contract with the company renewed, a possibility that at the same time would be detrimental to his reputation.

The people on board were paid on different bases. The licensed people, in this fleet called the "regulars," were paid partly by the shipowner on a fixed salary basis, partly as their share of the catch value on a percentage rate that differed according to their position on board; for instance, the master would receive more than the mate.

The unlicensed people, in this fleet called "fishermen," were paid exclusively from the value of the catch. The shipboard people shared 27 percent of the total value, as this was determined by weight and quality control administered by the company at the time of delivery. The price of landed fish differed with the season, and was from time to time determined by nationwide regulations.

As a consequence, the income of the crew was dependent on two factors: a good and able crew that knew how to find and take care of the catch and a dependable vessel that was not too much detained by days laid up for repairs.

The company's long-range objectives were to develop the resources of the two main instruments: the plant and the fleet. The plant had to face competition with the Common Market with a 20 percent handicap to overcome. They also had to live with the overheads required to run the 50-million-kroner plant itself, whereas this link was unnecessary to competitors who used factory ships instead. As for the fleet, the crucial thing was the continuity of supply. To have the plant fully in operation, the daily requirement was 250,000 pounds.

But there was also a third long-range objective: that of the viability of the surrounding community. The company was fully aware of the strong interdependence that existed between itself and the community and therefore actively supported community activities that could make it a better place to live. There were two reasons for this: one, that the company recognized the town as a main manpower source, the other, that the company was interested in the general welfare of its employees. The ties were further strengthened by the fact that quite a few company people were actively engaged in local political affairs.

The more specific objectives, however, were aimed at the two main instruments—the plant and the fleet. For years the shoreside plant had been in focus to improve its effectiveness, and the systems approach applied proved itself to be highly successful. With good return on investment, the company now felt that for a while it had tapped the main sources for improvement within the plant. So it turned to the fleet, where a cost reduction program could evidently contribute substantially to the company's economic situation.

A study was started, using the same engineering-methods approach as that applied to the plant. The study made it clear that substantial savings were within reach, reinforcing the impression that management had already, that a reduction in manning levels alone could bring about a saving of 3.5 million kroner a year. In addition the maintenance costs were frighteningly high, and so was the percentage of spoiled fish.

The report of the study concluded by suggesting new methods and equipment. However, the actual introduction of these remedies was not suggested. The reason given for this surprising reaction was that the necessary minimum of willingness to cooperate was simply not there. As long as this strong negative response prevailed on the ships, the reporter found it futile to attempt any implementation of the suggestions. The likelihood that it would all be sabotaged was too high. Finally the report stated that the systems approach that had been applied was not very well suited to the handling of this human-relations problem.

This being the situation, the company decided to postpone any introduction of new methods and equipment and to attack the low-morale problem instead. It wanted to have a social scientist to study the problems, and EIT (European Institute of Transnational Studies in Group and Organizational Development) was contacted. At the headquarters were people who were already familiar with Gunnar Hjelholt's work with the people manning a tanker. However, since this work was going to take place in Norway, it was assumed that it would be an asset to have a Norwegian fellow of EIT to do the field work. It was intended that this project director would work in conjunction with Mr. Hjelholt, and this did happen—with the main steps in the planning work taking place in Denmark.

SOCIAL SCIENTIST CONSULTANT'S PLAN

The usual steps were taken: data gathering, data analysis, report, and recommendations.

The collection of data started out in the company; the next source of data was supposed to be the ships themselves. What happened during the interviews, however, was that so many reactions toward the fishermen as fellow citizens were exposed that the community finally stood out as a relevant target for data gathering. This conclusion was heavily supported later by the way the fishermen reacted as well. It therefore became necessary to have two series of interviews: one before the trips out with the ships and one after.

The trips took place in December 1966 and February 1967. They were week-long trips, and three different trawlers were involved. The intention was to visit trawlers of different types and ages, and at different times—presumably when the fishing was good and when it was slow.

The gathering of the data led to four different sets of problem inventories: one as stated by the company, one by the community, one by the fishermen, and one by the consultant. First, the problems as stated *by the company:*

1. *High turnover of the workforce:* In a report from the company to the headquarters, a percentage of 800 was mentioned.
2. *Low morale:* A great concern to the company was the excessive drinking that had been observed. It had happened that it was necessary for a skipper to drop anchor behind a convenient island to allow the crew to sleep for a day before they could start working. Stealing could occur, as when the compass spirit was taken or fish sold in another town in order to buy liquor. Another discomfort for the management was what they labelled "general irresponsibility," which showed itself in really careless actions, like coupling a 220-volt current to a 110-volt motor, thereby causing it to burn out; or not uncoupling cables to the ship on departure, just cutting them by force as the ship left the quay; or not unhooking the gangway, but dropping it into the sea instead; or having fun with the steam by letting it out in the machine room.
3. *Impossible to experiment:* It is understandable when a young, dynamic management group, anxious to come up with results, feels impatient as they see chances for improvement come to nothing. This attitude revealed, however, that the whole endeavor was looked on as "their" experiment, and as such it was felt to be a problem not to see any opening for action.

Then, the problems as stated *by the community:*

1. *A group of troublemakers:* This reaction could be found at all levels. On the top official level the fishermen could be described as a bunch of bums, who could best be compared with left-behind seamen in Antwerp. Others said that they were people you were not supposed to know. Others again admitted that they would move if they happened to be seated beside one in the cinema, because they smelled so bad.
2. *Jeopardizing the economy of the community:* To have one of the main economic functions of the community taken care of by such a group caused some unrest in the community, and the need for a stable group of responsible people was expressed in different ways.
3. *Don't have the status they deserve:* Reactions in the community were not all negative. For instance, the mayor and the chairman of the board of the community-welfare committee both expressed views that clearly indicated a recognition of the fishermen's actual importance for the town. They were at the same time fully aware of the critical voices raised and would like to "do something" but were not quite sure how.

Third, the problems as stated by *the fishermen:*

1. *We are at the bottom of the ladder.* The fishermen had quite a few incidents to refer to in order to reinforce this feeling. For instance, the sanitary facilities on some of the ships were definitely below prescribed standards, and so much below that a most likely spontaneous reaction from a visitor would be: "You would never dare to offer this to anyone you considered an equal." Or to have to spend hours waiting at different places in the administration building before you could get your pay on the one day you had at your own disposal. Or not to be told how to handle the fish when the management was running an important experiment on a new and hopefully better way of handling them. (By the way this experiment did not turn out very well.)
2. *To be a fisherman is the same as being nothing.* This feeling was reflected in statements like: "The decent girls in the town won't mix with us"; or "it's your own fault if you have been silly enough to choose fishing as your work"; or "I'm not going to stay in this job, you know, it's only something I do in the meantime because there's good money in it."
3. *We need this night ashore, to get away from it all.* Once every 6 to 9 days each ship came in to land the catch and the fishermen were supposed to take off early next morning. Some few cafés and restaurants were selected as meeting places, and the girls who went there were selected in a way too. In addition, there were a few

families in the town who practiced a kind of "open house" policy which implied that a fisherman could be invited there, have something to drink, meet a girl or take with him a girl he had already met. The police were aware of what was going on, but the consultant—while out on the ships—learned about more places than the police apparently were aware of. Girls working in the plant were not engaged in this activity.

4. *You don't need to commit yourself, since you're not going to be a fisherman anyhow:* This—to shy away from declaring oneself as a fisherman—had quite a few practical implications. It influenced the motivation to attend the trawler course, to join the union, to settle down in the town, and to behave in a responsible way. So the trawler course was abandoned because of lack of attendance, and membership in the union was an insignificant 2 to 3 percent. For a while around 15 percent of the fishermen had been residents of the town and their behavior conveyed to an observer the attitude that there was not too much to be responsible for.

Finally, the problems as observed *by the consultant:*

1. *Key problem—the identity crisis in the group of fishermen:* With few exceptions, the general trend in the project findings was that the image of a fisherman was not very much of an image with which to identify when looking at the situation ashore. When out on the open sea, however, they worked really hard and with smooth collaboration but the people in the town were unaware of this.

2. *Forces promoting the identity crisis:* One force was low status—so low that it could hardly secure a minimum level of self-esteem. Another force was an insufficient sense of local belonging, with few ties in the town and very few possibilities to make contacts. This related to a third force—the feeling of being alien in the community, a feeling that stemmed from not knowing about events taking place, from not knowing how to use the resources of the community, and from the apprehension that they were not really welcome. A fourth was the existence of communication barriers, which created ample opportunities for the development of fantasies and mutual suspicions. A fifth and last force to mention was the forgotten continuity: When the trawler course was closed down, nothing was left to show that the shoreside people really cared about the development of the shipboard group.

THE CHOICE OF A COURSE OF ACTION

With four different ways of looking at a situation, what to do? Even if these views were not mutually exclusive, they still constituted a puzzle. In the search for alternatives, possibilities like these turned up: What about strengthening the pressure on the fishermen a little by enforcing the rules? Definitely not! How about discussing things with the police in order that they might understand the fishermen better? This would only take care of a tiny sector of the problem. How about inviting a group of girls and trying to persuade them not to be *that* rejecting? Impossible! But a big campaign, then, with the purpose of convincing the whole community about how important the fishermen were for them, how hard they worked, and that they deserved quite a lot of respect? Well, it might just be that the fishermen would not like it that way, and besides—it might not even work.

But instead of doing things *for* the fishermen, why not let them meet with groups or people germane to their situation? Right, but whom should they meet? Maintenance people who could inform them about the correct handling of equipment? People at the intake who weighed the fish and classified it and were suspected by the fishermen of cheating them? Or the tellers who were suspected of putting too little money in the pay envelopes? All these confrontations made some sense in that they might at least have the effect of reducing some incorrect and detrimental rumors. But still the soil was fertile for making up new rumors.

In the search for an answer these guidelines were followed: Whatever was done, it should enhance the possibilities for the fishermen to develop a sound and relevant identity. Starting from the fact that they represented a really important factor in the economic life of the total community, one guideline was that this had to be made evident. Another guideline was that we should not look for quick answers, but make time to allow processes to develop.

ACTION STEPS RECOMMENDED

1. Establish problem-solving discussion groups:
   a. Involving fishermen and company representatives.
   b. Involving fishermen and community representatives.
   c. Elect a representative from the fishermen to serve as a contact man, a coordinator of discussion groups.
2. Details:
   a. Representatives from both company and community should be top people for the group to be able—if necessary—to make decisions, and also in order to convey to the fishermen the impression that what they said is important enough for these people to listen to.
   b. Agenda to be set by the group, as well as frequency and place of meetings.
   c. The group process is supposed to be mildly helped by having the consultant sit in every third to fourth month.

The establishment of a communication device that should:
- a. Bring minutes from meetings and
- b. information about fleet and plant and
- c. reactions and ideas from the fishermen
- d. to every fisherman by way of a personal copy to each.

ACTION STEPS TAKEN

Figure 17–1 shows the composition of the groups. The ship-company group consisted of the managing director—head of the daily operation; the planning manager—who had daily contact with every ship and could tell them where to go and when to come in for landing; and the personnel manager—who aside from running the personnel function was the administrative link with the different community agencies. These three, with their deputies, formed together with the contact man the stable core of the group, which for each meeting was supplemented with three to six people that might be in town at that time from the ships.

The ship-town group consisted of the mayor—a very able and conscientious man; the director of the larger of the two banks in town—who could take care of some of the money that was so easily wasted; and the chairman of the board of the community-welfare committee for seamen—who at the same time was the elected representative of the seamen's union in that district. These three, again together with the contact man, formed the stable core in this group, and they were in the same way supplemented with three to six available fishermen.

The contact man was elected by arranging for all the ships to cable in their candidates for the position. At the time when this report was written, the second man on the list held the job, after the first had resigned. He gave this reason for resigning: "The job is important and I am not competent to hold it." The second contact man was both able and very enthusiastic about the project.

PROCESS DEVELOPMENT

In March 1967 the following sequence of events was formulated:

Ship-Company Group

1. Stage
   1967
   April
   May

   To come on speaking terms. Learn to know each other. Listen to each others' viewpoints and ways of thinking. Outline common problems. Learn each others' language.

2. Stage:
   June
   August

   Trust formation: Assurance about trusting each other. Ability to believe that the other group wishes to do a decent and reasonable job.

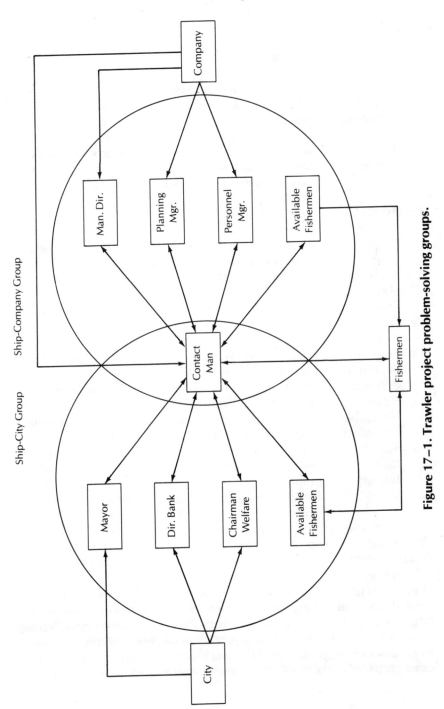

Figure 17–1. Trawler project problem-solving groups.

3. Stage: *Motivation.* Give real opportunity for coresponsibility.
   September   Training in decision making.
   October   Recognition through results.
4. Stage: *Problem solving.* Discuss problems of manning levels
   November   and relevant changes in wage agreements.
   December   Evaluate equipment and methods used. Suggestions.
5. Stage: *Established cooperation.* Maintenance of communica-
   1968   tion, trust formation, motivation, and problem solving
   January   through arrangements built into the organization itself.
               Daring and constructive personnel policy.

Ship-Town Group

1. Stage: *To come on speaking terms.* Learn to know each other.
   1967   Apprehend mutual expectancies.
   April   Grow familiar with each others' language.
   May
2. Stage: *Uncover needs.* Exchange of real wishes and experienced
   June   wants. Outline unsatisfactory arrangements.
   August
3. Stage: *Find a model.* Work on collected data in order to sug-
   September   gest alternative solutions.
   October   Creative period with room for revised thinking.
4. Stage: *Development of independence.* Acknowledge that the
   November   group itself must be responsible for implementations.
   December   Ability to act independently of the company.
5. Stage: *Establishment of community activities.* Develop nec-
   1968   essary arrangements for realizing the ideas of the
   January   group.
               Secure maintenance of the arrangements.
               Give attention to future circumstances.

Comparing these expectations with what really happened makes it clear that the actual events lagged behind the expectancies by about one month.

In the beginning the idea behind the groups had to be stated at meeting after meeting. Even if written information was given, people were not trained to use this. Slowly, however, a working model was established; and after six months a summary of the activities in the ship-company group took the form shown in Figure 17–2. As can be seen, the crews obviously learned to use the group; and it became pretty clear after a while that they came prepared to the meetings. So they were the ones to present problems

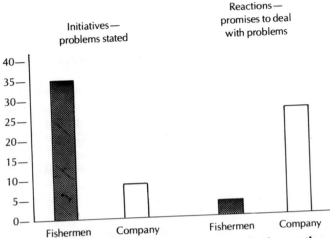

Figure 17–2. Relationships between initiatives and reactions from fishermen and company representatives after six months.

and cases, whereas the company ended up in the reactor's role, promising to look into the cases described and do something with the problems presented. The significance of this openness about decisive operational problems for the fleet was fully recognized by the management group, and it was decided to raise the frequency of meetings to once weekly.

The ship-town group also started by groping its way, and it took them longer to develop a satisfactory identity. The mayor put it beautifully when he once said in a meeting: "This is like coming unprepared to an examination." However, when this group started to meet in the town hall a remarkable change took place. Suddenly the fishermen stopped talking about the company, and then the growing independence felt by the stable members led them to seek ways of financing their share of the consulting expenses.

PROBLEMS STATED BY THE WORKING GROUPS

The following list indicates the types of problems brought forward in the group meetings:

1. Some shipowners fail in their responsibilities by keeping salaries back two or three months in order to gain interest, and by not paying the ship's chandlers, which risks the food supply to the ship.
2. Some ships are outdated. In fact, one sank one week after the crew in a meeting had characterized it as "doomed."
3. There is insufficient equipment for fishing and navigation. Generally this information was not new, but the needs became clearer and more specific.

4. There is no equipment for freezing or mixing food, a point made by the steward group.
5. Loading cases all in bad condition. They were supposed to be clean and sturdy, yet too many were dirty and broken and thereby were damaging the fish.
6. Variable ice qualities exist. From the more simple perception that ice is ice, it was now learned that there are different ices depending on how old, how grained, how crisp, how lumpy, and how flaked the ice is—and that some types are better than others to keep the catch in good shape.
7. There is high spoilage of landed fish: 12 percent when the project started.
8. Some holds are badly constructed and let the lowest layer of cases lie in dirty water.
9. Nobody is on the quay when the ships arrive.
10. There is insufficient quay space.
11. There is an inconvenient departure time: 2:00 A.M.
12. No bulletin or poster for arrival and departure exits. Even if 2:00 A.M. was the scheduled time, delays frequently occurred for different reasons.
13. Payment is badly organized, causing the fishermen to go from one office to another before they could collect their money.
14. No information about the community is provided.
15. A welfare center is needed. This idea was not new, but the formation of the ship-town group stimulated thoughts and actions around the idea.
16. There is no easy way to use the bank, aside from the fact that the fishermen were far from familiar with the institution in itself.
17. There are no wardrobes on shore in which to keep their best clothing away from the smell on the ship.

RESULTS OF ACTION STEPS

As Seen by the Company

1. In 1967 turnover of workforce was considerably reduced, from 800 percent to 25 percent in the spring of 1968.
2. Morale was substantially raised.
3. Fishermen are now perceived more as responsible coworkers.
4. Reduced manning experiment was started:
   a. on one ship
   b. in January 1968

    c. under special contractual conditions
    d. communicated to the rest of the fleet.

As Seen by the Community

1. Forum was established and viewed jointly as important.
2. Fishermen situation was better understood.
3. Greater responsibility in the community for handling its own affairs.
4. Greater responsibility among the fishermen to take part in community matters.

As Seen by the Fishermen

1. "They" finally listen to what we say.
2. The meetings are helpful.
3. We discuss real problems and something is done about them.
4. There is no natural place for "bums" in our group of fishermen.

As Seen by the Consultant

1. A positive self-image in the group of fishermen is developing. Identity crisis has been overcome.
2. Positive relationships were established both with company and town.
3. The fishermen have shown themselves to be constructive, inventive, and cooperative.

The factual basis behind these more normative statements is given below in a list of practical results prepared by the contact man:

1. Navigating instruments and trawler equipment being renewed where insufficiencies were located.
2. Spoilage down from 12 percent to 1 percent, heading for zero.
3. Problems with ice reduced—better loading, cleaning, and removal.
4. Cases sufficient and in better condition.
5. Arrivals and departures better organized.
6. Economic affairs taken over by company from reluctant shipowner.
7. Wage payments now made on board.
8. Quay space being expanded.
9. Wardrobe and showers provided.
10. Departure time changed from 2:00 A.M. to 4:00 A.M.
11. Equipment for freezing and food mixing furnished.
12. Renewal of fleet being planned more vigorously.
13. Welfare work intensified:

    a. Local paper distributed to all ships.
    b. Newsletter informing of coming events.
    c. Welfare center under active development.
14. Bank providing practical savings management.
15. Increased interest in settling down in the community.
16. Suggestion forwarded to town council on how to attract manpower to the community.

THE BOAT-POST

This little newspaper went through a tremendous development. The contents could after a while be classified under the following headings:

1. *Minutes of group meetings.* The minutes were specific to the extent that the names of the participants in each meeting were given, along with the names of the ships they represented. Then all the suggestions and questions were reported together with the reactions to them.
2. *Operating statistics.* These reports were given in different ways. One was to make a list that specified for each trawler how many days in a given period she had been out fishing, the average catch per day, the total quantity, and the value of the catch. Another mode of presentation was again to list all the trawlers; but this time the total catch was related to the number of landings and the percentage of spoiled fish.
3. *Official documents.* In Norway prices are settled on a nationwide basis by government agencies negotiating with relevant groups. These and other regulations of interest were communicated in the "Boat-post." So when a ship was due for landing, the crew could figure out how much money they had made on that trip; or they could read the regulations in force about fishing close to Soviet territorial waters, or the official text of the dispensation given for the experimental ship.
4. *News of community developments.* The need for this kind of information was largely reduced by having the ordinary newspapers distributed to each ship. Some special issues might be dealt with, however, like the negotiations with community officials about new quay space, or how the community housing projects were coming along.
5. *Internal communication.* This activity steadily grew. Naturally, the company was the most active participant, but there were notices from fishermen as well, especially when there was a dialogue going on, say, about assets and liabilities of particular fishing equipment.

Looking at the contents of this "Boat-post," especially the second and third points, this message could be taken to mean: This is the kind of information that would only be given to people who are expected to be interested, responsible, and understanding. Even if this message is not intended, it says something about the attitude of the sender; and there is reason to believe that this attitude somehow is conveyed to the fishermen either in the paper or in the meetings.

LOOKING BACK—REFLECTING

The intention of the project was to make possible the development of a climate suitable to problem-solving activity across formerly closed borders. It looks as if it happened in this way:

When out on the ships it became clear to the consultant that the stated problems were not located in the crews. They worked hard and with a spirit of mutual help and cohesion that was rare to meet. Even if the work was somewhat divided, they shifted positions in order to share the stress. Since each man felt responsible for the total process as well as for when and where to move, it is safe to say that they operated as autonomous groups. In this way there existed a unity between the man and the ship, and any unexpected installations or renovations could make him ask, "What are you doing to my ship?"

On shore there was a young group of executives, restless and impatient to get on, see results, make everything better. As the managing director said about the project: "It looks difficult, but exciting."

There was also the community, uneasy about the situation but also willing to try; only they did not know how. As the mayor once said: "Tell us what to do and we will do it."

Given these three forces, the consultant's main professional contribution was this: to establish a situation that made it possible for these forces to be freely and constructively exposed.

Was that a denial of the negative forces so abundantly expressed in the problem inventory? No. But it was not an encouragement to them either! So instead of dealing with troubles head on, this was the deal: I care and you care, so let us care together.

If this deal was seen as a challenge in the beginning, it nonetheless so happened that after a while the situation was used to its full capacity by an engaged management group, a rapidly maturing group of fishermen, and a community feeling more and more secure as to how to strengthen the relationship between the town and the important group of fishermen.

The most interesting experience, however, was that the trigger of the whole development was the description of the main problem as an identity crisis. Arranging the learning situations so that this problem could be dealt with made it possible for an abundance of practical problems to be handled as well.

Index

345

About the Editor and Contributors

Trygve Johnstad, who holds a degree in psychology from the University of Oslo, is Secretary General and chairman of the Executive Comittee of EIT. He has been a member of the Staff for the Development of International Trainers Program run by EIT since its inception in 1970. In addition, he is a charter member of the International Association of Applied Social Scientists, a member of the International Consultants Registry, and Director of the Norwegian Institute for Group Development and Organizational Psychology. The author of articles and textbooks in the field of group dynamics, Dr. Johnstad has served as a trainer for staff members of many consulting firms and has had long-term assignments with social service organizations in Sweden. He works primarily in Europe—in Scandinavia and in English- and German-speaking areas.

Harold Bridger is a psychoanalyst and applied social scientist in London. A founding member of the Tavistock Institute of Human Relations and of EIT, he is also European Member of the NTL Institute of Applied Behavioral Science (U.S.A.). Currently he is concerned with research and development in open sociotechnical systems and career development.

Kurt Buchinger is affiliated with the Institut für Tiefenpsychologie und Psychotherapie at the University of Vienna. In addition, he is a trainer with the EIT; a trainer-educator and member of the board of the Austrian Society for Group Dynamics and Group Pedagogics; and a member of the Vienna Psychoanalytic Society. Dr. Buchinger also works in cooperation with the Hernstein Institute for Management Training.

Arne Derefeldt is a certified psychologist and has worked as an industrial psychologist, consultant, and adviser in job participation and group-dynamics projects. Since 1958, he has been employed by the Swedish Council for Personnel and Administration, a nonprofit organization.

Peter Heintel has held various teaching assignments on national and international levels, has served on numerous scientific advisory boards, and is the author of numerous publications. A member of EIT and a member of the board of the Austrian Society for Group Dynamics and Group Pedagogics, he is professor of philosophy and group dynamics at Klagenfurt University in Austria.

Gurth Higgin holds the chair of continuing management education at Loughborough University in Leicestershire, England; before assuming that position, he spent twenty years with the Tavistock Institute of Human Relations in London. His chapter in this book is taken from the inaugural lecture he delivered at Loughborough University.

Hubertus Hüppauf, a member of EIT since 1973, is a freelance consultant and group counselor in Greifenstein-Odersberg, West Germany. The focal concerns of his consultancy are staff development and team building in educational institutions, supervision in clinical and social work and project development, and adaptation of general educational programs to local and client-specific conditions.

Svein M. Kile is professor of organizational psychology and head of the department in the Institute for Organizational Psychology at the University of Bergen, Norway. Previously, he served as professor of work psychology and personnel management at the Norwegian School of Business Administration in Gergen. Dr. Kile's main research interests have been management education and development, the quality of working life, and especially work environment and the evaluation of impacts of training and development efforts at all levels. He is the author of numerous articles and *Virker det? (Does It Work?)*.

Traugott Lindner became an independent management consultant in 195 after having worked in industry for five years. He has participated in research and training projects both in Europe and in the United States.

Dr. Lindner, a resident of Vienna, describes himself as a "social psychologist who applies his disciipline by consulting with management in the analysis of organizational structures and in the training of managerial personnel."

Ronald Markillie spends the major part of his time working as a psychiatrist or psychoanalyst both in the National Health Service and in private practice, and teaching in a university medical school. While serving as an army psychiatrist in World War II, he was introduced to group therapy and therapeutic communities. His subsequent work at the Tavistock Clinic and his association with the Tavistock Institute of Human Relations led him to consulting work in industry and institutions and to involvement in management-training programs and the training of social scientist consultants in international programs. Dr. Markillie, a resident of Leeds, England, has been chairman of the Membership and Standards Committee of EIT since 1971.

Ramon Meseguer served as professor of organizational behavior at the Institute Superior de Estudios de la Empresa, Barcelona, from 1964 to 1976. Previously, he was employed by the Institute of Sociology in Frankfurt am Main. A resident of Barcelona, he has been a member of EIT since 1971.

Max Pagès is professor of organizational social psychology at the University of Paris Dauphine. Recently he has engaged in research on "power phenomena within large organizations." He is also interested in developing methods of "existential animation" that favor individual and group responsibility at all levels—economic, political, ideological, and psychological. He is the author of numerous articles and of *L'Orientation Non-Directive, La Vie Affective des Groupes,* and *Le Travail Amoureux.*

Bernhard Pesendorfer received a Ph.D. in philosophy from the University of Vienna. He is employed as a consultant with the consulting firm Inter-Management, in Vienna. In addition, he is a member of the training staff of the Hernstein Institute of Management Development (also in Vienna) and a fellow of EIT.

Gerhard Schwarz is a lecturer in philosophy and the social sciences at the University of Vienna. He serves as a management consultant and is a fellow of EIT. In addition, he is a member of the Austrian Society for Group Dynamics and Group Pedagogics and of the staff of the Hernstein Institute for Management Training.

Eric Trist is professor of social systems sciences at the University of Pennsylvania. Previously, he was chairman of the Human Resources Centre of the Tavistock Institute in London.